D1546175

The Peace Conspiracy / *Harvard East Asian Series 67*

The East Asian Research Center at Harvard University administers research projects designed to further scholarly understanding of China, Japan, Korea, Vietnam and adjacent areas.

The Peace Conspiracy / Gerald E. Bunker

Wang Ching-wei and the China War, 1937–1941

Harvard University Press, Cambridge, Massachusetts 1972

© Copyright 1972 by the President and Fellows of Harvard Col-
lege. All rights reserved
Preparation of this volume has been aided by a grant from the
Ford Foundation
Library of Congress Catalog Card Number 78-180149
SBN 674-65915-5
Printed in the United States of America

7-11-77

With loving gratitude to G.M.B. and E.F.B.

Acknowledgments

I sat down in the library with the notion that everything was at hand to recapture a dark and tangled story from the shades of time. But it was not long before I learned that I must depend on the learning and experience of others to point each step of the way. The "community of scholars" is no longer an abstraction to me.

First, Professor Walter Gourlay guided me from the vast topic of the war in China, which had always seemed so mysterious and exciting, to the more manageable one of Wang Ching-wei's role in it. The second problem was to find reliable information. The late Mr. Liang Hsu and his colleague, Mr. Chi Wang, of the Library of Congress gave generously of their learning and leisure in directing my exploration of Chinese materials. Mr. Hisao Matsumoto of the Library of Congress Japanese Section helped me with equal kindness to find Japanese materials. Mr. Hirōō Wazaki procured for me a copy of Yashiaki Nishi's *Higeki no shōnin* (Witness of tragedy) and assisted me with interest and sympathy. My teacher and comrade in translating and interpreting the voluminous and often obscure Japanese archives and memoirs was Mr. Hong-kyoon An. His language skill and his political insight were indispensable. Nothing could have rewarded the lonely labors of the library more than the fellowship of a major actor and witness of the events which I had sought to bring to life from documents. After reading my first draft, Mr. Tsung-wu Kao, whom the reader will come to know well in the succeeding pages, consented to share with me his painful recollections. Professor Albert Craig time and time again has aided me with careful counsel and criticism.

In the matter of style I am indebted to my wife, Elaine, who read each of the interminable drafts and recensions hot off the typewriter, and to Mr. L. Michael Bell, who meticulously edited the manuscript. Miss Mary Jane LaBarge not only typed several versions of the manuscript, but also served as an editor, pointing out many inconsistencies, obscurities, and infelicities, and prodding me when I showed signs of flagging. Mrs. Lois Dougan Tretiak pursued gremlins through the footnotes and bibliography.

Others who have read the manuscript and made useful suggestions are: Professor Yoji Akashi, Professor Lloyd Eastman, Professor Shinkichi Eto, Mr. John Ford, Professor Han-sheng Lin, Dr. Andrew Nathan, Mr. Mark Peattie, and Professor Edwin Reischauer.

My debts to my teachers are inexpressible. I would like here to acknowledge special obligations to Professors Sterling Dow, John Fairbank, John Finley, L. Carrington Goodrich, Masatoshi Nagatomi, Ihor Sevcenko, Benjamin Schwartz, Zeph Stewart, Cedric Whitman.

Contents

Illustrations

The Peace Conspiracy

Prelude to Tragedy

1 Shots exchanged between Chinese and Japanese detachments on the night of July 7, 1937, at Marco Polo Bridge southwest of Peking precipitated, after decades of tension, what by all measures was the greatest war in East Asian history. Japan's despair at ending what was euphemistically called the "China Incident" — her war with China — led her directly toward Pearl Harbor. From that time on, her defeat by overwhelmingly superior forces could only be a matter of time. Following Hiroshima and Nagasaki, foreign conquerors were the masters of Japan for the first time in her proud history.

The eight-year war destroyed the moderate Western-oriented but nationalistic Kuomintang regime, which had sought for several decades to solve China's problems. Wartime chaos was the indispensable medium in which the Kuomintang's rivals, the Communists, were able to grow in numbers and strength, ultimately displacing them as China's rulers in 1949.

What follows is the story of the major effort by Chinese and Japanese to bring this conflict to a mutually acceptable conclusion before the logic of ongoing events would lead new men and new forces to take over after the old stage had become littered with corpses.

The men officially on top in the two countries did not want war in 1937. Nevertheless, through confusion and diplomatic ineptitude on both sides, efforts to stop the wide-scale fighting in north China, which followed the incident at Marco Polo Bridge, failed. Confidential talks were to begin in Shanghai on August 9. But before they could get well underway, a massive confrontation of the two nations' troops there ended for the time being the possibility of a negotiated settlement. Japanese forces broke the resistance of the Chinese troops and in December took Nanking in an orgy of rape and pillage which shocked a world not yet inured to such excess. At the same time the German government which enjoyed good relations with both adversaries, offered in vain its "good offices" to bring them together on acceptable terms.

Prime Minister Konoye's statement of January 16, 1938, that

henceforward the Japanese government would no longer have dealings with the National Government of China, personified by Chiang Kai-shek, seemed to mark the decisive rupture of communication between the two nations. If the Japanese would not deal with Chiang Kai-shek and could not overthrow his government, the two nations would be doomed to endless struggle.

It seemed to a small group of men with connections on the one side with Chiang Kai-shek and on the other side with Konoye Fumimaro that the only way to break through the impasse was to replace Chiang Kai-shek—with whom Konoye had apparently said he would "not deal" — with Wang Ching-wei.

Wang had been a leading associate of Sun Yat-sen and had played an important role in Chinese politics as the Kuomintang rose to power during the 1920's and as it sought to exercise power during the 1930's. He occupied a unique place among Chinese statesmen not only because of his background of prominence and service but also because of his personal magnetism and strength of character. While his role in the nationalist revolution put his patriotism nearly beyond question, he had stood for a policy of conciliation toward Japan — "resistance on the one had, negotiation on the other." If Wang would take responsibility for making peace with Japan — so the reasoning went — Konoye would be able to negotiate with the Kuomintang government without disavowing his January 16 statement, interpreted as a declaration that he would not deal with Chiang Kai-shek.

The advantages to the Chinese side were seen as twofold. First, China would receive better terms in a negotiated peace than if she waited until superior Japanese arms forced her complete capitulation and acceptance of dictated terms. Second, Chiang Kai-shek would not have to take responsibility for concessions to the Japanese which would be regarded by the Communists and other patriotic groups as treasonous. The feeling was widespread among patriots that it was better to fight on to the end rather than to permit further — perhaps this time final — erosion of Chinese sovereignty.

This peace scheme was originated not by Wang but by certain associates of Chiang, certain elements in Japanese military intelligence, and certain members of "liberal" Japanese political circles with connections to Konoye Fumimaro himself. At a certain point, Wang Ching-wei took up this scheme initiated by others, bet all his chips on it, and devoted the rest of his life to a futile endeavor to make it succeed. It is this story — to me one of grandeur, pathos, and ultimately tragedy — that the succeeding pages seek to recount.

In the end, the reader must answer his own questions about "treason" and "sincerity." But at the very outset it is apparent that the Chinese conspirators saw the Wang Ching-wei "peace movement" as a means to do what Chinese arms had been unable to do — halt the invader and ultimately drive him from Chinese soil. The Japanese conspirators were primarily motivated by the hope of causing a split in Chinese ranks and hence of cheaply purchasing the Chinese capitulation that Japanese arms had been unable to win.

As a result of conversations between Chinese conspirators who allowed the Japanese to think that they represented Wang Ching-wei and, on the other side, Japanese civilian go-betweens and army officers of equally doubtful authority, the Japanese military led the Chinese to think that the Japanese had committed themselves to military withdrawal within two years after the cessation of hostilities. The Chinese conspirators left the Japanese with the belief that powerful Chinese forces had agreed to rise in Wang's behalf against Chiang if the Japanese in fact publicly committed themselves to withdrawal.

The plan was for Wang to retire to a neutral area from whence he would issue a statement responding to the Japanese announcement of their terms, which would include withdrawal. Unfortunately, Wang's departure was delayed beyond the announced time, communications broke down, and the whole questionable structure collapsed. The Japanese failed to make the commitments that had been agreed upon, and thus Wang was left an exile and seemingly a traitor.

At this point Wang had several options. Rather than admit failure of his maneuver and return to Chungking or go into European exile, he chose to devote the rest of his life to a daring and excruciating effort to bring the Japanese to fulfill their "promises." The assassination of a beloved friend and disciple, perhaps by Chiang's agents, added to Wang's desire to save his country a less salutary desire for revenge. Passion overcame what hitherto had been a pragmatic maneuver, and Wang conceived the notion of realizing peace through the establishment of a rival Kuomintang government in Japanese-occupied Nanking. Despite the best that Wang and his comrades could do, this government became a powerless puppet government.

Pearl Harbor brought the United States into the war in the Pacific and completely altered the political premise upon which Wang's peace movement was based, namely, that Japan would inevitably win military victory in China. Although Wang's peace movement weakened the unity of the Chinese cause and made direct peace between Tokyo and Chungking more difficult, nevertheless, Wang's government acted as a custodian of Chinese interests in Japanese-occupied areas and as a buffer between the subject people and their conquerors. The hopes of Wang and his original collaborators to save China from a devastating war and to win favorable terms for China came to nothing. Those that survived the war were executed by Chiang's government; all have had heaped upon their memories the intense hatred of most of their countrymen. It is said, however, that when Nationalist troops returned to Shanghai after the war, many residents wistfully longed for the return of Wang and his friends.

Because history is made by men and not by mechanistic forces, no factor was so important in shaping the development of Wang's movement as the character of Wang Ching-wei himself. Others may see Wang as a pathetic figure swept along by forces that he could neither understand nor control. On the contrary, I see the whole story growing out of the tragic dimensions of Wang's character: his courage caused him to dare, his blindness to persevere, to stumble, and to fall. Undoubtedly, however, tragedy involves both the character of the protagonist and the nature of the situation with which he is confronted. Wang's actions grew out of his character. Fate faced him with tragic choices. Character and situation collaborated to bring about his disgrace and fall.

To review what might be termed the first four acts of the tragedy of Wang Ching-wei would involve a recapitulation of the history of the Chinese Republic.[1] In lieu of such a review, let us follow four themes which are the leitmotif of Wang's career prior to 1937 and provide the dramatic impetus for the events to be chronicled.

1. Wang's idealism and emotional search for heroic self-sacrifice and historical glory. He came to feel that the instrument of his apotheosis would be Sun Yat-sen's Kuomintang revolution.

2. The polarized political structure of Republican China — radical communism on the left and conservative militarism embodied in Chiang Kai-shek on the right. Thus Wang, a civilian moderate of the old mandarin type, was left with no ground to stand on as an aspirant for leadership.

3. The dilemma of the Kuomintang government trapped between native rivals — Communists and warlords — and the inexorable pressure of Japanese expansion. The unfavorable international situation exacerbated those difficulties.

4. The resultant of the above three factors: Wang Ching-wei's development of a political style and status peculiar to himself.

Wang's idealism. Wang was born in Canton, the scene of China's first contact with the West and the home of the Chinese revolutionary movement. He succeeded in passing the first of the traditional civil service examinations in 1902. The next year, however, he won a scholarship for study in Japan granted by the Kwangtung provincial government. There he was swept up in the tremendous tide of patriotic enthusiasm and indignation which seized Chinese students and intellectuals of the time — China had been humiliated by both the barbarians and her own Manchu rulers; bold innovative action on the part of young patriots was necessary to save China. It was the exposure to this enthusiastic patriotic atmosphere among Chinese students in Japan that set and fixed Wang's character. He continued to respond to contemporary situations in the light of values from the era of his youth.

The problem for Chinese patriots was to find a focus for their passion — some guide for constructive and consecutive action. Many Chinese intellectuals were to find in communism their principles for action; Wang was to find his in a more personal, less intellectual loyalty, to that most intrepid of Chinese revolutionaries, Sun Yat-sen, and to the Kuomintang party which accounted Sun its founder. Wang was swiftly drawn to Sun, a fellow Cantonese, and rapidly became prominent or notorious through his fiery anti-Manchu editorials in the *Min pao* (People's newspaper), the organ of Sun's T'ung-meng hui. These editorials were not distinguished by incisiveness or originality of thought; they were, however, elegantly and movingly phrased. This was characteristic of Wang: He was not really a perceptive and innovative thinker but rather was more sensitive to rhetoric and personality than to ideas.

Apparently, Wang grew impatient with the many failures of Sun's conspiracies. He deeply resented the obscurity into which the revolutionary movement had fallen — nothing could be more repugnant to the young hero who so earnestly desired to achieve at one stroke both China's salvation and his own apotheosis. Consequently, apparently under the influence of then wide spread anarchistic ideas and against the advice of his revolutionary colleagues, Sun Yat-sen and Hu Han-min, Wang embarked on a project to revive the revolutionary cause and his own through the assassination of some Ch'ing official. The prospective victim changed many times.

After many plans were made and abandoned, Wang, accompanied by Miss Ch'en Pi-chün, soon to become Madame Wang, and several other companions, proceeded to Peking. In January of 1910 this somewhat comic-opera troupe, carrying issues of the *Min pao* sewn into their clothing, attempted to assassinate two Ch'ing officials at the railway station but were unable to recognize them in the crowd.

On March 10 they determined to attempt the assassination of Prince Ch'ün, the father of the young emperor who was serving as prince regent. In the style of the Russian anarchists, the young conspirators mined a bridge over which the prince customarily passed. While they were in the process of so doing, barking dogs attracted a group of men who were out searching for an unfaithful wife and the bomb was found. Several days later the police observed that one of Wang's accomplices wore a false queue as he tipped his hat. They followed him back to the conspirator's headquarters. Wang immediately confessed everything, declaring: "Ching-wei wants to perform some extraordinary and sensational act for the purpose of arousing from the most important place (i.e., the capital) of the whole world (i.e., China) the people." Asked why he carried copies of the *Min pao* concealed in his clothes, he answered: "These articles were written in ink; I wanted to translate them into blood."[2] The case became a great cause célèbre. The regime did not execute Wang but, partly on account of his youth and promise, partly through fear of revolutionary reprisals, and partly perhaps through Japanese diplomatic intervention, reduced his sentence to life imprisonment. Fortunately for Wang, the empire was convulsed by the almost accidental insurrection at Wuhan in October, 1911, and he was released from prison in November. Wang sought for the rest of his life another like opportunity for sacrifice and glory.

The dark years from 1911 until early 1920's, which saw the failure of Chinese democracy, the rise and fall of Yüan Shih-k'ai, the decline of the nation into chaos and warlordism, Wang spent mainly in France. What (if anything) he accomplished there is not clear, since his command of French never advanced beyond a few phrases.

When at last the indefatigable Sun seemed to be having some success with his endeavor to establish a regime in Canton which might aspire to national leadership, Wang drew closer to Sun and permanently committed his life and his hopes to Sun's Kuomintang party and its revolution. He authored Sun's famous last testament by his deathbed in Peking in March 1925, which declared that the revolution was yet unfinished and that Sun's comrades must devote their lives to its fulfillment.

Chiang on the right, the Communists on the left. The period from Sun's death until the "unification" of China under the Kuomintang government in November 1928 was dominated by a struggle between the Communists, who wished to channel the revolution to their own ends, and Chiang Kai-shek, who wished a socially conservative nationalistic China under military leadership. Under Sun's leadership a tactical alliance had been formed between the two groups, but after his death and as victory seemed within the grasp of the revolutionaries, the inherent tension between those who accented nationalism and those who accented social revolution was exacerbated.

Wang Ching-wei was in between, sometimes cooperating with one, sometimes with the other. He had little independent power of his own — neither a party machine nor a military machine behind him. It is true that he enjoyed enormous prestige as a result of his long association with Sun Yat-sen, far predating that of Chaing's. Sun became deified in Kuomintang hagiography as the National Father; his close disciples thus carried and passed on the torch of legitimacy. But this relationship in itself is not a sufficient explanation for Wang's prominence.

Wang with Kuomintang Leaders

Above: from left to right: Wang Ching-wei, Chiang Kai-shek, and Ch'en Pi-chün (Madame Wang).

Below: from left to right: Yen Hsi-shan, Wang Ching-wei, and Ho Ying-ch'in.

The secret of Wang's continuing significance in Chinese politics lies for the most part in his personality. He was a handsome, youthful, and impressive-looking man who dressed with consummate elegance and taste. Despite suffering most of his life from ill health, he exuded an air of energy and vitality. In a rather prosaic age his rhetoric sparkled. He was undoubtedly the finest orator of his generation, no mean advantage for a politician. But most important was his gift for human relations. He always conveyed sincerity. Always at the fitting moment a tear came to his eye. Clearly, as will be illustrated by his dealings with the Japanese, this "sincerity" was premeditated and posed, a political tool. And yet he was a good and loyal friend. His kindness and fidelity to his friends — and his followers were his friends — inspired a type of devotion in return, for which it would be hard to find parallel.

Wang suffered his first reverse at the hands of the rising young Chiang in the Chung Shan Incident of March 1926. Supposedly directed against the Communists, Chiang's coup had the effect of forcing Wang into exile. Wang lost the next round too. After Chiang had taken Shanghai in March 1927 with the aid of the Communist-led laborers within the city, he invited Wang to return. After several days of apparently cordial conversation between the two men, Wang set out for Wuhan, whence the Kuomintang government had moved its headquarters. Wang seemed also anxious to keep up good relations with the Communists as well, for following his talks with Chiang, he issued a joint communique with the Communist leader Ch'en Tu-hsiu extolling Communist-Kuomintang cooperation. Outflanking Wang's maneuver, Chiang massacred the Communists in Shanghai, declared war on the Wuhan government, and established his own at Nanking. Chiang's bold strategy, reminiscent of Ts'ao Ts'ao and *The Romance of the Three Kingdoms,* did not enjoy complete success, and he was forced into temporary retirement in Japan.

The next move was Wang's. He established a regime in Canton and on that basis held unity talks with Chiang in December. But a Communist rising in Canton — the Canton Commune — destroyed Wang's power base. Chiang won this round too and Wang once again took up his travels. Wang contested Chiang's leadership two more times. He returned to China in early 1930 and associated himself with the efforts of warlords Yen Hsi-shan and Feng Yü-hsiang to set up a regime in Peking. Unlike Wang's other regime-forming attempts, this one was defeated on the battlefield. In the spring of 1931 Wang tried once again, becoming part of another abortive regime, again in Canton.

What is the meaning of this elaborate charade of endless new regimes played by all participants on the Chinese political scene? Basically it was China's search for a political system which would restore the unity and the legitimacy of the Chinese state lost with the fall of the empire. In the absence of political institutions which enable regular candidacy for the highest offices in the state, formation of a local regime was virtually the only way an aspirant could offer his services to "save China."

There was an important change in Wang after he returned from his long exile following the Canton Commune: he turned decisively against communism and became an apostle of order. He wrote: "Should the peasants be persuaded by the Communists to rob their landlords of their lands, the number of people to be killed will be ten thousand times that during the French and Russian Revolutions, and the terror and distress will also be considerably more acute than in France or Russia . . . At first they [the Communists] may succeed in instigating the peasants to follow them in creating disturbances. But later, when the economic structure has collapsed and there are no commerce and industry nor arable farmland, the peasants cannot but fight among themselves."[3]

Wang's change of stance doubtless stemmed from conviction. Nevertheless, the shift in the political spectrum to the right demanded it. There would be no future for a pro-Communist Kuomintang politician. The Communists, fighting for their existence in Kiangsi and later in Yenan, were beyond the pale of political respectability. Chiang had shifted to the right. The spectrum to his right was well filled with vested interests of the old order. The only position open for Wang was just barely to the left of Chiang where he could espouse party democracy, oppose Chiang's "dictatorship," and at the same time appeal to the moderate nationalistic interests. The outbreak of the Manchurian Incident in September 1931 unified Kuomintang factions against the foreign invader and muted temporarily factional strife.

The Kuomintang government trapped between enemies from within and from without. Disregarding patriotic sentiment which urged unity against foreign enemies, the Kuomintang continued all-out efforts to exterminate their erstwhile friends, now enemies, the Communists. Moreover, the Kuomintang's alliance with the warlords was on both sides one of opportunism. Despite the consequent tenuousness of its political position within China, caught between left and right, the Kuomintang government had to bear the responsibility for resisting the Japanese drive to undermine Chinese sovereignty, a drive with deep historical roots, which had mercifully somewhat abated during the 1920's and under Shidehara's diplomacy but which, from the Manchurian Incident on, continued relentlessly until it had burned itself out.

The basic policy that the Kuomintang government adopted to deal with the Japanese menace was the traditional imperial policy of barbarian taming — resistance in the last extremity, but wherever possible using diplomacy and superficial concessions to prevent a contest of military force in which China could only be the loser, and using time bought to build China's strength, garner foreign support, and wherever possible, to tighten up on the concessions previously offered.

One problem that made Chinese response to the Japanese threat difficult was that the Japanese could never be induced to make specific their demands upon China. The reason for this reticence was at least partially that the Japanese did not know what their objectives in China were; thus it was impossible to square them.

In January 1936 Foreign Minister Hirota Koki announced what became known as Hirota's "Three Points," namely: "cessation of all unfriendly acts or measures" by China toward Japan; recognition by China of Manchukuo; and Sino-Japanese cooperation for the eradication of communism.[4] In some sense these three demands were to remain in various recensions the minimum basis for Japanese accommodation with China. A major theme of the narrative soon to begin is the gradual emergence of these "Three Points" into concrete terms.

The Kuomintang government, faced with opposition from both sides of the political spectrum within China and with marauders from without, found also that another traditional resource of Chinese diplomacy, pitting barbarians against barbarians, was only of limited effectiveness. America was absorbed in isolationism; Europe was preoccupied by the growing crisis. The international stage was setting itself for a struggle between the nascent forces of communism and of fascism. The democratic Western powers seemed powerless to affect the flow of events. Moreover, these very democratic nations were those for the most part who had been the "imperialists" in China. Maybe China's cause lay with those nations who wished to alter the status quo. What was this emerging world scene going to mean for China and how should Chinese leaders react to it?

Wang develops a peculiar political style and role. The dynamics of internal politics had forced Wang into a position of constantly offering himself as an alternative to Chiang as heir of Sun in China's search for a viable political system to replace the old imperial system. The Japanese threat and the Chinese methods adopted to meet it necessitated a diplomatic and conciliatory leadership surrogate which would appear to alternate with a hard-line patriotic policy. The instrument of this seeming "soft" policy would necessarily have to endure intense popular opprobrium. Wang's desire for personal sacrifice and his history of genuine rivalry for the power of the state made him ideally suited for this role.

Wang undertook the dangerous and humiliating task of dealing with the Japanese, while Chiang, through his control of the military remaining the undisputed master of the state, devoted himself to "bandit suppression" and remained the unbesmirched focus of patriotic loyalties. In January 1932 at the time of the outbreak of the Shanghai Incident (Japanese attack on Chinese troops in Shanghai in response to widespread boycotts and patriotic outbursts), Wang assumed chairmanship of the Executive Yüan. Pursuing the traditional Chinese policy of "resistance and negotiations," he procured an armistice on March 5. Naturally, patriotic sentiment was unwilling to accept this settlement, and under pressure from Chang Hsüeh-liang, the Manchurian warlord now without a country, he was forced to resign in September and return to France.

But in early March of 1933 further Japanese aggression demanded his recall to take responsibility once again. The Japanese occupied Jehol, and there was no assurance that they would stop there. Wang returned from Europe on March 17 and was appointed concurrently chairman of the Executive Yüan and foreign minister. On May 31 the Tangku Truce was signed. It established a demilitarized zone between the Great Wall and a line running across Hopei just north of Peking. Although Chinese troops were prohibited, the Japanese continued to maintain troops there, somewhat stretching the terms of the Boxer Protocol. "In effect the truce gave the Japanese a hold on almost all of Hopei above the Peiping-Tientsin area, which enabled them throughout the next years to exercise military, political, and economic pressure against both the local administrations in North China and the Nanking government in an effort to gain even greater control over the Chinese nation."[5] No Chinese could rejoice at these terms, but at least this truce preserved China for the moment from the fate of Korea or Manchuria.

Wang personally took great satisfaction in "taking responsibility"; he craved more than anything else in his life the opportunity to serve his country as a hero. It was only during this period that he was really able to do so. The fact that he was a lone hero was also to his liking. He said in response to his critics: "Military officers have their responsibilities, and they cannot go away and say that they will not fight. Civilian officers have no responsibilities for fighting, and they of course can sing high praise for war. Who else besides me will tell the people the truth?"[6]

In March 1935 Wang took responsibility for signing the Ho–Umezu Agreement, which made further concessions to Japan in north China, in response to unbearable pressure. It seemed a matter of bending or breaking. Although this agreement was kept secret and even its existence was denied, Wang continued to bear the brunt of the opposition to the temporizing policy. Much of this criticism flowed from hearts fiery with patriotism and chagrin at China's humiliation, but a certain amount of it, particularly from warlord elements, was more oriented toward domestic politics. Naturally, it was far easier for those out of power to urge armed resistance to Japan than to carry out such a policy and be responsible for its consequences.

It must be emphasized that this hard-soft, Chiang-Wang policy was a joint policy. There is no sign of division between the two men at this time. There was complete accord as they both worked together toward their common objective — a strong

united China under Kuomintang rule. Symbolic of the cooperation between the two men was their mutual trust in the major
confidential agent in the humiliating but necessary negotiations
with Japan, Kao Tsung-wu. Kao's unique relationship with both
Wang and Chiang was to be a major factor in bringing the peace
movement of later days into being.

Kao came into his position of enormous trust and responsibility in his early twenties. Kao, like Chiang, a native of Chekiang,
returned to China in the spring of 1932 after his university studies
in Japan. Unlike most Chinese students in Japan, in addition
to his formal studies of law, he made hmself a student of Japanese character, life, and society. He visited geisha houses with
the rich and ate *udon* (noodles) with the poor.[7]

He launched himself onto the national political stage through
an article that he submitted to the prestigious Nanking newspaper *Chung-yang jih-pao* on the assassination in May 1932 of
Inukai Tsuyoshi, the Japanese prime minister whose son was to
be Kao's companion in the peace movement. That same year
Chiang invited Kao to join his own staff as a personal secretary.
Kao turned this offer down. In the summer of 1933 Wang Ching-
wei, impressed by an article which Kao had published, invited
him to lunch. This began Kao's association with Wang.

In 1934 Chiang, after requesting Kao's advice on Sino-Japanese
relations, offered Kao the critical post of consul-general in Seoul
with ministerial rank. Instead, discussions between Wang and
Chiang led to Kao's appointment at the age of twenty-seven to
the most important official post relating to dealings with the
Japanese, that of chief of the Asian Department (Ya-chou-ssu)
of the Chinese Foreign Office, hereafter referred to as the Wai-
chiao-pu.

Kao was able in his first important diplomatic mission, involving the restoration of postal service between Manchukuo
and China, to prove to both Wang and Chiang that he could be
depended upon to fulfill, whatever the pressures upon him, the
instructions he had been given.[8]

Having thus proved himself, Kao was entrusted with other
difficult negotiations.[9] He took the responsibility for parrying
the daily demands of the Japanese.[10] This was an emotionally
exhausting and humiliating enterprise. In the words of an American diplomat: "No Chinese official feels secure. At any moment

the visiting card of a hitherto unheard-of Japanese Major or Colonel may be presented to him and he knows that he is in for an interview with a man whose slightest opinion may become the active policy of the Japanese military, who are always ready to move."[11]

Those who dealt with the Japanese had not only to fear the Japanese but the Chinese as well. The bullet of a would-be assassin was to temporarily remove Wang Ching-wei from the political scene and cause in consequence a partial breakdown in the operation of the temporizing hard-soft policy. Whether the continued presence of Wang Ching-wei in the government could have delayed or prevented the buildup of tensions to the point of war is a question that cannot be answered.

In August of 1935 Wang had tendered his resignation, partly because of ill health and partly in response to the inevitable opposition to what some viewed as a sellout policy. There must have been a reservoir of appreciation, however, for Wang's work, since after lengthy debates, his resignation was rejected. This vote of confidence, however, did him little good because on November 1 he narrowly escaped death from gunshot wounds received in a confusing melee. He was soon well enough to undertake the voyage to Europe once again. Thus we may assume that political as well as medical factors motivated his withdrawal from the scene. When he returned to the stage of Chinese politics again, the situation had much changed. It was no longer possible for him to play his old role.

Wang demonstrated during the period from 1932 through 1935 a style of political behavior which incorporated his notions of national leadership. It is important to examine as well the political style of Chiang Kai-shek, not only because he is an important personage in the events to follow but because he more than any other man established the political system of republican China.

Whle Wang's style demanded at least the appearance of perpetual candor, Chiang favored an impartial inscrutability. It might be added that since Wang did not bear the responsibility for holding the unstable coalition of republican China together, he could more easily afford the virtue of candor.

It had only been at the fiat of the foreigners that an organ corresponding to a Western foreign office had been created to deal with foreign nations on the basis of equality rather than as barbarian tributaries. Under the republic the Wai-chiao-pu still had aspects of the traditional barbarian-temporizing organ and did not have full responsibility for the conduct of foreign affairs.

In the same way that in the days of the Chinese empire, the various bureaucratic organs of the government were coordinated at the level of the emperor, so under the Chinese republic, Chiang-Kai-shek was the only focus of decision making and co-ordination. Chiang's position, however, was more difficult because lacking the divine sanction which secured the emperor, he was surrounded by enemies and rivals eager to supplant him. He could only stay on top by playing one against the other. Thus Chiang owed his success more to his political abilities than to his military genius. No man had his ear or knew his mind. As a general rule, he played with his cards very close to his chest. This imperial inaccessibility was a key to Chiang's strength; it also is probably the key to his ultimate failure and rejection. Chiang would receive reports from various agents and agencies; very seldom would he give instructions. The responsibility and opprobrium of yielding to the superior force of the Japanese he left to others, to be disavowed if necessary. Confidential agents, therefore, with no political standing of their own were extremely valuable to Chiang. Successes could be acknowledged; failures disavowed. His agents, even high officials responsible for the conduct of foreign policy, were often unaware of what Chiang really intended to do. Nor, in the difficult position of "damned if you do and damned if you don't," was anyone eager to exercise initiative. It might well be argued that Chiang's style of political behavior was the most effective possible under the situation; however, it was frustrating and demoralizing to his subordinates.

Wang and Chiang played coordinated roles in a drama carefully contrived to manipulate the Japanese. Kao Tsung-wu, who acted as confidential agent, negotiator, and interpreter in the dealings of both men vis-à-vis the Japanese, asserts that from the beginning until Wang's defection there was no real difference between the policies of Wang and Chiang toward the Japanese. How then can Wang's defection be explained? In addition to the differences in personality and the personal rivalry of the two men, there was a basic difference in their attitude toward Japan. Both men had courage. But they differed as to how they should use their personal courage against the national enemy.

Chiang refused to make the least preparation for the possibility that China might be defeated by Japan. When most observers considered China's defeat a probability rather than a possibility, Chiang's attitude could not be called realistic. Of course he must have known that Japan might succeed in conquering his nation, but he would fight to the last and then in samurai fashion fall upon his sword rather than surrender. Thus the possibility of defeat had no meaning for him.

Wang, however, partly through the role he had played during the thirties in appeasing Japan, dwelt on the likelihood of Japanese victory. Perhaps this was the more realistic view. Wang's mission, his field for heroism, was to cushion China's defeat. It would not be just to say that he desired this defeat. Since it was only in defeat or national humiliation that his country seemed willing to give him responsibility to serve and to display those heroic qualities which embodied his personal ambition, it is only natural that he should have been more ready to deal with the possibility of defeat than was Chiang, who knew no other stance than "final victory."

China's foreign policy was naturally affected by internal developments and in turn influenced these developments. The Sian Incident brought Wang back to China and marked the crystallization of the new political situation in China. In accordance with the world-wide policy of "united front" to meet the fascist menace, the Communists had been pressing for a truce in the civil war so that they might join forces with the Kuomintang against the Japanese invaders. When Chiang visited the ex-Manchurian warlord Chang Hsüeh-liang in Sian in December 1936 in connection with yet another "bandit suppression" campaign, Chang, a patriot and not a Communist, but who had evidently been moved by the obvious logic of the Communists' slogan, "Chinese should not fight Chinese in a time of Japanese aggression," held Chiang prisoner. Chang and the Communists pressed on Chiang their "advice" that Chiang abandon internecine struggles and lead unified Chinese forces against the Japanese. In turn, they apparently offered their wholehearted support. It seems that Chiang agreed to make such a shift from attacking the Communists and temporizing with the Japanese to cooperating with the Communists against the Japanese.

Chiang was released, to national rejoicing, on Christmas Day, 1936. In the meanwhile, however, on December 23 Wang Ching-wei had departed from Geneva for return to China in response to urgent appeals from Nanking conveyed through China's delegation to the League of Nations.[12] What may we suppose his emotions to have been when he learned of Chiang's safety and he sailed once again into Shanghai on January 14, 1937, the man of the hour for whom the hour had still not come? Wang was met, among others, by Chou Fo-hai, a trusted behind-the-scenes factotum of Chiang's.[13] This is the first record of their contact, important for the story to come.

Although Wang asserts that he was never informed by Chiang or anyone else of the results of the Sian talks,[14] nevertheless, four days after his return he issued a statement urging the suppression of Communists before foreign invaders.[15] He questioned the Communist Party's sincerity and accused them of duplicity in their dealings with the Kuomintang since 1924. "It was not the Kuomintang which had misplaced its trust but it was the Communist Party which had broken faith."

There is little reason, however, to believe that Chiang had developed any more love for the Communists than Wang. The Sian agreements, whatever they may have been, were after all forced upon Chiang at the peril of his life. In retrospect, the Sian Incident seems to have been a turning point toward war. But it was only the subsequent events that made it so. Without the outbreak of war, Chiang would have returned to assault his political enemies as soon as he was able. Indeed, he did just that when the war with Japan stopped moving forward.

The immediate aftermath of Sian seemed to be very favorable. A new self-confidence, self-reliance, and unity seemed almost miraculously to quicken China, partly as a result of the Kuomintang-Communist united front which was being hesitantly fabricated behind drawn curtains. In addition, the Japanese government seemed to be taking a new and conciliatory course. On March 4 the new Japanese foreign minister, Sato Naotake, went so far as to declare that Sino-Japanese difficulties had been caused by a sense of Japanese superiority and promised that in the future negotiations would be on the basis of equality.[16]

Ambassador Kawagoe Shigeru was constantly engaged in negotiations in Nanking during that spring, which were rumored to deal with abolition of the Japanese client governments in north China. A number of anti-Japanese "incidents," for which the Japanese had been demanding wide-reaching concessions, were settled peacefully on the local level. The new seeming unity and solidity of China under the leadership of Chiang Kai-shek, a direct result of Japanese threats, took the Japanese by surprise; and it seemed for an instant as if they might halt their aggressive activities or even withdraw somewhat. The formation of a cabinet under the leadership of Prince Konoye Fumimaro, an aristocrat, reputed liberal, and friend of China, was viewed by the Wai-chiao-pu as a "matter of congratulation not only for Japan, but for China."[17]

In truth, the Japanese had little desire for, and less to gain by, full-scale war in China. They already possessed the lion's share of sovereignty in north China. Despite increased Chinese strength and unity following Sian, Japan's strength remained overwhelming in comparison. Second, it was the desire and interest of Japanese strategists to keep their hands free for possible war with the Soviet Union and to grasp whatever fruits the European crisis might drop into their laps. Since the Western powers to whom China had hitherto looked for support were preoccupied, Japanese aggression could only throw China into the arms of the Soviet Union, an eventuality contrary to the interests and desires of the Japanese military. Chiang, who had spent the last decade in mortal combat with the native Communists, would scarcely have made such a move if not forced to it.

Despite the many advantages of peace to both sides, previous events had made the situation unstable, difficult to maintain without changes which might come to have radical and undesirable consequences. The Japanese in China, like the Western imperialists before them, were a small armed force in a large country. Their position there depended upon "prestige," which the slightest setback would severely damage. Thus a partial retreat for them might mean a full retreat. Because of growing instability within the Japanese political structure, coordinated and limited response to the unexpected was very difficult. The Japanese military not only acted independently of the civilian arm but was also itself divided into semi-autonomous factions.

Chinese leadership was in a similar position. After Sian, Chiang owed his precarious position of political supremacy to the fact that he seemed the only man who could successfully unite the country against the Japanese. If he was to keep his position and preserve the simulacrum of new-found unity, he must not only not make visible concessions to the Japanese but must be constantly publicly pressing to roll them back; therefore, although neither side desired conflict, neither could yield nor abstain from pressing forward.

A decade of Chinese diplomatic maneuvering had exhausted Japanese patience and there was consequently a widespread feeling even among Japanese liberals that the "outrageous Chinese" should be taught a lesson. A decade of Japanese aggression and duplicity had virtually exhausted any hope that the Chinese might be able to appease them with finite diplomatic concessions.

Modern China had passed her entire existence in a twilight zone between peace and war. In addition to internal disorder, "incidents" with foreign powers were a constant fact of political life. Chinese statesmen had been forced to become habituated to the constant presence of violence and the threat of violence. Of course incipient violence is the reality which the facade of international relations always conceals. But the fact that foreign troops were actually stationed by treaty right within China proper made violent confrontation, encouraged by China's weakness, all the more likely. Usually these "incidents" were rather quickly resolved. In fact, the imperialist powers suspected that only violence would elicit from the Chinese government "respect" for their "interests," which, since the validity of foreign "interests" in China was just what Chinese nationalists denied and were devoted to extirpating, was perfectly true. It is true as well that because of the institutional inadequacies of the Chinese government as well as purposeful policies of evasiveness, diplomatic dealings with the Chinese government were trying on the patience.

Lines of communication and discussion between China and Japan, based upon both formal institutions like foreign offices and personal relationships of trust and honor, had been frayed by the events of the decade to the merest thread. Yet prompt, frank, and authoritative discussion between the two nations would be the essential factor in preventing a minor incident from becoming a major war.

The leaders of neither nation wanted war. Two factors, however, prevented either from paying the price for peace. First, the leadership of both Chiang Kai-shek and Konoye Fumimaro was rendered tenuous by widespread social revolution and the consequent weakness of the governmental institutions through which they sought to exercise leadership. Second, they both hoped to take advantage of the decay of the old international order dominated by western Europe to achieve nationalistic ambitions and thereby please and solidify their shaky constituencies. Thus they exacerbated the drift into chaos.

The situation in East Asia was at one with the world scene as the blindness, credulousness, and ambition of the world's leaders in the face of revolution in the international and social order caused what E. H. Carr calls the "twenty years crisis" to break out again into global war.

Opening Moves

2 The exchange of shots between Chinese and Japanese soldiers on the morning of July 7, 1937, some thirty miles southwest of Peking, was not itself a *casus belli*. It was only the occasion for war, the point when the mounting tensions within and between the two nations burst their bonds. The latest scholarly research,[1] as well as the observations of thoughtful diplomats of the time,[2] assert that the Marco Polo Bridge Incident was accidental and was not a preconceived campaign on the part of the Japanese military for further aggression in China.

Chinese patience, however, was exhausted. In the same way that internal tensions which had been developing within Japan pushed her on into foreign adventure, so did the forces of a century of the Chinese revolution and foreign oppression promote in the Chinese psychology an intense desire to wipe away national humiliation in a glorious defense of the homeland. Chinese leaders knew China's weakness. However, in part they were infected by the way of thinking described above, in part they felt that temporizing with the Japanese had failed; there was no way to meet Japanese force but with force of their own. At least Japan could be made to pay dearly for her conquests. But once the clash of arms had begun, the scope, aims, and outcome of the conflict became broader than ever anticipated. Chinese public opinion and Chinese leadership were virtually unanimous in supporting the government's decision to resist militarily further Japanese encroachment. But had they counted the cost and were they willing to pay it?

In contrast with, say, France, where the Petainists felt more in common with the foreign invaders than with Blum's socialists, in China there was no sympathy with the Japanese invaders, despite the many questions upon which Chinese differed, one from another. William Donald, the Australian newspaperman who had become one of Chiang's closest advisers, told a representative of the American embassy that there was "a large group of men around General Chiang who may desire avoidance of war at any price."[3] The sum of other evidence about Chinese councils, slight though it is, would seem not to support this report. Perhaps Donald, by hinting Chinese indecision, was fishing for an American statement of support for resistance. Nevertheless, various rumors suggested that some of the ex-warlords who had joined the Kuomintang were skeptical of the possibility of success against Japanese arms and even had contacts with the Japanese. General Han Fu-chü, for example, despite many strong statements about his intention to resist, allowed the Japanese an almost bloodless victory in Shantung. He was later executed for treason.[4]

In general, however, it would be not wrong to say that the real question before Chinese councils was not whether or not to resist, but whether this resistance should be limited with limited objectives, the traditional policy of simultaneous fighting and negotiations, or whether it should be all-out war.

On July 11 the mayor of Peking, General Ch'in Te-shun, signed an agreement with representatives of the Japanese Army for a "local settlement" of the Incident. A local settlement would have meant the further erosion of the authority of the Nanking government in north China and that was just what that government was anxious to avoid. Simultaneous with the negotiations in the north, Nanking had presented the Japanese with a note demanding the withdrawal of both armies to their original positions and furthermore had dispatched four divisions of the 29th Army under Sung Che-yüan to the north, a violation of the Ho-Umezu Agreement. Prime Minister Konoye, with the indecisiveness that characterized so many of his actions, announced on July 12 the "support" of his government for the "local settlement" but did so in a bellicose fashion. Patriotic fervor in both countries was fanned. It was the general belief that the Japanese had determined upon general mobilization.[5]

Thus the Chinese government, though it was anxious to avoid a local settlement, had every reason to believe that the Japanese government was not sincere in wanting one. Troops of both nations continued to move. Soon the fighting had spread all over north China; the "Marco Polo Bridge Incident" had become the "North China Incident."

The Kuomintang government was not known for making decisions by consensus. However, seeking the advice and support of leading citizens — politicians, educators, and others — in the face of the national crisis, Chiang called an unprecedented conference at Kuling (Lushan), his summer headquarters in the mountains of Kiangsi, in mid-July. Wang, who officiated at the conference, expressed the hope that the struggle with Japan could be delayed another five years while China built up her strength further.[6] The Communists, included in the councils of the government since Sian, also were much in evidence at the conference and certainly were in hearty agreement with the consensus of the conference: support for the government's policy of resistance.[7] Chiang expressed this consensus in a famous speech delivered during the course of the conference on July 19, in which he asserted that yielding Marco Polo Bridge would mean yielding Peking and yielding Peking would mean yielding Nanking.[8]

Chiang seems to have determined at this time to go beyond measured resistance to broad confrontation with Japan. He was to make his decision for war explicit in conversations with the American ambassador on July 25[9] and with Hu Shih on July 31, at which time he estimated its probable duration at six months.[10] The decision is, however, implicit in the Kuling speech several weeks earlier. In his speech Chiang set the four conditions on which his government would agree to settle the Incident: no infringement of sovereignty, no alteration of the status of the Hopei-Chahar Political Council, no removal of Nanking appointed officials, and finally, no limitation on where Sung Che-yüan's 29th Army might be stationed. This last condition represented an abrogation of the Ho-Umezu Agreement, which had restricted Nanking troops from north China, and thus would mean that the Japanese not only would have consented to a *status quo ante* but also would have allowed a reassertion of central government rights in north China. Chiang could not have entertained the belief that there was any chance that the Japanese would accept his conditions. Chiang went on to say that if these conditions were not accepted, China would have reached the "limit of endurance."

"But although a weak country, if, unfortunately, we should have reached that last limit, then there is only one thing to do. That is to throw the last ounce of energy into a struggle for national existence. And when that is done, neither time nor circumstance will permit our stopping midway to seek peace. We should realize that to seek peace after war has once begun means that terms would be such that the subjugation of our nation and complete annihilation of our race would be encountered. Let our people realize to the full extent the meaning of 'limit of endurance' and the extent of sacrifice thereby involved. For once that stage is reached we have to sacrifice and fight to the bitter end though with always the expectation of eventual victory. Should we hesitate, however, and vainly hope for temporary safety we shall perish forever."

It would be unjust to say that Chiang or anyone else in the Kuomintang *wanted* war; it was simply that he did not desire or was not able to pay the price for peace. If the Japanese were willing to pay his price, that would be fine, and he was not so foolish as not to have an interest in what the Japanese would demand in return. But he had a decade of experience to teach him to doubt that the Japanese would or could offer limited terms. There were many semi-official and nonofficial political brokers exploring peace possibilities, but since none had authority, this was so much idle chatter. Effectively during the month of July, the Chinese and Japanese governments were out of communication with one another. Events awaited armies on the battlefield. But Chiang's actions and nonactions (failing an unprecedented display of conciliation on the part of the Japanese) added up to a decision for all-out war rather than limited fighting accompanied by negotiations.

Why did Chiang make this decision? First of all, the internal situation forced him to it. He had the choice between civil war with the Communists without the support or even the compliance of his party and nation or war with the Japanese with the support of the Communists and popular patriotic enthusiasm. But equally important, China's capacity to resist was dependent more on the will of the Chinese people to resist than on the obviously inferior military forces at her command. This popular determination could only be mobilized by the government's resolution to resist. And yet such resolution might itself cut off the alternative of peace. Third, a traditional resource of Chinese defense had been reliance upon foreign powers who for various reasons were unwilling to see one of their number gain a paramount position in China. The Western powers, those associated with the League of Nations as well as the United States, had asserted an interest in world law and a hostility to aggression. However, it could be scarcely expected that China's friends would come to her aid if she were not making conspicuous and resolute efforts to defend herself. The supine policy had not been very successful in gaining assistance at the time of the Manchurian Incident.

These were forceful reasons. But did they justify escalating a war in which China was the weaker party? If war is indeed politics by other means, then must not wars have a feasible objective, peace on favorable terms? It was, however, inconceivable that Chinese arms could defeat the Japanese army. The best that could be hoped for was to make the Japanese pay heavily for their conquest and hope for some *deus ex machina* such as Western intervention to rescue China from her plight. Chiang's decision not simply to resist but to escalate the war was a leap of desperation. If the thought of further erosion of Chinese sovereignty was distasteful, all-out war with Japan might not only mean the destruction of Chinese sovereignty and the Kuomintang government but also would be certain to result in the physical devastation of the nation.

Although by the end of July Chiang had probably made the decision to extend the war to Shanghai,[11] during the month of July he neither committed his military forces in a full and resolute fashion against the enemy nor was willing to talk peace.

In a sense, the sea of East Asian politics was becalmed during July; the winds were about to shift, and in the meantime, China and Japan drifted. In a speech, "Frankness and Responsibility in Facing the Crisis," on August 4, Wang attacked both what he considered irresolution between war and peace and lack of ability to see what the probable outcome of conflict with Japan would be: defeat for China. "When China had been conquered at the end of the Sung and Ming dynasties, nobody was willing to fulfill responsibility, but everyone wanted to see how other people fulfilled theirs. When peace should have been made, everyone opposed peace; when war should have been declared, everyone opposed war, because in case of peace certain losses might be suffered; and in case of war, defeat was possible. The easiest way, therefore, was to put oneself beyond reproach by opposing both peace and war, and leave others to their fate."

In contrast, he cited the examples of Russia after Brest-

Litovsk and Germany after Versailles. "Both countries were able to preserve their national existence and revive, due to the fact that the people, facing extinction, were determined to save their countries. They were willing to speak frankly. They knew to secure peace there had to be certain losses . . . They knew that in case of war, defeat was possible, and they honestly admitted defeat, but after defeat they continued to fight. When they were again defeated they redoubled their efforts, until at last they saved their countries from extinction."[12]

It seems that in essence Wang was proposing his candidacy to lead China in defeat, which he saw as inevitable. It does not appear that he was opposing the war as such.

Wang was not alone in having some awareness of the cost of the war and in realizing that war once started must be ended. With political conditions and popular passions in the inflamed state that they were, it took courage to advise the Generalissimo to seek a negotiated peace. Wang's own advocacy was somewhat vitiated because he saw in it a fulfillment of his personal ambition.

It was Hu Shih, that exemplary scholar, educator, statesman, and friend of mankind, who took it upon himself to do so. Both Hu and Wang saw Kao Tsung-wu, one of the few persons experienced, willing, and able to conduct such negotiations with the Japanese, as the instrument of their hopes. Wang had hosted a dinner followed by a discussion of diplomatic problems, which Hu had attended on July 27 at Kuling,[13] but there is no evidence that they coordinated their démarches.

Kao himself had been fulfilling his function of feeling out the Japanese since the beginning of the Incident. July 7 had found him confined to a hospital bed in Shanghai with tuberculosis. Nevertheless, he received in his hospital room numerous Japanese visitors to discuss the crisis. By July 16 he was back in Nanking, for on that date he received the Japanese Consul Hidaka Shinrokuro who expressed to him the view that the Chinese government did not realize the gravity of the situation.[14] On July 18,[15] the day before the famous Kuling speech, Kao traveled to Kuling to see Chiang. Kao advised Chiang that since national defenses needed further strengthening, it was not an opportune time for war. He advised Chiang that the best course would be a prompt and firm military response coupled with negotiations. Kao frequently had advised Chiang, and it was a constant element in his own thinking, that war with Japan would enable the Communists to expand their own influence at the expense of that of the Kuomintang. Chiang did not prohibit Kao from exploring terms of peace with the Japanese, but, it seemed to Kao, in view of the intense popular feeling for resistance and against dealings with the Japanese, that he must wait for the situation to clarify itself before he made any further moves.[16] Although Kao was accustomed to undertaking his dealings with the Japanese on his own responsibility, since the government was unwilling to offer him instructions, he felt that in this case he dare not move.

Hu Shih came back from Kuling gravely concerned about the course his nation seemed headed upon. He deeply realized the tragedy that an all-out war with Japan would mean for China: the loss of decades of progress. From his knowledge of the United States gained through his American education and continued association with that country, he was fully aware of the thinness of support that China could expect from the West at this juncture.

Hu's distinguished career gave him immense prestige that assured that his words would at least gain the hearing of Chiang. Despite the fact that he had been somewhat critical of the Kuomintang in the past, respect for his character and accomplishments seemed to spare him at least in part from the suspicion of fishing in troubled waters for his own interest that might have attached itself to a lesser man. On the other hand, he was not personally acquainted with the political intricacies of dealing with Japan. It was natural then that he should seek the assistance of Kao Tsung-wu, who had this experience and whose views regarding the necessity of peace might be expected to coincide with his own.

Although he had only met Kao once before, Hu, in the company of Chiang Meng-lin, president of Peking University, and Mei I-ch'i, president of Tsinghua University, came to lunch with Kao Tsung-wu at Kao's home. Also present were Kao's friends and fellow officials Hsiao T'ung-tzu and Ch'eng Ts'ang-po.

Hu greeted Kao by asking, "Mr. Kao, what is your high (*kao*) opinion?" Kao replied, "My name may be high (*kao*) but my opinion is low." From this, according to one story, the "low tone club," a loose aggregate of individuals who favored a diplomatic settlement with Japan, got its name.

Kao told Hu that he believed that the government must begin to negotiate at once, for if the Japanese succeeded in conquering territory, then the diplomats would not be able to get it back by talking.

Hu proposed that Kao take action to begin peace talks.

Kao and his friends were able to persuade Hu that it would be better for Hu, outside the government hierarchy as he was, to attempt to persuade Chiang to begin diplomatic negotiations. Immediately Hu telephoned from Kao's house Ch'en Pu-lei, Chiang's personal secretary, and requested a meeting with Chiang. Chiang responded by inviting the three professors to lunch the following day, July 31.

This was to be an eventful day in the history of the incipient peace movement. The luncheon to which Hu and his colleagues were invited turned out to be a crowded one. Chiang made his announcement mentioned above that the decision for war had been taken. However, in leaving, Hu was able to say a few words to Chiang urging that diplomatic channels not be cut and recommending to him Kao Tsung-wu as a capable and responsible man. Chiang replied that he was well acquainted with Kao and that he planned to talk with him.

Chiang requested that Kao visit him that afternoon, and Kao repeated his advice that peace was better for China at the present time. Chiang agreed with Kao. Whether this agreement could be taken as any sort of authorization for negotiations is hard to say. In any case, Chiang did not express opposition.

After Kao's interview with Chiang, Kao received a phone call from Wang Ching-wei, who had just returned to Nanking from Kuling. Wang told Kao that he, Wang, was to receive the Generalissimo the next day, August 1. Wang asked Kao if Kao would like Wang to transmit anything to Chiang that Kao was unwilling to tell Chiang in person. Assumedly, what Wang meant was "Did Kao want Wang to express to Chiang on his behalf Kao's belief in the necessity of coming to terms with Japan immediately?" Kao replied to Wang that he talked freely with Chiang and that he had nothing which he wished Wang to convey. He did not take Wang further into his confidence at this time; nor as Chiang's agent would it have been proper for him to do so.

Kao then visited Hu and recounted his conversation with Chiang.[17] Was the stratagem of Hu and Kao and the sharing by Kao of Chiang's counsel with Hu fully consistent with Kao's responsibilities to Chiang?

Kao's working day was not yet over. That evening he met with Nishi Yoshiaki, the Nanking branch office chief of Mantetsu, the Japanese-owned Southern Manchurian Railway, headed by Prime Minister Konoye's friend and future foreign minister, Matsuoka Yōsuke. Nishi was one of Kao's many Japanese contacts. Kao told Nishi that when he had urged peace, Chiang had been silent and Wang had favored it. Not entirely seriously he urged Nishi to inform Matsuoka of the Chinese leaders' desire for peace and to attempt to persuade Matsuoka to intervene with Konoye. Kao may not have taken this request or Nishi very seriously, but Nishi did.[18] The story of Nishi's mission will be recounted in its place.

After Wang had in fact received Chiang on August 1, he telephoned Kao and asked him to come to his house. Wang told Kao that he had advised Chiang to work for peace through diplomatic channels and that Chiang informed him that he had already instructed Kao to do so. Kao was naturally embarrassed, since he had not shared this information with Wang on the previous day. He explained that the reason why he had not told Wang of Chiang's instruction was because he feared that Chiang might change his mind under such delicate circumstances and not carry through with negotiations. Wang told Kao that he need have no fear on this account: Wang Ching-wei himself would bear witness that Chiang had given Kao instructions to open peace discussions with Japan.[19] It was thus with Chiang's silent acquiescence and Wang's warm promise of support that Kao dared to open negotiations.

Hu also continued his efforts for peace. He visited Chiang once again and proposed a truce restoring the status quo, to be followed in three months by a peace conference in which all questions between the two countries could be reviewed.[20] Rumor also had it that some individuals were proposing to the Generalissimo that China offer to recognize Manchukuo in return for withdrawal of Japanese troops from north China.[21]

A complication was introduced into the possibility of beginning peace discussions by the fact that on July 8 Kawagoe

Shigeru, the Japanese ambassador, had left Shanghai for the Japanese concession in Tientsin.[22] There is some indication that the Chinese were applying pressure to get Kawagoe to return to Nanking, a victory of face for the Nanking regime.[23] Kao denies any such pressure on the part of the Chinese government.[24]

Be this as it may, the Japanese Foreign Ministry (Gaimushō) had itself developed an interest in negotiations. Kawagoe returned to Shanghai about August 5[25] and contacted a subordinate of Kao, requesting to meet with Kao.[26] This meeting took place on August 9. Kao immediately returned to report its content to the Generalissimo.[27] Kawagoe's instructions from the Gaimushō called for him to offer to the Chinese both short- and long-term proposals: the first dealing with truce negotiations, and the second, with a "General Adjustment of Sino-Japanese Relations."[28] Terms for peace would require a "demilitarized zone" in the Peking-Tientsin area; that is, no Chinese troops, but the Japanese troops could be stationed there under the terms of the Boxer Protocol. This concession would be balanced by Japanese abolition of the Hopei-Chahar and East Hopei puppet regimes and restoration of the Nanking government's sovereignty there as long as it was represented by officials friendly to the Japanese. Kawagoe was even instructed to suggest that the Japanese would be willing to consider abrogation of the Tangku Truce and the Ho-Umezu, Ch'in-Doihara Agreements. The "General Adjustment" was Hirota's "Three Points" warmed over; namely, Chinese recognition of Manchukuo, a Sino-Japanese anti-Comintern pact, and suppression of anti-Japanese activities. An important concession which was to be an issue for future discussion was the possibility that *tacit* recognition of Manchukuo by China might be acceptable to the Japanese.

The content of Kawagoe's instructions is of interest, however, only insofar as it reflects the evolution of policy within the Gaimushō itself because according to Kao, Kawagoe did not in fact present him with any specific terms. The two men merely discussed the desirability of and possibilities for localizing the conflict.[29] It is certain that such terms as those suggested in Kawagoe's instructions could not possibly have gained the consent of the Japanese military. Foreign Minister Hirota had strictly cautioned Kawagoe under no circumstances to allow any military personnel to gain any information with regard to

Wu P'ei-fu

the proposed terms, since he was certain of their opposition.[30] Perhaps, therefore, Kawagoe decided that it would be unrealistic to present the Chinese with the terms.

The existence, however, of such terms shows that there existed a certain will on the Japanese side for peace. There were a few men in the civil government and a few men in the military who did not share the general holiday spirit with which the Japanese nation went to war. They were able to see that it was not a matter of "punishing the insolent Chinese" but rather a matter of waging aggressive war. They had some awareness not only of the prospective cost in blood and treasure but also of the far-reaching and unpredictable changes that might result – the cementing of military rule in Japan, the forfeiting of the possibility of Chinese cooperation by standing in the way of Chinese nationalism, and not least, the possibility of advancing communism in China. They were aware too that the longer the war continued, the less willing the Japanese public and military would be to accept a compromise solution. In the civil government Prime Minister Konoye and Foreign Minister Hirota Koki must be included in this group. Konoye, according to one report, intended personally to fly to Nanking to confer with Chiang and solve the crisis.[31] According to another report, he sent a special representative.[32] This effort, or these efforts, were physically thwarted by the military. Konoye, that "supremely clever politician," imagined that he would be able to manipulate the military, but unfortunately, he did not have the courage or the strength to do so. He was a weak man riding a tiger. Even at this juncture he declared before the Diet on September 5: "The sole measure for the Japanese Empire to adopt is to administer a thoroughgoing blow to the Chinese Army so it may lose completely its will to fight."[33] Nevertheless, the efforts of Konoye and those associated with him to somehow engineer a settlement came to play an enormous role in the Wang peace movement to come. It was faith in Konoye's good intentions that sparked the hope of those Chinese who still continued to entertain the possibility of a compromise peace.

Perhaps more important than Konoye's persistent but low-pressure advocacy, there existed a powerful group within the military who desired peace and cooperation with China, although perhaps not on terms ultimately compatible with Chinese nationalism. Their views will find fuller development in the next chapter.

These relatively pacific-minded men in Japan, no more than Kao, Hu, or Wang on the Chinese side, were able to deflect the course of events. On August 12 the fighting spread to Shanghai and the raging conflagration ended the slight hope that diplomats could quench it with their words. The Kao-Kawagoe conversations never had any real possibility of success; Kawagoe could not speak for the military, Chiang too was undoubtedly preparing for war in Shanghai. Kao realized at the time that the hope for success was slim; nevertheless, he felt that it was worthwhile even grasping at a straw.[34] In retrospect he felt that if talks had begun sufficiently early, the war might have been prevented, although only to be followed by further incidents with the same danger.[35] But this would presuppose that the Chinese would have been willing to choose peace at a price at that time, which it does not seem that they were.

The shift of the fighting to Shanghai indicates a shift of strategy on the part of the Chinese government. From then until the end of the year, the primary endeavor of Chinese statesmen was to gain foreign support and intervention. This effort to gain foreign assistance was aimed primarily at the Anglo-American powers, partly individually and partly through the League of Nations; secondarily, at the Soviet Union, and finally, as a last resort, at Germany and Italy.

The war in Shanghai immediately involved the Western powers. (Germany and the USSR had no holdings; Italy only negligible ones.) It was, of course, in Shanghai that foreign interests and Western observers were centered. Chinese policy involved a two-pronged effort to hit the Western powers both in the pocketbook and in the heart. Wellington Koo presented China's case to the West: "It is clear that China, in vigorously resisting the Japanese armed aggression, is not only trying to defend her own territory and sovereignty, but in effect also to safeguard the rights and interests of the foreign powers within her territory. If China's efforts should fail for want of adequate support from this great institution dedicated to the cause of peace and security among nations [the League of Nations], or from those foreign powers whose special as well as general interests in the circumstances are the same as China's, then the menace of Japanese aggression will soon fall upon them and the burden of defence will have to be borne by themselves."[36]

Chiang squandered the best of his combat-ready, German-trained troops in a heroic defense and retreat, which indeed got headlines around the world. The Japanese obligingly furnished an exhibition of brutality and rapacity. China could ill-afford to lose her best troops. The thought guiding Chinese policy makers must have been, however, that perhaps a spectacular do-or-die effort might gain foreign intervention and prevent the further evolution of the war into mass resistance, which in addition to costing the peasantry dearly, might well bring down the Kuomintang regime.

Continuing this policy of seeking foreign assistance against Japan, China signed a Sino-Soviet nonaggression pact on August 21. Although the text of the treaty merely committed the parties to nonaggression and to abstention from aid to any third powers which should attack one or the other, undoubtedly it was accompanied by a Soviet commitment to aid the Kuomintang government with modest amounts of military supplies, which thereafter appeared in the China fighting. Both the difficulty of transport and the Soviet Union's own military weakness limited the amount of practical assistance. Stronger treaty terms would have possibly offended the Anglo-American powers.

The signature of the pact made compromise with Japan even more unlikely, since the Japanese proposal was for "cooperation" with the Kuomintang against the Chinese Communists within and the Soviet Union without. Moreover, the Japanese could no longer count on the opposition of the Chinese Communists to the Kuomintang. It was only natural that the Chinese should seek this agreement which they had heretofore rejected lest it might further offend Japan because China had no other foreign power that was willing to support her against Japanese pressures. Now that Japan had committed the bulk of its military machinery in a bloody fighting war, there seemed little use in sensitivity to Japan's feelings. Likewise, it was only natural that the Soviet Union should seek such an agreement. The Soviet Commissar for Foreign Affairs, Maxim Litvinov, told the American ambassador in Paris that he and his government were "delighted" about the conflict in the Far East and anticipated that Japan would be weakened and preoccupied for some time to come.[37] The conclusion of this pact with the Soviet Union was a decisive factor in causing the Japanese to decide that the success of their aims in China demanded the elimination of the Chiang government and the emergence of another regime or other regimes with which they could "cooperate."

Surely the hypocritical ineffectuality of the Western powers' response to China's need and the threat posed by Japanese aggression to world order more than justified Chiang's acceptance of Soviet aid. The Chinese government, continuing its heroic defense of Shanghai, appealed to the League of Nations on August 30 and September 12, urging sanctions against Japan under the League covenant. The League dillied and dallied and at length, after referring the matter to committee and subcommittee, extricated itself from having to make any embarrassing decision by suggesting that the matter be referred to an extra-League conference of the signatories of the Nine Power Treaty of 1922. This was to be the infamous Brussels Conference.

Invitations to the Conference were not sent out until October 15. Japanese refusal to participate could have been predicted. "As soon as the Powers understand the true intentions of Japan, and take suitable steps to make the Nanking Government reconsider its attitude, then and only then will a way be paved for their cooperation with Japan respecting the settlement of the present conflict."[38] The conference finally convened on November 3 and once again made a humiliating plea for Japanese participation, rejected by that nation on November 12. Wellington Koo eloquently pleaded for at least economic sanctions against Japan, but the conference closed by merely proposing that the participants "consider what is to be their common attitude in the situation that Japan does not share the interpretation of the other signatories of the Nine Power Washington Treaty."

The time and glory purchased so dearly by Chinese forces during the Shanghai campaign had been for nought. During the Brussels Conference, that is, mid-November, the superior Japanese military machine broke through the weary and battered Chinese troops and advanced with great swiftness up the Yangtze. The capital, Nanking, from which the Kuomintang government had withdrawn on November 20, partly to Hankow, partly to Chungking, fell in an orgy of rape and pillage on December 13.

Japan's conquest of the treaty ports and their hinterland, leaving ruin in its wake, destroyed the wealth and influence of the moderate Western-influenced upper class. It was just this group who would have pushed most strongly for compromise, not only out of personal self-interest to safeguard their property, but also because pragmatism was their business. When the regime was driven from Nanking to Hankow and from Hankow to Chungking, influence gravitated toward those who, having nothing to lose, were eager to risk everything. The wealthy Westernized treaty-port Chinese who had supported the Kuomintang and Chiang Kai-shek so extensively in earlier days, found that even if they fled the occupied areas, the cruel logic of politics meant that with the loss of their wealth, their support would have less value. And, of course, seeing their own positions destroyed, they too could move toward an all-out resistance point of view.

In company with the advance of Japanese arms, Japanese diplomats probed the possibilities for settlement. In part these proposals represented the sincere desire for peace of certain officials in the Gaimushō and elsewhere in the government. There still was very little likelihood that these officials could speak for the military, however, in whose hands the direction of affairs increasingly rested. In part these proposals were part of a political plot, in the first place to undercut China's efforts in Geneva and Brussels to obtain Western assistance, and in the second place, to cause dissension in Chinese ranks.

During October Foreign Minister Hirota made various proposals to the Chinese through the British ambassador, Sir Robert Craigie, a gentleman with pro-Japanese proclivities. This move undoubtedly improved Anglo-Japanese relations and worsened Anglo-Chinese relations, but because of the absolute opposition of the Japanese military to the prospect of Anglo-American mediation — after all, what they were fighting for was to drive Western influence out of China — it could make little contribution to the cause of peace.

The major possibility for peace from early November through the end of the year seemed to be in German mediation, since that nation enjoyed cordial relations with both combatants.

Why should the Germans have been interested in peace in the Far East? There are two reasons: one of sentiment, the other of interest. First, men like Ambassador Trautmann and many of his superiors in the German Foreign Ministry, career diplomats who were serving the Nazi regime as they had served its predecessors, felt a deep sympathy for China and an admiration for the Generalissimo. Because Germany had lost her special privileges in China as a result of her defeat in the First World War, she seemed to China no longer to be numbered among the imperialist powers. Germany, through its military missions in China, had made a great contribution to the strengthening of the Kuomintang regime and hence had a sentimental interest in preserving that regime; furthermore, the German diplomats saw a parallel between their own situation during the First World War and the Chinese situation at the present time. As they saw it, if Germany had accepted terms when defeat seemed inevitable instead of waiting for a punitive peace to be forced upon her, Germany would have been far better off. Thus they felt they were offering China wise advice in urging her to make terms with the Japanese while they were still willing, it seemed, to make peace on terms.

Second, out of political interest the German government had not given up the ambitions of its imperial predecessors to occupy a privileged economic and political position in China. But most important, from the point of view of the Nazis, Japan's involvement in what the Germans, privy as they were to intimate knowledge of China's military resources, correctly foresaw as an endless war in China, would effectively reduce Japan's value as an ally, or even as an independent aggressor, against Great Britain and the Soviet Union. What the Germans really wanted was to bring both China and Japan into close association with the Axis, and there were many reasons why they could believe these hopes might mature.

On November 3 Foreign Minister Hirota informed the German ambassador to Japan, Dirksen, of the following terms which he wished the German embassy in Nanking to communicate to Chiang. In Dirksen's view "Japan seriously desires peace on . . . [this] basis and . . . it is just as seriously determined on ruthless continuance of the war until the final overthrow of China in case the Nanking Government does not accept the conditions now."[39] The Japanese terms were as follows: (1) an autonomous government for Inner Mongolia; (2) a demilitarized zone along the Manchukuo border to a point south of the

Peking-Tientsin line; (3) a "common fight against bolshevism"; (4) various economic concessions and privileges. However, "The whole administration of North China would be left to the Nanking Government if peace were to be concluded at once, on condition that a pro-Japanese top official was appointed. In case an immediate conclusion of peace should not come about, and the necessity therefore arose of creating a new administrative agency for North China, this new administrative agency would be retained when peace was concluded later. Thus far the Japanese Government has abstained from the establishment of an autonomous government of any kind in North China."[40]

Ambassador Trautmann on November 5 reported these terms to Chiang Kai-shek in the presence of H. H. Kung. Chiang replied that (1) "he could not accept any Japanese demands so long as the Japanese were not prepared to restore the *status quo ante*" and (2) "it was impossible for him to take official cognizance of the Japanese demands because China was the concern of the powers at the Brussels Conference, and they had the intention, for their part, to work for peace on the basis of the Washington Treaty."[41] On November 8 Dirksen reported the Chinese reaction to the proffered peace terms. Two weeks later Hirota told Dirksen that "Japan expected the initiation of peace negotiations within a short time, with Germany participating. In spite of the recent military successes of the Japanese, the previously submitted Japanese demands would not be made more severe on the main points; in particular, autonomy in North China would still not be demanded."[42]

The report that despite their recent and impending victories, the Japanese would stick to their previous demands was communicated to H. H. Kung, then president of the Executive Yüan, by Ambassador Trautmann on November 28, according to information later revealed by Wang Ching-wei; and on the following day it was communicated to Wang Ch'ung-hui, the foreign minister.[43] The vice minister of foreign affairs, Hsü Mo, informed the Generalissimo of the apparent Japanese willingness to negotiate on December 2. That afternoon Chiang met with a number of the principal Chinese military leaders. Hsü Mo reported what Trautmann had said about the alleged Japanese terms. According to Hsü the military leaders favored acceptance.[44] As a consequence of this meeting, later that afternoon when Chiang met with Trautmann, Chiang stated: "1. China accepts the terms as a basis for discussion of peace. 2. The sovereignty and the integrity as well as the ... (group garbled) independence of North China may not be violated. 3. Germany is to act as mediator in the peace negotiations from the beginning. 4. Agreements between China and third powers may not be touched upon in the peace negotiations."[45]

Trautmann said that Germany could not participate directly in the negotiations but would do "what we could behind the scenes to help China."[46] The refusal of Trautmann and his government to mediate in the prospective negotiations left Chiang's acceptance of the terms as a "basis for discussion" in a somewhat ambiguous state, since Chiang's acceptance had been hinged on German mediation. The German government was certainly correct in refusing this responsibility, since it wished neither to force Japanese demands on China nor to strain her relations with Japan by supporting China against those demands. Undoubtedly Chiang was well aware that the Germans would not accept his request to put themselves in the middle, and thus he was making his acceptance purposely ambiguous.

Several days after Chiang's interview with Trautmann, while Chiang was away reviewing the troops, the Standing Committee of the Supreme National Defense Council met with Wang Ching-wei, the vice-chairman, presiding in Chiang's absence. After hearing Hsü Mo's report, they determined that peace negotiations should be continued.

Wang later asserted that Chiang did not take further action at this time because he cabled the Japanese conditions to Stalin and received a noncommittal response.[47] My own impression from the study of these documents is that Chiang was not interested in quibbling about terms; he did not trust the Japanese and did not intend to negotiate unless he was convinced the Japanese had performed a true about-face and henceforward were to permit China's continued existence as a sovereign nation. He was of course anxious both to preserve German good will and assistance and to maintain German involvement in the problem of Sino-Japanese peace, since the involvement of a powerful and friendly third-power could only work in China's interest. But whether or not Chiang truly considered peace at this time, it was soon to come out that once again the proposals of the Gaimushō did not have the backing of the military.

Anticipating that their careful and well-intentioned efforts were about to be crowned with success, German Ambassador Dirksen presented to Hirota on December 7 a summary of peace efforts under the German aegis to date, including the Chinese acceptance of December 2, as instructed by Berlin. "Hirota received the memorandum with thanks and the remark that he would now obtain the opinion of the Army and the Navy. Hirota doubted whether it would still be possible to negotiate on the basis drawn up a month ago, that is, before the great Japanese military successes. To my [Dirksen's] remark that as late as the middle of November, after the first successes, he had said to me that his basis remained unchanged, he replied that the last few weeks had brought about a different situation; the Field Army had become more exacting in its demands."[48]

Whether Hirota was absolutely justified in putting the blame for an intransigent policy solely on the military seems in great doubt. It appears from evidence presented in the next chapter that Konoye himself was instrumental in pushing this policy even over the opposition of powerful military leaders. The good faith of the Japanese diplomats is doubtful, since reports of the negotiations appeared in the press as soon as they transpired or even before. Because a precondition for successful negotiations was secrecy, such clearly deliberate leaks suggest that the real objective of the Japanese government in these negotiations was to embarrass the Kuomintang government with its domestic and foreign supporters and cause its internal collapse.

That these diplomatic conversations were not in good faith but were sheer political provocation is further illustrated by the fact that while China, in her expression on December 2 of a willingness to negotiate, shared the German notion that this would be shortly followed by an appeal by the Führer to both sides for an end to hostilities so that negotiations could continue, the Japanese plan was for hostilities to continue until a final settlement. Of course, should Chiang admit to be treating seriously for peace with the Japanese, the Communists would instantly rebel and China would be at Japan's mercy.

It was an essential element in Japan's China policy to manipulate the various regional and divisive forces within China and to take every advantage of the fragility of China's unity under

Kuomintang leadership. Konoye himself declared on November 27 that "long resistance would lead to the breaking up of the Central Chinese Government and the appearance of many separate regimes which Japan would support. If, as in the case of Spain, a separate regime controlled over half of China, Japan would consider recognizing it as the government of China."[49]

Whatever may have been the possibilities for peace in early November when the Chinese were still holding fast at Shanghai, after the fall of Nanking, the Japanese military made it clear by their public utterances that they had decided not to make peace with Chiang Kai-shek's government but to establish new regimes in China. Hugh Byas of the New York Times reported in an article datelined December 10: "Apparently the Japanese army has made up its mind not to treat with Chiang. Unless he resigns, moves his troops and ceases to resist, it is stated, he will be pursued and defeated wherever he goes, and as his government will no longer be recognized as the government of China, Japan will support movements for the establishment of a new regime."[50]

And if Chiang should resign, who would replace him? The answer in everybody's mind was Wang Ching-wei, who had emerged so often in the past to take responsibility when pressure from Japan had become unendurable. William H. Donald, Chiang's Australian adviser, told an officer of the American Embassy on December 6 that Chiang would not personally enter into negotiations with the Japanese but leave them to the so-called pro-Japanese group. Donald asserted that Trautmann had conveyed Japanese desires to see Wang Ching-wei and Chang Ch'ün prominent in the government; and Ho Ying-ch'in, as head of the army.[51] Press reports from Shanghai[52] asserted the same thing.

During the period of seeking Anglo-American and Soviet support, Wang Ching-wei had not been very visible, although he held the post of chairman of the Central Political Council. During October and November he had, however, made at least half a dozen nationally publicized speeches in which he supported the war of resistance most unequivocally. According to T'ao Hsi-sheng, a Peking University professor, long connected with Wang, who was later to follow Wang into the peace movement and then to desert him, Wang declared his intention at this time to cooperate with Chiang until the end of the war.[53] Privately, however, he continued to favor a peaceful diplomatic settlement with Japan at the earliest possible time.

As the Anglo-American oriented Chinese statesmen were exerting themselves at Brussels to get support for the Chinese cause, with the same end Wang tried to gain Italian support or at least to use the Italians to delay or prevent the Japanese from doing harm to the Chinese cause. Mussolini and his son-in-law Foreign Minister Galeazzo Ciano could be counted upon not to miss a chance to cut a *bella figura* on the stage of international politics, even though Italian interests in China were virtually nil. The facist statesmen identified the Sino-Japanese conflict with their own imperial endeavors in Ethiopia and thus were predisposed to support Japanese conquest and to urge the Chinese to submit.

Wang had reason to repose some hope in Ciano, however, for in the early 1930's Ciano had served as vice-consul, secretary of legation, consul-general, and minister in China, and at that period his "pro-Chinese sympathies" were "outspoken."[54] However, in August of 1937 Ciano confided to the American ambassador that he had advised a Chinese with whom he was intimate that China should make the best terms that it could for it was better "to lose a leg even though the operation was a painful one than the more vital parts of the body."[55]

In late October of the same year Ch'en Kung-po, at that time press and propaganda minister and formerly minister of industry, one of Wang's closest followers and by far the most distinguished to follow him into the peace movement, set out, appointed by the Executive Yüan, as head of a Chinese good will mission accompanied by the former ambassador to Germany, W. W. Yen "presumably for the purpose of enlisting the support of [the Axis] countries for China in the present conflict."[56] Wang in a speech in early December expressed his conviction that with Ch'en's visit as special ambassador to Rome, Italian-Chinese relations would be much improved and Italy would not openly aid Japan.[57]

Ch'en requested a large sum of money in order to take with him a certain woman from Shanghai who it was hoped would be able to influence Ciano.[58] It is not clear whether this money was not sent or the woman's charms were not effective. In any case,

Ciano's diary records that he gave little comfort to China's cause. On November 15 he told Ch'en that China's cause was hopeless and advised "direct negotiations through the mediation of Italy and Germany." The following day Ch'en met with Ciano once again, this time requesting Ciano to sound out Tokyo on conditions of peace and gave Ciano "to understand that the recognition of Manchukuo might be conceded."[59] Chiang must have got word of the counsels of defeat that these two emissaries were spreading and about the first of the year disavowed them, stating that Ch'en and others were visiting Europe as private individuals and had no connection with the National Government or himself.[60]

With the beginning of the new year, Chiang resigned his post as chairman of the Executive Yüan, H. H. Kung became chairman; Chang Ch'ün, vice-chairman. Chiang devoted his attention to military affairs. According to several sources,[61] the meaning of this move was that Chiang was preparing for peace with Japan.

One source claims that upon Ch'en Kung-po's return, Wang suggested the formation of a "privy council" above the Executive Yüan, which he would head. Thus Wang would take all responsibility for making peace. Chiang, however, rejected this solution, expressing the undesirability of having to flee from the Japanese to the northwest and thus becoming captive to the Communists.[62]

Our knowledge of the inner councils of the Chinese government at this period is based only on occasional rumor; the Kuomintang archives are still closed, and undoubtedly, considering the complexity of the scene, it would tax the abilities of a master historian with all the documents before him to untangle it. It seems fairly certain that the Chinese did not make a positive decision to reject peace talks with the Japanese but chose rather to let events take their course and hope for the best. The possibility that Chiang might resign, that Wang, as in the thirties, or others, might take responsibility for peace with Japan must have been discussed. Chiang might have adopted such a policy had the Japanese showed unambiguous evidence of their desire for a peace consistent with Chinese sovereignty. They did not.

On December 23 Hirota informed Dirksen of new and more extensive peace conditions. China was given only one week to make her decision, which in view of the delay occasioned by transmission via Berlin was a ridiculously short time. The Japanese could not have expected acceptance; indeed, some clearly hoped for rejection so that the already formed resolution to proceed with the elimination of the Kuomintang Regime could proceed. The conditions were as follows: 1. China must abandon her pro-Communist as well as anti-Japanese and anti-Manchukuo policy and cooperate with Japan and Manchukuo in carrying out their anti-Communist policy. 2. Demilitarized zones and special regimes shall be established in areas where necessary. 3. Agreements for close economic cooperation shall be concluded between Japan, China, and Manchukuo. 4. China shall pay Japan the required indemnity.[63]

This draft was the result of compromise between hard and soft liners. The vagueness of the terms meant in essence a dictated peace. Hirota told Dirksen in confidence that an autonomous "special regime" in Mongolia, and another for Shanghai, a "government with extensive powers but autonomy" for north China, demilitarized zones in Inner Mongolia, north China, the Yangtze area, indemnity to cover partial cost of war, compensation for destroyed Japanese property, and occupation expenses were intended.[64] It is even questionable if, had the Chinese yielded, Hirota could have kept the demands within these limits. Trautmann transmitted the four conditions to H. H. Kung and Madame Chiang, the Generalissimo being ill, on December 23. Gloom and consternation prevailed at Chungking.

It was not until January 13 that the Chinese foreign minister, Wang Ch'ung-hui, read to Trautmann the following for transmission to the Japanese: "After due consideration we have found that the altered terms are rather too broad in scope. The Chinese Government desires therefore to be apprised of the nature and content of the newly submitted conditions in order to make a careful examination and reach a definite decision."[65] Wang Ching-wei later claimed that the original draft of this reply, which was approved by the Executive Yüan, had appended to the above the assertion that the Japanese proposals might be accepted as a basis for peace negotiations, and therefore Japan was urged to formulate more concrete terms for further discussion. Kung, despite some members of the Executive Yüan who asserted that body was competent to decide, telegraphed

Chiang at Loyang. Chiang through his adjutant replied that these last two sentences should be omitted.[66]

That such a hint of compliance could have halted the Japanese from their chosen course is unlikely. Following several days of consultations between the various organs of the War Ministry and the General Staff,[67] the Imperial Conference (Gozen kaigi) had already met and formalized the decision not to deal further with the Kuomintang government. This decision, which was to mark a turning point of events to come, was announced by Prime Minister Konoye on January 16 in his famous *aite to sezu* statement, also referred to as the "first Konoye statement." "Even after the capture of Nanking the Japanese Government have till now continued to be patient, with a view to affording the Chinese National Government a final opportunity to reconsider their attitude. However, the Chinese Government, without appreciating the true intention to Japan, blindly persist in their opposition against Japan, with no consideration either internally for the people in their miserable plight or externally for the peace and tranquility of all Asia. *Accordingly the Japanese Government will cease henceforth to deal with that Government (Subete teikoku seifu wa kongo kokumin seifu o aite to sezu)* and they look forward to the establishment of a new Chinese regime, harmonious coordination with which can really be counted upon. With such a regime they will warmly co-operate for the adjustment of Sino-Japanese relations and for the building up of a rejuvenated China."[68]

Thus the first chapter of the China Incident was ended. From this point on the Japanese had burned their bridges. They had publicly resolved not to make peace with Chiang Kai-shek but to see his regime destroyed utterly. What were they to do if this remained beyond their power? Former Prime Minister Wakatsuki privately asserted that the statement had made the restoration of peace must more difficult. "First Prince Konoye wanted to utilize the military. But politics is a difficult thing. When one tries to use someone else, he ends up being used himself. And when he realizes it, it is too late."[69]

Japanese Intentions, Chinese Prospects

3 Wang Ching-wei, a student of Chinese history, had before him the model of Chinese statesmen who served barbarian dynasties. He observed the gradual amelioration and sinification of foreign rule. Indeed history seemed to show that, while barbarians may rule in the Middle Kingdom, China can scarcely be governed without Chinese collaboration and Chinese administrators. But the prospects for Wang and for other Chinese "collaborators" were dependent specifically on what plans the latest conquerors, the Japanese, had for China. Even several decades later, it is not at all clear what those intentions were. Plans for China evolved themselves out of the baffling flux of Japan's development during the modern era. The twin phenomena of Japan's expansion, which began shortly after the Meiji Restoration, and the later rise of military rule, which did not become very obvious until the 1930's, defy analysis.

It is natural that modern historians are questioning the simplistic generalities about conspiracies by junior officers and the like which seemed to grow out of evidence presented at the villian-seeking Tokyo war crimes trials. Anyone who has spent some time with the original sources of the militarist era will find it difficult to ascribe personal viciousness to the participants, so evident in the case of Goebbels, Himmler, and their cohorts. Nevertheless no amount of revisionism can remove from these men the responsibility for the war in China and the war in the Pacific, the costs of which in human and economic terms are incalculable. A point of view which sees them totally as automata driven by mechanistic forces is certainly more degrading to their human dignity.

Most historians would agree that the dominant motivation of Japan's expansion was a sense of insecurity. Korea, the Meiji leaders thought, was a "dagger pointed at Japan's heart." In consequence, Japan sought wars in 1894–95 with China and with Russia in 1904–05 to establish her hegemony in Korea. To safeguard the interests in Manchuria which she had obtained as a result of her victory over Russia, Japan became involved in successive adventures in north China, not to mention Siberia, Mongolia, or Manchuria itself.

Japan's nineteenth century imperialism was part of her vaunted modernization and Westernization. She was aping the Western powers who were competing to divide up the "uncivilized" world. Japan was praised by the Western nations for her success in building an empire and hence joining the club of advanced nations which was the arbiter of the international order. Yet Japan's political ideology, which drew heavily from ancient legend but which had never been codified as it was in the post-Restoration era, also contributed to giving Japan's imperialism a special character. Japan has historically had a racial and cultural homogeneity which combined with isolation to develop a sense of exclusiveness. While she received high culture in successive waves from China, it was impossible for her to accept that the Chinese emperor rather than the Japanese was the rightful ruler of all under heaven.

The militarism of the 1930's cannot, however, be seen as simply reemergence of the military dominance of the shogunal eras. A half-century had passed since the Restoration and Japan had undergone tremendous social and economic changes. The samurai of old were no more and the new military elite were drawn from the secondary schools of the new educational system. The same factors that caused many Europeans to abandon the attempt to order themselves with free and democratic institutions were operative also in Japan: the example of Western moral bankruptcy occasioned by the First World War, the seeming weakness, corruption, and self-serving of politicians, the privations and inequities brought about by the great depression.

Events of the 1920's and 1930's such as the San Francisco School Board case, the unsatisfactory outcome of the Washington Naval Conference, the growth of tariff protectionism led many Japanese to feel that the world was closing in on them and that the Western nations would never accept them as equals.

During the Meiji period, some Japanese formulated the notion that Japan's *kokutai* (national polity) based on her unique emperor system was superior, at least for Japan and East Asia, to Western polities. This notion — under the stress of a sense of presumed rejection – contributed to Japan's decision in the 1930's to go it alone and to attempt to eliminate Western influence from East Asia. The growing dominance of *kokutai* thought helps explain both the assumed high moral tone of Japanese officials, and also, how, without an overarching plan such as Hitler articulated in his *Mein Kampf,* one unlicensed act of violence could lead to another with what seemed to outsiders to be malignant persistence.

Since the emperor was the source of all morality, it followed that his servants — especially the Imperial army – could do no wrong. The spread of the rising sun could be nothing but the spread of virtue. In the words of Maruyama Masao, "The just cause and national conduct invariably coexist. In order to spread the just cause, it is necessary to act; conversely, when the nation acts, it is *ipso facto* in the just cause."[1]

Decisions are made by men in human contexts. Discussion of factions, hierarchies, organs, powers behind the throne, and the like are to some extent an excuse for hiding our ignorance of the essential human realities. Getting to these realities in the Japanese case is particularly difficult because decisions are made collectively and by consensus. Though one man may be behind a decision, he rarely takes full responsibility for it. The members of the power group may not be readily discernible from the posts they hold. Therefore the government's official structure may be at some remove from power realities.

The question of who ruled Japan became more complex during the 1930's as the military rose in influence and interpenetrated the Japanese polity until, by the early 1940's, they were the masters of Japan. How then can one delineate the respective spheres of the military and the civil authorities? The Western historian who has made the most thorough study of Japanese foreign policy formation during the 1930's says that the civil authorities maintained control of decision making and continued the policies of their predecessors. He eloquently argues that "it is unfair to the responsible leaders of the Imperial government, as well as to the policies they pursued, to view the authoritarianism and imperialism of the 1930's as the consequence of the thoughts and deeds of right-wing ideologues, zealous junior officers, conspiratorial field commanders, and subordinate staff officers who manipulated the ministers of state as if they were *bunraku* puppets."[2]

Though in fact the continuity of the civil government — the

bureaucracy, the cabinet — continued unbroken, nevertheless, the military held the upper hand. The basis of its power was its ability to refuse to provide army and navy ministers — who had to be active duty officers — without which a cabinet could not be formed or continue. The military's power infinitely expanded once the military adventures began, for the "prestige" of the Imperial army became an unanswerable argument. Even decisions made by civilian officials had to be formulated so as to be acceptable to the military. These decisions, made under military intimidation, either explicit or implicit, have in large measure to be laid at their door.

Military bureaus and offices proliferated at the center. The War Ministry and the General Staff both had their own separate but overlapping bureaucratic apparatus. As the Incident spread and Japanese forces assumed the role of occupying armies, the regional commands in north, central, and south China became vested interests and assumed a degree of autonomy. Military organs, both new and old, simply rose in influence relative to the already established pillars of what Professor Maruyama calls the Japanese "oligarchy." This diffusion of authority among various military and civilian offices created an atmosphere of indecision inappropriate to resolving a difficult political and military crisis in which hard choices had to be made.

"The individuals who composed the various branches of the oligarchy did not regard themselves as active regulators but as men who were, on the contrary, being regulated by rules created elsewhere. None of the oligarchic forces in the country could ever become absolute; instead they all coexisted — all of them equally dependent on the ultimate entity [the concept of the emperor] and all of them stressing their comparative proximity to that entity."[3] Coordination therefore between the military and civil organs was weak. Irregular Renraku kaigi (liaison conferences) were held between top military and civilian leaders on matters of high policy. Naturally the preparatory work had already been done by lower-level staffs.

The device adopted as the military crisis deepened to give the appearance of decisiveness was the Gozen kaigi, the imperial conference held in the presence of the emperor. The imperial presence was supposed to make a decision "irrevocable" but more often papered over the lack of decision. Wang Ching-wei's misunderstanding of a Gozen kaigi decision caused the initial miscarriage of his peace movement. Another sort of civil-military coordination was for political leaders to back factions within the military in return for their support. This was a two-way street for military bureaucrats toyed with politicians in the same way.

The nature of the factions within the Japanese military is still not clear. Evidence before the Tokyo war crimes tribunal — the memoirs of Konoye and the testimony of General Tanaka Ryūkichi — led many writers to portray the whole militarist era as dominated by the struggle between the Tōseiha (control faction) and the Kōdoha (imperial way faction.)[4] Modern studies have demonstrated that this bipolar analysis is a questionable oversimplification. Factions were important in military politics and hence in national policy. They were based on personal loyalties and affinities as well as on shared ideas and attitudes. Naturally differing views of how to "solve the Incident" found their place within the factional system.

The present narrative outlines a peace conspiracy between Chinese politicians and Japanese soldiers with political connections. The Wang Ching-wei peace movement depended on a group within the Japanese army who at least conveyed the appearance of desiring peace. We are seeking here to define this group.

Peace might be sought because intrigue might gain the desired ends better than guns or because Japanese armies should be in readiness to strike at their old enemy to the north, the Soviet Union, or to seize the weakly defended holdings of the Western imperialists to the south. Undoubtedly these practical arguments had their weight. But most of what we tentatively call a "peace" or "nonexpansion" clique felt also that there existed a natural cultural and racial affinity between the two great nations of East Asia and that the war between them was based on tragic misunderstanding.

The man who inspired this line of thinking was Ishiwara Kanji.[5] Ishiwara had been prominent in the Manchurian conspiracies of the 1930's but had undergone a change of heart. At the time of the Marco Polo Bridge Incident Ishiwara was serving in the important post of chief of the Military Operations Bureau of the General Staff. He strongly argued that although the Japanese could not concede their position in Manchuria, Chinese sovereignty should be restored south of the Great Wall.

Ishiwara's influence had been gravely compromised by his implication in an attempt by the so-called "Manchurian faction" to dictate the composition of the Hayashi cabinet the preceding December. The failure of this political maneuver eventuated in January of 1937 in a personnel shake-up unfavorable to those who had been involved. Although Ishiwara maintained his own post for the time being, his subordinates and supporters were transferred. As a result, Ishiwara's strength in military politics was broken. He could not find a hearing for his views on limitation of the Incident. In November he was transferred from his influential post in the capital to the Kwantung Army. Ishiwara's influence on the later development of the military's search for peace was largely through his followers.

Ishiwara's views, later to be expressed in the pronouncements of his Tōa renmei (East Asian league) were not very different from what became the official orthodoxy — the "new order in East Asia." The difference was that Ishiwara really believed in literal Sino-Japanese cooperation, albeit a cooperation in which Japan would clearly be the "elder brother." Ishiwara seems to have favored a somewhat more equal community of the East Asian nations than that envisaged in the orthodox "Greater East Asia co-prosperity sphere." But he never had a chance to put his ideas into practice.

Naturally, some of those who counted themselves disciples of Ishiwara found in his slogans justification for Japanese aggression. Itagaki Seishirō — a prominent proponent of "peace work" who served as war minister and chief of staff of the China Expeditionary Army — could be placed in this group. On the other hand, Kagesa Sadaaki, the soldier most committed to the Wang Ching-wei movement, found the teachings of Ishiwara inconsistent with Japanese military rule of China.

Other Wang movement cadres influenced by Ishiwara were Horiba Kazuo, chief of the War Guidance Section of the General Staff, and Imai Takeo, assistant military attache in Peking at the time of Marco Polo Bridge.

Though many of these who had been associated with Ishiwara in the "Manchurian faction" also opposed expansion of the war, the so-called "anti-expansionist clique" was by no means coextensive with the former. For example, General Tada Hayao, the vice-chief of the General Staff and Ishiwara's superior, was the leader in the struggle to prevent the break with Chiang but was not a particular intimate of Ishiwara.

The "anti-expansionist clique" lost the struggle at that point, but they continued to hold considerable power within the Japanese military structure. In large part the same people who wanted peace negotiations with Chiang went on to support negotiations with Wang in the hope that they might accomplish the same thing.

Japanese plans for China were influenced by her previous experience in building and administering an empire. Japan directly administered her nineteenth-century conquests, Taiwan and Korea, without employing cooperative local leaders to maintain the appearance of independence.[6] On the Asian mainland, the situation was somewhat different. Japanese strength was not so overwhelming in relation to the numerous local population and to the foreign powers which had deeply entrenched interests there.

From the Manchurian Incident on, the Japanese endeavored to provide legitimacy for their presence on the continent through client governments of various complexions. As the late Mary Wright remarked, the Japanese resurrected all the possible political institutions from the museum of Chinese history. They restored the Manchu Ch'ing dynasty in Manchuria, the Tuan Ch'i-jui government in Peking, and finally set up a Kuomintang nationalist revolutionary regime in Nanking.

The concepts which dominated Japanese policy for "solving the China Incident" took shape in late 1937 and early 1938. The War Guidance Office of the General Staff (Sanbō honbu) drafted a plan for the "central government of China" on November 21, 1937.[7]

Japanese thinking was torn between notions of dividing China so that it could not be a threat to Japan, and on the other hand, of unifying it to fulfill some kind of historical mission. The essence of Japanese strategy for ruling China is contained in the phrase *bunchi gassaku*, loosely translated "federation of local regimes." Specifically, this meant the establishment of local governments throughout China which would eventually coalesce into a "central government." This "central government" would "cooperate" with Japan. Its formation would represent the "solution of the Incident."

The contradiction between "divide and rule" and the establishment of a central government stems as much as anything else from Japanese military thinkers' study of Chinese history. The Japanese China specialists believed that they understood Chinese politics so well that they could rule China by playing one region or faction off against another, much as Chiang Kai-shek did. But the Japanese "China hands" also combined a great deal of condescension toward contemporary Chinese with a very romantic view of the Chinese past. They longed to recreate the grandeur of imperial China, the dragon throne this time to shine in the reflected light of the rising sun.

The *bunchi gassaku* formula also came to be the framework for Japanese military politics in China. Since each of the various regimes established in China were the cats-paws of different commands, the pressure for a "central government" reflected in part the rivalry between the respective commands for the leading position in China.

Japan's power to work her will in China was blocked by one man, Chiang Kai-shek. It was Japan's incompetence in facing this that caused her to fail to "solve the China Incident" and consequently to take those desperate steps which led to Pearl Harbor.

While the *bunchi gassaku* doctrine might offer a polite formula for Chiang's capitulation — Chungking could join the federation of local regimes — Konoye's *aite to sezu* statement that Japan would "not deal with the National Government" made it difficult to see how this might happen unless Chiang and his government simply evanesced.

Japanese arms might bring about Chiang's destruction but they never succeeded in doing so. My view is that Japan did not succeed in this because of a weakness of will caused by an ambiguous attitude toward Chiang. I believe that Japan's strength was more than sufficient to take Chungking and effectively destroy Kuomintang resistance. After Pearl Harbor, the Japanese empire swept to the bounds of India, Australia, Hawaii. As Hitler's admiration for the British and his hope that racial consanguinity would bring them to join him caused him to hesitate at the critical moment of Dunkirk when England might well have fallen to an all-out assault, so Japan hesitated after the fall of Nanking.

It may be, as is more commonly believed, that Japan never made an all-out assault after 1937 because she feared Russia to the north and that she feared that Chiang would simply retreat further, keeping the spark of resistance alive. Whatever view correctly explains Japan's military failure, Konoye's statement cut off the possibility of making peace with Chiang. The Japanese were never able to reach a settlement until one was dictated to them on the decks of the Missouri.

The outbreak of the China war, and more particularly, the issuance of the *aite to sezu* statement mark a decisive turning point in the evolution of Japan's expansion and also of her domestic life. Expansion in China from the Manchurian Incident on had been haphazard and uncoordinated, a product more of local decisions by lower-level officers than a matter of national policy, but henceforward Japan's imperial concerns would dominate national life.

The domestic scene in the 1930's had been fragmented. A rising socialist vote coexisted with rightist assassinations. After the decision not to compromise the war in China as previous incidents had been compromised, national life underwent a qualitative change. The few who opposed the drift into war and totalitarianism were suppressed without noticeable popular outcry. The nation assumed the appearance of unity and of national paranoia which was to lead it to Pearl Harbor and through the tremendous and heroic exertions made necessary by the Pacific War.

It appeared that the formulation of Japanese policy was monolithic and that will to conquest was its only component, but actually in December 1937 there was a division of counsel, with the nonexpansion group favoring a negotiated peace with Chiang and with Konoye and preponderant military opinion for throwing over Chiang in order to create a "new order" in China.

The self-serving account presented to the International Military Tribunal by Marquis Kido blames the break on the Chinese. "The Foreign Minister [Hirota] reported to the cabinet that Chiang Kai-shek's regime had shown no sincerity in desiring to continue their negotiations whatsoever, and was still very vague and ambiguous, and that there was no point in continuing the negotiations."[8] As Ambassador Dirksen pointed out to Hirota, the Japanese terms were too vague to permit a definite Chinese answer.

Another averred reason for the decision to break with the nationalist regime is that Wang K'o-min, the leader of the newformed Provisional Government in Peking, or the Japanese backers of his regime, solicitous for its future, demanded the action.[9] This may well be so, but one would not suppose that their influence in Tokyo was sufficient to carry the day on a matter recognized as being of such great importance.

General Tada Hayao of the General Staff, representing the views of the nonexpansionists, demanded a series of liaison conferences beginning on December 14, in which he forcefully put forward his view that, on the model of Prussia after the Franco-Prussian War, Japan should offer conciliatory terms to Chiang. These terms would be those which Hirota had transmitted on November 3, before the fall of Nanking, to which Chiang had returned a hopeful response.

Konoye, by new appointments to his cabinet of hard liners and with the undoubted support of many of the military, outmaneuvered Tada. The Imperial Conference of January 11, the first since the Russo-Japanese War, which Tada had hoped would hold the hard liners and the field armies in check by endorsing a decision to negotiate, instead endorsed the decision to establish a new order in China.[10]

The nonexpansionists fought the decision all the way down to the line. Horiba Kazuo even went so far as to urge his superior Kanin no Miya, the chief of the General Staff, to appeal to the emperor himself to prevent the issuance of the statement. The emperor's advisers thought it wisest for the emperor not to interfere in what appeared to be an already reached government decision.

Konoye's statement was artfully ambiguous. Various interpretations of the phrase *Kokumin seifu o aite to sezu* (not to deal with the National Government as a partner) formed the area of maneuver for future efforts to "solve the incident" and at the same time save Japanese face. Perhaps the most significant ambiguity for the present narrative is contained in the phrase *kokumin seifu*, National Government, the appellation of the Kuomintang regime. *Kokumin seifu o aite to sezu* came increasingly to be interpreted as *Shō Kai-seki o aite ni sezu,* that is, "not to deal with Chiang Kai-shek." Konoye himself is quoted as referring to the statement in these words.[11] Perhaps this was the meaning originally intended, at least by some; perhaps it was an interpretation to meet changed conditions. The significance of this interpretation is that it left the possibility that the Kuomintang government could make peace with Japan on condition of Chiang's resignation. Upon this possibility Wang Ching-wei's peace movement was to be built.

The second great ambiguity is in the meaning of *aite to sezu,* "not to deal with as a partner." Its meaning apparently stopped somewhat short of a traditional break in diplomatic relations; just how short is difficult to determine. The Gaimushō prepared a document which asserted that *aite to sezu* meant not a severance of national relations (*kokkō danzetsu*) or denial, nonrecognition, (*hinin*) of the Nationalist Government but rather meant to "ignore" (*mushi*) it. It was a "political prediction to proceed to the establishment of a new government."[12] The official statement captures well the arrogant spirit of Japanese bureaucracy at the time: "New phenomena . . . are emerging from the present situation. International law is the result of precedents and Japan's actions are now forming precedents for the future."[13] The Chinese ambassador, Hsü Shih-ying, in fact, left Japan, although the Gaimushō stated that Japan would continue to "accord diplomatic and consular privileges to diplomatic and consular officials representing the National Government."[14] It appears, however, that Chinese representation did cease and official diplomatic contact was cut off, to be replaced by unofficial, and consequently often unreliable, contacts.

The ambiguity of the statement was partly a result of Japanese "resolution without resolution," Horiba's phrase, which so well characterizes Japanese policy; partly it was the result of Japanese internal dissension; and partly it must have been fashioned as a political weapon. Konoye's Cabinet Secretary Kazami Akira criticized the statement as having no legal meaning but merely as being an insult.[15] In any case, it surely failed to clarify anything.

These two policies, *bunchi gassaku* and *aite to sezu,* determined that Japanese political strategy, before it could proceed to substantive negotiations, must be dominated by the task of developing secret contacts with influential Chinese. The aims of these contacts were dual: first, to find Chinese with sufficient ability and prestige who would be willing to join local "puppet" regimes which would "cooperate" with the Japanese, at the beginning in the occupied areas, and later, it was passionately hoped, in the hitherto unoccupied areas as well; and second, to maintain contact with the Chungking government or forces within it, since the route of normal diplomacy had been cut off by the *aite to sezu* statement. These two goals were very closely related because the real ambition of the Japanese in contact with the Chungking government was often to find some faction within that government which would betray it, or indeed to persuade the Chungking government, even possibly under Chiang's leadership, to associate itself with the network of local "puppet" regimes that the Japanese were in the process of establishing.

The Ministry of Foreign Affairs and several foreign ministers, legally responsible for the conduct of Japan's foreign relations, made several attempts to negotiate with influential Chinese after the failure of the ministry's diplomacy in the Trautmann mediation. Foreign Minister Ugaki negotiated with H. H. Kung and Foreign Minister Matsuoka tried to negotiate with Chiang through the Chinese bankers, Chou Tso-min and Ch'ien Yung-ming.

In reality however, the military, through its many intelligence organs, usurped the role of conducting negotiations with China. Since the 1930's and perhaps earlier the Japanese military had prosecuted its political warfare by means of specialized semi-autonomous small bureaus called *kikan* (organs) or *tokumu kikan* (lit., special work organs). Their activities were associated with intelligence work, both of the information-gathering and "dirty tricks" variety. Generally each *kikan* was centered around a leader who would have a small personal staff and would be focused on some particular Chinese individual or group. Each *kikan* would pursue such an endeavor, called a *kōsaku* (work). The *kōsaku* were generally referred to by code names; for example, the *kōsaku* aimed toward Wu Pei-fu (see below) was known as the *ran* (orchid) *kōsaku*, the *kōsaku* aimed at T. V. Sung and Sung Mei-ling (Madame Chiang) through their "brother" Sung Tzu-liang was known as the *kiri* (paulownia) *kōsaku*. Sometimes they were known by the names of the individuals through or toward whom they worked; for example,

Stuart *kōsaku*, for John Leighton Stuart, president of Yenching University. The *kikan* were named after the Japanese officer whose personal organ they were; for example, the Doihara kikan, headed by that grey eminence General Doihara, which practiced the *ran kōsaku*, and Colonel Wachi's Wachi kikan, which conducted *kōsaku* toward the southwestern leaders Pai Chung-hsi and Li Tsung-jen. These *kikan* were financed by seemingly unlimited and unaudited funds from the military budget, were very loosely controlled either by Tokyo or by the local commands, and tended more often than not to pursue their activities in competition rather than in cooperation with one another.

The term *tokumu kōsaku* (special work) was used to describe the activities of these various *kikan*. *Tomuku kōsaku* also connotes the full associated range of secret activities of the Japanese army: assassination, blackmail, bribery, opium traffic, racketeering.

Since the *kikan* were regarded as official but clandestine, the Japanese government and military (if indeed one can speak of such a loose aggregation as a unit) were not accountable for any promises made, which had to the Japanese only the value of *ruses de guerre* in which their honor was not in the least involved. The Chinese were not exactly novices at this game either. The rough-and-tumble back-stabbing maelstrom of Chinese internal politics was a hard school, and they had been toughened by long years of attempting to tame the Japanese and other barbarians with diplomacy's subtle arts. Imai Takeo, one of the leading participants in *wahei* (peace) *kōsaku*, bitterly complained that Chinese leaders were wont to send out any number of retainers, who would each represent the view of his patron to fit the hearer, and the patron would be free to disavow any he chose.[16]

Wang Ching-wei was the last rather than the first Chinese politician to attempt to practice his profession on the unlikely ground of occupied China. The activities of his predecessors helped shape the scene which he had to face and also, by their fate, gave some indication of his prospects.[17]

It was extremely difficult for the client regimes to recruit the quality of men necessary to inspire even the slightest shade of public confidence. Feeling against the Japanese generally remained strong, and cooperation with the Japanese, however necessary for the continuation of daily life, seemed impossible to distinguish from treason. Those elders who had been used to adjusting themselves to the violent shift of events in modern China and who might otherwise have been willing to hold office were discouraged by ruthless campaigns of assassination directed in large measure from Chungking, which would surely prevent them from drawing a further easy breath.

For the most part, the Japanese Army attracted as collaborators at the lower level the worst type of humanity — dope peddlers, pimps, petty extortionists, racketeers — the only ones who were interested in the Japanese Army's massive campaign of vice in China, which was the most conspicuous evidence of the Japanese presence. Naturally, a respectable politician would be less than enthusiastic about such associates. Above all hovered the doubt whether risk of one's honor — for one who had any to lose — and one's life actually stood any real chance of gaining any corresponding benefit for the Chinese people. The Japanese extended to their client officials little trust and less authority. Might the little that a man could do to mediate between the Japanese militia — truly not all evil men — and their unwilling subjects be outweighed by the consequent legitimization of Japanese conquest? What is amazing is that a handful of men of fine character were willing to risk their honor and their lives in the uncertain enterprise of appeasement.

There is a certain irony in the fact that peace with Chungking and withdrawal of Japanese troops, which seem to have been the genuine objectives of the leaders of the major occupation regimes in intramural China, would inevitably lead to their own executions. Certainly, Wang K'o-min, the leader of the Provisional Government in Peking; Liang Hung-chih, the leader of the Restored Government in central China; and Wu P'ei-fu, T'ang Shao-i, and Ts'ao Kun, who were prospective "puppet" leaders, were all gentlemen and patriots, men of honor and courage. They were all, however, of the "old school"; they had held responsibility before the Northern Expedition and the rise of the Kuomintang. Generally, they had been associated with the Peking Government, which was the recognized Chinese government during the late 1910's and the early 1920's, associates and successors of Yüan Shih-k'ai and Tuan Ch'i-jui. Liang Hung-chih was a member of the old Anhwei clique, Wang K'o-min,

Wu P'ei-fu and Ts'ao Kun had belonged to the Chihli clique, two of the many groups whose struggle comprised the political life of the old republic.

All these men were conservative, traditionally and classically oriented. These qualities were what the Japanese regarded as the traditional Chinese virtues which they admired and wished to cultivate, as opposed to the "uppity" arrogance of the Kuomintang nationalists. The extreme of this Japanese proclivity is found in their unsuccessful efforts about the same time to induce K'ung Te-ch'eng, the seventy-fourth lineal descendant of Confucius, to accept a position under the Japanese, even, rumor had it, as emperor. These old men whose support the Japanese sought had been relegated to obscurity by the rise of the Kuomintang, which they had opposed. Naturally, they had little sympathy for it and even less after the Sian Incident and the cooperation of the Kuomintang with the Communists.

Generally, neither the lower echelons of the "puppet" regimes nor the myriad "peace preservation committees," which sprang up after the Japanese occupation like mushrooms after a shower, possessed men of comparable background or comparable character. Perhaps there were worthy men among these too. However, although conditions at the important political centers in China, Peking, Nanking, Shanghai, are relatively well recorded, there is much less documentation of conditions in the interior. The general condition in the occupied areas was thus described by a foreign relief official who had traveled widely in those areas: "Maladministration is widespread and thorough. And it seems that the new puppet officials, by way of compensating for the keenly felt loss of honor and the daily risk of life, pursue a policy of getting rich quick by ruthless exploitation of a population that is already bled white."[18]

Of the pre-Wang Ching-wei "puppet" governments, the North China Provisional Government is by far the most important, its leader Wang K'o-min the most significant. Japanese-educated, he had devoted himself after the Northern Expedition to mediating between the Chinese government and the encroaching Japanese in north China. He held such posts during this period as "acting chairman of the Peiping Political Readjustment Committee."

After their conquests of the summer of 1937, the North China

Area Command of the Japanese army wished to restore the Chinese political capital to Peking and to have the regime under their tutelage grow to be the central government of China. Accordingly, General Terauchi, the commander, and his associates were most eager to proceed to establish a regime there. Wu P'ei-fu was probably their first choice to head the regime, but since he was unavailable, they turned to Wang K'o-min.

At the time of the outbreak of the Incident, Wang K'o-min was in Hong Kong. The North China Area Command dispatched representatives to contact him. On November 24, 1937, Wang came to Shanghai. Apparently, he had not yet decided to head a regime, but after a trip to Japan on December 6, he consented to "emerge from retirement."[19] Undoubtedly the fall of Nanking influenced his decision, and he must have received certain promises of support in Japan. Accordingly, on December 14 his regime was established in Peking. This regime made massive economic commitments to the Japanese, readopted the five colored flag of the old Peking Chinese Republic, and adopted a platform of Confucian revival and vocal opposition to Kuomintang nationalism and to communism alike. The regime was a creature of its military masters, its every move manipulated by Japanese "advisers." No matter what the excellent personal qualities of the few old men who composed the regime, it was clear that even if they had any real power, they were inadequate to solving any problems. Their only roots were in the distant past. Even the Japanese gave them only partial and grudging support. Despite pressure from the Japanese North China Command, the Provisional Government was not recognized as the government of China by Japan.

Paradoxically the weakness of Wang K'o-min's government was his personal strength. He was the only man of substance in the regime, and it was clear to all that, should he disappear from the scene, that frail entity which he headed would become so insubstantial as to be untenable. Wang was well aware of this, and the fact that he was virtually indispensable to his Japanese backers enabled him to refuse to be completely compliant with their wishes.

To the south the Central China Army Command went ahead with its plans for the creation of its own puppet regime in Nanking, its candidate for the central government of China. Many months before, however, the Great Way (Ta tao) municipal government had been established on December 5, 1937, in the parts of Shanghai not included in the foreign concessions. Since Shanghai was the locus of wealth in central China and since each regime became a vested interest with Chinese and Japanese supporters difficult to dislodge, the existence of an independent government in Shanghai necessarily conflicted with any attempt to set up a central government in Nanking. Despite this opposition and that of the North China Army, Major General Harada and Colonel Kusumoto of the local *tokumu kikan* engineered the establishment of the Restored Government in Nanking on March 28, 1938, headed by the gentlemanly and scholarly old-school politician Liang Hung-chih. Liang had been secretary-general of Tuan Ch'i-jui's Provisional Government in 1924 and had sought safety in the Japanese legation when that regime collapsed. The Restored Government was even more inconsequential than the Provisional Government. Immediately after its "inauguration," the whole body of officials returned to Shanghai where they would enjoy better protection, leaving the Japanese to administer their new government.[20] Before the establishment of his government, Liang had communicated to Chiang Kai-shek that his intention was merely to act as a caretaker regime and that he would welcome nothing more than Chiang's return to Nanking in triumph.[21]

Reflecting the relatively less activist leadership of the Central China Area Command, the program of the Restored Government was somewhat more mild than that of the Provisional Government. Though the Nanking Restored Government shared with Peking the slogan of anti-communism and the use of the archaic five-bar flag, its opposition to the Kuomintang, whose capital it occupied, was much less pronounced than that of Peking. It attacked the Kuomintang on the charge of "driving an untrained populace to fight in an unequal combat" rather than on ideological grounds.

Thus *bunchi* (division) was easily accomplished. There were now three major client regimes — the Provisional, the Restored, the Ta tao — within intramural China as well as a multitude of local "committees." To the north beyond the Wall was Manchukuo and the recently formed "autonomous" regimes in Mongolia. *Gassaku* (cooperation), which was supposed to accompany *bunchi*, was to remain an elusive goal.

The Restored Government asserted that it had no intention to compete with the Provisional Government in the north. "As soon as communications are restored on the Tsinpu and Lunghai Railways, the Reformed [that is, Restored] Government will amalgamate itself with the Provisional Government. It is not our desire to have rival governments functioning within the same country."[22] An impending merger was rumored; Wang K'o-min and Liang Hung-chih exchanged visits in April of 1938, but no action was taken until the formation the next autumn of a "joint committee" (rengo iinkai) for coordinating the two regimes. The committee existed largely on paper.

The formation of a "joint committee" was the first step in the Japanese blueprint for establishing a new central government as outlined in a resolution of the Five Ministers Conference of July 13, 1938. If the Chiang regime were to split or fall, the pro-Japanese elements in it would be made a constituent element of the new government. If the Chiang regime were not defeated or did not split, a central government would be organized from the existing regimes. Such a regime would not be recognized, however, until it showed real power.[23]

The prime requisite for the formation of a central government, particularly in the more likely case that it did not include Chung-king elements, was able and prestigious leadership which could give the appearance, at least, of capacity. Of course this prospect was dimmed by a paradox: the Japanese did not wish to support a regime which was not capable, and yet they were eternally unwilling to offer a client government the freedom to exercise capacity.

In any case, the main endeavor of Japanese political strategy at this time was to find a head for their prospective central government, who would then rally Chinese forces to himself and with whom the Japanese could make a peace settlement. Ts'ao Kun, a former president of the old Chinese Republic, died leaving two major prospects, Wu P'ei-fu and T'ang Shao-i. Both these leaders had been contacted by separate Japanese organs.

T'ang was educated in America as a member of one of the first such educational missions supported by the imperial government. Later assigned to Korea, his abilities attracted the attention of the rising and ambitious Yuan Shih-k'ai, under whose patronage he served in a number of important posts connected with foreign affairs. After the revolution of 1911 he was unable to support Yuan's pretentions to the throne and shifted his support to Sun Yat-sen.

His political complexion within the kaleidoscope of political maneuvering during the 1920's and 1930's is not easy to define exactly. By 1936 however he had come out definitely in support of the Kuomintang Nanking government. Partly because of old age (he was 78) and ill health, he did not retreat with the government but remained in the French concession of Shanghai. A grand old man of Chinese politics whose life had denied him the major role he might have played in a more orderly situation, T'ang still cherished a hope that he might be the one to "save China." He differed from the other Japanese candidates to form a "central government" in that a government that he might form would undoubtedly contain Kuomintang members.

At first he turned a deaf ear to Japanese proposals, since he felt that the Japanese were either going to make a compromise peace with Chiang Kai-shek or would establish a puppet government.[24] But by the summer of 1938, he seems to have decided that he was the man of the hour. He told Bos, the Chinese secretary of the Netherlands legation, that he would become head of the Restored Government "if the Japanese authorities should display anything like a reasonable attitude . . . Seemingly, T'ang believes that the Japanese are so anxious to obtain a man of his prestige and experience to take the lead in the new government that they will go far towards meeting his requirements."[25] T'ang's son-in-law, who was a classmate of Konoye, reportedly visited Japan and north China, arranging T'ang's emergence.[26] Apparently, the plan at this time was, as stated above, for T'ang to head the Restored Government. General Doihara, Japan's prince of intrigue who had been deeply involved with engineering the Manchurian Incident and who continued to operate in north China his own Doihara kikan, which had generally been devoted to securing Wu's emergence, got the idea in August 1938 of setting up T'ang as the political leader and Wu as the military leader.[27] This plan received its *coup de grace* when T'ang was brutally murdered by an axe-weilding intruder on September 30.

Wu P'ei-fu, then in retirement and engaged in devotions to the Buddha, dominated the stage while he waited in the wings. Wu, one of the most colorful and interesting personalities in modern Chinese history, seemed to stride on to the stage straight from a Chinese opera or popular novel. His had been the major military force in the Chihli clique, and he, along with Feng Yü-hsiang, dominated the history of the warlord era. He was distinguished from most warlords by a lack of interest in politics, by the comparative purity of his personal life, and by his authentic classical learning. He was indeed a figure from the great tradition. Wu had been regarded by the Kuomintang and allied militarists as the real obstacle to the extension of Kuomintang power to the north. After the Kuomintang victories, he took up the life of a religious recluse in Szechwan.[28]

Despite his retirement Wu enjoyed enormous prestige among both Chinese and Japanese. As a soldier and scholar and as a man with a reputation for courage and incorruptibility, he appealed greatly to the Japanese military and was very adroit in dealing with them. He was certainly their favored candidate for leadership of the "central government." He graciously received visitors at his modest compound near Peking and listened politely to what each had to say. Like an artful woman he coyly charmed and stimulated their ardor without ever committing himself or giving them what they wanted. Despite Doihara's fond hopes, it is clear that from beginning to end Wu had absolutely no intention of taking responsibility unless Japan agreed to withdraw her troops, in which case his emergence would permit the saving of Japanese face.[29] He had been in contact with Chiang's government since the commencement of hostilities.[30] Needless to say, the constant rumors of Wu's impending emergence were extremely rattling to the Provisional Government, which was already on shaky enough basis; consequently, Wang K'o-min's regime, most especially its Japanese supporters, viewed Wu and his backers with suspicion.

To summarize, the political situation in occupied China consisted of the two regimes, the Restored and the Provisional in Nanking and Peking, respectively, each supported by the local Japanese armies while Wu P'ei-fu waited in the wings — the center of all hopes for the future. All these forces were, under their respective Japanese promoters, semiautonomous and competing. Japanese policy looked for the emergence of a "central government," but these local interests, in the Japanese feudal tradition and also in the tradition of Chinese regional separatism, not only made the coming into being of a "central government" unlikely but also suggested that if one did emerge, it would not enjoy unified support even from the Japanese, whose capacity for acting constructively and consecutively was crippled both by conflicts among themselves and by inner contradictions in their policies. Wang's prognosis, should he throw himself into the politics of occupied China, can therefore only be described as gloomy.

Tung and Kao Go to Japan

4 By early 1938, after the failure of Trautmann's mediation and after Konoye's *aite to sezu* statement, diplomatic contact between China and Japan had been broken, and peace seemed only possible in the case of Chiang Kai-shek's capitulation. There were Japanese who regretted their nation's course; there were Japanese who hoped that political manipulations in China could win a costless victory. There were Chinese who sought to spare their country further devastation. There were both Chinese and Japanese who sought political intelligence regarding the plans and intentions of the other side. Individual foreigners, and foreign governments alike with diverse machinations, sought to play a mediatory role. Thus it was that quite a number of tentative feelers were extended in the vacuum left by collapse of authoritative negotiations between the two countries.

The feeler which was to lead into Wang Ching-wei's peace movement grew out of the meeting of Kao Tsung-wu and Nishi Yoshiaki, the Nanking branch office chief of the Southern Manchurian Railroad, on the night of July 31.

Nishi was a man of generosity, warmth, and candor. He was motivated by a sincere idealism, a sympathy for Chinese nationalism, and faith in the possibility of harmony between China and Japan. He was one of the few Japanese to put this into practice on the personal level. Unlike most Japanese stationed abroad, he did not mingle much with fellow Japanese but sought out Chinese as his close friends, whose trust his sincerity and goodwill swiftly won. Nishi's idealism often crossed the borderline to sentimental romanticism. Like many other political go-betweens, he saw himself playing a grand role in world history. His account of his activities is thus somewhat overblown.

Kao met with Nishi that evening in the home of Wu Chen-hsiu. Wu Chen-hsiu was director of the Nanking office of the Bank of China and representative there of the Chekiang bankers who had been so useful to Chiang Kai-shek in his rise to power. Wu was a graduate of Tokyo University, and apparently as a result of his studies in Japan he became converted to the cause of

Sino-Japanese friendship. He made his home a center for like-minded young men, for the most part Japanese-educated Chinese and Japanese, to meet. He repeatedly urged upon Chiang a policy of moderation and conciliation toward Japan so as to strengthen the hand of the civil leadership vis-à-vis the young officers who threatened disaster to both countries.[1] Kao appealed, only half seriously, to Nishi to persuade his employer, Matsuoka Yōsuke, then director of the Southern Manchurian Railroad, to convince Konoye of the sincerity of the desire of Chinese leaders for peace.[2]

Matsuoka has been seen by Westerners as a warmonger. Secretary of State Cordell Hull called him "more crooked than a barrel of fishhooks." Matsuoka made his debut on the international scene as the fiery spokesman who led Japan out of the League of Nations; he also, as foreign minister in Konoye's second cabinet, tightened Japan's association with the Axis. Actually, Matsuoka's intentions, if not his actions, seem to have been more pacific than commonly supposed; it was his notion that he was a new Bismarck. The Axis alliance would neutralize the United States, and Japan's nonaggression pact with Stalin would neutralize the Axis. Despite his foolish vanity and posturing, he was certainly endeavoring to find, within the straitened means available to a foreign minister in militarist Japan, some way to avoid the approaching holocaust toward which the military were so inexorably driving their nation. The Wang Ching-wei peace movement, which he was helpful in initiating, turned out in the end to foil his plans for peace as we shall see.

When Nishi succeeded in reaching Dairen, where the main office of the Southern Manchuria Railroad and hence Matsuoka were located, the fighting had already spread to Shanghai. Receiving Nishi in his bath at dawn, Matsuoka, according to Nishi, responded to Nishi's pacific message with passion. "Are you day-dreaming in Nanking?" he shouted. "Do you think Prince Konoye can do anything? What country do you belong to, anyhow? Why don't you quit being a Japanese?" Calming himself, he explained to Nishi how the situation had deteriorated. Nishi's resolution to fulfill the trust of his "Chinese comrades" remained firm, and seeing this, Matsuoka said at last: "What has been done is done. That is, a predestined fate has been imposed upon the peoples of Japan and China. What is destined must come to pass. The fire in hell must be burned out to the last. But when the opportune moment comes, someone who is so destined must begin to reconstruct peace for the two countries out of the fire and ashes. You have been to Nanking and have inspired so much trust in the Chinese. Therefore you are the one to await the opportunity."[3]

Matsuoka gave Nishi a large sum of money, released him from his official duties in connection with the railroad, and authorized him to devote his full time to pursuing contact with his Chinese comrades when and where he chose. Bearing a letter from Matsuoka to Kazami Akira, Konoye's cabinet secretary, Nishi went to Japan. The political situation there as the war continued to escalate did not give him much encouragement. He returned to Shanghai on December 30. His endeavor got under way, however, with the unexpected visit of Tung Tao-ning, an old acquaintance who was chief of the First Section (Japan) of the Asian Bureau of the Wai-chiao-pu, in other words, a subordinate of Kao Tsung-wu. Thus Nishi hoped through him to reestablish contact with Kao, and through Kao, with Chiang.[4] Tung had grown up in Yokohama and graduated from Kyoto University and felt himself as much a Japanese as a Chinese. He was, because of his warm nature and command of Japanese, an ideal "accompanying guest" for Chinese-Japanese contacts. Tung, however, was not a man of much political sophistication. His view scarcely went beyond the personal and emotional.

When the Chinese government had been forced to move from Nanking, government staffs had to be cut drastically. Tung asked to be relieved of his responsibilities at the Wai-chiao-pu. He was thus in Shanghai as a private citizen with no connection with the government.[5]

Tung was rather incoherent during his meeting with Nishi, but Nishi surmised that Tung had come to Shanghai to contact Kawagoe in connection with Ambassador Trautmann's attempted mediation, upon Kao's instruction. Nishi was struck with the notion that by persuading Tung to come to Japan he could at once convince Japanese authorities of the Chinese will for peace and at the same time open a route of communication with the Kuomintang regime through Kao. He told Tung that if he went to Japan, "It will be different from ordinary diplomatic dealings or bargaining for conditions. It will show the sincerity of the Chinese people breaking through the bigotry of the Japanese and communicating the consanguinity of the two peoples. The present tragedy is caused by lack of trust between the two peoples. Your flying to Tokyo would teach the Japanese that the Chinese trust them. That would be a beginning."[6]

The *aite to sezu* declaration followed Nishi and Tung's conversation by a few days. Nevertheless, Tung yielded to Nishi's persuasion. Nishi feels[7] that Tung was partly motivated by a desire to outshine Kao, his former superior and yet ten years his junior. Alas, Tung wanted to play in a league for which he was not qualified. The obvious purpose of a trip to Japan at this time would be to ascertain the seriousness with which the Japanese would hold to the *aite to sezu* declaration.[8] Wu Chen-hsiu, the friend of Tung, Kao, and Nishi, encouraged Tung to make the trip.[9] Nishi went ahead to prepare the way for Tung's visit. He arrived in Nagasaki on January 19 and the next morning knocked at the door of Kagesa Sadaaki, then a colonel and chief of the Eighth Section of the General Staff. The Eighth Section was the *bōryaku* (conspiracy) section which had been especially established for "solving the Incident."

The story of Wang Ching-wei's peace movement is as much the tragedy of Kagesa Sadaaki as it is the tragedy of Wang Ching-wei. To those who knew him and to those who try to evaluate his life and motivation, Kagesa is a controversial figure. To Inukai Ken, who volunteered many years and his personal savings to aiding him, Kagesa was little less than a saint, selflessly devoting himself to the cause of Sino-Japanese peace. To Kao Tsung-wu, he appears no more than a run-of-the-mill military intriguer.[10]

Kagesa's whole career centered around China. The early years of his military career were spent in China as a student of the Chinese language and Chinese affairs. He was an assistant military attache in China during the 1930's, at which time he knew both Nishi and Kao. At this time he was known as favoring a hard-line policy towards China. As previously mentioned, he fell under the influence of Ishiwara Kanji, who had come to espouse Sino-Japanese cooperation. The cooperation envisaged by Ishiwara gave a primacy of place to Japan and undoubtedly could only be unacceptable in the end to Chinese nationalists. Nevertheless, Ishiwara's doctrine was far more compatible with

Chinese feeling and Chinese national existence than was the prevalent view which looked for complete conquest of China.

Ishiwara held the post of chief of the Military Operations Bureau of the General Staff, and it was under his sponsorship that Kagesa was appointed chief of the Eighth Section. When, with the constant flux of Japanese military politics, Ishiwara was given an "Irish promotion" to become vice-chief of staff of the Kwantung Army, Kagesa was left in Tokyo as the leading figure of the nonescalation faction. His influence at this time was much greater than might be surmised from his level in the hierarchy, for it was at the colonel level that the real decision-making power rested. Nishi was able to persuade Kagesa that the coming of Tung, a Wai-chiao-pu official, to Japan was an opportunity for peace which should by no means be overlooked.

Tung's companion on his voyage was to be Itō Yoshio. A graduate of London University, through acquaintance with Matsuoka, he secured a position as an official of Manchukuo stationed in Nanking. Since this post made him persona non grata with the Chinese, he became, through Nishi, a "specially attached" employee of the Southern Manchurian Railroad. He was Nishi's constant associate, and where Nishi was impractical, he was the tireless and practical organizer and expediter of the peace movement. Kao feels that Itō was an agent of Japanese intelligence.[11] Somehow Itō managed to get Tung to Nagasaki, unbeknownst to all but the smallest number of Japanese. They arrived on February 15. Tung met with Kagesa in the New Grand Hotel in Yokohama on the afternoon of February 17. Kagesa was taken aback by Tung's almost childish naivete and sincerity but was moved by it as well.[12]

Kagesa wrote many years later: "I was greatly moved by the passion and courage of Mr. Tung who came into enemy territory . . . He told me that some kind of movement to stop the Sino-Japanese conflict must be made and in China the atmosphere of both civilian and government circles was filled with a desire for peace. He passionately demanded the effort and understanding of the Japanese side for peace. His attitude not only influenced me but his passion and sincerity moved me deeply. I felt I must endeavor to fulfill what Mr. Tung expressed. I told him 'Inquiry into who is responsible for the China Incident is like reckoning the age of a dead child. Japan must make self-reflection and so must China. Unless we mutually discard our bad feelings and solve the Incident, it will harm China and Japan forever.' "[13]

After this meeting with Kagesa, Tung went with Itō to Tokyo, where he met again with Kagesa and with Colonel Imai Takeo, who was at that time the China Office Chief of the General Staff. With Kagesa's introduction, Tung also met with Vice-Chief of Staff Tada, a leader of the nonescalation group who had vigorously opposed the *aite to sezu* declaration.[14] Tada told Tung that despite the *aite to sezu* declaration, the Japanese army desperately wanted peace[15] and conveyed to him the impression that consequently the *aite to sezu* statement might be modified or abrogated. It is uncertain, but not improbable, that Kagesa, Imai, and Tada suggested the obvious, namely, that the way the *aite to sezu* declaration might be circumvented was for Chiang to resign and for Wang Ching-wei to take his place.

The Japanese did not know whether Tung had a real connection with Chiang Kai-shek or other Chinese leaders, which of course would be necessary if he were to be of use to them in establishing contact with the Chungking government.[16] And in fact, according to the testimony of Kao Tsung-wu, neither he nor anyone else in the Chinese government had any foreknowledge of Tung's trip.[17] Despite this uncertainty about Tung's *bona fides*, Kagesa gave Tung a letter to Kagesa's classmates, Generals Ho Ying-ch'in and Chang Ch'ün, who were among Chiang's most trusted and most powerful military associates. Kagesa did not address Chiang directly because he felt it would be presumptuous to do so; moreover, the *aite to sezu* statement had just been issued, and it would have been inappropriate for him to disregard it completely.[18]

There are two texts for this letter: one given by Nishi; the other given by Kagesa himself in his memoirs written in Rabaul, New Britain, in 1943 after his and the peace movement's failure. Nishi's text is undoubtedly the more authentic, but Kagesa's is worth citing because it expresses movingly what in retrospect he considered his true intent to have been. "The solution of the Incident cannot be basically achieved through the exchange of conditions. Japan and China must embrace naked. We must discard all the past and express our sincerity. If we embrace each other, Japan, the country of samurai, would come to an understanding with your country. That is my belief."[19]

The text given by Nishi is far more careful and diplomatic;

nevertheless, it was an act of considerable courage to send such a letter to the leader of an enemy country in wartime. "When the unfortunate war between the two peoples of Japan and China came to its peak, it resulted in the imperial government's statement of January 16. We must say that the destiny of East Asia came to a dead end. A great Wang Lun[20] must appear to correct misunderstanding in our country and enable us to break through this impasse. Tung Tao-ning has now come and himself conveyed the sincerity of your country, and we are much moved, and thus the first step to breaking through the present misunderstanding has occurred. It is wished that someone should follow Tung and attempt a further enlightenment, and it is wished to expect the exchange of the sincerity of your country and the emotion of our country. [Signed] Col. Kagesa Sadaaki"[21]

The vague and elliptical style of the letter is clearly designed to convey Kagesa's meaning without subjecting himself to a charge of treason should the letter become known to his colleagues. Kagesa sought in the Aesopian language of the letter to persuade Chinese leaders that, despite the abruptness of Konoye's *aite to sezu* statement, peace was still possible. Peace, he suggested, now depended on a Chinese initiative. His own efforts to swing Japanese councils toward peace would be greatly aided if a Chinese leader would seek to mediate or if the Chinese would dispatch a negotiator to take advantage of the good will created by Tung's visit. Undoubtedly, as is so evident in the language of the letter which Kagesa himself gives, Kagesa's vision of Sino-Japanese relations was by no means compatible with Chinese aspirations for independence and national sovereignty.

On March 7 Tung, bearing Kagesa's letters, the first glimmer of a possible Japanese change of heart, embarked in the company of Nishi and Itō for Dairen, landing there on March 10. The three dined with Matsuoka, who, through his support of Nishi and Itō, was the sponsor of the whole project. After being treated to Matsuoka's usual heady ebullience, Tung, again accompanied by Itō, departed for Hong Kong on March 13.[22] There he met Kao Tsung-wu, and he gave Kao the letters for Ho and Chang. Kao had been in Hong Kong and Shanghai collecting intelligence on Japanese movements and intentions. Kao took these letters from Tung immediately to Chiang Kai-shek, to whom he showed them in person. Chiang read them without comment. He returned them to Kao without criticism of their substance and directed Kao not to deliver them to their addressees.[23]

Kao was pessimistic about the chances of peace at this time, the spring of 1938. His friend Matsumoto Shigeharu attempted to persuade him that if he, Kao, were to go to Japan, he would be able to see many more people and accomplish much more than Tung, since his position and political acumen were much higher. Matsumoto told Kao that Kagesa had come under the influence of Ishiwara Kanji and accepted Ishiwara's view that while Manchuria should properly remain under Japanese control, Japan should recognize Chinese sovereignty south of the Great Wall.[24] Kao considered that Chiang would recognize the Japanese puppet regime in Manchuria if he could be assured that Japanese expansion would end there. Thus it seemed to Kao that it was worth following up Tung's contact with Kagesa. On the other hand, Kao was reluctant to accept Matsumoto's advice to follow Tung's path to Tokyo, since he felt that the possible loss in case of failure and disclosure was far greater than the likely gain.[25]

Matsumoto Shigeharu, at this writing (1970) is still bringing people together, presently as director of the International House of Japan, which deals with educational exchange. He is reported by all who know him to be of shining and exemplary character. As the peace movement began, Matsumoto was the director of the Shanghai office of Dōmei, the official Japanese news agency. But he was no ordinary journalist. He was related to the aristocratic Matsukata clan, which had intimate ties with Konoye. After a brilliant record at Tokyo University, he studied further at Yale. He had high standing in the worlds of society and of scholarship as well as of journalism. Around Matsumoto revolved a brilliant circle of Chinese and Japanese intellectuals who sought a basis for a mutual understanding and cooperation between the two countries. The leading Chinese intellectuals associated with the Shanghai circle were Professor Chao Cheng-ping of Chinan University and Professor Fu Shih-shuo of Ta-hsia University. Fu, who had a close relationship with Ch'en Li-fu of the C. C. clique, had discussions with officers of the Japanese consulate as well as with Colonel Imai Takeo and Major General Harada. A Professor Toyama Ken'ichi visited Shanghai, and Chao and Fu discussed with him the possibility of harmonizing the "Greater East Asia" idea of Japan and the "Three People's Principles" (san-min chu-i) of the Kuomintang.[26] In association with Matsumoto they arrived at a theoretical synthesis which they called zenmin shugi (principles of all people) and attempted to launch a zenmin shugi undō (zenmin shugi movement).[27] Also associated with Matsumoto's circle were the influential bankers Ch'ien Yung-ming, chairman of the Bank of Communications, and Chou Tso-min, chairman of the board of the Chin-ch'eng Bank. All these men were to be intimately involved during the years ahead in the work for peace.

Matsumoto, as long as he was able, attempted to play a mediating role between the two nations, even to the extent of supplying Kao with estimates of Japanese intentions, which he was able to formulate on these basis of his entree into high government circles.[28] Matsumoto had previously served as intermediary many times during Kao's negotiations during the 1930's.[29] It was Matsumoto that Kao really respected and trusted. More than anything else it was Kao's trust in Matsumoto that prompted Kao to continue to try to further open up the route to Kagesa that Tung had originated. The other Japanese were Kao's professional contacts, which, as any diplomat must, he discounted. Matsumoto was his friend.

Nishi describes a meeting in his Hong Kong hotel room on March 28, attended by himself, Itō, Matsumoto, Tung, and Kao. According to Nishi, the five men consecrated themselves comrades to work for Sino-Japanese peace. They were to form a "third force" to work for the emergence of progressive forces in the Japanese government and to mediate for peace. Nishi quotes Kao as saying that peace had been at hand during the Trautmann mediation, that only the aite to sezu declaration had prevented the restoration of peace. He quotes himself as saying that Kagesa and Konoye, who desired peace, had been defeated by the expansionists; Tung's mission had greatly aided those who were working for peace; the Chinese must aid them by further demonstrations of sincerity. The Japanese were apparently under the misapprehension that Kagesa's letters to Ho and Chang had not been delivered to Chiang. They urged Kao to take them to him, and he declared, according to Nishi, his intention to do so.[30]

Nishi reports that on April 16 Tung and Kao returned to his hotel room and that Kao, dismissing Tung from the room, gave orally Chiang's reply to Kagesa's letters.[31] Kao had long previously delivered the letters to Chiang and Chiang had made no reply to Kao. Kao firmly asserts that he could not and did not transmit any reply to Nishi.[32]

According to the reply alleged by Nishi, Chiang was represented as saying: "I consider that the true objectives of Japanese operations in China are two; (1) guarantee of security against the Soviet Union, and (2) economic development and cooperation. In principle I accept these two items. The first item may be subdivided into (a) Manchuria, (b) Inner Mongolia, (c) Hopei and Chahar. We will talk about Manchuria and Mongolia in later days. But Hopei and Chahar must absolutely be returned to China. We wish you to respect Chinese territorial integrity and administrative rights south of the Great Wall. Upon the understanding of the above, we would enter into truce and then into peace negotiations with the above conditions as the basis."[33] These terms are fundamentally the same as Chiang seemed willing to accept during the Trautmann mediation and that he was to continue to insist upon — no formal recognition of Manchukuo but tacit acquiescence, no loss in principle of Chinese sovereignty in north China but willingness to make economic concessions and to cooperate in anti-Communist activities. We may conjecture that perhaps Kao suggested on his own initiative that such was probably Chiang's thinking and that Nishi mistakenly inferred that this reply came from Chiang himself.

About this time, in March or early April, Kao returned to Hankow and presented to the Generalissimo the results of his intelligence research in Shanghai and Hong Kong. Kao, sharing afternoon tea with Chiang, suggested that he, Kao, would perhaps be able to be of more service to the government if he should resign his official post and work for peace as a private citizen. Thus, if he should make a misstep, the government would not be embarrassed. Chiang agreed; Kao's resignation was accepted and his old post filled at the Wai-chiao-pu. Kao opened an office of his own in Hong Kong and continued to report to, and receive financial support from, the General-issimo.[34]

On May 25 Konoye reshuffled his cabinet, and it appeared that the political climate in Japan might be becoming more favorable for peace with China. Two relatively liberal and pro-Chinese ministers assumed office, General Ugaki Kazushige as foreign minister and General Itagaki Seishirō who replaced the hard liner General Sugiyama Gen as minister of war. It was indeed Konoye's intention by these two appointments to make a resolute effort to bring the Incident to a close by making parallel efforts both through the Gaimushō and through the military. He told Ugaki that his goal was to correct the error of the *aite to sezu* statement, and he instructed Ugaki to begin negotiations with the Chinese government. Ugaki chose to do this through contact with H. H. Kung.[35] Chinese delight at Ugaki's appointment was shown by the fact that Chang Ch'ün, the vice-chairman of the Executive Yüan, wired him congratulations upon his appointment.[36] Itagaki's appointment seemed even more significant, since it looked as though in the military, which everyone realized was the center of power, the nonescalation clique had come to power. Konoye appointed Itagaki on the advice of Ishiwara Kanji, the founder of this clique.

Accompanying the Itagaki appointment, Kagesa Sadaaki was transferred from his post as chief of the Eighth Section of the General Staff to chief of the Military Affairs Section of the War Ministry (*gunmu kachō*). In this position, even though on paper subordinate to the office of chief of the Military Affairs Bureau (*gunmu kyokuchō*), he was in fact, both because of his personal relationship with Itagaki and because of the peculiar nature of Japanese bureaucracy, Itagaki's prime adviser and, as such, was able to influence the course of the War Ministry, at least to the extent that it was susceptible of leadership.

Konoye, who initially opposed the nonescalation group's desire to make a compromise peace with China, apparently had changed his mind about the possibility of a rapid military victory there. He now sought to collaborate with the nonescalationists in order to outmaneuver those who favored a hard line and in order to reach a political settlement.[37]

Kagesa had a key position in Konoye's strategy. In addition to Kagesa's post at the nerve center of military decision making he also maintained intimate connections with Kazami Akira,

Konoye's cabinet secretary, and through him, with Konoye himself. Kazami paid Kagesa's expenses out of a secret fund known only to the prime minister and a few other high cabinet officials.[38] Konoye told Harada that Kagesa, accompanied by Captain Oka of the navy (First Section Chief of the Military Affairs Bureau), had weekly secret luncheon meetings with Konoye's secretary, Kishi.[39] Kishi told Konoye that without the knowledge of even War Minister Itagaki himself, Kagesa was going to bring Kao Tsung-wu to Japan. Matsumoto and Kagesa were clearly coordinating their efforts through Konoye and his office.

In retrospect, the fact that these efforts to move toward peace had to proceed as a conspiracy within the Japanese government cannot but make one doubt that there was any real chance that the disparate elements of that government could be brought to accept any kind of compromise peace.

Although the details of Japanese internal shifts must have been unknown to the Chinese, it was surely not lost upon them that a general shift had taken place. Kao denies that he was persuaded to go to Japan by the shift in the Japanese political climate.[40] Nevertheless, Nishi records that it was on June 14, after these changes, that Kao announced to him his decision to go to Japan.[41]

What were the real factors motivating Kao's decision? A primary consideration was Kao's view of his role in Chinese politics. Possessed of great personal courage and also a certain measure of ambition, he considered it his role to undertake the dirty but necessary job of dealing with the Japanese, which no one else in the government was willing to undertake. He hoped that he saw the true interests of his country and that perhaps he could save her where no one else had been able. What, from beginning to end, was important for Kao were the terms of peace which Japan would offer to China. Kao and Matsumoto conducted conversations in Hong Kong about peace conditions. They agreed that the sine qua non was Japanese withdrawal.[42] In conversations with Kao, Matsumoto had suggested that Chiang's temporary resignation and replacement by Wang Ching-wei might be the basis for peace consistent with the *aite to sezu* declaration. Matsumoto also raised this possibility in conversations with Matsuoka.[43] If the form, titular leadership, could buy concessions on the substance, the actual terms, then it seemed to Kao wise to explore the possibility of buying peace at the price of Chiang's resignation.

Kao, although he always reported on his activities to Chiang, practically never received precise instructions from Chiang. Kao felt that his work, conducted with Chiang's understanding, had his tacit approval. Kao served Chiang by attempting to ascertain what Chiang's position was or should be and then acting in a manner consistent with that position. Kao, unlike some other of Chiang's advisers, considered that in the long run the struggle against the Communists was more important then the war against Japan.[44] Kao considered that Chiang too really wanted peace with Japan and that it was up to himself to arrange it if it possibly could be arranged. This he believed was not only in Chiang's interest, but in China's interest.

As had been his custom, Kao reported his plans to go to Japan through Chiang's personal secretary, Ch'en Pu-lei. And, as had been his custom, Chiang expressed neither approval or disapproval.[45] Other members of the government, whether through informal contacts or through their official positions, were also aware of Kao's intention to go to Japan. This number probably included Wang Ching-wei and his chief-of-staff to be, Chou Fo-hai. Kao, however, went to Japan on his own initiative and responsibility with the intention of gathering direct information on Japanese plans in continuation of his work of the previous five years.[46]

Wang spoke with Kao several times, inquiring about Kao's work and encouraging him. He expressed his willingness to take responsibility for peace with Japan if Chiang wanted him to. But Kao was in no sense acting as Wang's agent.[47] As Kao points out, Wang Ching-wei had no military strength of his own; Wang could only assume titular leadership with Chiang's support and approval. Thus in no sense did Kao consider exploration of the possibility of Wang's assuming leadership to be a betrayal of Chiang.[48] He felt the closest personal loyalty to Chiang, who had favored him with great responsibility and trust. Chiang too, despite all that was to transpire, was to indicate to Kao his respect for Kao's courage and loyalty, which he surely would not have done to someone he felt had betrayed him. Kao's situation from beginning to end was extremely delicate.

Matsumoto, with the assistance of Itō, took responsibility for the practical details of the trip, which because of the necessity of maintaining secrecy from the Chinese public, the Japanese public, and large factions within the two governments was a complex task. Matsumoto also arranged through his wide acquaintance in the political world that Kao meet important and congenial people upon whom he might have the greatest effect.[49]

On June 22 Kao, accompanied by the ubiquitous Itō, left Hong Kong for Yokohama abroad the *Empress of Japan*.[50] Kao arrived on July 5 and received a large welcome by military and civil police, which, although it was undoubtedly meant to protect him, in the light of the secrecy of his mission endangered both his life and his cause.[51] Kagesa had arranged for a car to take him to Tokyo and for lodgings at an inn, the Kachō, which was guarded by military police.[52] He must have wondered whether he was being guarded or imprisoned. Indeed, in view of the record of the Japanese military for treachery, he must have rightly feared for his life, dependent as he was upon Kagesa's support against the many hard liners in the military establishment.

Matsumoto introduced Kao, Nishi, and Itō to the *beau monde* of Japanese society, a small group of liberals called the Asameshi kai (breakfast club), which held weekly meetings. Kazami was the organizer of the meetings, but the group included such distinguished members as Prince Saionji's grandson, Saionji Kinkazu. Everyone in this group was opposed to the expansion of the war. Here Kao met Inukai Ken, a young Diet member and son of late Prime Minister Inukai Tsuyoshi, who because of his efforts to settle the Manchurian Incident, had been assassinated on May 15, 1932. The Inukai household had long received Chinese revolutionaries with warm hospitality. Inukai had been asked by Kazami to set up a small office in the prime minister's mansion to do research on China. Because of the press of his professional duties and failing health, Matsumoto could no longer participate actively in the peace movement; and Kao, upon Matsumoto's recommendation, asked Inukai to take his place as a liaison between the Chinese comrades and liberal-minded Japanese in the military and in civil life. From this point on, Inukai devoted himself to the peace work. Although Kao has high regard for Inukai's sincerity, he believes that he was more easily manipulated by the Japanese military than Matsumoto. He believes that the switch of Inukai for Matsumoto was a shell game perpetrated upon him by the military.[53]

One of the most striking things about the Wang Ching-wei peace movement is the seeming cooperation of a small group of Japanese — Nishi, Inukai, Matsumoto, Itō as civilians, Kagesa, Tada, and others in the military—with a small group of Chinese to work toward peace which the government of neither nation seemed willing or able to procure. Were these few Japanese sincere? Kao feels that since the army realized that the trust of the Chinese government in the Japanese military was very low, they used men like Nishi and Inukai to deceive him, Wang, and others. He noticed a pattern in his dealings with the Japanese: they would send one hard-line man who would make demands, and another with him who would be mild and who would try to establish personal bonds. Thus he feels that men like Nishi and Inukai were serving the interests of the military.[54] It is clear that Nishi, Inukai, and Matsumoto must have enjoyed good relations with the military; otherwise, they never would have been able to carry on political activities, certainly not political activities contrary to the desires of the military. If the military were using them, so far as one can judge from extant memoirs, these civilians were also trying to shape the course of military politics toward peace. There is no one in this story who was not seeking to manipulate others.

During the three weeks that Kao was in Japan, he met with Kagesa and with Colonel Imai Takeo, then chief of the China Section of the General Staff. Through Kagesa he also met with War Minister Itagaki, Vice-Chief of Staff Tada, and Naval Minister Yonai. Kao was not able to meet Ugaki, the foreign minister, who was himself conducting direct negotiations with the Chinese government through talks between Nakamura, the Japanese consul-general in Hong Kong, and Ch'iao Fu-san, the secretary of H. H. Kung, then chairman of the Executive Yüan. Konoye had told Ugaki of Kao's coming, but Ugaki, believing it was a military conspiracy, reacted phlegmatically.[55]

The proposals that Ugaki put before Kung showed no change from those the Japanese had insisted upon the previous December — Chinese recognition of Manchukuo, stationing of Japanese troops and advisers, establishment of "special areas," including north China, and the payment of an indemnity. Kung's answer also displayed no change from Chiang's original position — while China might consent to keep silent and thus tacitly recognize the Japanese position in Manchuria, she could not recognize any infringement of her sovereignty south of the Great Wall.

The basic issue in the Ugaki-Kung exchanges was the same as that which dominated Kao Tsung-wu's conversations with Japanese officials — the *aite to sezu* declaration. "The Japanese nation regards Chiang Kai-shek in the light of an enemy, saying it will have no dealings with him," said Ugaki.[56] But, as Kung said, "If Chiang was made to retire, there would be no one strong enough to put a treaty into effect — whoever made it."[57] That Kao's conversations with military officers and Ugaki's contacts with Kung were conducted in isolation or even in competition vitiated the effectiveness of Kao's mission. Because Kao's mission seemed to be sponsored by the military and because his official contacts were only with the military, the confidence of civilian liberals close to the throne in Kao, and after him, in Wang, was undermined.

Ugaki himself, because he viewed Kao's trip as another military intrigue, did his best to torpedo it. At his summer home on July 8, just a few days after Kao's arrival, he disclosed Kao's trip and criticized it to a group of news reporters.[58] This publicity both endangered Kao's security and discredited his work in the eyes of those civilian liberals who should have been its staunchest friends.

If Ugaki and the Ministry of Foreign Affairs can be faulted for failure to cooperate with the military's efforts to open up negotiations with China, it is equally true that blame must be alloted to the military as well. Kao himself says that he did not meet with Ugaki because Kagesa prevented it. Kao responded enthusiastically to Matsumoto's initial proposal of a meeting with Ugaki. Matsumoto did not raise the possibility of a meeting again. To Kao's inquiries, he replied that the time was not right. Matsumoto's changed attitude toward meeting Ugaki, thinks Kao, was based on Kagesa's opposition.[59]

Kagesa himself came to regret that he had not coordinated his work with the efforts of the Gaimushō but offered as his reason the need for preserving secrecy.[60] He must also have been influenced by the Japanese military's traditional jealousy of what it considered its prerogatives and by the traditional military distain for the civil government. But the basic responsibility for the failure to coordinate the two approaches to the Chungking government lies with Konoye himself. Both Kagesa and Ugaki were reporting to him and it was on his behalf that they were making these approaches.

While Kao came to Japan with the sole intention of gathering information about Japan's intentions, nevertheless the result of the trip was the first serious articulation of the Wang peace movement — a joint Sino-Japanese plot to end the China Incident. Kao's responsibility for this development is hard to determine. The impression that Kao gained from his conversations was that Japanese policy had not solidified and that they might change their decision not to negotiate.[61] But as the conversations more and more associated abrogation of the *aite to sezu* decision with the emergence of Wang Ching-wei, the more it came to seem to the Japanese that Kao was an exponent of such emergence. Kao, in retrospect, feels that the Japanese lured him to Japan to compromise him and to force him to cooperate with Japan. Kao thought that he fully realized the danger that the Japanese army would use any dealings that he might have with them to force him to cooperate with them. Kao felt that he could face this danger and withdraw if it should become necessary.[62] In fact Kao did withdraw, but did he withdraw in time?

Just who, in these discussions, first raised the possibility of Wang's assuming responsibility is unclear. Kao recounted to Inukai that Imai told him in response to Kao's inquiry about the possible abrogation of the *aite to sezu* statement, "This is a permanent position of the Japanese Government. We cannot cancel the statement of a prime minister so easily. Even though the General Staff opposed it, there was originally ample reason to issue such a statement. These reasons cannot be eliminated in one or two months." Imai and Kagesa proposed, as a second-best plan, to ask Wang, who was of even more senior standing in the Kuomintang than Chiang, to come forth as head of a peace movement; and with his assistance, it would be possible to deal with Chiang Kai-shek.[63]

According to this story, it was the Japanese military who proposed Wang's emergence to Kao. Kagesa asserted, however, in his affidavit for the defense counsel in the Tokyo trials that Kao made the proposal that Wang emerge and that the Japanese government merely "seemed to have no particular objections to Mr. Kao's plan."[64] Of course in the circumstance Kagesa naturally had every reason to deny Japanese responsibility.

In any case, Harada, Saionji's secretary, recorded that Kao had said "If the Japanese government will promise to support and assist Wang Ching-wei, then Chiang Kai-shek will resign."[65] This was the Japanese view of the substance of the conversations with Kao. A statement of this nature by Kao would definitely seem to go beyond the mere gathering of intelligence. At some indefinable point hypothetical discussion of possibilities for peace led into discussion of a plan for Wang's emergence. It is at that point perhaps that Wang's peace movement began.

Japanese sources almost uniformly reflect the inference that Kao had a great deal more faith in the prospects for peace than his recollections actually show. They seem to have believed that Kao was an advocate of Wang's emergence. Undoubtedly Kao consciously projected enthusiasm in order to draw out the Japanese and get them to commit themselves. But in so doing, as often happens in discussions, he, as he had feared, committed himself perhaps more than he would have liked and perhaps more than was wise.

Harada states in his diary that Kao requested that Konoye give him a secret letter for transmittal to Chiang promising that if Chiang resigned in Wang's favor, the Japanese government would cooperate with him.[66] For Konoye to write any sort of letter to Chiang would be an ipso facto abrogation of his *aite to sezu* statement. Again according to Harada, Konoye refused and said that War Minister Itagaki might write a letter instead.[67] Inukai quotes Kagesa as saying that Itagaki would give Kao a letter. Kao himself states that he definitely did not request a letter to Chiang. He states, however, that he may have received a letter from Itagaki addressed not to Chiang but to Wang, but he does not remember either what it said or what happened to it.[69] It is more likely that in view of the *aite to sezu* statement, the Japanese would be willing to send a letter to Wang.

Kao's mission took place in a strange shadow world of intrigue. Kao represented neither Chiang nor Wang nor did he claim to do so. However, the Japanese were interested in talking with him on the assumption that he in fact did have connections with the two leaders. Just whom or what Kagesa and the others with whom Kao spoke represented was equally unclear. Kagesa claimed that he received information of Kao's coming from Matsumoto Shigeharu as a "private individual," and he received Kao as an individual. "But after talking with him and the subject of general peace came up, then my position changed from that of an individual to that of an official and in that capacity [I] reported my information gathered from the Chinese to my superior officers."[70]

Moreover, the Japanese failed to fully endorse the proposal to deal for peace with Wang if Chiang should resign. Kagesa reported his conversations with Kao to Vice-Chief of Staff Tada, and as he told the Tokyo Trial interlocutors gathered around his hospital bed: "Tada reported it to the Minister of War [Itagaki], the War Minister reported it to the Five Ministers Conference and no one entertained any objections . . ."

Q. Do you mean that they favored Mr. Kao's plans of general peace?

A. No, that there was no opposition, no objection to the plan.

Q. Did they stop only there and didn't go any further?

A. Yes, that is so.[71]

In other words, insofar as the Japanese had an attitude, it was a passive, wait-and-see attitude.

Kao returned to Hong Kong on July 21 and reported in great detail to Chiang on all his activities and conversations in Japan, even including the Japanese desire for his resignation.[72] Chiang undoubtedly assumed, since Kao's conversations had been exclusively with the military and even they had failed to commit themselves to anything, that this was another plot to split his government and cause the collapse of Chinese fighting strength. Moreover, so Kao was told, someone had brought to Chiang's attention a report in a Japanese newspaper, leaked by the Communists, that Kao Tsung-wu was in Japan as his representative to negotiate peace with Japan. Kao had, however, been extremely careful not to make such a claim. Chiang, for whatever reasons, received the report of Kao's trip very unfavorably and ordered Kao to cease all peace work.[73]

Perhaps because of the strain and tension that he had endured, Kao's tuberculosis exacerbated. Spitting blood, he was confined to his bed in Hong Kong.

The Peace Movement Quickens, Approaches Victory, and Is Betrayed

5 Wang Ching-wei, since the beginning of the incident and before, had been for peace; his role in Chinese politics was and had been to present the peace-loving and accommodating face of the Kuomintang toward Japan. In the same way, other leading figures in the Chinese government specialized in relations with one or another of the countries with which China had to deal: Sun Fo with the Soviet Union; T. V. Sung with the United States. Although these specialists would naturally come forward in turn like carved figures on a cuckoo clock as China turned from one power to another for support, nevertheless, there was no reason to doubt the basic devotion of each to the interests of China and the Kuomintang regime. The existence of these various "area specialists" gave Chinese foreign policy flexibility. Essentially, it was a method whereby the government could maintain good relations with various competing nations at the same time, while not being fully responsible for promises to any. Diplomats of all the powers with interests in the Far East endeavored to keep in contact with the various factions and personalities of the Kuomintang, attempting both to influence and to predict the direction of Chinese policy. The Japanese had of course no official diplomatic contact, but since peace with Japan was China's number one diplomatic problem, it is not surprising that they were able to open some tangled subterranean passages to various Chinese leaders.

Neither the Japanese nor, to tell the truth, the representatives of the other powers could tell, when they approached or were approached by a Chinese dignitary who relayed some information, or at least one degree or another of warmth or coolness of attitude, whether they were in contact with the government itself or with a possible dissident faction, or whether they were simply being fed purposeful prevarication. The Japanese yearned to deal directly with what they rightly or wrongly conceived of as factions of the Kuomintang. They were not quite so childish as to believe that money or arms could buy the new-style nationalists as they had the warlords; the Japanese did hope, however, that if they could establish direct contact with a "peace faction," they could break the unity of Kuomintang councils.

Wang Ching-wei was naturally a leading object of Japanese hopes in this regard. But he gave his suitors no encouragement. Despite his role in the Kuomintang foreign policy machinery as conciliator of Japan, Wang not only coordinated his work for peace with that of his government, but also, so far as we know, rebuffed all offers to deal with the Japanese directly. He had enough experience to know Japanese techniques. Among the better documented examples is the following: in July, 1938, T'ang Shao-i's daughter visited Hankow, and after extending praise on behalf of her father to the Generalissimo for his resistance to Japan, she called upon Wang Ching-wei and invited him to come to Hong Kong to confer with T'ang with regard to peace mediation. Wang saw in this approach a Japanese scheme for dividing the Chinese camp; he informed the Generalissimo and insisted on Miss T'ang's immediate return to Hong Kong.[1]

It was well known that Wang Ching-wei deplored the "scorched earth policy" and the alliance with the Communists with its implications for mobilization of the masses.[2] Despite — or even because of — these views he was appointed to high office, *fu tsung-ts'ai* (vice-president, titular second-in-command to Chiang Kai-shek) and chairman of the People's Political Council (an advisory organ drawing from all sections of political opinion and designed to promote unity in face of Japanese aggression) by the Extraordinary National Congress of the Kuomintang held at the end of April 1938. Wang's occupation of these prestigious, if not very powerful, posts signalled two things to observers of Chinese politics, both inside and outside China: the unity of all factions in the war of resistance against Japan; and the possibility of a settlement with Japan and rupture of the united front should conditions so warrant.

But Wang was not going to emerge from the cuckoo clock without the agreement and support of Chiang Kai-shek and the top leadership of the Kuomintang. This could only be brought about by some very powerful demonstration that a diplomatic solution was not only possible but more desirable than a military one. The Japanese seemed to know this well; there were no serious plans laid upon the expectation of the desertion of leaders of the rank of Wang Ching-wei. Such quixotic activities were left to military intelligence.

It was general Kuomintang policy, since China was the weaker party, to avoid direct talks with Japan but to make every effort to protect China from unlimited Japanese ambitions by involving other powers. Such was the Trautmann mediation as well as the many attempts to bring about British or American mediation. It was in accordance with this general policy that Wang Ching-wei during the spring and summer of 1938 sought Italian mediation in the Sino-Japanese struggle. Wang's follower, Ch'en Kung-po had failed the previous autumn to bring back encouraging news from Rome; perhaps now, however, China would be willing to pay a higher price for peace. The real inside story of these negotiations, looking toward an Italian-mediated peace in which presumably Wang would come to office in China and, as the price of peace, align China with the Axis powers, is not known; and it seems unprofitable to rehearse the tangle of rumors here. Suffice it to say, these efforts came to naught when a press leak in London exposed them to the world, seriously embarrassing both Wang and the Kuomintang government.[3]

As the autumn wore on, the complete triumph of Japanese arms seemed more and more imminent. Partly, some say, as a result of the Munich Conference, Japan no longer held back from invading Kwangtung, the backyard of Hong Kong and traditionally a British interest. The Japanese landed at Bias Bay on October 12 and, marching virtually unopposed, captured the great city of Canton on October 21. General Yü Han-mou, who was responsible for the defense of Canton, had, after extensive negotiations during the months before, agreed to yield it up to the Japanese without a fight.[4] Hankow, from which the last government organs had withdrawn to Chungking, fell on October 27. From now until the end of the war, the Chinese regime was to be landlocked, isolated from foreign aid and contact, in a remote and backward province. The American ambassador felt that the situation was "most precarious." "Best informed foreign military opinion is that Government cannot hope to continue organized resistance on any effective scale for more than six months and doubt is expressed concerning effectiveness of guerrilla activities."[5] Was the policy of holding on, holding out, and hoping for a change in the international situation going to be able to prevent China's conquest and the crushing of the Kuomintang government?

Apparently, it was at this juncture that Wang felt that he might have to move independently if China were to be saved from defeat. Several weeks before the collapse of Wang's Italian scheme, he had learned of the results of Kao's mission to Japan: that Japan might make peace if Chiang would resign in Wang's favor and that Chiang had prohibited Kao from further exploration of the possibility. Kao, through Kagesa, had succeeded in reaching the nerve center of the Japanese military; and through Inukai and Matsumoto, he had succeeded in reaching Prince Konoye himself. Therefore, Wang felt that of the numbers of informal communications lines that might be opened up, that which Kao had pioneered was the most promising. The twin factors of fear for China's fate and the spark of ambition consequently motivated Wang to urge Kao, against Chiang's express orders, to resuscitate the parley he had begun.[6] He conveyed his desire to Kao in Hong Kong via coded telegram.[7] Thus Wang took over the peace route which Kao had reconnoitered on behalf of Chiang. The Kao route, however, remained but one string on Wang's bow, and he left the management of it to his new-found collaborator, Chou Fo-hai, while he devoted himself to higher-level statecraft.

Chou Fo-hai, Japanese-educated, early joined and quit the nascent Communist party of China and gained through his popular exegesis of Sun Yat-sen's doctrines, the patronage and favor of Chiang Kai-shek. In 1937 he was made vice-director; in 1938, acting director of the Kuomintang propaganda department. Chou had early been opposed to escalation of the war and around him gathered a casual group of intellectuals who shared this view, the "low tone club" (ti-t'iao chü-lo-pu).[8] The "low tone club" seems to have coalesced after and partly as a result of the Kao–Hu démarche. Kao and Hu, as well as T'ao Hsi-sheng, Chang Chi-luan, editor-in-chief of the Ta kung pao, and others, were members of the circle which used to meet socially and for discussions of national affairs in Chou's Nanking bomb shelter.[9] The club itself was not cohesive nor did it have any real political character. It was Chou Fo-hai who moved from discussion to conspiracy. Despite Chou's official position, he never was in a position to advise the Generalissimo on matters of war and peace; his function was propaganda.[10] Chou felt that his talents were worthy of the most important affairs of state. Perhaps it was frustration with lack of influence in national policy that made him seek out Wang Ching-wei and his group, for there he might expect to find both agreement with his views on the war and the resources to promote them and himself. At first Wang suspected that, since Chou was known as a retainer of Chiang, Chou had been sent as an agent provocateur to spy upon him.[11]

The instrument Chou employed to gain Wang's confidence and to carry out his own diplomatic maneuvers was a literary research society (I-wen yen-chiu so), in reality a creature of the propaganda ministry and thus of Chou himself. He appointed Wang's longtime friend and supporter, T'ao Hsi-sheng, general secretary of the society. Through T'ao's good offices, Chou gained entrance to Wang's circle.[12] By autumn of 1938 Wang and Chou were working closely together and Chou, never a man to be bashful, had taken over management of Kao's direct route to Japan, even acting independently of Kao himself. Wang apparently received reports on these activities only at Chou's pleasure.

That Wang would leave the Kao route in the hands of a new follower tends to buttress the view that Wang at this point felt simply that the Kao route was an iron which should not be allowed to cool. Wang's conviction was that the whole endeavor of the Chinese government should be to make terms with Japan at the earliest possible moment both for the sake of the parts of China which were under Japanese rule and for those parts which might with great suffering soon fall under the Japanese yoke. The Kao route might be useful in the task of opening negotiations, but far more difficult and critical, he evidently felt, was the problem of persuading his own comrades and fellow citizens that this was China's best choice.

Probably, though there are no documents to prove it and both personal and political relationships were enormously complex, Wang's advocacy of peace was a trial balloon to test national and international opinion, sent up in consultation with his colleagues in the government. In other words, Wang's point of view, although contrary to the government's avowed policy of the moment, nevertheless represented an alternative toward which it might tack. For example, after the fall of Canton on October 21, his birthplace and center of influence, Wang stated to the Reuters correspondent in Chungking: "If Japan offers peace terms which do not hamper the existence of the Chinese nation, we may accept them as the basis for discussion, but otherwise there is no room for discussion . . . So far as China is concerned, we have never closed the door to mediation . . . All depends on the terms offered by Japan." Chungking sources vociferously denied that this was the government's view, and yet we know that at this very time, as well as before, the Chinese government was vigorously seeking to discover Japanese terms and to induce foreign mediation of the conflict. Hu Shih revealed several months later when he had become ambassador to the United States that during this period after the fall of Canton, that is, late October, "There were talks of peace — that is, there were serious thoughts of giving up the fight. In fact, our enemy too, made it quite clear that they wanted peace. But this period of hesitation was also a period of great decisions. It did not take very long for our leaders to come to the conclusion that it was impossible for China to have peace at the present moment simply because there was not the slightest chance for a peace that would be reasonably acceptable to my people. After serious considerations of all difficulties and potentialities, our leaders have definitely decided to continue our policy of resisting the invader and to fight on."[13] American diplomatic records indicate that this attempt on the part of the Chinese government to obtain terms from the Japanese was through the medium of British mediation.[14]

Wang undoubtedly put all his political strengths and abilities into swinging the Kuomintang councils towards peace, but the decision went against him, both because Chiang and his associates had no faith in Japanese sincerity and because they feared the internal political consequences of a dishonorable peace.

The Japanese had indeed been re-examining their policy under pressure from Ishiwara's disciples and, though no change was really made in its substance, the formulation and trappings it was given at this time were to shape the Wang Ching-wei peace movement and to imbue Japanese imperialism henceforth with its characteristic moral tone. It was the locus of the "new order in East Asia."

Because Kagesa and his fellow Ishiwara disciples felt that "what Japan desired was co-existence and co-prosperity through cooperation from the heart between Japan and China"[15] and because they foresaw that the longer the war went on without formulation of a real plan for peace with China, the more difficult it would be for the Japanese military to accept a peace which would permit a cooperative relationship with China, they pressed for an official codification of Japanese policy. As a result of this reasoning, Colonel Horiba Kazuo of the War Guidance Office of the General Staff prepared a draft of a new, supposedly conciliatory, China policy. This draft, which was presented to and accepted by the war, navy, foreign, and finance ministries at the end of August, was entitled *Nisshi shin kankei chōsei hōshin* (Policy for the adjustment of the new relationship between China and Japan). This document was to be the foundation of Japanese China policy up to the time when her defeat in the Pacific War became imminent. It may have struck its authors as being on a high moral plane *(daijōteki),* but to concur in their assessment one must share their peculiar moral framework. Japan, Manchukuo, and China were to cooperate on the basis of *zenrin yūkō* (neighborly cooperation), *kyōdō bōkyō* (cooperative anti-communism or anti-Comintern cooperation), and *keizai teikei* (economic cooperation).

Zenrin yūkō is spelled out in practical terms as Chinese recognition of Manchukuo and pursuit by the three countries of unified foreign policies, that is, China's foreign policy would be subservient in every respect to Japan's. She could not pursue an independent policy toward third powers. The political form of the new China would be *bunchi gassaku.* Japan would send "advisers" *(komon)* to the new central government, to the police, and to the army, which would be strictly limited. Shanghai, Tsingtao, and Amoy would have special governments in which Japanese control would be even tighter. *Kyōdō bōkyō* was spelled out as the stationing of Japanese troops in Mongolia, in north China, and in the Shanghai-Hangchow-Nanking triangle. There they would have a political, economic, and strategic stranglehold. The Chinese would contribute to the occupation expenses. The two nations would sign an anti-Comintern pact and repress Communist elements in the interior. The Japanese would have control of transportation and communications within the areas where they stationed troops as well as free navigation on the Yangtze and along the Chinese coast. *Keizai teikei* meant that the Japanese would be given special concessions to exploit the natural resources of north China. The economy of China would be integrated with that of the Japanese empire and would be devoted to supplying what the empire needed rather than what might be most advantageous for China.

In general, then, the liberal and conciliatory aspect of the *hōshin* was not in its substance but in its rhetoric. There were two concessions, however, upon which hopes of a compromise peace were to be built: the Japanese promised after the restoration of peace and order to withdraw their troops from the areas, such as they were, where their presence was not specified, and second, they promised to "consider" the abrogation of their extraterritorial privileges and the return of their concessions.[16]

Wang could know nothing of the existence or content of the *hōshin*. He was apprised, however, of a possible shift in Japanese councils by Prince Konoye's radio address made on November 3 (sometimes called Konoye's second statement). Although written in celebration of Japanese triumphs in Canton and Hankow, this speech seemed to signal a new tone to Japanese policy and, in particular, a new interest in the formula of Chiang's resignation.

Konoye's second statement had been the goal of many months of work by Nishi, Inukai, and Matsumoto. Nishi and Inukai had each written drafts for the speech, but the text selected had been written by Konoye's speechwriter, Nakayama Yu.[17] The statement as it appeared disappointed those who were looking for a mutually acceptable basis for peace because although it suggested vaguely the possibility of brotherly cooperation with the Chinese and the National (Kuomintang) Government, it also suggested that this government must be radically changed. What Konoye did in this speech was to suggest officially that the *aite to sezu* statement might be interpreted not as refusal to deal with the Kuomintang government whatsoever but merely with that government so long as it was headed by Chiang Kai-shek. It might be read as the official endorsement of the plan which had been discussed during Kao's visit to Japan — Wang's emergence in turn for Japanese support — that Konoye had refused to give in July.

Konoye claimed that "what Japan sincerely desires is the development and not the ruin of China." "No country," he said, "desires or understands as Japan does perfection of China as an independent state and China's racial aspiration and sentiment." He explained the current conflict as having been caused by the Kuomintang government's flirtation with racially alien Western ideas and nations and by that government's failure to suppress communism. "If," he concluded, "the National Government regains the original spirit of the Chinese race, effects changes in the policy it has pursued and the personnel and emerges as a new administration for the reconstruction of China, Japan would not reject the participation of the National Government.[18]

Wang, then, at about the same time, experienced failure in his efforts to sell the idea of immediate peace to his comrades and yet also received encouragement from Konoye's statement to believe that the Japanese might in fact make peace if he came forward. Several weeks later he received even more convincing evidence from the Kao route he had reopened, namely, what appeared to be a Japanese promise to withdraw their troops from China.

This surprising promise lay at the end of a long string of events which, despite rather full documentation, remains difficult to untangle convincingly. Wang had taken the initiative in reopening the Kao route, but it was Chou Fo-hai and his assistant, Mei Ssu-p'ing, rather than either Wang or Kao who saw through the enterprise of making a secret agreement with Japan.

Mei had previously achieved moral success but personal financial failure as administrator of a model hsien (county) near Nanking.[19] Chou dispatched him to Hong Kong putatively to open and serve as director of the international affairs institute (Kuo-chi wen-t'i yen-chiu so), a branch of Chou's literary research society, with the mission of reporting on the foreign press.[20] Mei's real role was to be Chou's personal operative in contacts with the Japanese. Unlike Kao or even Wang himself, neither Chou nor Mei had any experience in diplomatic dealings with the Japanese. The ambitious Chou was not unwilling to take command; the Japanese military for their own part anticipated that they could deal more easily with greenhorns.[21]

The responsibility on the Japanese side for resuscitating the Kao route seems to lie with Matsumoto Shigeharu, the man who had persuaded Kao to go to Japan in the first place. According to a Japanese statement based on information apparently conveyed to the author by Matsumoto himself, Matsumoto visited Kao in August and brought with him a draft of peace conditions which allegedly Konoye himself had helped prepare. These conditions, perhaps reflecting the development of the *Nisshi shin kankei chōsei hōshin,* at the same time were quite liberal and even provided for Japanese withdrawal.[22] Although Kao was still ill, he met frequently with Matsumoto. He says, however, that in these discussions Matsumoto never touched on specific peace conditions.[23] It appears then that Matsumoto, probably on the instructions of military intelligence, took up dealings with Mei Ssu-p'ing without Kao's knowledge. The details of how this came about are unclear, because for one thing Mei and Matsumoto could not speak a common language.[24] Matsumoto gave Mei the purported draft of Japanese peace terms. In turn, Mei gave Matsumoto a draft supposedly containing Chinese minimum conditions.[25] Neither the content nor composer of this draft is known. Matsumoto returned with the Chinese draft to Shanghai, where he was stricken with typhus.[26] As a consequence, it fell to Nishi and Itō to take the Chinese conditions to Tokyo. One source says[27] that on the contrary they gave this document to Imai, who flew then to Shanghai for discussions with Mei. However, Imai, a precise, diary-keeping man, states that he was not acquainted with this document until later.[28] But whatever the exact details, it seems clear that the two sides had exchanged drafts of peace conditions. These were combined into a joint Mei–Matsumoto draft which Mei took back to Chungking on October 21, the date of Canton's fall and Wang's press statement.[29]

Following a pattern characteristic of *wahei kōsaku,* the Japanese pressed for a "conference." Matsumoto receded into the background and who should take his place but intelligence operatives from the Japanese army! These intrepid colonels felt at last they had a straight line direct to Wang Ching-wei.[30] But did they? The answer seems to be a definite no. According to the authoritative testimony of Kao Tsung-wu, Wang did not authorize Mei or Kao to represent him, and he knew nothing whatsoever of the conference.[31] Indeed, both Chinese and Japanese sides were playing a confusing game, the real character of which was further obscured by an aura of "comradeship." Kao[32] asserts that this comradely spirit was a Japanese fabrication, but neither side lacked either self-assurance or skill in the age-old East Asian art of personal relations.

Apparently after receiving word from Chou in Chungking, Kao informed Kagesa that Mei and he would come to Shanghai and requested that the Japanese send a responsible negotiator. Nishi, Itō, Kazami, Inukai — the comrades associated with the prime minister's office — and their military associates, Imai and Kagesa, took counsel; and subsequently, the General Staff decided to dispatch Colonel Imai with Itō Yoshio as his assistant to meet with the Chinese in Shanghai.[33]

In order to avoid suspicion, Mei left Chungking on November 2 for Hong Kong, arriving there on November 9. He went to Shanghai on November 12 aboard a French ship, and Kao arrived from Hong Kong via an Italian ship on November 13. Imai and Itō were awaiting them, having arrived on the ninth of November.[34] Also present as interpreter was Chou Lung-hsiang, an old friend of Kao's and the former chief of the Russo-Japanese section of the Wai-chiao-pu information office. Chou, who spoke "better Japanese than a Japanese,"[35] was to play an unobtrusive but important role throughout Wang's peace movement and peace government.

The place chosen for the conference was the Jūkōdō, the former mansion of a rich Chinese official, in the "badlands," the Japanese-occupied sector of Shanghai. The Jūkōdō had been previously used by Doihara but now was vacant. Imai had requisitioned it for several days, borrowed furniture and kitchen utensils, and employed several maids.[36] All the delegates went about with bare feet and Japanese yukata (robes) as if at a Japanese hot spring resort.[37]

There were as many views of what the Jūkōdō conference was to accomplish as there were participants. The understanding of the Japanese civilians as represented by Nishi was that it was a meeting of peace comrades with the objective of moving the Japanese government to make concrete the abstractions of Konoye's November 3 speech.[38] The Japanese army, and assumedly its representative, Imai, viewed the conference as a negotiation similar to many Japanese intrigues with Chinese leaders in the past, bargaining with Wang Ching-wei to cause him to rebel against Chiang and split the enemy camp.

There were also two points of view on the Chinese side: that of Kao and that of Mei. Kao did not take the conference very seriously. He regarded it as "just a few people getting together" to explore hypothetical solutions to the war. He had every expectation from his past experience that the Japanese would not truly commit themselves, but he hoped that perhaps there might be some point in further fishing for concrete Japanese peace terms.[39] Mei Ssu-p'ing and behind him Chou Fo-hai were more interested in taking immediate practical action which at once would bring peace to their nation and personal advancement to themselves.

It was between the points of view of Imai and Mei that bargaining was really possible — both were interested in action. In fact, despite the presence of the others at the conference, the discussion and negotiation took place between Imai and Mei. Kao, the other Chinese representative, and Imai had already come to regard each other with thinly disguised suspicion.[40]

The talks got off to a slow start because Mei and Imai disagreed about what should be the basis of their discussion of terms. Mei had come under the impression that the draft which he and Matsumoto had agreed upon was what the Japanese wished to discuss. Imai claimed on the other hand that he had never seen this draft and was in no way bound by it. He intended to be guided by the *Nisshi shin kankei chōsei hōshin,* a far less conciliatory document.[41]

By the night of November 14, however, Imai and Mei had succeeded in putting together a joint draft entitled the *Nikka kyōgi kiroku* (Sino-Japanese consultative record and understanding). In accordance with Imai's desire, the principles of the *Nisshi shin kankei chōsei hōshin,* namely, *zenrin yūkō* (neighborly friendship), *kyōdō bōkyō* (mutual anti-communism) and *keizai teikei* (economic cooperation) were made the basis of the agreement. The Chinese agreed to the recognition of Manchukuo;

the signature of an anti-Communist agreement modeled on the anti-Comintern pact which would permit stationing Japanese troops in north China and Inner Mongolia for defense against communism; to Japanese freedom of residence and trade and certain economic priorities in north China; and to compensation for the losses suffered by private Japanese citizens during the war.

In return, the Japanese promised to begin the withdrawal of their troops *immediately* upon restoration of peace and progressively as order was restored in the interior and to complete this withdrawal within two years. The Chinese government would be responsible for guaranteeing the re-establishment of order during this period. Not only did the Japanese hint future surrender of extraterritorial privileges, but also the concessions that they had gained from the Chinese side were hedged about with restrictions: Japanese troops were to be stationed in north China only in the Peking–Tientsin area "in order to safeguard lines of communication to Inner Mongolia"; the stationing of troops in Inner Mongolia was to be limited to the term during which the proposed anti-Communist pact would be in effect; further, Japanese economic priority should only take effect when all the powers offered China equal terms.[42]

In summary, under the terms of the *kiroku,* China would leave the war, in which she had been all but militarily crushed, with her sovereignty more intact than when she had entered it.

But what was the price that had to be paid? The last section of the *kiroku* read as follows: "When the Japanese Government issues statements concerning the above conditions for solution, Wang Ching-wei and other Chinese comrades will immediately declare that they are severing their relationship with Chiang Kai-shek. In order to construct a New Order in East Asia they will announce Sino-Japanese cooperation and anti-communist policies. At an appropriate time they will establish a new government."

The Chinese interpretation of this was that if the Japanese government changed its aggressive policy and Konoye made a public address in which he offered peace on the terms stated in the *kiroku* — Japanese withdrawal within two years and Chinese recognition of Manchukuo — Wang would leave Chungking in order to gain freedom of speech and would publicly "respond" to Konoye's offer of terms supporting Chinese acceptance. Thus it would appear that it had been Japan which had sued for peace.

The Japanese interpretation of the *kiroku* was that in return for the promise of eventual withdrawal, Wang would organize and lead a military conspiracy to overthrow Chiang's government and replace it with a pro-Japanese regime. It is hard to feel that the text of the *kiroku* does not support the Japanese interpretation.

In the light of the divergence of what they were really willing to accept, it was perhaps unscrupulous for both sides to put their signatures on this document. Kao opposed signature at the time, but the Japanese, since they were anxious to mobilize a conspiracy, pressed for signature not, they said, as an agreement but as a *kiroku,* that is, conversation record.[43] These different interpretations of the *kiroku* go back to the inception of the Kao Tsung-wu route. According to all reports, not merely his own, Kao's intention never was to oust Chiang Kai-shek; it was to make an acceptable peace with Japan even at the price of Chiang's resignation. The major intention of the Japanese military was to topple Chiang, and they might be willing to make some concessions, or hints of concessions, in order to do so.

With the *kiroku* draft in hand Imai flew back to Tokyo, where coincidentally a joint conference of the War Ministry and General Staff was in progress. Present were War Minister Itagaki, Vice-Chief of Staff Tada, Chief of the Military Affairs Section Tanaka, Chief of War Affairs Section of the War Ministry Kagesa, Chief of the Operations Section of the General Staff Muto Akira, among others. This meeting thus included the leadership of the Japanese military bureaucracy. Imai reported to the assembled company on the Jūkōdō conference. After the high officials had retired, the staff officers continued to meet privately. One said to Imai: "I think you have been cheated by the Chinese." Imai replied, "I don't believe so. But if that is the case, I feel I have nothing to regret and I would gladly be cheated." Tension filled the air. Finally, Tanaka, the senior officer present, broke in and said: "Let us not talk about whose responsibility it is. Let us all take responsibility and act resolutely together." And the staff officers decided to send Imai, this time accompanied by Kagesa, back to Shanghai to sign the agreement for the army — Imai representing the General Staff and Kagesa, the War Ministry.[44]

What was the significance of this little drama? Certainly, it was not that the masterminds of the Japanese military machine had agreed to accept the *kiroku* as the basis of peace with China. Since responsibility for any of their actions was exactly what they never could accept, the word rings curiously from their lips. Kagesa, who was about to join the group at the Jūkōdō, admitted later that although there was complete agreement among himself and Kao and Mei with regard to the withdrawal of troops, there had been absolutely no communication with the commanders of Japanese forces in China.[45] Second, later developments make clear that it was understood on both sides that before events could move, both Wang Ching-wei and the Japanese authorities had still to give their consent. Third, it would have been impossible for the Japanese military so quietly to agree to see the fruits of their aggression, which had been bought for much toil and blood, surrendered. It appears, therefore, that the joint meeting was merely giving its approval for Kegesa and Imai to sign the *kiroku* "as comrades." They were giving consent that the conspiracy be continued to see what might result: whether it might not split the Chinese government. But like so many other Japanese "decisions" of those trying years, it was vague and unclear what, if anything, had been agreed upon.

Nishi and Inukai accompanied Kagesa and Imai back to Shanghai, where Mei and Kao awaited them. After the day was consumed in establishing authoritative texts in the two languages, at 7 PM on November 20 the *kiroku* was signed. After the signing, Kagesa called for glasses and drinks. Raising his glass in toast, he said: "With long painful work we have reached agreement. But for the future of China and Japan there are many harsh obstacles. I hope for your cooperation in the future."[46]

Essentially, signature by either side, neither of which had any real authority to commit anyone, of a "conversation record" had no meaning. Somehow, however, in the weeks to come, the *kiroku* became what seems to have been understood on both sides as an agreement.

It was only after the conclusion of the conference when Mei brought the *kiroku* back to Chungking that Wang himself learned of the activities of Chou, Mei, and Kao, who had been bargaining in his name. Exactly how much Chou and Mei told Wang is not known. Wang seems to have believed, however, that he was merely to "respond" to an offer by Konoye of peace on the terms of Japanese withdrawal. Did he fully realize the commitments the Japanese believed his followers had made in his name?

As was the pattern in the many secret negotiations between China and Japan, each side was trying to dupe the other. The Japanese, at least the authorities in Tokyo, were trying to buy a cheap victory. The Chinese, and perhaps their civilian Japanese comrades and Kagesa, were trying to maneuver the Japanese government into committing itself to withdraw Japanese troops from China. The Chinese were able to play upon the weakness of the Japanese for thinking that they "understood" China and Chinese politics. The Japanese were familiar with Wang's political history before 1931 and thought he might well be willing to plot a military revolt and the establishment of an anti-Chiang regime.

Apparently, the Chinese not only let the Japanese think that Wang would organize an anti-Chiang military rising, but they told them so. According to a written account of Chinese intentions which Imai says he and Kagesa received from Mei and Kao after the Jūkōdō meeting, once Wang had responded to Konoye's statement, the armies of Szechwan and Yunnan would rise. The tone of the document implied that it would be difficult to keep these forces from rising prematurely.[47] This scheduling of a military revolt would imply a prior conspiracy involving military leaders in these regions. The Japanese firmly believed in the existence of this prior conspiracy; it was the raison d'être for the kōsaku.

Kao Tsung-wu says that there existed no military conspiracy and that the Japanese were not given any written promise that one existed.[48] Logic and probability support the first assertion. Wang's influence was insufficient to organize a military conspiracy. A military conspiracy of the sort that the Japanese hoped for — leading to a Chinese capitulation — would run counter to Wang's patriotic objectives. First of all, it is most unlikely that any sane military politician would lay his career and his life on the line for the sake of unlikely promises from the duplicitous Japanese merchandised by the powerless Wang Ching-wei. Further, these military leaders were not in a position to rebel even if they wanted to. Military supporters of Wang in the early republican era like Chang Fa-k'uei, were, like all forces that were not commanded by Chiang's closest adherents, closely supervised. Because of the presence of central government armies, rebellion in Szechwan would have been virtually impossible. Second, as mentioned above, not only was Wang's political strength so nonexistent as to render his capacity to organize a military conspiracy virtually nil, but also, judging from both his past and future actions and from what one can construe of his character, it would be unthinkable that he would plot to destroy his country and government. Wang's interest was in obtaining satisfactory peace terms for his country, not in destroying his country's capacity to resist the Japanese.

All evidence suggests that there was no widespread conspiracy and also that even many of Wang's faithful and respected followers were neither informed nor consulted prior to Wang's departure.[49] Only Chou Fo-hai, Mei Ssu-p'ing, Ch'en Kung-po, T'ao Hsi-sheng, and Madame Wang were in on the plan.[50]

The original plan, which had taken shape during Kao Tsung-wu's trip to Japan and in prior discussions, called for Chiang's temporary resignation and Wang's assuming responsibility for making peace with Japan. When Chiang proved unwilling to accept this plan, it had to be altered only to the extent that Chiang would have to be forced temporarily to surrender his leadership to Wang, in his own and China's interest. As Wang, Kao, and others saw it, they were acting in Chiang's interest and doing what Chiang would have done if he had not been, as they saw it, a prisoner of the Communists. It was the intention of Kao and Chou, servitors of Chiang, to bring Wang forth only to establish peace, and then it was the hope and intention of all three to return the leadership to Chiang, perhaps, of course, with their own positions enhanced.

If Wang did not conspire with military leaders beforehand, his plan nevertheless required that his hoped-for success in securing a promise from the Japanese to withdraw within two years would gain him the active backing of those military leaders who enjoyed power independently of Chiang. Because of the very nature of politics in republican China, Wang perforce had to depend on those who had guns. Without their support he would be in a position neither to negotiate peace with the Japanese or to persuade Chiang to temporarily resign. Thus it was

that the Japanese imagined the Wang Ching-wei peace movement, which had been originated by Kao Tsung-wu, would split
China into warring factions, but in the eyes of the Chinese comrades, it would end in a united Kuomintang government and
the withdrawal of Japanese forces from China.

Did the Chinese give the Japanese written or definite verbal
promises of Wang's intention to organize a divisive military conspiracy as Japanese sources claim that they did? Or were these
promises the products of a fetid imagination fed by Chinese
hints? My own conjecture is that Mei, perhaps on Chou's instruction but without Kao's knowledge, actually gave the Japanese such assurances.

Mere inspection of rumors in the press during the period
makes it clear why the Japanese were willing to believe in the
existence of potential rebellion in Yunnan and Szechwan. The
politics of Szechwan at this period were certainly stormy. Suffice
it to say that the old warlord Liu Hsiang, whose power had
barely been touched by the Kuomintang revolution, had died in
early 1938, and a many-cornered struggle was going on between his officers and various nominees of Chiang Kai-shek —
outsiders of course — for the rule of Szechwan.

Yunnan had become accustomed to virtual autonomy under
its colorful leader, Lung Yun, a Lolo tribesman and a self-made
man. Supplies from the Burma Road, the only overland communications route except the desert tracks to the Soviet Union,
passed through Yunnan. The province possessed vast resources
of tin which the National Government needed for foreign exchange and for the war effort. Moreover, if the Japanese should
gain control of Yunnan, they would have a strategic stranglehold on the National Government from which it could not escape. Thus it was natural that Chungking should encroach upon
Lung Yun's autonomy and just as natural that Lung should resent
it. He had cooperated with Chiang and had supported the defense effort, but the relationship between the two men was
somewhat touchy. Lung was to spend a number of postwar
years as Chiang's unwilling guest.[51] Lung desired peace; he had
great respect for Wang Ching-wei. Wang reposed great hopes
in Lung for the success of his movement.

The plan was that Wang would leave Chungking in order to
gain freedom of speech; Konoye would announce peace condi-

tions; Wang would respond. To set these events in motion, Wang had to be assured of Japanese acceptance of the peace conditions; the Japanese, of Wang's consent to the plan.

What was most in question, of course, was whether the Japanese government would accept the unprecedented peace conditions outlined in the *kiroku*. The story of the Japanese "acceptance" is a tangled one.

On November 21 Kagesa and Imai returned to Tokyo and reported the outcome of the Jūkōdō Conference to War Minister Itagaki and Vice-Chief of Staff Tada. On the following day Kagesa, Imai, and Itagaki went to Konoye's official residence and reported to the Five Ministers' Conference what had transpired. Imai says that the Conference "came to a resolution that the content of the Sino-Japanese consultative record should be announced as the third Konoye statement."[52] Mei was so informed and returned with the news to Chungking on November 27.[53]

At this very time the press was full of reports that the Japanese cabinet was changing its "fundamental policy for regulating Sino-Japanese relations"[54] and that this was to be formalized by an Imperial Conference (Gozen kaigi) attended by the cabinet and the military, the function of which was to make decisions as immutable as holy writ. On November 30 the word came out that the conference had indeed been held and had resolved upon a new China policy.

Wang's group naturally assumed, or rather were led to believe, that this Imperial Conference had accepted the *Nikka kyōgi kiroku,* most especially the clauses dealing with Japanese withdrawal and limitation on stationing troops. If we accept Imai's statement that the Five Ministers' Conference had decided that the *kiroku* agreements should be announced by the prime minister as national policy, then between the Five Ministers' Conference and the Imperial Conference, which would be expected to formalize the decisions of the former, some kind of flim-flam was performed. What the Imperial Conference passed was the *Nisshi shin kankei chōsei hōshin,* prepared, as we recall, by the military the preceding August without reference to the Wang *kōsaku,* which, despite idealistic rhetoric, was a blueprint for the practical subjection of China. The only changes effected by the Imperial Conference were to make the imperialistic intent of the document more plain. The phrase "on the basis of construction of Far Eastern culture and morality" was replaced by "construction of the New Order in East Asia." Horiba, its drafter, felt that this change of wording changed it from an idealistic to an interest-motivated document.[55] What could show the superficiality of the Japanese bureaucratic mind more poignantly? Horiba was among the most clear-minded and well-meaning of bureaucrats. Then Privy Council Chairman Hiranuma proposed further restrictions on the meaning of the *hōshin,* stating that Japan had no intention of returning concessions or abandoning privileges until the European powers did likewise.

In any case, Kao affirms that the Chinese peace comrades were to continue to labor under the misapprehension that the Japanese government had formally and at the highest level accepted liberal peace conditions when it had done no such thing.[56] Do we say that they were deliberately tricked or that their Japanese comrades failed to accomplish their objectives and, rather than halt the work that had gone so far, decided to move forward and hope for the best?

Japanese acceptance of the *kiroku* was even shallower than the above would suggest. We recall that Wang was to approve the *kiroku* for the Chinese side and Prince Konoye for the Japanese side. However, in the first place, Konoye's attitude toward the negotiations with Wang was that it was a conspiracy (*bōryaku*). As such, it naturally had the flavor of being underhanded and dishonorable. High court officials and the emperor himself were unanimous in this view, which inevitably influenced Konoye. Prince Saionji expressed the view of the court: "Japanese diplomacy and politics are very low quality... *Bōryaku* are not appropriate for the diplomatic and political activities of civilization."[57]

But more serious than the slight distaste with which Konoye viewed the secret negotiations was the fact that his own position, upon which the Japanese side's acceptance of the *kiroku* conditions was to rest, was rapidly deteriorating. The military acted without consulting or informing him. For example, the only information that Konoye received prior to the Hangchow landing in November 1937 was an oblique and belated hint from the military that "there may be a new landing for a Nanking offensive."[58] Konoye was also distressed at the pressure of the military to strengthen cooperation with Germany and Italy against England and France.[59]

For these reasons, in late October Konoye instructed his Cabinet Secretary Kazami Akira to prepare a draft announcing his resignation. Kazami submitted this to him on November 3, the day of the second Konoye statement. In Kazami's view Konoye would undoubtedly have resigned with the Imperial Conference decision of the "new relationship policy" on November 30 if it had not been for the prospect of Wang's emergence, for which he felt responsible.[60] On December 12 Konoye told Kido Kōichi, then the education minister, that he wished to "resign when the long-term construction begins its first stage because he could not rely on the conspiracy practiced by the army [the Wang kōsaku?] and the situation is not going smoothly." Kido argued that in light of the possibility of Wang's emergence, Konoye should not resign, lest he expose Japan's "internal instability."[61]

In summary, the Gozen kaigi did not endorse the kiroku; Konoye, in whose trust the Chinese had put their faith, regarded the plan with great suspicion; what trust he did have was nullified by the fact that his own position was precarious. Thus the Japanese commitment to Wang Ching-wei was a sham.

There are questions also about the extent of Wang's endorsement of the kiroku; he seems to have agreed only to respond to Konoye's statement promising conciliatory peace, not, as the kiroku clearly (if the text quoted in genuine) states, to organize an anti-Chiang regime. Whatever the real content of his approval, whether he realized what the Japanese expected him to do or whether he simply felt that any way he could change the political situation would be a change for the better, he caused the green light to be flashed to the Japanese.

This decision was not reached without agony. T'ao Hsi-sheng describes the scene in Wang's Chungking quarters at the Shang-ch'ing temple. Mei, the bearer of the Jūkōdō tidings, Chou Fo-hai, and Ch'en Pi-chün (Madame Wang) were present; the devoted Ch'en Kung-po was earnestly summoned from Chengtu; T'ao himself gained admittance only with difficulty. Ch'en passionately opposed accepting the Jūkōdō kiroku; T'ao privately reminded Wang of his promise to support Chiang for the duration of the war and Wang seemed to accept his remonstrance. Ch'en Pi-chün from the beginning favored accepting the *kiroku*.[62] From the days when she had joined Wang in the attack on Prince Ch'ün, Madame Wang was always a passionate activist. She meant well for Wang; she meant well for China. Her quick and fiery temper was compounded with noble courage, steadfastness, resolution, and energy. She could not endure to sit still while Wang languished, while China seemed about to fall in flames. Alas, however, true courage sometimes requires patience; this was a virtue that she did not have. Although Wang's courage was often fired by her own, Madame Wang, perhaps as much as any single person, bears responsibility for pushing him into the series of events which were to lead to his doom. To her advocacy was added that of Chou and Mei who later in conversation with Kao gave themselves credit for persuading Wang.[63] Kao himself returned a noncommittal reply to Wang's query of Japanese sincerity.[64] Wang's counselors, then, were divided. He himself must have made the final decision.

Perhaps the most important factor in Wang's decision was frustration, both with his own position and with that of China. In the peace debate alluded to by Hu, Wang undoubtedly put his political prestige on the line and lost. Everywhere Chiang tightened his control over both civil and military affairs. Any discussion of peace was suppressed. Wang had simply exhausted the limit of political action within the Kuomintang system and felt he had to move outside as he had in the '20's.

What brought to a head the frustration he felt for his country was the burning of Changsha on November 13. He expressed this frustration in a speech on November 24. Changsha was fired by its own defenders, who, upon a false rumor of Japanese attack, applied the "scorched earth policy." The responsible authorities thereupon fled, leaving the city to smolder for days with great loss of life and property. Was continuation of the resistance policy going to lead to more of the same?

From Chungking Mei brought to Kao in Hong Kong a somewhat guarded message, not exactly that Wang endorsed the *kiroku* but rather that Wang would reply to Konoye's statement if it fulfilled Japanese promises. Kao transmitted this message to Nishi.[65] Other stories are that Chou Lung-hsiang brought the reply to Nishi,[66] that Mei brought the reply to Nishi and Major Ota Umeichiro of the Japanese General Staff on December 1,[67] and that Kao Tsung-wu's brother brought the reply to Itō on December 2.[68] In any case, through the diverse channels of this tangled conspiracy, Wang's message of "acceptance" made its course. According to Imai, the text of the Chinese response ran as follows:

1. Wang Ching-wei approves the Sino-Japanese Consultative Record of the Shanghai Jūkōdō Conference.

2. In the Konoye statement it is necessary that the Japanese promise not to exercise economic monopoly nor to interfere in internal affairs.

3. Wang Ching-wei will depart from Chungking on December 8 and is scheduled to arrive in Kunming on December 10 via Chengtu.

4. Because of the need for preserving secrecy at this time, the Chinese side desires that the statement be issued about December 12.

5. Wang Ching-wei will announce his resignation either in Kunming, Hanoi, or Hong Kong.[69]

The Chinese were telling the Japanese only what they needed to know in order to time their announcement. Actually, according to Kao, it had been definitely decided that Wang would go to Hanoi.[70] The plan was that Wang would go to Kunming, preceded a few days by his followers, to await the Japanese statement. If the Japanese fulfilled their promise, he could ask for Lung Yun's support and then proceed to Hanoi, where he could say what he wished freely and without fear of embarrassing Lung. If the Japanese reneged on their statement, he could return to Chungking with only the loss of his efforts.

Chou Lung-hsiang expressed to Nishi Kao's fear that things might go badly and that it might be necessary for Wang to take refuge in the Japanese consul general's office in Hong Kong. How it was foreseen that Wang might find himself in Hong Kong is unclear. Consequently, Kao, through Chou, requested Nishi to ask the Japanese government to send a consul general they knew and trusted, Tajiri Yasuyoshi, former second secretary at Shanghai, an able and not uncritical political observer. This was about December 2, and Wang was expected to arrive about December 10. On the tenth the new consul general arrived aboard a Japanese gunboat.[71] Perhaps this was an attempt on the part of Kao to test Japanese sincerity; it was virtually the last promise the Japanese kept.

In early December a deathly quiet fell upon the East Asian political scene. All observers expected something to happen — perhaps the long-awaited "new central government" — yet no one knew quite what. The fact that the Japanese slackened their military offensive after the fall of Hankow and the burning of Changsha, doubtless because they felt that their political maneuverings were going to lead to the disintegration of the Chungking regime, actually gave the Chungking forces a breathing spell to regroup militarily and psychologically. Without this pause it is doubtful if the Chinese could long have withstood the Japanese juggernaut. Unquestionably then, this is one service Wang performed for his country.

The Japanese privy to the conspiracy awaited impatiently the word of Wang's departure; Imai intended harakiri if the movement should fail.[72] Konoye planned to make his statement in Osaka at the City Hall on December 11 or 12. He seems to have been seriously worried about the public reaction to his statement, lest these "light and easy conditions" would be difficult for the public to accept after such extensive sacrifice.[73] The moments passed anxiously until December 10 when Wang's loyal publicist Lin Pai-sheng in Hong Kong cabled the alarming news that Wang's departure would be delayed several days.[74] Another version states that the information reached Tokyo via a telegram from the chief of staff of the Taiwan army on the dawn of December 9. Wang had wired Kao about midnight of December 7 that Chiang had unexpectedly returned on December 6 and the departure could not take place as planned on December 8. Chou Lung-hsiang transmitted this information to Nishi on December 8, who then probably forwarded it through Colonel Ota via the Taiwan army.[75]

What should the Japanese do about the promised statement? Should they issue it as scheduled or should they delay it as the Chinese side asked? There was a general fear among Japanese officials that they were somehow being cheated by the Chinese. Konoye said: "I do not think we are being deceived by them, but since the other party is Chinese, perhaps we might have been deceived all this time. I am quite concerned with this and have reported to the Emperor . . . I do not think we have been cheated and strung along by the Chinese. But in the worst case, perhaps so . . . If we have been cheated, the war minister and I are responsible. This is a grave responsibility of the government, even though the public does not know about it."[76]

But just how the Japanese understood they might be being cheated is a bit confused. It is clear that some understood that the Japanese statement was a quid pro quo for Wang's emergence. To make the statement before Wang left Chungking would perhaps endanger Wang's freedom of action if not his life, and it would run the risk that Wang would not fulfill his part of the bargain. Strangely enough, however, Foreign Minister Arita, in the Five Ministers' Conference of December 9, argued that the statement should be issued as scheduled regardless of Wang's delay.[77] "Why should we deal with those people? Why should we not declare our policies?" he exclaimed.[78]

Konoye at first postponed his statement to December 14 on the excuse of illness and then later cancelled it entirely. Kao repeatedly cabled reassurances that Wang was resolved as ever and was waiting for a favorable time to escape.

According to a Japanese report, Kao asked for a Japanese military offensive to distract Chiang from Chungking; this Kao heatedly denies.[79]

Finally, however, word arrived that Wang had escaped on December 18. An explanation of the delay may lie in the last several weeks' events in Chungking.

In preparation for Wang's arrival there on December 8, Chou Fo-hai had flown to Kunming, the capital of Yunnan, on December 5 on the pretext of official business. He was to discuss with Lung Yun the publication in Kunming of the Central Daily News, a Kuomintang organ and the establishment there of the Kuomintang news service.[80] In other words, Chou's supposed mission was to assist in Chiang's larger policy of bringing Yunnan under Kuomintang control. Whether Chou had contact with Lung Yun at this time or whether he was merely making the practical arrangements for the projected stay of the Wang party is unknown. T'ao also awaited Wang in Kunming.[81]

It was at this point that the plan broke down. As Kao told the Japanese, Chiang unexpectedly returned to Chungking on De-

General Lung Yun

cember 6 and this was felt to make Wang's departure impossible. On December 7 Chou received a telegram from Chiang's secretary, Ch'en Pu-lei, conveying Chiang's instruction to return to Chungking immediately. Chou thought that all had been discovered. His fears were heightened when Wang did not come as scheduled on the eighth. Chou considered fleeing alone to Hanoi or to Hong Kong. However, he felt that such a move might further jeopardize Wang. He cabled Wang asking whether his flight would so affect him. Wang cabled back that the connection between himself and Chou was unsuspected.[82] Chou and T'ao remained in Kunming until Wang finally arrived on December 18.[83]

The delay meant that the timetable that had been worked out with the Japanese had broken down. Perhaps because of Lung Yun's attitude, perhaps because of the furor his departure from Chungking had made, Wang was not able to stay in Kunming to await Konoye's statement. He had to leave China and trust everything to Japanese promises.

While he had been waiting in Chungking, Wang had made a final attempt to sway Chiang to his position by once again proposing peace negotiations with Japan at the meeting of the Central Political Council on December 9. But once again Chiang failed to be convinced. A private encounter between the two men is reported to have taken place on December 16. According to some accounts, the discussion ended with Chiang and Wang no longer on speaking terms. According to others, the question of peace was not even broached.[84] Wang had already made his plans but these apparently unpleasant encounters with Chiang may have strengthened his determination to carry them out.

The details of Wang's successful departure from Chungking are unclear. One account says that Wang escaped while Chiang was giving a lecture to the members of the Central Committee of the Kuomintang which Wang, as vice-president, was not required to attend.[85] The Japanese were told at the time that Wang went to Chengtu at the invitation of the president of Szechwan University, Ch'eng Tien-fang, former ambassador to Germany, who may have shared Wang's views with regard to a détente with Germany, and of Ch'en Kung-po. According to this account,[86] Wang, after stopping in Chengtu, proceeded by air to Kunming with Lung Yun's assistance.

The two other accounts involve a direct flight to Kunming. The report which seems most trustworthy because it is ascribed on good authority to Wang himself is that he obtained tickets through the assistance of Lung Yun's chief of staff, who gave him several tickets to Kunming.[87] The other story is that Wang ordered the tickets from the vice minister of communications, P'eng Hsüeh-p'ei, his longtime follower. P'eng, however, was unaware of the use to which Wang intended to put the tickets. Departure permits were generally required, but because of Wang's high position and his relationship to P'eng, P'eng did not question him. For security reasons the names of the passengers were not revealed to the airline company. Wang was accompanied by his wife, Ch'en Pi-chün, his secretary and disciple, Tseng Chung-ming, and Mrs. Tseng. Because of Wang's position, the security officer inspecting the plane before departure did not ask any questions either.[88] Kao Tsung-wu confirms that Wang was not questioned because of his fame and position but states that, so far as he knows, P'eng was not involved.[89]

When Wang and his party landed in Kunming, Lung Yun met the plane at the airport and consulted with them for several hours. The main topic was the possibility of Japanese withdrawal.[90] Lung was undoubtedly skeptical that the Japanese, close to military victory, would be about to announce the withdrawal of their forces. The original plan would have called for Konoye to make this announcement while Wang was in Kunming. Then with this evidence of Japanese willingness to make peace with a government under his leadership, Wang intended to ask for Lung Yun's military and territorial support. Though Lung held out the possibility of his future support in case Wang should be able to win such promises from the Japanese, he could not incur Chiang's suspicion and wrath by allowing Wang to await in Kunming something as unlikely as a statement from Konoye announcing Japanese withdrawal. Lung chartered a plane to take Wang and his group to Hanoi. After their departure, Lung cabled Chiang Kai-shek, who was on an inspection tour in Chengtu, that Wang had unexpectedly come to Kunming and made peace proposals.[91] Lung was thus running with the fox and with the hounds.

Wang, Chou, Tseng, and others arrived in Hanoi on December 19. For the moment the Wangs were quartered in the house of a friend, and other members of the party, at a hotel in Hanoi. After several days, however, the whole party proceeded to a mountain resort near Hanoi, because of the season deserted except for their group.[92]

The news that Wang had left Chungking to negotiate with the Japanese soon leaked to the world press, which speculated widely on its significance. But since there were always so many Japanese-inspired rumors circulating with regard to the development of a peace faction in Chungking, many observers did not credit the story. Others felt certain that Wang's move was with the knowledge and under the instructions of Chiang Kai-shek. When Wang's flight was verified, international confidence in China's intention to continue resistance was gravely shaken — and foreign support for China's cause was based on confidence in China's resolution. British Ambassador Sir Archibald Kerr expressed the consensus of his colleagues that if any of the key generals should support Wang, it would mean "serious trouble" for the Chiang regime.[93] Donald made representations to the British and American governments that "nothing that Wang Ching-wei might do or say represented the Chinese Government in any way."[94]

The Chinese press featured a variety of ingenious stories to explain Wang's trip to Hanoi. One suggested that he had gone to visit Lung Yun and, falling sick on the way, had proceeded to Hanoi where his personal physician was staying.[95]

Chiang publicly reiterated what Donald had told the ambassadors: that Wang was in no way authorized to represent Chiang, the National Military Council, or the Kuomintang government.[96] On the other hand, he praised Wang's "sincerity" and his "unselfish devotion" and asserted that Wang would "surely display a spirit of cooperation" in sharing responsibility for the solution of national problems.[97] Chiang hoped that the differences between himself and Wang might still be bridged, as the two men so often in the past had separated and come together again.

Who knows what might have happened if the Japanese had really fulfilled their promise to announce the withdrawal of their troops from China in exchange for minor concessions? Might not Chiang himself have been delighted to have Wang take responsibility if he could win such conditions from the

Japanese? Alas, when Konoye finally made his statement — the so-called "third" Konoye statement — it failed to contain the withdrawal promise. The statement followed the *kiroku* up to the critical point. It enumerated the familiar *hōshin* slogans of *zenrin yūkō, kyōdō bōkyō,* and *keizai teikei.* Japanese demands for troop stationing in north China and for economic privileges and priorities were touched on, and in turn, the Chinese were offered a peace without loss of territory or indemnity. "Japan not only respects the sovereignty of China, but she is prepared to give positive consideration to the questions of the abolition of extra-territoriality and of the rendition of concessions and settlements — matters which are necessary for the full independence of China."[98]

However, what appeal these promises might have had for China — if indeed they had any meaning at all — was completely negated by the first paragraph: "The Japanese Government are resolved, as has been clearly set forth in their two previous statements issued this year, to carry on the military operations for the complete extermination of the anti-Japanese Kuomintang Government, and at the same time to proceed with the work of establishing a new order in East Asia together with those far-sighted Chinese who share in our ideals and aspirations." Thus in no sense could the Konoye statement be called a basis for peace; it was a basis for capitulation. The attempt of Wang and his Chinese and Japanese collaborators to change the course of Japanese militarism had completely failed.

Chiang was swift to point out the hollowness of the statement. "We must understand that the rebirth of China is taken by the Japanese to mean destruction of an independent China and creation of an enslaved China. The so-called new order is to be created after China has been reduced to a slave nation and linked up with made-in-Japan Manchoukuo. The aim of the Japanese is to control China militarily under the pretext of anti-Communism, to eliminate Chinese culture under the cloak of protection of Oriental culture and to expel European and American influences from the Far East under the pretext of breaking down economic walls. The formation of the 'tripartite economic unit' or 'economic bloc' is a tool to control the economic lifeline of China. In other words, creation of a new order in Asia means destruction of international order in the Far East, enslavement of China and domination of the Pacific and the whole world."⁹⁹ If Wang had left Chungking to propose peace on terms such as these, he was a traitor indeed!

How did it happen that the agreements of the Jūkōdō had metamorphosed into such a warped form? Kao Tsung-wu had persisted and apparently won Wang's approval that all contact with the Japanese should be through him alone. In the same way as he had tried when he was serving Chiang to keep all peace routes in his hand and thus prevent the Japanese from playing one against the other, he now hoped to control Wang's movement and to prevent it from going too far or too fast.¹⁰⁰ Thus it was he who informed Imai in Hong Kong of Wang's urgent desire that the Konoye statement be issued by December 22 at the latest. Imai's telegram arrived at 7:10 PM on December 21.¹⁰¹ At noon on December 22 the three ministers — army, navy, and foreign affairs — met.

From this point on we have to choose between several accounts of the castration of the Konoye statement. According to Inukai Ken, the original Konoye statement, which was to have been issued on December 11, was to be in the form of a press interview, and as such merely required the approval of the "three ministers" — war, navy, and foreign affairs. However, now for some reason a press statement was required which necessitated agreement of the three ministers on the text. Work began on this text at noon on December 12. But much more serious, Major General Tominaga had been transferred to the General Staff, and although his predecessor had approved the withdrawal promise, Tominaga would not "permit any such dishonorable statement that the victorious country promises the vanquished country a time of withdrawal. How can we face the officers and men fighting at the front?"¹⁰²

Inukai was waiting in the anteroom of Konoye's office in the late afternoon of December 22. Kagesa telephoned Inukai from another room — to which he had withdrawn in order to prevent being overheard by his colleagues — to say that the General Staff was meeting and had reached a deadlock because of Tominaga's opposition. Konoye, resting in his office and awakened by the phone, called Inukai in. Inukai told him that Kagesa had called and reported Tominaga's opposition to the withdrawal promise. Konoye said, "But isn't that the first condition from the beginning of the talks with Kao and others?" Inukai replied, "That is correct. Why don't you put pressure on Prince Kan'in, the Chief of Staff? Why don't you speak to Kagesa further? He is a man of sufficient capacity to work even as a secretary of the cabinet. And he is an expert writer. No, Kagesa is thought to belong to the clique favoring peace and General Tominaga is most unfriendly to him." Konoye: "Then let's wait a little longer. All these small troubles and disturbances are the disease of the army. But unless the situation is adjusted this evening, since there are reporters waiting outside, the General Staff will be humiliated. Then Tominaga would be the man responsible. But he doesn't want to take responsibility. Well, something can be worked out. Let's take a little nap and wait."

About eight o'clock Kagesa, accompanied by Oka Takazumi, the chief of the First Section of the Military Affairs Bureau of the Navy, came in. Kazami came out of his office, and the three of them went into the prime minister's office. After a delay, Kazami called a secretary and announced there would be a press statement at 8:20 PM. Kagesa gave Inukai a copy of the compromise statement, which left out the withdrawal clause. After the press statement, Inukai and Kagesa, defeated and in dejection, went down the back stairs to avoid being seen and off into the night.[103]

Nishi affirms the sense of Inukai's account in that he says that the deletion of the withdrawal clause was not the result of a "deep plot" to deceive Wang but rather was the "shallow and frivolous political sense" of Japanese military bureaucrats (gunbatsu).[104]

The verisimilitude of Inukai's account makes it difficult to disbelieve. There is, however, a directly contrary story presented by an otherwise convincing authority. The story presented is that Konoye wrote the speech completely alone, although Nakayama Yu, his speechwriter, had earlier submitted a draft. Kagesa and Inukai came and asked to see the draft but were refused, as were others in the military, on the pretext that because the prime minister had been entrusted with the statement by the Three Ministers' Conference, consultation was not necessary.[105] Such determination, however, does not seem to be consistent with Konoye's general pattern of behavior.

But whatever the true story about the composition of

Konoye's statement, there is no question that it left Wang in a very awkward position. The Japanese explained to Wang's representatives that the reason the withdrawal clause had been left out was the opposition of the military, and they held out the hope that withdrawal might later be offered.[106] In his dilemma, Wang asked for advice from Kao. Should he issue a statement in response as he had promised? Kao advised him not to do so but to make every effort to find out exactly what peace terms the Japanese were willing to offer. Kao felt that if the Japanese were not willing to accept the *kiroku* conditions, the best thing would be for Wang to go to Europe.[107]

Wang made the decision that for China's sake he could not turn back. He could not let slip from his grasp the chance that Japan might be willing to allow China to maintain her national existence. He felt that he had exhausted his political resources in Chungking; his counsel carried no weight where only arms mattered. He must launch his appeal from outside. Only from a neutral position could he hope to bring the two sides together. He would accomplish this through the only power that he had, that of rhetoric. He must convince his countrymen both of the possibility for peace and of his own patriotism; he must convince the Japanese to restore the sovereignty of China to China.

Confined to his bed in his desolate mountain exile by a leg injury he had suffered in a fall,[108] Wang penned as his response to the Konoye statement the *yen tien* (December 29 telegram), which he dispatched on that date to the Central Executive Committee of the Kuomintang and the Supreme National Defense Council. Says Kagesa in his memoirs, "I detect the hard deliberation of Mr. Wang in this statement."[109] Wang then sent Ch'en Kung-po and T'ao Hsi-sheng, who had come with him to Hanoi, to Hong Kong; and he instructed Ch'en to publish this telegram without any alterations.[110] Ch'en and T'ao showed the *yen tien* to Ku Meng-yu, a scholar and government official who was the most prominent and most gifted of all Wang's past followers. Ku severely castigated Ch'en and T'ao and bitterly opposed publication of the telegram. Ch'en who shared Ku's views, cabled Wang and urgently requested Wang to reconsider his decision.[111] Wang rejected Ch'en's appeal and demanded that the telegram immediately be published in accordance with his previous instruction. The Japanese were not consulted nor informed before the appearance of the telegram in Lin Pai-sheng's newspaper on December 31.[112]

In the *yen tien*, Wang respectfully argued that Konoye's statement of November 3 had abrogated his *aite to sezu* position of January 16 and that the National Government should "exchange views with the Japanese Government in order to restore peace" on the basis of the three principles of the third Konoye statement of December 22, namely, the familiar neighborly friendship (*zenrin yūkō*), anti-Communist collaboration (*kyōdō bōkyō*), and economic cooperation (keizai teikei). "These three points constitute the principles of peace." Wang made it quite clear, however, that he considered implicit in these principles "that the withdrawal from China of the Japanese Army in its totality must be prompt and universal in all directions." *Kyōdō bōkyō* could only mean cooperation against communism on the international level; no troops could be stationed under the projected agreement except in Inner Mongolia. "This affects China's sovereignty and administrative independence and integrity, and only by this restriction will China be able to carry out the work of post-war rehabilitation and reconstruction of a modern state."[113] He made it clear that he was by no means proposing capitulation to Japan; he envisaged long and hard negotiations — "As to the terms of peace, we must take them into careful consideration in order to assure their appropriateness."

He reaffirmed his position as a patriot and his support for the war of resistance. But "The object of China's armed resistance is to secure its national existence and independence. In the course of the present war, which already has lasted more than a year, great suffering has been inflicted upon the country. If we are able to re-establish peace in conformity with justice, then the existence and independence of the nation may be maintained and the aim of armed resistance is reached."

Wang's colleagues and countrymen knew nothing of the Jūkōdō. They did not notice the subtleties in Wang's telegram. What was clear to them was that Wang was endorsing a demand by the enemy for capitulation. Perhaps he had even been conspiring with the enemy. There was little doubt that he had turned traitor.

On January 1 an Emergency Joint Session of the Central Ex-

ecutive and Supervision Committees of the Kuomintang expelled Wang from the party permanently and dismissed him
from his posts. Chou En-lai said, "In my twenty years' association with Wang, I have always known him to be a quitter."[114]
General Pai Chung-hsi gave what seems to have been the general estimate by thoughtful men in Chungking of Wang's action, an estimate not without a large element of truth, even if
it does not tell the entire story: "Wang proved too weak for the
travails of wartime conditions . . . He left his responsibilities at
Chungking on his own initiative, an action improper for a Chinese of his position in a time like the present. His real intention
is to attempt a compromise with the Japanese, but he can
achieve nothing because he does not represent any following
in the Kuomintang or among the people. Wang represents only
himself."[115] Another Chungking source declared, "Wang is better out of the government than in it for he was a source of weakness and uncertainty."[116]

Wang's situation was already desperate, but the final coup
de grace to the peace movement as originally conceived was
dealt on January 4, 1939, when Konoye and his cabinet resigned. Not only did the promise of withdrawal fail to material-
ize, but Japanese spokesmen seemed to repudiate even the
ambiguous offers which the Konoye statements had made: respect for Chinese nationalism, "no annexation and no indemnity," and possible restoration of concession areas. Those who
had worked so hard for the Japanese acceptance of the Jūkōdō
conditions and Wang's emergence — Kagesa, Inukai, Nishi —
were aghast and in despair.

Konoye's position and his resolution had been steadily becoming more and more shaky. He had continued in office
solely for the sake of the Wang conspiracy. Now that Wang had
come out and the statement had proved to be a failure, Konoye
was determined to resign at last. On the night of December 29
War Minister Itagaki spent two hours trying to persuade
Konoye to change his mind. "The Wang conspiracy has been
successful so far. Wang depends on the cooperation of the
Army and the Konoye Cabinet as the basic premise of his activities. Therefore, if the Prime Minister should resign, then the other
party [Wang] would be totally affected."[117]

About December 30 War Minister Itagaki and Chief of Staff

Prince Kan'in no miya, had audiences with the emperor telling him that the solution of the situation in China necessitated Konoye's remaining in office and urging him to refuse to accept Konoye's resignation. The emperor refused to make such a departure from precedent. "That would be very difficult," he said. Prince Chichibu, who was a brother of the emperor, also attempted to persuade Konoye. Konoye said that the internal political situation made resignation imperative, but he agreed on the prince's urging that he remain in the cabinet as a minister without portfolio.[118] This, however, did little to change the general impression that the policies of Konoye toward China, with their at least slight hope for conciliation and cooperation, were repudiated.

From Hanoi to Shanghai

6 The fatal lacuna in Konoye's statement immediately followed by Konoye's resignation, compounded by Wang's action in issuing the *yen tien* against the advice of his closest friends and counsellors, left the peace movement in an impasse. If courageous, it was imprudent of Wang to maneuver himself into a position where he could neither move forward nor backward. As the situation appeared in January 1939 Wang had to choose whether to return to Chungking, remain in Hanoi, or go into exile in Europe. None of these seemed to offer much hope for aiding the cause of peace. The shock of a friend's murder and his own narrow escape from death pushed him into a fourth course — a mad attempt at revenge and at saving China by venturing unarmed with heroic passion into the very camp of his enemy. This chapter chronicles Wang's voyage through indecision to tragic resolution.

Shortly after the *yen tien,* Chou Fo-hai and Mei Ssu-p'ing left Hanoi and joined Ch'en, Kao, and T'ao in Hong Kong. In the fetid atmosphere engendered by inactivity, Wang's comrades debated what they should do. Since counsels were divided — Kao, T'ao and Ch'en favoring exile in Europe, Chou and Mei reluctant to abandon what had been begun — the only consensus that they could reach was to pursue all alternatives at once, which as so often in compromise solutions, boiled down to watchful waiting.[1]

Wang, surrounded only by his personal staff, removed himself from the mountains to a residence in Hanoi where through many means he attempted to assay the situation in Chungking and to sway feeling there toward peace. There was a constant flow into Hanoi of political agents from Chungking and other parts of the Chinese world. Kao, in Hong Kong, remained in charge of bringing the Japanese to mediation, but after the failure of Konoye's statement followed by Konoye's resignation, there was little cause for optimism. Utterances from Tokyo scarcely made credible Wang's claim that the Japanese were in a conciliatory frame of mind. Typifying the tone of the statements of Japanese spokesmen, Itagaki Seishirō, the Japanese war minister and a supposed supporter of the Wang *kōsaku* and the *kiroku,* declared on January 30: "I believe you may take it that in general troops will be stationed in China for a substantially long period . . . Since the issuance of the official statement of December 22, a rumor has been current that the army intends to withdraw the forces now in Central China and South China. This is sheer propaganda. The army has no intention whatever of taking any such action."[2]

For his part, from Hanoi, Wang in public and private left nothing undone in his efforts to sway his former comrades. On January 8 Lin Pai-sheng published a second statement which Wang had sent to the Kuomintang Central Executive Committee. In it, Wang reviewed the representations he had made privately to Chiang and the views he had expressed in the telegram of December 29, namely, that the time to compromise for peace was now, when the Japanese were conciliatory. "With regard to the internal situation — with the exception of the Communist Party, and a minority that would like to see China doomed, the National Government overthrown, and the Kuomintang collapse — I can see no proper reason why anybody should be opposed to honorable peace."[3]

Wang did not have much chance of directly affecting the political situation within China, but he might indeed shake the confidence of China's foreign friends in China's determination to resist, which would of course make them reluctant to aid China in her struggle against Japan. Many observers, both in high position and amid public opinion, generally were convinced that Wang was acting as an emissary for Chiang. Even as late as April 24, the British ambassador told an American official that such was the view of British intelligence.[4] One factor which seemed to favor this point of view was that Wang's two leading subordinates, Kao Tsung-wu and Chou Fo-hai, were thought to be Chiang's personal followers.[5]

Chungking, after an initial reaction of shock, chagrin, and efforts to conceal what Wang had done and intended to do, took a policy of carrot and stick. The purpose of the carrot was to persuade Wang either to indicate his solidarity with the Kuomintang and his support of the resistance policy by returning to Chungking or, if he could not do this, to remove himself from the East Asian political scene by going into exile in Europe. The stick was to let Wang know what would happen if he did not yield to the blandishments of the carrot.

The first sign of the carrot was a request that all Chinese newspapers who supported the Kuomintang line refrain from further criticism of Wang.[6] Chiang followed this up by sending a member of the Kuomintang Central Committee who was close to Wang to Hanoi to tell Wang that if he would return to Chungking, not only would another ad hoc conference be called to reinstate him in the party and in his various posts, but also the government would be reshuffled to include members of his clique, thus guaranteeing both his security and his influence.[7]

The first blow of the stick fell on January 17 as Lin Pai-sheng, Wang's publicity agent and editor of *Nan hua jih pao* in Hong Kong, was seriously beaten by assailants armed with hammers.[8] The intention was not to murder Lin, which would have been simple enough, but to intimidate Wang and his would-be collaborators.

Wang dealt with the Chungking agents who visited him with his usual courtesy, but he soon made it clear to them that he could not return to Chungking; his return at that time would only cause dissension; his purpose in leaving Chungking had been to gain the freedom to express his views freely. Now it was up to the government to choose between peace and war. Wang assured his visitors that if the government chose to continue the resistance policy, he would yield to the government's desire and once again go to France with his family and close friends to await the hour when he could serve his country.[9]

The fundamental reason that neither Wang nor any of his group considered the possibility of return to Chungking was that Wang had bet all his chips there and lost them. The effect of Wang's departure on Chungking politics had been to strengthen Chiang's position and to weaken further those who advocated peace. Wang was the only figure who could have provided previously a real alternative to Chiang, both in terms of personality and of policy. On January 20 Chiang himself assumed Wang's post as president of the People's Political Council. On January 26 the fifth plenary session of the Kuomintang Central Executive Committee created a Supreme War Council, a virtual military government with authority over party, army, and nation, headed of course by the Generalissimo.[10] Even the Communists rallied with increased enthusiasm now that the threat of Kuomintang compromise with Japan represented by Wang had disappeared.

Despite the fact that the political climate made Wang's return to Chungking impossible, Wang made it absolutely clear in his public statements, in his interviews with Chungking representatives, and in communications to his own confidants[11] that he differed from Chiang only on the question of the desirability of suing for peace; he displayed no personal political ambitions.

In accordance with his assurances to Chungking, hand in hand with his political probings, Wang prepared paths for European exile. Whereas France was probably always the number one possibility, according to the report of the German ambassador in Tokyo on January 24, Ch'en Pi-chün, Madame Wang, had applied on Wang's behalf for visas to England and Germany as well.[12]

There is a story that Wang considered in January the possibility of mediating the East Asian conflict from Europe; he would conduct model peace negotiations in Paris with Tani Masayuki, the former "minister at large" in Shanghai who had just been appointed Japanese ambassador to France. France, however, rejected Tani's appointment on the grounds of Tani's "non-cooperation" with the French when he served in Shanghai.[13] Thus this plan came to a dead end. Another story is that Chiang had applied pressure on the French to reject Tani.[14] Tani later became ambassador to Wang's Nanking government, so undoubtedly there is some substance to the story of his intimacy with Wang.

Chungking did everything possible to expedite Wang's travels. The British embassy in Chungking had requested Chiang's approval before granting his visa. On February 1 an official of the Wai-chiao-pu confirmed to a member of the American embassy staff that Wang had been issued a passport "at the specific instructions of General Chiang Kai Shek."[15] Wang later confirmed that a "member of the Central Executive Committee" had brought him a passport "in the middle of February."[16] Other reports assert that the passport was accompanied by a grant from the Chungking government of a large sum for "travelling expenses."[17] Chungking even tried to hurry Wang along through constant rumors in the Chinese press reporting his imminent departure; he was going to Italy; he was going to France.[18]

Wang did not limit his political contacts to Chiang's representatives. Naturally, he made every effort to gain the support of those who had been associated with him in the past or might be in sympathy with his present objectives. It would seem that many were more willing to return conciliatory "wait-and-see" answers privately than they were in public. What the Japanese were interested in, of course, was not the pacific yearnings of random intellectuals and bureaucrats but military support for Wang, which would weaken the Kuomintang government. Wang was to maintain, in his discussions with the Japanese and with his anticipated Chinese allies in the occupied territories, that somewhere between two fifths and two thirds of Chinese military forces were waiting to rise with him against the policy of cooperating with the Communists.[19] Since Wang's movement never was successful enough to test this hypothesis, we cannot really know how much truth there was in it. Probably Wang used such prospects to entice the Japanese; their own intelligence reported time and time again, however, that there was no chance under existing circumstances of military risings in Wang's favor.

Wang's emergence had weakened rather than strengthened his former military supporters; they were under constant suspicion. Chiang was able to utilize their embarrassment to further his program of unification and centralization. Chang Fa-K'uei, although he remained and was confirmed in high position, was carefully watched by Chiang, who surrounded Chang with men loyal to himself. Wang did establish contact with him, sending a special messenger in late March to tell Chang that his plan was to discard the Provisional and Restored Governments, cause the withdrawal of the Japanese army and the restoration of Chinese territory.[20] Undoubtedly Chang viewed the possibility of Wang's achieving these objectives with some scepticism; nevertheless, Wang continued to tell the Japanese that the possibility of Chang's emergence was great. Events of August, 1939, were to raise the question once again of whither lay Chang's loyalty.

Lung Yun, unlike Chang Fa-k'uei, enjoyed a powerful independent territorial position, and he was to remain restive until it was clear that the Allies were going to win the Pacific War. Lung Yun was under particular suspicion because of his involvement in Wang's escape. Pressure was brought to bear on him until at length on May 2 he made a speech claiming that he was astonished when Wang appeared in Kunming.[21] On May 6 Lung

Yun wrote Wang an open letter. Although Lung advised Wang to go into exile and not to associate himself with the Japanese enemy, he, nevertheless, took a very warm, gentle, and friendly tone — something very unusual in Chinese political circular telegrams.[22] At the same time Lung sent a messenger to Wang to tell him that he had sent the letter only under pressure.[23] The wily old fox was trying to remain on good terms with both Wang and Chiang so as to hedge his bets and to be prepared for whatever might come.

While Wang was thus engaged in various contacts designed to move the Chinese from a resistance policy toward a peace policy, what was the course of Kao's dealings with the Japanese? This is probably the single most vexing question in the history of the peace movement, because the evidence offers two stories which on their face are directly contradictory. The Japanese (Inukai, Nishi) state that Kao, chagrined and crushed by feelings of personal responsibility for the failure of Wang's emergence to create a "third force" to mediate for peace, urged the Japanese army to undertake an offensive designed to force Lung and other Chinese leaders to rally to Wang, creating this "third force," an independent regime in south China.[24] Kao himself categorically denies that either he or Wang pursued such a policy or could possibly have entertained it.

The Japanese story is as follows: Kao, plagued by guilt for Wang's failure, conceived the plan outlined above to save the "Kao Tsung-wu route." Kao arrived to visit Wang in Hanoi on February 1. The two men determined upon the establishment of a "National Salvation Anti-Communist League" (Chiu-kuo fan-kung t'ung-meng-hui) and an army as nuclei around which a "third force," possessing actual military and political power, would coalesce. They also decided upon the abolition of the Provisional Government in north China and the Restored Government in central China.[25] Kao, according to Inukai Ken, who was his constant companion during the trip, then went to Japan with the prime purpose of persuading the Japanese army to rescue Wang's movement. This endeavor failed because Kagesa had been transferred from the General Staff to the War Ministry and no longer had influence over operational plans. The General Staff was severely offended at the suggestion that any advice from the outside might influence the plans for military operations. The "command channel" guaranteed by the Meiji constitution must at all costs be kept inviolate; thus Kao's request was summarily rejected.[26]

Further possible evidence for the existence of a proposal of this sort is the so-called "Wang-Hiranuma secret agreement," which Chungking, when relations with Wang had considerably worsened, alleged that Wang had signed with the Japanese prime minister. This document claimed that Wang had suggested Japanese military action in south China.

Kao's account is that he never advised Wang to emerge or to be optimistic that the Japanese would fulfill any promises; consequently, the decision to emerge was Wang's; Kao had no reason to feel guilt. He did come to visit Wang in Hanoi in February. There was no discussion of military matters or organizing an army. They discussed, however, the establishment of a political movement with the slogan of "peace, anti-communism, reconstruction." Wang instructed Kao to go once again to Japan to investigate the current political situation there. Had the Japanese at last decided upon concrete peace terms? Wang told Kao to tell the Japanese that if they wished peace, they must negotiate with Chiang Kai-shek.[27]

Kao returned to Hong Kong from his conference with Wang and sent word to Kagesa that he desired to come to Japan. This was welcome news to all those who had been involved in the Wang *kōsaku*. Kao, accompanied by Chou Lung-hsiang, arrived in Nagasaki on February 21 and was met by Inukai, whom Kagesa had dispatched for the purpose. Kao's first move when he arrived was to visit his fellow townsman (from Wenchou, Chekiang), old friend and mentor, Huang Chün. Huang, three decades Kao's elder, had been associated with Liang Ch'i-ch'ao in the early days of the Chinese Republic in Peking. The rise of the Kuomintang had brought his retirement. Kao showed Huang all the documents concerning the peace movement. The two men sat up talking until 4 AM. Huang said that despite his own troubles with the Kuomintang, in the face of Japanese aggression all Chinese must support that government. Huang and Kao agreed without reservation that the most important thing was not to help Japan divide China.[28] Kao's account of his meeting with Huang is authenticated by a poem in Kao's possession, seen by the author, memorializing the occasion and the sentiments exchanged.

Following his meeting with Huang, Kao met with Prime Minister Hiranuma and Foreign Minister Arita, who gave Kao their polite assurances that the Japanese government was solidly behind the Konoye statement.[29] These assurances were meaningless, unless behind them lay the assumption that the withdrawal promise was not dead. But such a hint was not enough to engender genuine hope. Kao also met with Konoye and Itagaki,[30] with Imai,[31] and extensively with Kagesa and his associate, Colonel Usui Shigeki.[32] Kao's impression was that the Japanese were very evasive in their discussions with him and that they still had made no decision about their policy.

Since Kao's tuberculosis was once again troubling him, he did not feel able to return to Hanoi. Therefore, he prepared a complete report on his discussions with the various Japanese and forwarded it to Wang through Chou Lung-hsiang, his assistant and friend. Again, the conclusion of Kao's report was that the time was not yet ripe for a peace movement and that Wang should either wait in Hanoi or go into exile in Europe.[33] How can these two divergent accounts be reconciled? An easy way, since there is no question that the Japanese *thought* Kao was promoting Japanese military action, is to say that Kao has prevaricated. This hypothesis I do not accept because it runs counter to my general impression of his candor and because judging from the character and actions of Wang and Kao, it is improbable that they could have been parties to a proposal not only treasonous but also probably inefficacious.

If we accept Kao's veracity, how do we explain the Japanese inference that he embraced the plan? Nishi, according to his own account,[34] believing that he "truly understood the development of Kao's state of mind," wrote at the end of January 1939 a long letter to Kagesa expressing what he thought Kao wished. Perhaps this letter of Nishi's is the source of the Japanese belief that Wang wanted Japanese military intervention. Kao, in fact had told Nishi that if Wang Ching-wei was to be able to make peace, Wang must be beyond Japanese influence.[35]

Whichever account of Kao's trip to Japan one chooses to accept, they both agree that it was a failure. The political scene of neither Japan nor China was responsive to Wang's appeals. Furthermore, the situation in Hanoi was becoming more and more untenable. The French had high regard for Wang personally, but his presence in Hanoi embarrassed their relations not only with the Chungking regime but also with their European allies who were also supporting Chiang; therefore, they put considerable restriction upon his political activities. Wang seemed about to admit failure for the time being and return to exile in France. Before these plans could see fruition, a dramatic act of violence was to alter the course of the peace movement.

In charge of plans for Wang's French trip was Tseng Chung-ming. Tseng, bound to Wang both by ties of family and by discipleship, was Wang's personal secretary. Political humorists called him the "handbag of Wang Ching-wei." He had earned a doctorate in literature in France during Wang's former stay there and was familiar with the language and country. No other member of Wang's entourage — including Wang himself, despite his long residence there — had these skills.

Unable to endure Wang's procrastination any longer, agents (there is every reason to believe) of the Kuomintang, broke into Wang's Hanoi residence about 3 AM on the morning of March 21. In attempting to assassinate Wang Ching-wei, they succeeded in killing Tseng Chung-ming. This produced two results: Wang became deeply embittered against Chiang Kai-shek, both because Chiang had tried to kill *him* and had caused, so Wang believed, the murder of his dearest disciple, who had been closer to Wang than his own sons, and second, because the death of Tseng cut off the possibility of exile to France.

The story of the murder was as follows: the Wang group lived in a modest two-story house in the Hanoi suburbs. Wang was convinced, partly by the negotiations that he had been conducting with Chungking and partly by his long service to his country, that Chiang would not threaten his life; therefore, he had rejected the French offer to station guards at his home and had taken few security precautions. There were two rooms on the second floor; the larger one was used as a bedroom by night by Mr. and Mrs. Tseng and during the day by Wang as an office and reception room. The smaller room was used by Mr. and Mrs. Wang as a bedroom. Any visitor, neighbor, or spy might observe that Wang received guests in the larger room, which also contained a bed. The assassin, therefore, naturally sought Wang in that room where the Tsengs instead of the Wangs were sleeping. The assassin climbed the fence, went up the back stairs, broke the glass in the door, and sprayed the room with submachine gunfire. Tseng had risen, hearing the footsteps, and received the fire full on. He was gravely wounded in the heart and intestines. Mrs. Tseng, hiding behind the bed, received less serious injuries. The assassin, hearing the body fall, fled down the stairs, wounding with further shots an assistant who had been roused by the gunfire.[36] Tseng died the next afternoon in a French military hospital.[37] His dying words were: "For matters relating to the state, there is Mr. Wang Ching-wei; for matters relating to my family, there is my wife: my mind is at peace."[38]

Despite Tseng's last words of equanimity, his death signaled the end of the peace movement as originally conceived — a rational and controlled endeavor to bring the two countries to peace. Wang was no longer content with playing the role of comrade seeking to sway his party to what he considered the better course. Henceforeward his aim to bring peace was mixed, not altogether consciously, with a desire to see Chiang's humiliation. Wang's own health was precarious — he suffered from chronic diabetes, and a bullet from his wound of 1935 remained to torment him. Tseng's death pushed him over the edge into tragedy — the rest of his life was to be spent in a desperate final attempt to seize glory, the fruit of which was slow, painful humiliation and failure.

Wang's first hysterical move was to send a telegram to Kao and others in Hong Kong stating his desire to go immediately to Peking to assist Wang K'o-min, chairman of the North China Provisional Government and an old friend. Kao was able to persuade Wang of the impracticality of such a notion.[39] Wang abandoned it only to seize upon another, wilder one. Prior to Tseng's death, Wang had not considered associating himself with a regime in Japanese-occupied territory, much less establishing his own metamorphosis of the Kuomintang "central government" in Nanking.[40] This notion first appeared in the councils of the Wang group in the few weeks following Tseng's assassination. The instrumentality for planting and nourishing this seed seems to have been Chou Fo-hai.

Fretting from anonymity and inactivity in Hong Kong,[41] Chou had several weeks before gone to Shanghai, the political marketplace as well as commercial entrepot for East Asia, doubtless to see what support for Wang could be drummed up there. When

he got to Shanghai, he first made contact with the circle of idealistic intellectuals associated with Matsumoto Shigeharu. But as
soon as it became clear that, despite these men's personal virtues and noble ideals, they could do nothing for him, Chou's
interest shifted to the Japanese army's *tokumu kikan* (special
service agency) in Shanghai, which had been led by General
Doihara and which had been promoting the candidacy of first
T'ang Shao-i and then Wu P'ei-fu as heads of the proposed "new
central government." Undoubtedly the Japanese intelligence
officers conveyed to Chou some intimation of the Japanese desire for a "new central government." Chou, probably led on by
them, conceived the notion, hitherto not entertained in Japanese councils, that Wang might become head of the "new
central government." This would be a Kuomintang government
in legitimate succession from that founded by Sun Yat-sen, and,
by means of this instrument Wang would mediate for peace
and save China.

Wang's first act of public retaliation against Chiang for Tseng's
murder was to release a statement on March 27 entitled "For an
Example," revealing details of the December 1937 Trautmann
mediation discussed in Chapter 2. Wang felt that proof that the
possibility of peace had been entertained in high councils would
both strengthen his case and embarrass Chiang and his colleagues with their internal and external supporters. The revelations, being of a somewhat distant historical nature, did not
make much of a noise in the political world; but this "betrayal
of state secrets" confirmed the general belief that Wang was a
traitor.

With what undoubtedly was considered a suitable counter-
blow, the Chungking daily *Ta kung pao* published on April
5 the alleged terms of a so-called "Wang-Hiranuma secret
agreement," already discussed above. Although not authentic,
it must have come from Japanese sources; perhaps Ozaki
Hidemi, a secretary in Konoye's office was responsible.[42] Ozaki
worked with master spy Richard Sorge, who supplied the Soviet
Union with the top secrets of the Axis.

The Chungking-controlled press accelerated its propaganda
attack, demanding Wang's arrest as well as that of most of his
collaborators in Hong Kong and Shanghai. All hope of persuading Wang to return or to go into exile seemed abandoned.

Wang in Hanoi

Top: Wang Ching-wei admires a famous antique screen in Japan.

Bottom: Wang and his entourage in Hanoi. From right to left: Tseng Chung-ming, Wang Ching-wei's daughter, Wang Ching-wei, Ch'en Pi-chün (Mrs. Wang).

Wang responded to the *Ta kung pao* accusations by accusing that newspaper of being a tool of the government and suggesting that the charge that he had instigated the Japanese to attack in south China was an effort on the part of the government to escape responsibility for the defense of those areas. As for himself, he said: "Nobody can question my loyalty and love for the Republic founded by the late Dr. Sun Yat-sen. My heart bleeds to see China perish at the hands of ignorant people. It was for this reason that I announced my proposals, disregarding all difficulties and dangers. My only desire is to see that the peace terms will not lead to the extinction of China, and that China may regain her breath and retrace the path to prosperity. These views I will maintain to the last, even if I have to sacrifice my life. Neither threat nor slander will make me falter."[43]

After Tseng's assassination and Wang's narrow escape, the Japanese refused to brook any longer the monopoly Kao Tsung-wu attempted to maintain on their communication with Wang. They suspected Kao of collaboration with Chiang; they had no confidence that he was justly representing Wang's replies to them. In fact Kao was loyal to Wang. He rejected the request of Chiang's agent that he serve as a Trojan horse in Wang's camp.[44] On the other hand, he profoundly distrusted the Japanese. He felt that Japanese direct contact with Wang would inevitably lead to Wang's becoming a Japanese puppet like Manchukuo's pathetic Henry Pu-i.

The news of Tseng's assassination reached Tokyo on March 22, and the Five Ministers' Conference met that very day, undoubtedly at the demand of the military authorities, and entrusted General Kagesa, who had been associated with the Wang peace work ever since Tung Tao-ning came to Japan, with the task of rescuing Wang. The appointment of Kagesa to undertake this mission was the beginning of the organ (*kikan*) set up for guiding the Wang work (*kōsaku*). But Kagesa wanted this *kikan* to be different from all other *kikan* in that it should be devoted to Sino-Japanese cooperation for peace: a continuation of the activities of the peace comrades. It angered Kagesa when informal parlance applied his name to it, on the model of other *kikan*, dominated by military figures. It was his claim that the Ume "plum" kikan (*ume* being another reading for the first character in the name of the building in which it was situated, Baikadō, "plum blossom hall") was not a personal fief subject to his whim but a collegial group of representatives not only from the army but also from the navy, the Gaimushō, the Kōain (China affairs board), and the civil government.[45] For the mission to Hanoi he did not quite get a full complement. Yano Seiki, concurrently a secretary in the Gaimushō and the Kōain, was assigned to the duty. Kagesa also requested Inukai Ken, to whom we are indebted in part for the following narrative, to accompany him in the role of Diet member.[46]

The reactivation of the Wang movement got another boost on April 1, when the Kōain decided to grant Wang three million yuan per month for the next six months from the maritime customs surplus revenues collected in occupied ports.[47] One advantage of this arrangement was that Wang could claim, to himself at least, that he was not accepting money from the Japanese but rather using funds that rightfully belonged to China.

The Italian consul general in Hong Kong informed Tajiri confidentially that he had word that Kuomintang authorities had decided to send two agents to Hanoi to make contact with French Indochinese authorities, to make a final attempt to persuade Wang to go abroad, and concurrently, to prepare for his assassination.[48] Whether or not there was any truth in this rumor, there was no time to lose lest Wang be beyond the rescue of any man.

A ship, the 5500-ton freighter *Hokkōmaru* of the Yamashita Steamship Company, was made available for Kagesa's mission through the generosity of Kagesa's friend, Yamashita Kamesaburo, president of the steamship company that bore his name. Captain Tsuji of the *Hokkōmaru* was ordered to obey Kagesa's instructions.[49] Following these preparations, on April 6 the *Hokkōmaru* departed from Omuta in Fukuoka bearing Kagesa; Inukai; Dr. Ōsuzu, a military surgeon; Warrant Officer Maruyama, a military policeman who was friendly with Kao and who became connected with the peace movement; several other military policemen; and a German shepherd to guard Wang's Hanoi residence.[50]

Kao made every effort to halt the mission of the *Hokkōmaru*. On his way to Hanoi, Secretary Yano stopped in Hong Kong and conferred with Kao. According to Yano, Kao urged that the

Hokkōmaru stop at Hong Kong so that he, Kao, could consult with Kagesa.[51] Apparently, Kao hoped to dissuade Kagesa.[52] Kao urged Yano not to go to Hanoi, telling him peace could only be made through dealing with Chiang Kai-shek, not Wang Ching-wei.[53] Continuing these efforts at deterring the Japanese, Kao sent via Wang in Hanoi a telegram addressed to Kagesa and Inukai telling them to keep hands off Wang Ching-wei.[54] The only result of Kao's démarche was to win Wang's resentment and the increasing suspicion of the Japanese, thus becoming the man in the middle feared and distrusted by both sides.

It was on the evening of April 16 that *Hokkōmaru* arrived in Haiphong, the port for Hanoi.[55] Kagesa had been ill for most of the voyage. An elaborate cover establishing the passengers of the *Hokkōmaru* as employees of the Taiwan Colonialization Company had been concocted. Yano had arrived by air from Hong Kong. The ubiquitous Itō Yoshio had somehow made his way privately by boat to Hanoi on April 15 and was already in contact with the Wang group. Oya Kasuo, a Dōmei representative in Hanoi, had done likewise at the instruction of Matsumoto Shigeharu.[56] In charge of the official arrangements for the reception of the *Hokkōmaru's* party was the military attache in Hanoi, Major Kadomatsu. Thus it was quite a heterogeneous company which had gathered to rescue Wang Ching-wei.

In the evening of April 17 Itō brought the news that Kagesa, Inukai, and Yano were to meet with the Wang group in Wang's residence at 1:30 PM the next day. They were to go to a suburban race track and stand in the ticket line. A young Chinese who spoke Japanese would greet them as old friends by saying "How are you?" in English. Then they would all leave in the Chinese agent's car. Kagesa demurred, requesting a personal letter from Wang, both because he feared a ruse by the Kuomintang "Blue Shirt Agency" to abduct them and because he felt it necessary to uphold the prestige of the Japanese delegation.[57]

It is unclear whether Kagesa actually got such a letter, but in any case, the next day as planned, Kagesa, Inukai, and Yano drove to the race track. As they arrived, another car drew aside them; a young man, who turned out to be none other than Chou Lung-hsiang, got out and greeted them. The three Japanese got into the Chinese car which after elaborate detours to avoid being followed arrived at the Wang residence. The iron door swung open to receive the car and closed behind it. Wang himself came out to greet his visitors.[58]

Kagesa began the interview by announcing that he had been instructed by government order to take Wang to a safer place. Wang replied slowly and with courteous reserve, thanking Kagesa for coming so far and admitting that his situation in Hanoi was "not only dangerous but meaningless" because of the threat of Kuomintang terrorists and French restrictions on Wang's political activities.[59] An apartment on the third floor adjacent to Wang's house had been rented by the European Asian Airlines, a Chungking corporation associated with the Sung family.[60] Thus the Wang group and their visitors were under constant surveillance by Chungking agents and under constant threat of further attempts against their lives.

Wang said that he had been informed by Kao of Japanese intentions, so that discussions could begin on a substantive basis. Wang went over with Kagesa what had been his public contentions: that Chiang was prevented from appealing for peace by the Communists, and, therefore, Wang had left Chungking in order to appeal to public opinion for peace on the basis of the Konoye statement.[61] Wang said nothing at this point about any plan or desire to establish a government, and perhaps he had none. If Chou Fo-hai had been intriguing with elements of the Doihara kikan to this end, Kagesa, who had been dispatched by military bureaucrats in Tokyo, would have known nothing of it.

Wang thanked the Japanese for their trouble in coming to rescue him and announced to their surprise that he and his associates had already made plans to go to Shanghai. Wang told Kagesa that he had rejected the possibility of going to Canton. He feared, he said, that the Chinese public might feel he was a creature of the Japanese and consequently would not respond to his movement if he should set up his headquarters in his birthplace and traditional political base, now under Japanese military rule. In the foreign concessions of Shanghai he could maintain his independent stance and would be free to carry on political activity. Although he realized that the danger of assassination was great there, he felt that he would be more likely to "gain the people's heart" by risking his life.

Wang announced that the Chinese side had already chartered a small French-registered freighter, 760 tons, called, as well as we can guess from the Japanese transcription, something like *Von Hohenhoffen. Hohenhoffen* means, appropriately or ironically, "high hopes." Wang's intention in procuring his own craft was to maintain his independence. There were great dangers attendant upon such a voyage in a small boat, especially since Wang could not dare risk hugging the China coast because of the possibility of Chungking attacks. Wang requested that the Japanese follow in the Hokkōmaru so they could call upon the Japanese ship for assistance in case of need.[62] The only problem that remained was gaining French approval for the departure.

Kagesa gave Wang letters from Foreign Minister Arita, War Minister Itagaki, Kōain Director Suzuki, and a calling card (*meishi*) from Naval Minister Yonai. Wang promised to reply to them as soon as he reached Shanghai.[63] After these exchanges, Wang retired and an assistant replaced him for two hours of administrative discussion. Translation naturally consumed much time. At the close, Wang reappeared and bade his Japanese guests farewell, showing them with quiet eloquence the black-ribboned bed where Tseng had been shot. It is Kao's view, based on what he was told by Chou Lung-hsiang, who was present, that Kagesa's tears on this occasion won Wang's heart and persuaded him to entrust his fate to Kagesa.[64]

The return drive to the Japanese consulate in Hanoi was just as frenetic as the arrival. Kagesa, who had been having acute pains in his stomach, at last said he could stand it no longer. He demanded to get out of the car. Inukai stayed with him and left Yano to go with the driver to get Dr. Ōsuzu. Kagesa lay on his back in a nearby park and Inukai lay down next to him. Kagesa looked at the sky and said, "Ken-san, we finally met with Wang Ching-wei. Today is April 18. We have just begun."[65]

Wang felt that he could maintain his independence of action while still in the last extremity depending on Japanese protection. Unfortunately this proved impossible because, as Kagesa assumed a certain responsibility for Wang's safety, he also came to exercise an element of control over Wang's actions. For example, Wang's intention was to keep the Japanese at arm's length and if possible rely on the French for security; he would travel on a French ship to the French Concession in Shanghai where he owned a home.[66] In the same telegram in which Kagesa told Tokyo that the above had "been decided," he asked that other hideouts be prepared in the International Settlement, which could be guarded by Japanese police. In the next telegram, Kagesa announced that Wang's stay in the French Concession was to be very temporary and efforts should be concentrated on preparing several maximum security residences in the International Settlement[67] in areas controlled by the Japanese. In the final telegram of the series, Kagesa stated that Wang was not to be taken to the French Concession at all but directly to a Japanese-controlled hideout.[68] From whatever motivation, Kagesa was already constraining Wang's freedom of choice before they had even left Hanoi.

The Japanese, always somewhat nervous in foreign countries, spent the two days succeeding their meeting with Wang in anxious fear, both for themselves and for Wang. They sensed assassins everywhere. But finally, at about noon on April 20, Oya, the Dōmei reporter, called and said that the French authorities had received instructions from the French Foreign Office in Paris. They would soon be in touch with Wang. The Japanese continued their vigil until about 10 PM. Then Oya called to announce that the French would assign a police guard to conduct Wang to the *Von Hohenhoffen* at 9 AM the next morning.[69] Since loading, hiring of crew, customs clearance, and so on, was sure to take several days, it was agreed that the two ships would rendezvous off Nightingale Island,[70] about five miles out of the port of Haiphong, on the afternoon of April 25.[71] Yano[72] and Itō[73] were dispatched to Shanghai to help with arrangements there.

But all was not to go smoothly. Kagesa, Inukai, Ōsuzu, and the others aboard the *Hokkōmaru* arrived at Nightingale Island about noon and circled it until 4 PM, when dusk and fog reduced visibility to nearly zero. The radio operator of the *Hokkōmaru* kept repeating the code signal that had been agreed upon between the two sides. Soon a message came from the French naval station in Haiphong demanding cessation of code transmission; therefore, there was nothing to do but to begin slowly cruising around the outer shore of Hainan Island toward Shanghai with the hope of finding the *Von Hohenhoffen* en route. Three days went by without word from the *Von Hohenhoffen*. Kagesa telegraphed asking the assistance of the Japanese navy in finding the lost boat.[74] He lay in his bed, his illness aggravated by anxiety and grief. "We have killed Wang Ching-wei. Even the emperor knows about this affair through the Five Ministers' Conference. I am very sorry," he agonized.[75]

Captain Tsuji suggested that perhaps since the *Von Hohenhoffen's* radio was old, if the ship had taken the route through the Hainan Straits, radio communications would have been cut off. On the next day the *Hokkōmaru* would have rounded Hainan and perhaps contact could be made. Inukai tried to cheer up Kagesa with this possibility. The next day, April 29, was the emperor's birthday. About noon the *Hokkōmaru* passed the mountains of Hainan and the radio operator recommenced transmission. About 3 PM he received a reply saying "our side safe." The signal became louder and stronger and agreement was made to meet in a small harbor near Swatow, considerably north of Hong Kong, the next day, April 30. The *Hokkōmaru* arrived at the agreed rendezvous first, at night. They were astonished upon awaking to find fortifications and men all about them, Chinese fishermen-pirates. The Japanese had only two rifles aboard but did their best to give a show of strength by having one of the soldiers give a marksmanship exhibition, a feat in the samurai tradition.

Finally, in the afternoon the *Von Hohenhoffen* steamed up beside them. Chou Lung-hsiang came over in a small boat and gave the explanation that the Chinese had been late for their rendezvous off Haiphong because of delays occasioned by outmoded facilities and a dock strike. When they had reached the island it was dark, and because of the smallness of the boat, they had been forced to go through the Hainan Straits rather than attempting the passage along the outer shore. Moreover, the *Von Hohenhoffen* had proved slower than expected.[76]

Was the story that Chou told the Japanese the true one? Had Wang really decided upon Shanghai, that amoral entrepot, as against the staid and respectable Hong Kong, a possibility that he had not even mentioned to Kagesa? The debate had raged among the comrades concerning where Wang's East Asian refuge should be. Kao, T'ao, and Ch'en — the moderates — favored Hong Kong, where Wang might pursue genteel contacts some-

Wang's journey from Hanoi to Shanghai

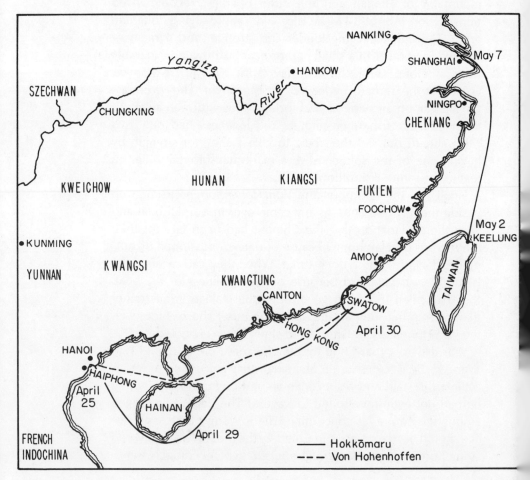

what insulated from the passions of the mainland; Chou Fo-hai, we assume, favored Shanghai, where anything was possible or, at any rate, could be attempted.

It is my hypothesis that between April 18, when Wang met with Kagesa and his entourage, and April 30, when the seasick passengers of the *Von Hohenhoffen* were transferred to the *Hokkōmaru,* the decision to finally reject the alternative of going to Hong Kong and the decision to take up working toward the establishment of a peace government in Nanking were made.

Let us treat the first part of the hypothesis first. There is evidence that Wang was making preparations for a possible sojourn in Hong Kong. On March 31, nine days after Tseng's death, Kao told Tajiri in Hong Kong that Wang was coming to Hong Kong.[77] Kao had requested the approval of the British authorities. Even though on April 18 Wang had told Kagesa of his intention to go to Shanghai, on April 22 a spy among the Chinese comrades, "P. L.," reported that Wang would make his decision whether to go to Hong Kong or Shanghai on the basis of the British reply.[78] And it was on April 30, the day when the two ships met, that Tajiri reported to Tokyo that the Hong Kong government had politely discouraged Wang's presence there.[79]

Second, according to the telegram dispatched by Kagesa when radio contact was first established with the *Von Hohenhoffen,* the *Von Hohenhoffen* was at that time in the vicinity of Hong Kong.[80] As illustrated by the attached map, although the *Von Hohenhoffen* was slower than the *Hokkōmaru,* the route that it took was shorter. Further, the *Von Hohenhoffen* may not have delayed after the missed rendezvous as did the *Hokkōmaru* and, therefore, may well have been in the vicinity of Hong Kong, as Kagesa says it was, by the time the *Hokkōmaru* rounded Hainan Island. If we assume that Wang's representatives got the word from the British before Tajiri did on April 30, which seems a warranted assumption, then it is perfectly possible that Wang and the others on the *Von Hohenhoffen* were awaiting word of the British response before they made the final decision to go to Shanghai rather than Hong Kong and consequently established radio contact with the *Hokkōmaru.* The Chinese side had previously acted independently while giving a minimum of advance information about their plans to the Japanese. There is no reason to believe that, if the British response had been favorable, Wang could not simply have wired Kagesa and told him politely that their plans had changed — they were going to Hong Kong.

In any case, whatever the merit of the above speculation, Hong Kong was not chosen; Wang did proceed to rendezvous with the *Hokkōmaru*. He went to Shanghai and prosecuted there the plan to establish a Nanking peace government. The decision to go to Shanghai rather than Hong Kong was a sign that the moderate comrades in Hong Kong — Kao, T'ao, and Ch'en — were to be heeded even less, and Chou Fo-hai and the associates he was collecting about himself in Shanghai were going to dominate the direction of the peace movement from this time on. The basis for the second part of the hypothesis, namely, that the resolve to establish a peace government was also made during this period, is the fact that Wang brought up this possibility for the first time, to the apparent surprise of his Japanese "rescuers," in conversations with Kagesa aboard the *Hokkōmaru*. Second, the decision to go to Shanghai, while not necessitating the peace government policy, was a premise of that policy.

Wang told Kagesa and Inukai that his original intention had been to organize a Kuomintang-centered group which would argue that "peace was the only way to save China and thus East Asia."[81] But now it was clear that words alone were not going to sway Chungking's resistance; therefore, Wang wished to establish a "peace government" with Japan's cooperation. His government must have military strength if it were to be effective.[82]

Anger at Tseng's death had moved Wang from the position of cooperation with Chiang Kai-shek, which he had taken since the Manchurian Incident, back into the role of holding himself out as a competitor for the leadership of China. Of course the policy of cooperative alternation between Wang and Chiang had its ambiguities and tensions too. By the same measure, one should not exaggerate the extent to which Wang was separating himself at this time. Although anger and resentment had led to an estrangement from Chiang, nevertheless, Wang's objectives remained as they always had been — peace and a united China under the leadership of his beloved Kuomintang. He believed that the only mechanism left to him within the framework of

Chinese politics, now that peaceful efforts at persuasion had failed was the establishment of another regime, not with the objective of supplanting the existing government, but rather of influencing it.

As Wang explained to Kagesa: "I have repeatedly expressed the objective of my movement. It is to do nothing else but achieve peace. Once peace is achieved, I do not care who holds power. The objective of my peace movement is to bring the Chungking government to suspend resistance and to accept the argument for peace. Therefore in case the Chungking government comes to cooperate with our movement, then the objective is achieved and I would not hesitate resolutely to resign. I want to make this clear to you."[83] Wang insisted that to be effective, his projected government needed armed forces; nevertheless, these forces would never fight against the Chungking forces in civil war. "My purpose is not to defeat the Chungking government. It is my ideal to realize total peace by coalition with them. This is the fundamental difference between my movement and ordinary anti-Chiang Kai-shek movements."[84] The aim of Wang's movement then was a reunion of the two branches of the Kuomintang, like those following divisions and differences on policy in the past, under a platform of peace.

Wang, in proposing that he establish a regime, made quite clear to Kagesa that he was by no means condoning Japanese aggression or suggesting that he sympathized with Japanese objectives rather than those of his former colleagues in Chungking. He made it clear that the success of his plan depended upon a change in Japanese policy. "What I ask the Japanese people to understand is that for the Chinese, the argument for peace is an expression of patriotic spirit and the argument for resisting Japan is also an expression of patriotic spirit. Anyone who has either of these beliefs loves his country and desires the prosperity of the people. Therefore the difference between these two theories of peace and resistance to Japan is caused by differences in understanding of Sino-Japanese relations in the Far East. It is impossible for Japan to correct, by using military power alone, the understanding of those who believe in resisting Japan. I want you to understand that the best means for the Japanese to change their policies is through changing their own policies."[85]

Whether or not Chou Fo-hai had discussed the peace government plan with the Doihara kikan in Shanghai, nevertheless, it was Wang who took the initiative in proposing the same to Kagesa. From this point on Wang personally took upon himself the "do or die" responsibility, first selling to the Japanese and afterwards effecting the plan for establishing a central government in occupied China. Thus the initiative rested with him and not, as in the case of the other kōsaku, with the various army kikan. He needed support from the Japanese to accomplish his plan, but even when that was unbelievably grudging and half-way, he would not take no for an answer.

After he had heard Wang's dramatic new proposal, Kagesa seems to have been a little nonplussed and to have expressed a certain degree of skepticism. Kagesa replied that his instructions had only ordered him to rescue Wang, and therefore he could not make an official reply. Kagesa and Inukai frankly advised Wang that his plan depended on Japanese execution of the Konoye statement, by which they probably meant the omitted withdrawal clause as well. According to Inukai, Kagesa and Inukai expressed delicately their doubts that this would occur.[86] According to his own account, Kagesa was a little less impolitic. He says that he told Wang that the Konoye statement was not only an expression of opinion by Konoye himself but also a declaration of the Imperial Government which would continue to remain in force, despite the change of cabinet. Kagesa expressed the views that Japan *should* stand behind the statement and that the formation of a government before the achievement of peace "would be well understood by those who know the situation."[87] However, Kagesa expressed his considered judgment at the time: His feeling that if the Konoye statement were in fact fully carried out, the formation of a government would be able to bring about total peace; but that if the statement were not carried out, the government would be a failure. Wang's trust would be betrayed; therefore, he thought it would be wiser to establish a peace movement without establishing a peace government.[88] A peace movement would mean propaganda activities on behalf of peace rather than establishing a government. Despite his personal skepticism, Kagesa agreed to forward Wang's proposal to the authorities in Tokyo.

On May 1, still aboard the *Hokkōmaru*, Kagesa asked Wang

for more detailed information on his plans. Wang replied that the plan uppermost in the councils of his comrades was a proposal that he go to Tokyo in early June to discuss the problem of Sino-Japanese peace with Japanese leaders. His advisers were of two minds about it. The new plan enjoyed the warm support of Chou and Mei, and the opposition of Kao. Wang had also asked the advice of three old friends, the most intellectually distinguished of all his past associates, though at the moment they were not actively participating in his movement: Ku Meng-yü, Ch'en Kung-po, and T'ao Hsi-sheng. They all advised Wang to reconsider and reflect. More plainly, they opposed the plan.[89] Friendship was to bring T'ao and Ch'en to join Wang; T'ao later deserted him; Ch'en was loyal to the grave. Ku could not bring himself to associate with Wang's new venture in any way. Wang, however, had already cast behind him all counsels of hesitation.

On May 2 the *Hokkōmaru* docked at Keelung, Formosa, to take on supplies. Kagesa had wired ahead to make arrangement that there be no customs inspection for the Wang party.[90] When the *Hokkōmaru* arrived, Nishi Yoshiaki was waiting to make a last attempt to dissuade Wang from his chosen course. Nishi had learned of Wang's new plans through conversations with Chou Fo-hai in Shanghai. Nishi questioned Chou whether Wang could be successful in bringing peace through establishing a government where the existing Restored and Provisional Governments had failed. If the Japanese government really wished peace, there had been many opportunities to fulfill the ideals of the Jūkōdō *kiroku*.[91] In Chou's view it was worth one more effort. He was the author of Wang's new plan: Wang must go to Tokyo and demand political independence from the Japanese leaders. "You get a tiger cub only by going into the tiger's lair," he said. If the Japanese government refused, then Chou felt that Wang and his comrades could give up the plan for establishing a government and devote themselves to propaganda work.[92] But would it be that easy to escape from the tiger's den?

When the *Hokkōmaru* arrived in Keelung, Nishi met Wang for the first time. His good and sentimental heart was overwhelmed when Wang greeted him as Tarō-san, eldest son, the nickname Nishi had been given at the Repulse Bay meeting. Nishi conveyed Chou's proposal, of which Wang was well aware, but added to it his own views, namely, that Wang should regard the Konoye statement as an absolute minimum. More than that, he should demand the return of the China mainland. If the Japanese government did not yield, Wang should go into exile in France or America.[93] Wang, said Nishi, was too great a man to be made a tool of Japanese military bureaucrats. Nishi told Kagesa that it would be difficult for him, Nishi, to continue to assist the Wang *kōsaku* if it turned into a scheme for a government within Japanese-occupied territory. After Nishi left, Kagesa turned to Inukai and said with envy, "Ken-san, we were bawled out. Nishi is free and how nice it is!"[94]

Chungking agents in Shanghai would be gunning for Wang. Even if they did not succeed in taking his life, the constant threat of assassination would inevitably hamper Wang's freedom to pursue political activities. He had to have armed protection. Giving up living in the French concession meant he had no claim to French protection. While ultimately he had to depend on Japanese arms, he had to avoid giving the impression that he needed Japanese gendarmerie to protect him from his own people. The Japanese dispatched professional terrorists to counterattack Chungking agents sure to mass against Wang; Kagesa ordered their return.[95] Chou Fo-hai "solved" the problem of personal security by making an alliance which Wang later ratified with Li Shih-ch'ün and Ting Mo-ts'un — like Chou, ex-C.C. clique members — renegade Kuomintang agents and gangsters who had gone over to the Japanese. This alliance with Ting and Li was Wang's greatest mistake. Although Ting and Li did provide Chinese guns for hire which Wang needed sorely, they demanded a quid pro quo: freedom to practice their vice and violence under Wang's auspices but not his control. Their devious dealings not only with Shanghai vice but also with the opposing agents, their ex-colleagues, and even with the Communists — Li was a graduate of Moscow University — tarred Wang's movement with petty self-interest.

On May 6 Colonel Imai, dispatched from Tokyo to discover more fully Wang's intentions, met with Wang aboard the *Hokkōmaru* somewhere near Shanghai.[96] Wang spoke eloquently along much the same lines as he had to Kagesa; however, he added an important new point; namely, that the new government which he wished to establish would not be a new government at all in a sense, but would succeed to the legitimacy of the present Kuomintang government with the title of Chung-hua min-kuo kuo-min cheng-fu, the government of the Republic of China; hence the establishment of the government must take the form of returning to the capital at Nanking; it must take the *San-min chu-i* as its official ideology; and it must use Sun Yat-sen's "blue-sky white-sun" flag which had been the traditional Kuomintang flag.[97] Imai returned to Tokyo to inform his superiors of these details in Wang's scheme. Both Wang, self-styled successor to Sun Yat-sen, and Chou, who owed his rise to his reputation as a Kuomintang political theorist, confused symbols with realities; what was important was not flags or titles but whether and on what terms Japan would make peace with China.

A certain elation filled the air aboard the *Hokkōmaru* as the comrades elaborated their schemes for transforming the political situation in East Asia. It was proposed that they not land at Shanghai at all but spend the month of May in continuous conference as they sailed the Pacific. Kagesa felt that the *Hokkōmaru* was too small; thus this plan had to be dropped.[98]

Japanese agents ashore in Shanghai frenetically made preparations for the disembarkation of the Wang party, while the *Hokkōmaru* extended its short voyage from Formosa. Finally it anchored at Woosung on the afternoon of May 7,[99] but the Chinese passengers were not permitted to land; the entire Shanghai staff of the Tokyo *Asahi shimbun* had turned out to witness Wang's supposedly top secret arrival. The information had leaked out of the Five Ministers' Conference in Tokyo.[100]

Kao Tsung-wu had come up from Hong Kong a few days previously to await Wang, and he went out to visit with Wang on the *Hokkōmaru*. Wang asked for Kao's views on Wang's proposed trip to Japan. Wang already knew that Kao was opposed. Kao replied that while a political agent like himself had nothing to lose by venturing into the enemy camp, Wang was too important a figure to risk coming under Japanese control. Wang said Kao, should only go to Japan on condition that he resolve to extract from the Japanese their peace terms and take them straight to Chungking. Kao would accompany Wang if he should do so. Wang was sadly caught between his passion for peace and his fear and hatred of Chiang. Chiang wanted to kill

Wang. "How could Wang deal with him?" flared Ch'en Pi-chün.[101]

It was not only at Kao that Madame Wang lost her temper that day. Leaving Wang and his party aboard the *Hokkōmaru,* Kagesa and Inukai went to the Jūkōdō where Chou Fo-hai, Mei Ssu-p'ing, and Kao Tsung-wu were awaiting them. As they were dining, Madame Wang called on the telephone from the *Hokkōmaru* and demanded that she be permitted to spend the night in the French Concession, even threatening to swim there. The thought of the obese Madame Wang doing such a thing amused the party at the Jūkōdō. She had become angered, since the original plan had called for the Wang party to come to the French Concession and Kagesa was thwarting it. He would not even let them off the boat. Kagesa yielded to her wishes. Kao too announced his intention to spend the night with his brother in the French Concession, and when Kagesa protested, Kao also lost his temper. "What right does Kagesa have to shout at me, a Chinese? I am also risking my life . . . for the peace movement."[102] Despite these indications that the comrades were chafing under Japanese efforts to arrange their affairs for them, they allowed themselves to be settled the next day in a temporary residence near the Jūkōdō.

Wang himself was not altogether pleased either with the situation in Shanghai or with Japanese "protection." About the middle of May he inquired separately of both the French and the Italians whether he might reside in their respective concessions in Tientsin. The French replied that he might live in their concession but that he must not engage in any political activity.[103] The Italians, who had both a desire to meddle in the China Incident and a high regard for Wang, were very eager to have Wang come to their concession; however, they inquired first of the Japanese what their attitude would be. The prospect of Wang's taking up residence in a foreign concession violently displeased Japanese officials. The Japanese reasons for rejection were, first, a fear that Wang's presence in Tientsin would complicate their relations with the North China Provisional Government (that is, with the Japanese military supporters of the same) and, second, it would involve the Italians in the settlement of the Incident, whereas it was a major objective to eradicate Western influence.[104] Wang "voluntarily" withdrew the proposal, and the Japanese told the Italians that so far as they knew the Wang clique had no intention of moving to Tientsin.[105] Chou Fo-hai articulated to the Japanese further details of Wang's scheme in a lengthy document, "concrete method for handling the situation," which he submitted on May 28. This "concrete method" was the basis of the comrades' discussion in May, of negotiation with Japan in June, and of the endeavor to establish a peace government during the succeeding year.

The first stage of establishing or "returning" the government was to be the holding of a Kuomintang National Congress. Since China was still in the "tutelage" stage, the second in Sun Yat-sen's three-stage blueprint for China's progress to democracy, the Kuomintang was indistinguishable from the government itself. If the forms of legitimacy were to be maintained, the Kuomintang National Congress at once offered a connection of the present with the past and, as well, a method of legitimizing change. Thus a congress to endorse Wang's new course would be of the greatest importance if his new course were to receive the validation of the republican tradition.

This congress would confer authority on Wang and empower him to organize a Central Political Conference. The conference was to include members belonging to all anti-Communist parties and those without party affiliation. In this way Wang hoped to answer the Japanese and others who accused the Kuomintang of "one-party dictatorship." The conference would vote the return of the government to Nanking; it would declare the San-min chu-i (redefined to avoid any confusion with communism); it would establish the traditional Kuomintang five-yuan government. When the Kuo-min cheng-fu had returned to Nanking, the Provisional and Restored Governments would "voluntarily announce completion of their mission and cancellation of the names of the governments." The conference would declare all succeeding acts and agreements of the Chungking government null and void. All official employees of the Chungking government would be required to report to Nanking within the year. Troops were to stop fighting and await orders. The Japanese embassy was to return to Nanking and those of the other powers should be encouraged to do likewise. Interests of friendly powers would be respected. A popular assembly would be convened to inaugurate the final of Sun Yat-sen's three stages, constitutional democracy. This assembly would make peace with Japan and proclaim peace, anti-communism, and reconstruction as the basis of national policy.[106] Peace, justice, and harmony would be restored to the Middle Kingdom.

The Japanese were perplexed about what use they should make of Wang and his flamboyant plans now that he had thrown himself into their arms. Actually, although the notion of a "new central government" to "solve the Incident" continued to enjoy a shadowy existence in their minds, never, so far as documents disclose, had Wang been envisaged as its head; that officer and gentleman of the old school, Wu P'ei-fu, was the leading candidate. The Wang *kōsaku*, but one of the many *kōsaku*, had seen Wang's emergence as a mode of splitting the Kuomintang, not of ruling occupied China. The Wang *kōsaku*, however, had been more successful than the other *kōsaku*; Wang had come out. Kagesa's *kikan*, with its connections in high places and its moralistic intentions, had been organized to follow up what had been begun. Despite the fact that it was unclear what Wang could do for the Japanese — since he had no connection with Chiang, dealing with Wang would make later dealings with Chiang, the sine qua non for "solving the Incident," more rather than less difficult — it was unthinkable to the Japanese, especially to those who had been associated with the Wang *kōsaku* and thus had a chance to advance their careers, to do nothing with the great Chinese leader Wang Ching-wei, now that he was in their hands.

The Ume kikan had to sell the scheme to its competitors; Kagesa had urged Wang, as he reported on May 23, to send emissaries to the Restored and Provisional Governments, and to Wu P'ei-fu as well, informing them of his intentions and requesting their cooperation[107] and the understanding of their Japanese Svengalis.

The immediate question that the Japanese had to decide was whether or not Wang should be permitted to come to Japan to discuss with Japanese leaders his plans for establishing a regime. Behind this was the broader question of what Japan's attitude would be toward this proposed regime. Many middle-ranking officers opposed Wang's trip; if they allowed Wang to come to Japan, perhaps he would trap them into supporting him as head of the "central government."[108] Others could see no larger implications in allowing Wang to come to Japan. "Since Wang is unmistakably in the position of a traitor, it is no longer necessary to hide his relations with Japan. It is advisable to bring Wang to Tokyo and search out his intention directly,"[109] said Colonel Usui. A third line of opinion refused to agree to bring Wang to Tokyo or to allow him to establish a regime. Colonel Horiba believed passionately that the way to use Wang Ching-wei to solve the China Incident was to send him as a peace emissary to Chungking. To set up a rival government was not a way to bring peace but rather to prepare for long-protracted war.[110]

It was a compromise suggested by that Wang *kōsaku* veteran, Colonel Imai, which carried the day. Actually, like so many compromises, it merely proposed delaying a decision until later. However, a decision to defer decision usually works to favor one alternative over another. Imai proposed that Wang be permitted to come to Japan and that he be encouraged to establish a government. Japan, however, would not be committing herself to support or recognize this regime nor to support Wang as the leader of the "new central government." No change in the *bunchi gassaku* policy would be necessary; if Wang were successful, perhaps his regime would replace the Restored Government in Nanking. The Japanese might let Wang have his way on use of the name and flag of the legitimate Kuomintang government. Establishment of such a Kuomintang regime in Nanking would not affect Japanese dealings with the regime in Chungking.[111] Imai envisaged that the question of negotiations with Wang could be separated from commitment to Wang. In fact, while Japanese commitments were so shallow as to betray all the hopes of Wang and his comrades, they were substantial enough to commit Japan to an elaborate charade which contributed nothing to the "solution of the Incident."

In meetings in Tokyo on June 2 and 3, the supporters of the Wang *kōsaku,* almost entirely associated with the military bureaucracy in Tokyo — the War Ministry and General Staff — met with officers dispatched from the Japanese Area Commands in north and central China. These officers were brought to accept the idea of a "new central government" with Wang Ching-wei as its head, which was to be established in Nanking by the Double Ten Festival (October 10, 1939) at the latest. Despite the urging of the Tokyo bureaucrats that Wang be given at least a shadow of power,[112] it was decided that, at most, only the names of the existing regimes might be changed; the governments themselves would continue to exist with their present personnel.

Wang's "new central government" was to be merely a paper coalition including the existing governments and Wu; further, the absolute military, political, and economic control over all of China, which Japan had declared as her basic policy the preceding November and had implemented through various "agreements" with the existing regimes, was to be preserved and expanded.[113] Imai's proposal that Wang be permitted the externals of the Kuomintang, that is, the name *Kuo-min cheng-fu* and the "blue-sky white-sun" flag, was rejected; even Wang's beloved *San-min chu-i* was to be revised. On June 6 the Five Ministers' Conference formalized what the military officials had already decided but hypocritically declared their complete support of the Konoye statement and Wang Ching-wei.[114]

To one perusing these records of Japanese deliberations, it appears that Wang's chance of procuring the merest simulacrum of Japanese support for his plans, much less the reality, was virtually nonexistent. The Japanese showed at this time no desire for peace or conciliation, with or without Wang. Wang, however, as Hong Kong Consul Tajiri said, was "likely to face the negotiations with a resolution to risk even his life."[115] It was May 31 according to one report,[116] (according to another, June 4[117]) when Wang and his troupe of eleven — including Chou Fo-hai, Mei Ssu-p'ing, Kao Tsung-wu, Chou Lung-hsiang, and surprisingly our friend from long ago, Tung Tao-ning — were flown to a military airport about 50 miles from Tokyo.[118] On the flight Wang occupied himself with composing a classical Chinese poem about the mountains and the sea, not betraying in the least the tension that he must have felt. He drove with Nishi and Chou Lung-hsiang to Tokyo, all the time engaged in a cultivated conversation about literature, politics, nature, and history.[119] This capacity of Wang's to express himself, even in the times of greatest stress, in elegant and harmonious sentiment was one of those qualities which convinced all who knew him that he was an extraordinary person.

Chungking's reaction was to order Wang's arrest, thus making the breach more unbridgeable, Wang's hopes to mediate between Tokyo and Chungking more untenable.[120] The Chinese party, all except for Kao Tsung-wu, were housed in a Tokyo mansion owned by Baron Furukawa. Kao, suspected by both sides as an agent of Chiang, was given separate quarters on the pretext of his illness. Only Inukai's last-minute intervention saved Kao from falling victim to a Japanese plot to poison him.[121] Kao's position was not an enviable one.

The actual negotiations between Wang's group and the Japanese were double-layered. Wang met with cabinet members while Chou Fo-hai, as Wang's chief-of-staff, met with the middle-ranking officers who held the real power. Wang's talks with the members of the cabinet were extremely amicable. It is the custom in Japanese negotiations for the top man always to avoid unpleasant haggling, leaving that for others, and to exude an air of friendly cooperation. Wang Ching-wei was a politician himself and doubtless he was no stranger to this technique. Nevertheless, he seems to have overvalued both the sincerity and the influence of the Japanese cabinet.

Wang's first meeting, on June 10, was with Prime Minister Hiranuma. After Hiranuma had made some remarks on the desirability of peace between the two countries, a peace based on "virtue," Wang responded with his proposals. Three different methods of working toward peace, he said, were conceivable. The first possibility would be to establish a peace policy by dealing with nonofficial and non-Kuomintang personalities. The second possibility would be to deal directly with Chiang Kai-shek and the Chungking Kuomintang government for the solution of the Incident. The third possibility would be to proceed together toward peace "hand-in-hand with those who accept peace and are concerned about the future of the country, regardless if they are Kuomintang or not and regardless of whether they are government officials or not."[122]

"If you are to take the first measure, although I would not be able to take a public stand, I would like to render as much assistance as possible behind the scenes. If you should adopt the second method and negotiate directly with Chiang Kai-shek, to regain peace, as a member of the Nationalist Party myself, I would not hesitate to mediate between Japan and him. And if the third measure is to be adopted, I should like to directly embark into the peace movement myself and become its control[ling] figure, but which way is Japan intending to take?"[123] Hiranuma answered: "This is a problem of China. There is no way except to take measures which China feels to be most proper. It is very excellent, however that a person like yourself would embark positively on a peace movement as its control[ling] figure." Wang emphasized to Hiranuma that the government must be a Kuomintang government in legal continuity with Sun Yat-sen's party and government. All this seemed agreeable to Hiranuma. Similar interviews followed with other top civil government figures. Wang received the *appearance* of support. But at best all he received from these august personages was passive acquiescence.

On June 12 Navy Minister Yonai assured Wang that Japan would not interfere with Wang's activities and that Japan would cooperate for mutual benefit. The next day Treasury Minister Ishiwata emphasized that Japan had no intention of monopolizing China's economy. Foreign Minister Arita on June 14 was as friendly and reassuring as his colleagues.[124]

The same day, Wang had an interview with Prince Konoye, whose supposed desire for compromise peace with China and whose personal support for Wang Ching-wei had been the cardinal features of the Kao route. Wang and Konoye conversed with an interpreter for one hour and alone without interpreter for two hours.[125] The interpreter reports that during the hour that he was present, Wang told Konoye of his faith in the Konoye statement and of his plans for establishing government.[126] Konoye said that he was very gratified that there had not been any widespread public dissension over the Konoye statement like that over the Portsmouth Treaty ending the Russo-Japanese War in 1906.[127] Wang told Konoye that his guiding principle was to continue Sun Yat-sen's work. Konoye expressed his admiration for Sun and his pleasure that Wang was following a course that Sun would have wished.[128] Little is known of what happened during the third hour when the two statesmen communicated by writing Chinese characters; Kao reports that later Wang told him that, in response to a question of Konoye, he, Wang, had answered that the attitude of Kao Tsung-wu was pessimistic; Wang did not think, however, that Kao would move against him.[129] This hour of private written conversation must have been very important, however, because Kagesa said that Wang appeared to gain great courage and be reinforced in his efforts as a result of his conversation with Konoye.[130]

Could Konoye really have been so duplicitous as to encourage Wang in the belief that the Japanese would, under any other condition than their own defeat, withdraw their troops from China and tolerate a sovereign Chinese government?

Since the Wang kōtsaku was almost entirely a military project the responsibility for talking brass tacks to Wang fell on War Minister Itagaki. Itagaki told Wang what had been decided in the earlier military conferences, namely, that the existing regimes must not be abolished in actuality and hence that Wang's regime would at best be some sort of meaningless coalition under the bunchi gassaku policy; that Wang's treasured San-min chu-i, "blue-sky white-sun" flag, and Kuo-min cheng-fu were all unacceptable to the Japanese.

Wang, easily Itagaki's superior in experience, intelligence, and poise, was no mean negotiator. He had come to the tiger's den, and he didn't plan to leave without the tiger's cub. The first conference on the morning of June 11 opened with a polite joust on the topic of communism in China. Wang asked if "joint defense against communism" was merely another name for Japanese aggression, a justification of invading China. The only answer to the menace of communism in China, Wang asserted, was a strong and unified China under the Kuomintang. Itagaki countered by saying that he was all in favor of a strong central government, but after all, several governments and autonomous areas had already emerged. "A certain respect must be paid to such facts and factors. Thus to strengthen the unity of China and Japan in respective areas is not to make the central government weak, but to strengthen the position of the central government by strengthening the unity of China and Japan," continued Itagaki. Wang didn't have a moment to force down this elegant logic before Itagaki suggested the revision of the San-min chu-i.[131]

Itagaki himself and the clique he represented, which enjoyed temporary preponderance in the central military bureaucratic organs, the War Ministry and the General Staff, were eager to utilize Wang and were willing, in order to keep Wang active, to make the superficial compromises on the matters of form which meant so much to Wang. In making these compromises, Itagaki and his colleagues did not consult the representatives of the field armies who were adamantly opposed to them.

Apparently as a result of Chou's negotiations with middle-level officers, a compromise was reached on the flag question before Wang's next meeting with Itagaki, which took place on the evening of June 15. Inukai describes his discussion of this compromise with the Chinese comrades in the conference room of the Furukawa mansion: Chou Lung-hsiang was just drawing with a flourish the "blue-sky white-sun" flag and below it, a yellow triangular pennant with the characters "peace, anti-communism, reconstruction." Chou said, "How do you like the design? I do not much care for this small pigtail triangle." Inukai replied, "A triangle is a triangle, but yellow is the color of the Ch'ing dynasty." Chou: "Should we say that it was made in the Ta-ch'ing Ch'ien-lung period and give it to the Ueno Museum?" Inukai: "Well, it is tied by a string and easy to take off. That was the final concession the *Koain* would make. On national celebration days and on Sun Yat-sen's birthday, I want to take off the pigtail." Wang, in the background, said in Chinese: "We must keep our promise but no more than one year."[132]

In the second conference with Wang, Itagaki replied to the "concrete plan for handling the situation," which Chou Fo-hai had submitted to the Japanese in May. Itagaki expressed acquiescence in the Chinese desire to make the capital of their regime Nanking and in their plan to hold a Central Political Conference. On the basis of the interim discussions, Itagaki this time agreed to permit the "blue-sky white-sun" flag as long as it was flown along with the yellow pennant. At this time Itagaki added a new proviso: the army of the new government would not be permitted to use the "blue-sky white-sun" flag but only the yellow pennant. Wang vehemently protested this restriction and a heated argument ensued, only put aside for the moment as Wang tactfully agreed to give the matter further consideration.

Itagaki, after explaining the Japanese position on the existing governments — only the *names*, not the entities, might be abrogated — proceeded to give Wang a full and frank account of Japanese policy and intentions towards China. "Considering the present situation in China, we consider that the appropriate political form should be in line with the *bunchi gassaku* idea. This means to make Sino-Japanese relations close, reflecting the special situation of each locality." Itagaki made his meaning clearer, spelling out in detail Japanese territorial ambitions. North China would be a "special Sino-Japanese area for defense and economy"; Mongolia and Singkiang would be special anti-Communist areas; the Yangtze delta area would be an area of Sino-Japanese economic cooperation; the coastline would be a defense area.[133] In other words, as might be expected, Japan, like other conquerors, had no intention of relinquishing any measure of control over the territory she had conquered.

Wang ignored Itagaki's revelations of the extent of Japanese territorial demands, perhaps because he did not want to hear them, and limited his reply to the question of the existing governments. "If it is necessary to maintain the actual existence of the two governments, then there is no other way but to postpone the organization of the central government. The Kuomintang will organize a government with a specific territorial base, and await the right opportunity before forming a central government."[134] This was one hundred per cent bluff; Wang had no territorial base nor any likelihood of obtaining one. Itagaki did respond by modifying his statement somewhat, saying that what must be preserved were not the governments but the agreements with those governments which formally rendered to Japan absolute control over the wealth and power of occupied China.

Wang lectured Itagaki on the importance of Japanese respect for Chinese nationalistic consciousness; discussing the Chungking political scene in detail, he encouraged Itagaki to believe that there were large sections of the Chungking military who were in sympathy with Wang and who would surely join him if only the Japanese showed a cooperative and conciliatory spirit. Wang urged upon Itagaki the necessity that his government be permitted normal diplomatic contact with foreign powers; only in such a case would the legitimate succession of the new government be recognized. Existing agreements, no matter how displeasing both to the new Chinese government and to the Japanese, could be altered by peaceful diplomacy alone. Wang's intention was that once foreign diplomats were accredited to his Nanking government, they would tend to balance the overwhelming Japanese presence. The Japanese were pathological in their desire to extirpate foreigners from China; no solution to this problem took place during the Wang-Itagaki meetings or afterwards.

In the end and on paper Wang and Chou succeeded in winning from Itagaki and his subordinates compromise on several points. These points involved form rather than substance. It was agreed that the Nanking Restored Government might be abolished on condition that its members be absorbed into the new Kuomintang government in Nanking; the north China regime would remain as it was but with a different name, the North China Administrative Council. Wang won Japanese acquiescence in his desire to use the name *Kuo-min cheng-fu* and to promulgate the *San-min chu-i* merely reinterpreted rather than rewritten. These concessions, formal and insignificant as they appear, were nullified by the fact that the expeditionary armies with whom Wang would have to deal in China bitterly opposed them.

Chou submitted a list of further demands on July 15 (requests concerning the realization of the principle of respecting the sovereignty of China, *Chūgoku shuken sonchō gensoku jikō ni kanshi Nihon ni taisuru yōbo*).[135] The Japanese were not to send political advisers to either the local or national governments. All matters between the Chinese and Japanese governments would go through normal diplomatic channels. The Japanese army should withdraw from all pacified areas, letting Chinese troops bear the responsibility for keeping order. A foreign military adviser group should be formed. One half of this group was to be Japanese, the remainder German and Italian. Foreign military advisers should not be assigned to local units, should confine themselves to instruction, and under no circumstances should undertake responsibility for command functions. Chinese-owned factories, houses, and railroads should be returned to their rightful Chinese owners as soon as possible. Japanese interest in joint-stock companies could not exceed 49 per cent.[136] The Japanese side indicated that they accepted these demands "in principle." It was not only naive, it was stupid of Wang's group to believe on so little evidence that the Japanese had so altered their designs upon China.

From the Japanese point of view, catapulting Wang out onto the political stage of occupied-China could do them no harm — they made no commitments — and it could do Chungking no good.

The purpose of Wang's trip to Japan had been to discover whether Japan would offer her cooperation in Wang's endeavor to make peace between China and Japan through establishing a model regime in Nanking. Japan was not willing to offer cooperation; the only hope held out was that it might acquiesce if Wang himself proved able to establish a "new central government." The Japanese gave every indication that they would yield nothing; this government could have no independent strength. Wang was led by his passionate resolution to misinterpret shallow concessions on relatively formal matters offered by a single clique within the Japanese military as evidence that, though powerless, he could single-handedly conciliate the Japanese.

There was little talk in Tokyo of the all-important questions of peace conditions and withdrawal of Japanese troops. Wang said he told Hiranuma, "At present in discussing peace between Japan and China we must attend to it in all sincerity. It will be difficult to realize peace if customers insist on seeing goods and merchants try to decide the price beforehand."[137] Wang believed, or hoped, that if somehow he could unite the Chinese in a policy of cooperation with Japan, he would be able to bring the Japanese to grant magnanimous conditions, such as those of the *kiroku,* which would permit China to maintain her sovereignty. Wang was one of the most daring brokers in history: he would persuade the Chinese of a virtually nonexistent Japanese desire to cooperate; he would persuade the Japanese of the legitimate demands of Chinese nationalism; and he would hope that if both could be brought to the bargaining table, each could be made to fulfill in fact what he had asserted of them in hope. The first step was no less improbable than the last; on the basis of his personality alone, he was to develop independent political strength within territory which the Japanese army had conquered and continued to rule behind a frail facade of Chinese "governments." Was it courage or madness that made him set out for Tientsin on June 18 to beard Wang K'o-min and Wu P'ei-fu in their respective northern dens?

From Shanghai to Ch'ingtao

7 Returning from his trip to Tokyo with its ambiguous results, Wang forged on with his plan to realize peace. During the summer of 1939 Wang and his handful of comrades were active everywhere. Wang was campaigning for the support of the existing regimes in north and central China. He was intriguing to establish a local regime based on "partial truce" in Canton. He was building up a political machine in Shanghai by drawing together his own "orthodox" Kuomintang and by penetrating local organizations and gaining the support of local interests. He sought contact with Chungking and appealed for the sympathy and support of the Chinese people and foreign powers. For the moment he animated the sluggish and dreary scene of occupied China.

By autumn it was sadly clear that this animation was only a disturbance on the surface rather than an indication of movement in the sullen depths of the static political situation. Following the outbreak of war in Europe, the Japanese made it unambiguously certain to Wang that, far from seeking a compromise peace and respecting Chinese sovereignty, their only interest was in solidifying and expanding their conquests. Thus Wang and his associates were faced with a terrible dilemma. If by constituting themselves a Chinese "government," they accepted Japanese demands, then they might hope to soften the ultimate and inevitable triumph of Japanese arms and save something for China. Others would read signing away of China's interests as treason. If Wang's group refused to sign, they would be throwing away the dream of their movement to save China. If some chose to continue and some to withdraw, those who refused would seem to be betraying their comrades. It was a tragic choice.

Before the dark winter of doubt was the halcyon summer of hope. The first task that the Japanese had set for Wang was winning the cooperation of the two existing governments — the Provisional in north China, the Restored in central China — and, equally important, of that charismatic old warrior who in retirement was the most powerful Chinese in occupied China, Wu

P'ei-fu. Itagaki and the "China clique" — Imai, Horiba, and others — were not enthusiastic about Wu, but Wu enjoyed enormous support among the hard liners in the expeditionary armies and in the Kōain. The supporters of Wang K'o-min and the North China Provisional Government and Liang Hung-chih's Restored Government in Nanking were less influential and less vocal; nevertheless, unless they were squared, the "central government" stood little chance of coming into being, much less of fulfilling its name in any sense. Further, Wang's endeavors with regard to the existing governments were ambiguous in their results; with regard to Wu P'ei-fu, they were completely unsuccessful. Concomitant with these political challenges was the imperative to make Wang's aspirations credible by giving him a public aura of leadership — in Wang's own phrase, "winning the people's heart."

Wang set forth from Japan on June 18 accompanied by those stalwarts from the Ume kikan — Kagesa, Inukai, Shimizu Tōzō of the Gaimushō, and the gentle Admiral Suga of the navy.[1] Like his hero, Sun Yat-sen, fleeing the Manchus, Wang arrived in Tientsin in disguise on June 24. The next day his old friend Wang K'o-min, who had come from Peking, formally welcomed him there, an act of considerable courtesy in the Chinese context.[2] Wang K'o-min was a veteran in Sino-Japanese "cooperation" and he was weary; in mid-August he was to ask American assistance to escape to Chungking.[3] He certainly was not unwilling to pass on the torch. Consequently, the interview between the two men on June 25 was very successful.

Wang K'o-min asked Wang Ching-wei to relate to him the answers to three questions: What had been Wang's past activities? What were his future plans? What was it he wished to ask of Wang K'o-min? Wang dealt with the first two questions on this occasion. He emphasized to Wang K'o-min that while he wanted to form an independent and free central government with the Kuomintang flag and ideology, he wished to do so in cooperation with others.[4] When the two men met again for lunch on June 27, Wang answered Wang K'o-min's third question: What part did Wang want him to play in the new government? Wang K'o-min agreed to assist Wang Ching-wei by being present at various meetings he was planning — the Kuomintang Representative Congress and the Central Political

Conference — but he refused to assume a post in the "new central government." He rejected Wang's proposal that they establish a code for their private communication.[5] He was too tired for theatrics. Wang K'o-min warned Wang that his desire to use the "blue-sky white-sun" flag and the *San-min chu-i* was going to receive a very cool reception in north China. Wang K'o-min's North China Provisional Government used the five-bar flag of the old Peking Republic and mechanically attempted to promulgate a conservative, classically oriented political philosophy, the title of which aped that of the Kuomintang's — *Hsin-min chu-i* (New people's principles) instead of *San-min chu-i* (Three people's principles). Wang K'o-min knew very well that these archaic pseudo-Confucian mouthings had no power to win modern Chinese in comparison with nationalism and communism.[6] It was the Japanese who entertained the conceit that the clock could be turned back in China. In general, Wang K'o-min evidenced an encouraging though passive attitude toward Wang Ching-wei's plans. The prospect of Wang K'o-min's cooperation was an important premise upon which Wang continued.[7]

During their second meeting, Wang K'o-min had strongly advised Wang to reach an understanding with Wu P'ei-fu. "It would be inexpedient to increase your enemies," he said.[8] This advice proved impossible to follow. Wu had long been playing a game similar to Wang's but perhaps a little more sharply. He had asserted his willingness to come out for peace and assume administrative responsibility, but only on condition that the Japanese withdraw their forces from China. Although he played a very coy game with the Japanese, letting them think he might at any time agree to their demands, one thing was very clear: he would under no condition play a secondary role to Wang Ching-wei. The Wu guidance organ had undoubtedly received instructions from Tokyo to guide Wu into cooperation with Wang; thus it was in rather halfhearted fashion that Colonel Osako, apparently in charge of such things, had an interview with Wu P'ei-fu on June 18, the very day that Wang had left Tokyo.

Osako asked Wu to "come out and be charged with handling the situation." Wu pretended to take this to mean that the headship of the two existing governments would devolve upon him and that, as such, he would be head of a sovereign power, equal, as he said, to the Japanese emperor, and his ministers would be equal to Japanese ministers. On this basis he would begin negotiations for peace with Japan. He indicated a willingness to cooperate with Wang but implied that Wang would assume a very subordinate role.[9] Wu not only stood up to the Japanese in private but also leaked to the press that his demand was not equality between his prospective Chinese government and the Japanese government, but rather that Japan should take an attitude of humble respect toward the "elder brother" China.[10] Wu well realized that the Japanese had no intention of setting up a sovereign Chinese state in occupied China. What he was doing was refusing to emerge and refusing to cooperate with Wang.[11] The enthusiasm of Wu's Japanese supporters was, if anything, enhanced by his arrogance. A striking evidence of the rōnins' devotion to Wu was the fact that a retainer of Colonel Oseko was sent to assassinate Wang about this time. A Gaimushō official learned of it and warned Kagesa.[12]

Wang considered it essential, if his prospective government was to bring peace through merger with the Chungking government, that the post of president be reserved for Lin Sen, who held that position in Chungking. Wu, however, communicating with Wang by messenger, had demanded the presidential post for himself, in addition to that of commander-in-chief of the army and leader of the proposed "anti-Communist national salvation league."[13] Wu's ambitions thus were incompatible with Wang's. Wang did not credit Wu with motives other than the desire to secure his own position,[14] and Wu had no higher opinion of Wang. Despite this fundamental rivalry and irreconcilability of points of view, the Japanese supporters of both were eager to get the two to cooperate, the backers of each envisioning their respective protege in the leading position. So if they should meet, neither could afford to lose face in relation to the other. The result of all this backing and filling, jockeying for position, and exchange of messages was that the planned meeting between the two men never came off. It was scheduled for June 26 or 27. Wu would not stir from his residence to meet Wang at a place appointed by the Japanese army. He felt that Wang should play the guest, the petitioner. Wang agreed to call upon Wu on condition that Wu return the call. This Wu refused to do, and the meeting was called off amidst re-crimination.[15]

Wang's supporters placed the blame directly on Wu for the failure to establish cooperation between the two Chinese leaders and hence to promptly realize the "new central government." Wu's failure to cooperate was a knife that cut both ways. It left Wang Ching-wei as the only really promising personality in occupied China who seemed likely to cooperate with the Japanese. In retrospect, however, the reason Wang was not able to get a foothold in north China was his failure to capture the support of Wu.

Was Wu's cool policy of letting the Japanese come to him wiser than Wang's policy of seeking out and manufacturing agreement where none existed? Could the two of them together have created a real Chinese government within occupied China? There is no question that with Wu's cooperation, the new government conceivably could have organized military forces, virtually a sine qua non for political strength.

Wang returned from his northern expedition on June 28 and the next day started in on his next task — establishing a cooperative relationship with the Restored Government and its Japanese supporters. There was inevitable tension in this encounter, since it was Wang's avowed purpose to see the Restored Government dissolved and to take its place. On the morning of June 29 he met with Liang Hung-chih, the head of the Restored Government, and in the afternoon with Liang's second-in-command, Wen Tsung-yao, an elderly American-educated ex-imperial official. Sometime later he was to meet with Ch'en Chün, the third major personality.

Wang opened his interview with Liang by relating his adventures in the cause of peace and humbly asking his cooperation. Liang was extremely eager to know if the Mongolian and the north Chinese regimes were to remain autonomous, and he was unwilling, if they were to do so, to see his regime dissolved. Wang avoided giving a direct answer, with the excuse that such details would be decided by the Central Political Conference, one of the preliminaries in his plan for government formation. He did, however, reassure Liang that the officials of the Restored Government would be included in the new government in positions of appropriate dignity.[16] Essentially, Liang favored the original plan of having the "new central government" come into being through something like the already existing joint committee (*rengo iinkai*), which would provide the form and name of a central government without disturbing any incumbents.[17]

Wen Tsung-yao, the chairman of the Judicial Yuan, took a considerably warmer attitude toward Wang's endeavor. He urged Wang not to put off the formation of the new government lest the moment of opportunity pass. He urged Wang to ignore the interests of the Restored and the Provisional Governments but by all means to make contact with Wu P'ei-fu.[18] Ch'en Chün, a Japanese-educated ex-Kuomintang official, Liang's interior minister, also took an extremely positive attitude toward Wang's plans. Wang and Ch'en seemed to disagree about policy toward Chiang Kai-shek. Whether attempting to anticipate Ch'en's view or whether truly stating his own opinion, Wang began by saying: "In essence our purpose is to destroy the Chungking government which is carrying out the policy of uniting with Russia, cooperating with the Communists and resisting Japan." Ch'en demurred, saying that he differed in direction from the Chungking government and Chiang Kai-shek but did not believe in criticizing them as others had done. Wang modified his earlier position, asserting that his hostility was not directed toward Chiang but toward his policies. "If he abandons his present policies and comes to follow us, I have no reason to criticize him."[19]

Wang sought to gain the support not only of the Chinese in the two governments but also that of the Japanese officers who created and supported the governments. In Peking he met with General Sugiyama, who headed the North China Area Command,[20] and in Nanking with General Yamada, who held the same post in the Central China Area Command.[21]

After his individual meetings with the leaders of the two existing governments, Wang met with both of them at Ch'ingtao about July 11.[22] The Restored Government had suggested Ch'ingtao as a site, since they felt that it would be a blow to their prestige if the meeting were held in Peking or Tientsin,[23] sites presumably preferred by the Provisional Government. Little is known of this meeting, since Wang's movements were shrouded in secrecy to prevent assassination. It must have been at this time that the above-mentioned assassination attempt was to take place, for this is the only occasion from the beginning of the Wang *kōsaku* to Wu's death that the three leaders met in Ch'ingtao, as described by the reporter of the incident.[24]

Everyone was tired and bored with the stagnant and frustrating political situation in occupied and semi-occupied China. There was no hope for change. There was no leadership, no spark of life. Chungking was interested only in a war with the Japanese that she could not foreseeably win. The foreigners were concerned with the burgeoning European crisis. Occupied China and its isolated concession areas had been forgotten. Thus, it is not surprising that when Wang Ching-wei left Chungking and began bustling around trying to effect some changes in the occupied areas, a certain reservoir of interest and enthusiasm soon was generated. By July Wang was receiving twenty to thirty callers a day eager for news of his plans and inquiring about possibilities to participate.[25]

By the first week in July, Ting and Li's "special work" had proceeded to the point where it was deemed safe for Wang to publicly make known his presence. Consequently, Wang moved to the mansion at 1126 Yu Yuen Road that had been prepared for him in western Shanghai. He launched his appeal for popular support in a speech broadcast by Japanese radio on July 7, the second anniversary of the Marco Polo Bridge Incident.[26] This speech, entitled "My Basic Concepts and Objectives Concerning Sino-Japanese Relations," rephrased his prior pronouncements.[27] The next day Chiang Kai-shek countered in a broadcast to the occupied areas branding the peace movement as "traitors' peace" and reasserting that Wang in no way represented the Kuomintang.[28]

The fledgling Wang group also began to move to establish a constituency in the great city of Shanghai, the largest and richest of Chinese cities. One of their first objectives was to gain the support of educators. Unfortunately, this project was placed in the hands of the Ting-Li gestapo. The methods of persuasion used were abduction and blackmail; a subsidy for support, murder for refusal. Some principals favored Wang's cause; few could resist the arguments of Ting and Li. When the educators would announce their support of Wang, or if they were even half-hearted in their condemnation of Wang, the students, among whom patriotic and anti-Japan sentiment ran strong,

Wang's official headquarters and residence in Shanghai, 1126 Yu Yuen Road..

would riot and demand their resignation. The students were encouraged in their criticism of their teachers' political attitudes by inflamatory articles in the Chungking-influenced *Chinese American Daily News*. The result was disruption of education and, ultimately, a grave loss of prestige for Wang's movement among the educated classes.[29] Japanese intelligence reported in July that the Wang group, through its involvement with Ting and Li and their hangers-on, was coming to be regarded as corrupt opportunists.[30]

By mid-July, in face of Wu's refusal to cooperate and Wang's failure to convince the public of his ability to transform the situation, the "new central government" was as far away as ever. Wang felt the reason for the general reluctance on the parts of puppets, puppet-masters, and public to respond to his appeal was a feeling that it was absurd for him to assume leadership with neither territory nor army behind him.[31] So he determined upon stronger expedients; he would persuade his old supporters, Generals Chang Fa-k'uei and Teng Lung-kuang, to set themselves up with Japanese cooperation as warlords in the Canton area. Their support would give him the political basis he needed to set up his central government in Nanking. The "local peace" established in Canton would gradually spread over all of south China. This Canton scheme is similar to what the comrades had hoped would follow Konoye's statement and Wang's emergence. Again the line between treason and patriotism was a thin one; peace would benefit the whole nation, but could it be bought at the price of reawakening old tendencies toward southern regionalism — in line with Japanese schemes for *bunchi gassaku* — and away from the ideal of Chinese unity for which the Kuomintang had been fighting for so long?

For a considerable time the Japanese South China Area Command had wanted to have its own Canton-based regime parallel to and competing with the pet regimes of the north and central China armies. Consequently, when Wang, accompanied by Yano Seiki from the Gaimushō, journeyed to Canton to begin negotiations with General Satō Kenryō, vice-chief of staff, he found Satō extremely enthusiastic.[32] The success of the Canton scheme would give the South China Expeditionary Army the predominant influence over the "new central government." The Japanese promised that if appropriate armed forces came over from the Chungking side, they would yield to them order-keeping functions within Japanese-held territory. The reconstruction of Canton would swiftly follow the success of the enterprise.[33] Plans for the composition of the government and a schedule for its formation were drawn up. Wang whetted Japanese hopes by reporting to them, truly or falsely, that Ch'en Pi-chün had been meeting with Chang Fa-k'uei in Hong Kong and that Chang had displayed great interest in the plan.[34]

Since the Japanese were being so cooperative, Wang decided to press for a little more: could Wang contact the British consul in Canton? True to form, the Japanese expressed their displeasure at Wang's request.[35]

Before his return from Canton to Shanghai at the end of July,[36] Wang sought to win back the support of his old friends and comrades, Ch'en Kung-po and T'ao Hsi-sheng, whom he had invited from Hong Kong to meet with him in Canton. He earnestly requested them to come to Shanghai and actively participate in his movement. T'ao agreed to come; Ch'en temporized.[37]

Less than a fortnight after his return, Wang launched the Canton scheme in a speech on August 9 broadcast not only to south China but also to Southeast Asia, where the powerful overseas Chinese were mainly Cantonese in origin. "If," he said, "Chinese forces in Kwangtung . . . express their will for peace and their opposition to Communism, Lieutenant-General Ando will agree to not only halt the attack of the Japanese Army on the Kwangtung forces, but gradually to turn over the duties of peace maintenance and economic administration in the occupied areas to the Chinese."[38] Chinese everywhere, especially the Cantonese, who felt that they were bearing a disproportionate share of the sacrifices, were profoundly weary of the interminable and seemingly hopeless war. Wang's plan was logical; there was no other hope for peace on the horizon. His appeal was not without some effect.[39]

The real question was whether Chungking forces would defect. Again the question divides itself into two parts: would military leaders wish to risk their lives and careers on the promises of a discredited and renegade politician, and second, if they desired to do so, did they possess the means? There is no way of knowing the true feelings of these leaders. In any case,

Chungking lost no time in making sure they could not move. The Military Affairs Committee authorized the political affairs officers of each military unit to report directly and independently any sign of disaffection.[40] In August Chang Fa-k'uei, along with other generals of Cantonese origin, issued circular telegrams denouncing Wang and his scheme. The Japanese were told that Chang informed Wang that his anti-Wang statement was only a result of Chungking pressure.[41] Nevertheless, by mid-August Wang had to admit that the "general reception" of his plan had not been very good.[42]

Quickly Wang shifted gears and turned his attention to the upcoming "Kuomintang Representative Congress," as stated in Chou's May memorandum, an essential step toward the establishment of the peace government. Vigorous politicking had gathered two hundred and forty "delegates," most of whom had little or no previous association with either the Kuomintang or the geographic areas which they were supposed to represent. After Chinese guards had searched the assemblage — for fear of assassins — the "Sixth Kuomintang Representative Congress" convened in Wang's heavily guarded residence on August 28. In the front of the hall was a massive portrait of Sun Yat-sen flanked by crossed party and national flags. The assemblage rose to sing Sun Yat-sen's long-forbidden national anthem — San-min chu-i, wo tang so tsung (the San-min chu-i are the aim of our party) — and scarcely an eye was dry. Perhaps, one might think, Wang had won something for the Chinese, because at his demand not a single Japanese was present.[43]

The Chinese further asserted their independence by listing on the roster of delegates those from Manchuria as "absent," thus denying the legitimacy of the Japanese puppet Manchukuo.[44] Kagesa feared for his job. However, the statement, with which the Congress closed on August 30 declared that the Manchurian issue could be settled on the basis of the manifesto of the Kuomintang Emergency Congress held in the spring of 1938 and on the basis of Chiang's own statement that "in the event of Japan guaranteeing to refrain from further encroachments upon Chinese territory and sovereignty after the solution of the question of the Four Eastern Provinces [Manchuria], I myself [Chiang] will bear the responsibility of effecting the solution."[45]

The Congress declared acts of the organs of the Chungking

government since January 1, 1939, to be null and void. The constitution of the Kuomintang was to be amended by abolishing the post of *tsung-ts'ai* held by Chiang Kai-shek in favor of a central executive committee, the chairman of which was to exercise the powers of the *tsung-li*, president. Naturally, Wang was elected to fill the post. This amendment was intended to give the appearance of collegial leadership as opposed to the dictatorship of Chiang Kai-shek.

Anti-communism was declared the basic policy of the party; the *San-min chu-i* were declared incompatible with communism; Sino-Japanese relations were to be readjusted and normalized; a National Assembly was to be convoked and a constitution put into force, thus entering the last of Sun Yat-sen's three stages of government. It was once again declared that Japan wished a peace on the basis of no claims for territory and no indemnity and of signature of an anti-Comintern pact similar to that in force among Japan, Germany, and Italy. All treaties were to be respected; good relations were to be cultivated with the powers; playing one power off against another was denounced. Wang was empowered to convene a Central Political Conference composed of "persons of outstanding virtue and great wisdom" irrespective of party. This was to be the second and penultimate step toward the "restoration" of the government.[46]

In Chungking the fourth session of the People's Political Council, of which Wang used to be head, was held from September 9 to 18. Tajiri felt that with the recent developments in the world situation, Wang, had he not left Chungking, might have gained control of the council and swung a large segment of the Kuomintang government toward peace.[47] Instead, the People's Political Council closed with Chiang Kai-shek's declaration that China's resistance must continue and that she could never recognize the activities of traitors or the existence of their regimes. Chiang also declared that Chungking would soon establish a constitutional form of government. Was this an answer to Wang's claim to have abolished one-party tutorship and be about to move on to the democratic state of government?

After the Kuomintang Congress, the next step toward formation of the new government was agreement on the representatives from each regime to the Central Political Conference,

Wang's activities during the summer and autumn of 1939.

Upper left: Wang delivering his broadcast speech in Shanghai on July 7.

Center left: Wang as guest of honor at a banquet given by Lieutenant General Yamada of the Japanese Central China Area Command.

Lower left: Wang entertaining Yamada at his own residence. Chu Min-i is the second figure from the right.

Upper right: Wang Ching-wei (center) confers with Liang Hung-chih (right) and Wang-K'o-min (left) in Nanking at the end of September.

Middle right: Wang Ching-wei -confers with Lieutenant General Ando Commander-in-Chief of the Japanese South China Area Command.

Bottom right: Liang Hung-chih meets with Sado Kadomatsu, a Giamushō official who had close contact with the Wang comrades.

which in turn would establish the "new central government." Since the conference was to be formal only, all details had to be settled between Wang and the regimes in advance. By the end of August Liang had come around to looking with more favor on Wang's plans, partly as a result of Japanese "internal guidance" (*naimen shidō*). Wang in turn would publicly ask for Liang's assistance and invite members of the Restored Government to join the new government, thus saving their face.[48] Wang K'o-min, however, was cooler than before to Wang's project.

Wang Ching-wei and his cadres traveled to Nanking and, always under heavy guard, met with Liang and Wang K'o-min on September 19, 20, and 21. Before the "three heads" could meet, their respective advisers had to meet to resolve their claims. In this, they were not completely successful.[49]

The participants in the conference suffered from assassination nerves. During the pre-conference banquet it seemed that Kao Tsung-wu's many enemies had finally succeeded in liquidating him; he became violently ill and was rushed from the banquet hall. To the relief of all the collaborators, it proved nothing but indigestion.[50]

Wang began the meeting by submitting a "practical method for organizing the Central Political Conference" This did not provide Liang with the detailed assurances which he craved.[51] Wang got his way with regard to the allotment of representatives to the Central Political Conference — one third to the Kuomintang, one third to the two existing governments between them, the final third to Mongolia and other "autonomous" areas — but the three could not agree on an agenda for the coming conference. Wang K'o-min and Liang Hung-chih assured Wang of their *personal* support; it was only their Japanese advisers who could not agree.[52]

Wang and his followers felt disheartened and humiliated by the failure of the meeting, attributing it as they did to the lack of courage of the other two leaders and the faithless meddling of the Japanese.[53] Nevertheless, after the meeting closed, Wang issued statements — worked up at great effort during the previous few weeks — praising the two regimes.[54]

The intent of the meeting had been to provide an opportunity for the existing regimes and their advisers to relinquish part of their power. It is not surprising that they were reluctant to do so. Kao Tsung-wu offers another perspective on at least Wang K'o-min's failure to cooperate, and indeed his withdrawal from the encouraging attitude he had taken in June. Without Wang Ching-wei's knowledge, Kao had visited Wang K'o-min immediately on his arrival in Nanking. Kao advised Wang K'o-min to do everything in his power to prevent or delay the establishment of the new government, which he said would hinder rather than promote the realization of peace. Wang K'o-min told Kao that he had heard from General Kita of the North China Area Command that Kao was working on behalf of Chiang Kai-shek to sabotage Wang Ching-wei. Kao denied this allegation, saying that the only reason he had joined Wang in Shanghai was to save Wang from the Japanese. Wang K'o-min expressed his agreement with Kao's views about the inefficacy of Wang's central government plan; it was easier, he said, for Wang, Kao, and himself to deal with one another, because they were civilians and friends, than with Chiang; yet it was Chiang who held political and military power; it was only Chiang who could make peace.[55]

Whether or not Wang K'o-min turned away from Wang Ching-wei on the advice of Kao Tsung-wu, there was always existing and steadily increasing resistance in north China to the establishment of a new regime. It was not only the feudal tendency that the Japanese armies demonstrated to carve out private empires for themselves and a deep resentment of the Kuomintang, of which Wang had been a leading figure, which motivated the North China Army's opposition to Wang's central government. There was sound logic behind their skepticism. General Tada was conducting promising contact with Chungking, using J. Leighton Stuart, the president of Yenching University and later American ambassador, as intermediary. The terms being discussed involved Japanese withdrawal to a position north of the Great Wall.[56] Tada regarded the establishment of a new regime as a barrier to peace with Chungking.[57] "What is the use," he asked, "of making government after government when the prospects for the war are not yet clear?"[58]

After the "three heads" meeting in Nanking, the peace movement declined. Wang's activities had caused a movement on the political waters, but the deeper currents flowed against him.

The outbreak of the European war seemed to favor Wang and his movement, but that Europe too chose bayonets and bombs as its arbiter really made Wang's position more difficult. Wang's prospects might seem better because those of Chungking seemed worse; in defeat Wang might save something for China. The outbreak of the European conflagration had, however, two very important effects upon the political situation in East Asia: it intensified the drift toward extremism in Japan, and it bound the Western powers to support of Chungking — because now, without question, China and the Western powers were engaged in a common struggle.

Because of a complicated series of events, the first effect of the new war in Europe upon the political situation was just the opposite of its ultimate effect. Japan had been fighting with the Soviet Union on the Mongolian border (the Nomohan Incident) at the same time as she was carrying on negotiations with Germany for an alliance. Germany and Russia signed a nonaggression pact on August 23. After suddenly halting the hostilities at Nomohan on September 16, the Soviet Union reached agreement with Nazi Germany on September 28 to divide Poland between them. The alliance of their would-be friend with their enemy made fools of Japanese diplomats. The broader meaning of these events, however, was that the prevailing world order was breaking up and that the revolutionary enemies of the status quo were everywhere victorious. Consequently, despite the shock of the Russo-German rapprochement, prospects for realizing the "new order in East Asia" were brighter than ever. Since full and complete achievement of all their desires seemed within their grasp, the Japanese had less inclination than ever to compromise with the Chinese, either with Wang or with Chiang.

These changes in the world situation were reflected in a governmental reorganization in Japan; the Hiranuma cabinet was replaced by one led by General Abe, and a widespread transfer of personnel took place in the military. Whether these shifts represent, except temporally, a step toward Pearl Harbor is a moot question. They did, however, affect the future of the Wang movement profoundly. The "China clique" in the central military bureaucracy, the leading figure of which was Itagaki, was removed wholesale from its position of power. But in typically Japanese fashion its members were not cashiered, retired, or sent to more military, less political posts; rather an entirely new organ, the Shina hakengun sōshirebu, the "China Expeditionary Army Supreme Headquarters," usually called the Sōgun, was established on September 12 in Nanking to be their domain. They continued semi-independently of Tokyo to prosecute their various *wahei kōsaku*, political schemes for tricking the Chinese into surrender, chief among which remained the Wang *kōsaku*. General Nishio Toshizō, former inspector-general for military training, became commander-in-chief; Itagaki as chief of staff held the real power.[59] Their followers — Imai Takeo and Horiba Kazuo, among others — soon followed them to Nanking. The meaning of the establishment of the Sōgun for the Wang group was that they no longer had supporters in Tokyo.

Wang and his advisers were trying to interpret the significance for their cause of the events in Europe and in Japan. Wang's own immediate reaction to the outbreak of the war was to see it from his anti-Communist bias. In a signed article in his Shanghai newspaper, *Chung-hua jih-pao,* he called for peace, blamed Germany for the war because of her nonaggression treaty with the Soviet Union, and suggested a new alliance of European and East Asian powers — Japan and Italy linked with Great Britain and France against Germany and the Soviet Union.[60]

In order to check their standing in Tokyo after the change of cabinet, Chou Fo-hai was sent to Japan on October 1 to "congratulate" the new cabinet and to carry letters from Wang to the members of the Hiranuma cabinet, all of whom had assured him in June of their personal support. The Japanese dignitaries whom Chou saw were instructed to reassure him of Japanese support and to urge the swift formation of a central government by gaining the support of Chungking, Wu P'ei-fu, and the existing governments.[61] It was a fairy-tale wish to imagine that Wang could do anything of the sort without some very tangible promises from the Japanese.

Consequently, Kagesa, probably in consultation with Wang, felt it necessary to procure some detailed account of Japanese terms; he pressed his government, therefore, to open negotiations with the Wang group for an informal agreement (*naiyaku*) which would be the basis of a permanent peace between China and Japan. He thought that Wang's ability to form a government would be greatly enhanced if Japan would promise, even in the indefinite future, to withdraw her troops from China, a promise which in Kagesa's mind lay behind Konoye's statement in the form of the *kiroku*.[62] Kagesa was aware of the drift of events, and he knew that the longer the delay in gaining a firm commitment, the more difficult it would be to acquire one.

Kagesa's demand for detailed negotiations was bitterly opposed by some, especially Horiba, who claimed that it was better to let the Chinese continue to believe that Japanese policy would be based on the generalities of the Konoye statement. To go into detail, Horiba maintained, would only cause dissension and allow Japan, the stronger party, to be manipulated by China, the weaker party.[63] Horiba's point of view was that it was in Japan's interest — and in the interest of peace in the long run — to maintain Wang and his group in a state of readiness, to be utilized as the changing situation seemed to warrant, while not making any specific commitments to Wang or constraining Japan's freedom of action.

Because the launching of the peace movement had been based on divergent purposes, Horiba was quite correct in feeling that detailed negotiations which would make this divergence explicit might well torpedo the Wang movement.

From Wang's point of view the fundamental purpose of the peace movement was to demonstrate, through negotiations with Japan, that Chiang Kai-shek was mistaken in embracing the Communists and rejecting peace negotiations with Japan, and that Japan was in fact willing to make a peace consistent with Chinese nationalism. Peace negotiations between Wang and Japan would be a "model" of Sino-Japanese cooperation; the terms arrived at would have to prove to Chiang and Chungking that an honorable peace was possible.

From the Japanese point of view the purpose of dealing with Wang, as well as with the many others with whom they attempted to intrigue, was to gain verification from the Chinese of the legitimacy of Japanese rule in China. *Bunchi gassaku* meant just that. The intended effect of negotiations with a powerless client on Chungking was to provide Chungking with a formula for surrender. Therefore, they should present their client negotiator with a complete list of Japanese demands upon China.[64]

If Japan were successful in conquering China, then Wang's prior arrangements might be the best of a bad bargain for China. If, however, the Japanese forced Wang to accede to their list and then were unable to gain Chungking's acquiescence, they would have to negotiate, offering better terms, directly with Chungking, thus making Wang appear both a traitor and a fool.

In accordance with Kagesa's request the many echelons and bureaus of the Japanese military bureaucracy began to grind out a draft to guide him in negotiating a model peace treaty. Horiba, from his vantage point at the war guidance office, warned Kagesa in September that it would be treason for Wang to agree to the developing draft.[65] The document was given its final form by the Kōain, "China Affairs Board," which, being a committee drawn from the various branches of the military and civil government, was well suited to compiling a list. Horiba brought it in person to Kagesa in Shanghai about the end of October.

The next question was what Kagesa was to do with this draft. According to Horiba, he told Kagesa that the draft was simply for his information; Kagesa was not to go into details with the Chinese but presumably compose with them another homily on neighborly friendship, anti-communism, economic cooperation, and so on. Horiba's statement does not make much sense. It does not explain why so much trouble had been expended on compiling the draft. It must have been that the Tokyo authorities wanted Wang's group to endorse the detailed Japanese demands. The Wang-Ume kikan negotiations were to begin on November 1, and another meeting of Wang with the heads of the existing governments was scheduled at Ch'ingtao for November 8. This meeting would resolve the final questions involving the Central Political Conference and the formation of the new government. Therefore, the Kōain must have expected Kagesa to get the Wang group to quickly rubber-stamp the Japanese demands.

Kagesa did nothing of the sort, however. On the contrary, when the Chinese comrades assembled together with the Ume kikan in the tatami-floored[66] conference room of the Wang mansion, Kagesa not only distributed copies of the entire text but he urged the Chinese to debate at length every point in the hope that they could achieve some basis for Sino-Japanese rapprochement. "In the future as we talk there will be quite a difference of opinions. However, in order to achieve our great objective of readjusting the relationship between China and Japan, we should go beyond considerations of present gain and loss. We should take up what we should take up and discard what we should discard, trusting each other frankly and proceeding in our discussion[67] . . . The Japanese side also feels deeply that there are points to be revised . . . Therefore, your side should not take a defensive posture but freely and voluntarily make proposals for revisions."[68]

Kagesa, according to the devoted Inukai, saw the negotiations as not really Sino-Japanese but rather as between Japan and Japan.[69] He hoped that by putting meaning into these negotiations, which were not intended to have meaning, his own government could be won to commit itself more fully to Wang. He hoped that the threat of delaying the new government so eagerly awaited by Japanese military planners might persuade them to grant some concessions.

Kagesa was like Wang in many ways; perhaps that is why the two men got along so well. Like Wang, he had a penchant for sacrifice and glory. "Once the negotiations are over, we all will be transferred, demoted, or retired. Therefore for the one memory of our life, why do we not pour out our noble ideals and leave this record to future generations?" he declared.[70] Kagesa could not have acted completely alone; he had the support of Itagaki and of the Sōgun, who had hitched their star to the Wang kōsaku.[71] Nevertheless, Kagesa's support of Wang's demands was an act of personal courage. Was he motivated, as he and his friends say, by unalloyed altruism, or did he wish, as Kao says, to be a "second Doihara"? Nashimoto Yūhei, civilian adviser attached to the Ume kikan, inclines to the second view: "General Kagesa was a man of intelligence and with good common sense. This was rare for a soldier. But he could not suppress his desire for promotion and glory. This was the pernicious army tradition. He was deeply conscious that the establishment of the basic treaty [between Japan and the Wang regime] would be his highest achievement, and therefore he promoted the conclusion of the basic treaty."[72]

From the fact that it was a codification it follows that there was nothing really new in the Japanese draft. It followed the lines of the *Nisshi shin kankei chōsei hōshin* of the preceding November. Itagaki had informed Wang of Japan's territorial desires in June, but Wang had ignored them. The Kōain draft, like the *hōshin*, the *kiroku*, and Konoye's (third) statement, was organized around the principles of neighborly friendship, anticommunism, and economic cooperation. Under these categories, it provided for complete political and economic peonage. Neighborly friendship meant the dispatch of "advisers" to the new government, no independent dealings with third powers, and suppression of anti-Japanese propaganda. Joint defense against communism, as before, was the wedge excusing Japanese stationing of troops: a "necessary number" in north China and Mongolia. Although Japanese troops, other than those for defense against communism, were to be "promptly withdrawn in accordance with developments in the general or local situation, those at present stationed in north China and along the lower reaches of the Yangtze River shall be stationed . . . until peace and order are definitely restored." North China and Mongolia were to be virtually autonomous on the basis of the existing Japanese occupation; Hainan Island was to be a Japanese naval base. Furthermore, Japan reserved "the general right to demand and supervise railways, airports, postal services, principal harbors and waterways in areas where Japanese troops are stationed."

In those areas where Japanese troops were to be stationed, that is, almost everywhere, there were to be a "minimum number" of Chinese troops and police. These Chinese forces would be armed, "advised," and "instructed" by the Japanese. Under the rubric of "economic cooperation" the original Jūkōdō provision to allow Japan limited preference in exploitation of north China natural resources was expanded to give Japan the right to direct all economic activity in China. Customs duties were to be adjusted for Japanese benefit; a separate puppet regime was to be established in Shanghai. The new government would, moreover, confirm all the various concessions that had been conceded by the existing client governments.[73]

Wang himself was not present at the *naiyaku* negotiations. When his comrades brought him the draft, he took the Japanese terms very hard. The Japanese, he said, had the power to conquer China easily. Before they accomplished that, they wanted him to sign a contract selling out his motherland. This he felt he could not do.[74]

The peace movement had succeeded in obtaining a full and detailed account of Japanese ambitions in China, a task in which a generation of Chinese negotiators had failed. No compromise between Japanese imperialism and Chinese nationalism was possible. Was it not time now to beat a retreat? This was the counsel of Kao Tsung-wu. Kao advised Wang that he had three choices: leave Shanghai and expose Japanese demands in detail; call in Kagesa and tear the draft up in front of him, telling him that there was no possibility of further talk, that he, Wang, was wrong and Chiang was right; or stay in Shanghai, be polite to the Japanese but simply refuse to conduct further negotiations.[75]

Kao did not trust to words alone to defeat what he considered a Japanese plot. He had obtained the means to torpedo Wang's scheme if, contrary to Kao's constant advice, he proceeded along a course which, as Kao saw it, could only lead to treason. Wang had asked Kao's interpretation of the Japanese draft as he had that of the other comrades. Kao's opinion was especially significant, since he had conducted negotiations with Japan for the past decade. In fact, Kao Tsung-wu was the link between the peace movement and the previous policy of the legitimate Chinese government.

The Japanese usually collected the documents carefully after each day's negotiation. On this first day, however, Kao had been able to prevail upon Wang to allow him to study the draft overnight. That evening in their home in the French Concession, Mrs. Kao photographed the draft of Japanese demands. If Wang accepted these demands, Kao would make them known to the world. Kao's hope and constant endeavor was that Wang himself would repudiate them.[76]

At this juncture Wang and the other comrades were not ready to give up. As Wang had said, the Japanese were about to conquer China. Would it not be cowardly for him to quail in facing them now? The negotiations went on still with the expectation that a new Nanking regime would shortly follow. Since, T'ao said, the establishment of the central government would advance the cause of peace, the Chinese and Japanese comrades must be content to make the revisions in the draft which were possible in present circumstances and go on with extablishing the government "giving people the impression that we may revise certain things."[77] Although the Chinese were willing to continue the negotiations on this basis, Mei Ssu-p'ing made it crystal clear to the Japanese that they were agreeing only to negotiate on the basis of Konoye's third statement, Wang's conversations with Japanese leaders in June, and the "minimum demands for respecting Chinese sovereignty," all of which the Japanese, they believed, had accepted. By Konoye's third statement, Mei said, the Chinese side meant not only the statement as Konoye had issued it but also the Imperial Conference decision which had preceded it based as they believed on the promises of the Jūkōdō *kiroku*.[78] The Chinese negotiators under Chou Fo-hai's energetic leadership proceeded to do just as Mei had said: at enormous length they raked over the Kōain draft, protesting and discussing in detail every aspect of Japanese demands inconsistent with the *kiroku*. Kagesa was no less tireless. Every evening Inukai, as Kagesa's representative, would continue the discussions with Chou Fo-hai in an effort to smooth the next day's conference.[79]

Underneath all the detail of the *naiyaku* negotiations, the basic issue as always was the withdrawal question.[80] The Chinese made it clear that they realized that Japanese operational freedom could not be jeopardized *now*; what they wanted was again the promise that the Japanese would withdraw within two years *after* peace had been concluded. With that promise in hand they hoped to win Chungking's consent.

Naturally, in this discussion all the ambiguities of the Jūkōdō came home to roost. Who had promised what to whom? Kagesa told the Chinese that he would insert in the draft as his personal opinion the specification that Japanese withdrawal would be concluded within two years; actually Horiba, when he had brought Kagesa the draft, had told him that was his understanding too.[81] Mei Ssu-p'ing protested that Kagesa's personal opinion was inappropriate; the Japanese state had officially accepted the proviso in the Imperial Conference decision preceding Wang's emergence.

If Kagesa's personal responsibility did not offer much food for Chinese hopes, neither did Wang speak for anyone but himself in accepting the *kiroku* which called for recognition of

Manchukuo and the like. Could he reasonably expect the Japanese government to make any binding commitment to him personally, either at the time of the *kiroku* or at the time of the *naiyaku*? It surely could not be said that Wang's constituency had grown much in the meantime. Kagesa, although he must have been well aware of these points, could scarcely have thrown them in the face of the Chinese, since he personally had promoted Wang's emergence, although not, in truth, the plan to organize a government.

Whatever the exact blend of Kagesa's motives, there is no question that he made every effort to sell Tokyo on making concessions to Wang. A sample Ume kikan telegram put the case as follows: "Originally the purpose of the establishment of the new government was to form the basis for Chungking *kōsaku* in order to solve the Incident. Therefore if we are to have the [Wang side] Chinese accept what would not be accepted by Chungking, then this would be only a Japanese self-indulgence. If we are to make concessions in the future to Chungking, then it will be said that Chungking and Chiang Kai-shek were correct. This would result in complete defeat for Japan and the Wang Ching-wei side."[82]

No less intensely did the peace comrades labor to convince Chinese and foreign opinion that the negotiations were genuine, the prospects hopeful, and that although all details could not be revealed at present, Wang could be depended upon not to sign any agreement which would not be in China's interest. A constant theme was that the "reorganization" of the Kuomintang government and its "return to Nanking" was subsidiary to Wang's main concern, peace. If Japanese conditions did not permit Chinese sovereignty and independence, he would not form a regime; if Chiang Kai-shek wished to come out for peace, he would not form a regime, Peace, however, was China's greatest need and China should be prepared to pay some price for it.

Wang also dared to address the Japanese public directly in an effort to clear away the mists of misunderstanding between the two nations. In an article in the respected intellectual journal *Chūō kōron*, he explained the psychology of Chinese hostility toward Japan. "The greatest concern of the Chinese to-day is the fear that Japan might be going to overthrow China. Ag-

Wang and the Sōgun

Top: Wang Ching-wei flanked by General Nishio Toshizō, Commander-in-Chief of the Sōgun (left) and Lieutenant General Itagaki Seishirō, Chief-of-Staff of the Sōgun and former War Minister.

Bottom: Wang with Vice Admiral Oikawa Koshirō, Commander-in-Chief of the Japanese China Sea Fleet aboard the latter's flagship.

gression and communism each has its terrors, but the annihilation of China by Japan would be the more dreadful. The Chinese know very well that the Japanese are opposed to communism, but the Chinese have never been acquainted with the fact that the Japanese are opposed to aggression also. The Chinese also labor under the belief that Japan is a land-grabbing country... This being their preconceived idea, the Chinese jump to the conclusion that . . . 'construction of a new order in East Asia in a synonym for China's ruin.' "[83]

As might have been expected, the Tokyo authorities were not in the least influenced by the agony and care expended both by the Ume kikan and the Chinese comrades in the *naiyaku* negotiations. On November 13 the vice-minister of war ordered the Ume kikan to persuade the Chinese to accept the draft as submitted and to put aside for later discussion those elements upon which agreement could not be reached. Wang was slated to proceed without delay to the Ch'ingtao conference with Liang and Wang K'o-min, which would precede the establishment of the government.[84]

The attitude of Japanese officials in China and their client governments toward Wang's ambitions, never very favorable, worsened as the negotiations went on. In an absurd contretemps Wang's "special work" forces under the control of Ting and Li clashed with the soldiers of Liang Hung-chih's similar organ. Peace was only restored between the contending puppets by the intervention of the foreign-controlled Shanghai Municipal Police. The Restored Government agents feared that the inauguration of Wang's government would mean the loss of their jobs.[85] The Japanese military in north China, who had always felt that Wang's ambitions ran counter to their own, kept up a barrage of cables to Tokyo opposing concessions to Wang.[86] After the situation had been "explained" to them, many officials of the Provisional Government declined to serve in Wang's new government.[87] Rather than preparing to yield any sort of power to the new government, the Provisional Government moved to solidify its control. Anti-Kuomintang propaganda was expanded and Wang's agents were rigidly excluded from north China.

Following in the train of these discouraging events, on November 24 the Kōain finally replied formally to the "minimum demands" which Chou had submitted in June. The reply ruined every hope that the Japanese might allow the new regime any freedom to manage its own affairs or to deal with foreign powers.[88] Thus by the end of November Wang felt that he had come to the end of the path which had begun with the *kiroku*. The Japanese would yield nothing. The comrades let it be known to the Japanese that they were no longer willing, as T'ao had originally suggested, to form a government leaving many questions pending. Privately, despair reigned within the Chinese camp. A desperate proposal to send the fledgling "Anti-Communist National Salvation Army" to Canton to try to establish a territorial base was considered and rejected.[89]

Finally Wang felt that he could go on no longer. He called in Kagesa and told him that he desired to suspend the peace movement and retire to his residence in the French Concession. Kagesa's demeanor on this occasion again reinspired Wang's hope in Sino-Japanese cooperation and caused him to reverse his decision. While Wang told him his plans, Kagesa, weeping continually, wrote down every word in his diary. He promised to make immediate plans in consultation with the French authorities for Wang's proposed move. He offered to go immediately to Tokyo and ask Prince Konoye personally to intervene. Kagesa proved his sincerity by actually mobilizing the French police. At the meeting of the comrades that afternoon, T'ao's suggestion that Kagesa's tears were "fish tears" was most coldly received.[90] Kagesa was able to dissuade Wang from a decision to retire from politics because there still burned in Wang that other aspect of his passionate determination to save his country, namely, ambition, which, as when he attempted so long ago to assassinate the prince-regent, could never endure obscurity.[91] Wang's hopes for the future were also revived by the presence of Ch'en Kung-po who had finally left Hong Kong to join Wang. Ch'en continued to oppose the peace movement and peace government as he had from the beginning, but he could sit idle no longer while Wang was in need.[92]

As he had promised, Kagesa went to Tokyo in company with Imai Takeo.[93] Whether he saw Konoye is not known, but he did see War Minister Hata. He warned Hata that the talks were on the verge of collapse. Hata agreed to procure Kōain approval for certain revisions in the Japanese demands.

What the Japanese military bureaucrats did was exactly what they had done in the case of the Jūkōdō *kiroku*; they allowed the Chinese side to list their demands alongside the Japanese demands. Thus a document that both sides could "sign" would emerge and the conspiracy could continue. Since the *naiyaku* negotiations had lost their character of real negotiations, they proceeded swiftly during the month of December. Wang and Kagesa signed the resultant *Nisshi shin kankei chōsei yōkō* (Important points for adjusting Sino-Japanese relations) on December 31. The revised draft, had it ever been put into effect, would have represented a great victory for Wang. Although, like the *kiroku*, it still ensured that Japan would be the most influential power in China; nevertheless all the promises of the *kiroku* were put into writing and spelled out in detail: withdrawal after two years, troop stationing only under an anti-Communist agreement, limitation on advisers, Chinese ownership of the railroads.[94]

Always the Wang Ching-wei peace movement had depended on bringing China and Japan together by selling each on the nonexistent conciliatory spirit of the other. There were, by its very nature in the *yōkō*, elements that each side could not accept but which were the other's inalterable demands: China would not accept the stationing of Japanese troops or the recognition of Manchukuo; Japan could not agree to withdraw nor to permit the activities of third powers within China. If the *yōkō* was to serve its function of bringing the two sides together, Wang must advertise to Chungking and to the Chinese public those elements in the agreement favorable to the Chinese cause whereas the Japanese side must emphasize the elements favorable to itself. The *yōkō* represented, as Kagesa put it, a post-dated check which could only be cashed if the new government succeeded in "solving the Incident."[95]

In a joint conference between the War Ministry and the General Staff, on January 5, 1940, the Japanese military bureaucrats narrowed to practically nothing what they would give the new government even in the unlikely event of its success. According to their deliberations; they would ignore a secret understanding stating that "north China," wherein the Japanese could station troops would be limited to only the areas of Hopei, Shansi, south of the Great Wall, and Shantung. In the passage under "mutual anti-communism" which read "Japan shall station its army, as necessary, in the specified areas in Mongolia-Sinkiang and in north China," "specified areas" were to be decided as necessary by the Japanese without consultation with the Chinese side, that is, anywhere at Japanese pleasure. In the passage "Japan shall begin withdrawal of troops, except those agreed [for anti-Communist stationing], after the restoration of peace, and complete it within two years as peace is restored," "withdrawal after the restoration of peace" would be "executed based on the subjective view of the Empire," and "complete it within two years *as* peace is restored" was to be interpreted as "complete it within two years *after* peace was restored."[96]

This trick had been foreseen by the Chinese side in the *naiyaku* negotiations — if absolute order was required as a precondition for withdrawal, then the Japanese could always find some incident to claim that order had not been restored. The time for "return" of the railroads to Chinese management would be decided upon by the military, that is, put off indefinitely. The following day, January 6, the Kōain "endorsed" the yōkō and gave instructions to proceed to the next step toward the establishment of the new government, the Ch'ingtao conference. The Kōain declared at the same time that Japan would support this new government only if it were successful on its own.

The value of the yōkō as any sort of binding agreement was further depreciated by the fact that Kagesa was fundamentally an army bureaucrat. The Kōain, the War Ministry and the General Staff which had been involved in the decision to accept the amendments to the Japanese draft desired by the Chinese side, were composed of, or in the case of the Kōain dominated by, army bureaucrats. The officers of the field armies with whom Wang's regime would have to work were not consulted and continued to oppose any concessions to Wang whatsoever. Even the navy, supposedly the "liberal" branch of the Japanese military, opposed concessions to Wang. Rejecting Kagesa's claim that his Ume kikan represented the entire Japanese government, Naval Minister Yonai ordered Admiral Suga, hitherto attached to the Ume kikan, to conduct direct and private negotiations with the Wang clique to secure its acquiescence in the navy's desires in China, especially for a naval base in Hainan.

War Minister Hata telegraphed Kagesa that neither he nor any other army member of the Ume kikan was to be involved.[97] Ch'en Kung-po volunteered to conduct these negotiations with Suga. Ch'en probed to see what assistance the Japanese navy might be able to give the new regime but in the end had to acquiese to the navy's demands with regard to Hainan.[98]

Even though, based on the hollow yōkō, the real strength and prospects of Wang Ching-wei's peace movement were at as low an ebb as they had yet reached, during December the peace movement inspired its peak of public and international confidence. Partly this efflorescence was due to the darkening of the world situation for the allied powers, partly it was due to the energetic public relations campaign launched under Wang's auspices. Wang himself told a German correspondent that the inauguration date for his Kuomintang government, which would become the only legitimate government of China, had not been determined, "as the discussion of honorable and concrete peace terms, acceptable to both China and Japan, will take some time." These negotiations had been based on the Konoye statement and his own December 29 telegram. He expressed the hope that "the Chungking government will join my peace movement" and warned if it continued to refuse to discuss peace, only regional withdrawal of Japanese troops could be effected "as arranged last August with the Japanese supreme commander in South China."[99]

Wang's Shanghai newspaper, the Chung-hua jih-pao, vigorously asserted that Wang was taking an independent stand against the Japanese. The reasons for the delay of the negotiations were that Wang was demanding a peace treaty before he would establish his government; he was demanding return of the railroads, the customs service, and Chinese-owned factories; he was demanding partial withdrawal of Japanese troops upon the establishment of the regime and guarantees of eventual complete withdrawal.[100] Japan was unable to defeat China militarily and must cooperate with Wang or withdraw.[101] On December 10 a further Chung-hua jih-pao editorial declared that "the new China would not agree to support Japan in any future war in which Japan may be involved." The Japanese must be able to understand that it is impossible for them to attain military and economic control of China because of the United States and Great Britain, the editorial continued.[102]

China's political structure was, asserted the newspaper, a matter for Chinese to settle among themselves. "The central government cannot be reorganized by Japan, nor can the Chiang government be overthrown by Japan. To abandon the Chiang regime and redevelop the central government under the Kuomintang are matters concerning the Chinese and only Chinese may with determination and energy deal with the matter at their own initiative. What we hope from Japan is that Japan will respect Chinese determination and efforts and help the Chinese in what they want to attain rather than direct the Chinese in how to do it. Only through a central government formed with the determination and efforts of the Chinese and by the determination and efforts of the Chinese may peace be effected as a whole and automatically solve the problem of the Chungking government."[103]

In December Chou Fo-hai said, "The establishment of a new Central Government is not a question of time but a question of terms. If the terms are conducive to the salvation of China, we should proceed immediately. Otherwise, we should never attempt to do anything of the sort." He added more soberly: "What China can strive at is only to get back what she has lost; she has nothing to give in return. Therefore, even should the establishment of the central government not directly benefit China, it certainly cannot harm her in her prevailing condition."[104]

A logical next step for the comrades was to initiate diplomatic dealings with the foreign powers whose recognition and support would be so greatly needed by the new government. Chu Min-i, Wang Ching-wei's brother-in-law and director of the *Institute Technique Franco-Chinoise,* was chosen as the front man for these contacts.[105] Chu's activities were not welcomed by the Japanese. Consul General Tajiri entertained the notion of many of the Japanese associated with the Wang *kōsaku* that Wang and his group were not cooperating with the Japanese because it seemed temporarily necessary and expedient but rather because they shared the Japanese view of "Sino-Japanese cooperation" as synonymous with the Japanese imperial mission. Thus Tajiri told Chou Fo-hai with regard to Chu's efforts, "In your heart it seems that you hold Japan in the same position that you hold Great Britain and the United States. We can even suspect that you plan to establish diplomatic relations with Europeans and Americans and use them against us." He urged Chou to "grasp the true meaning of the great policy of Sino-Japanese cooperation."[106] Despite Tajiri's rebuke and ill-humored rumblings and denials by the newspapers connected with the Japanese North China Area Command with regard to the declarations of Wang's press, these vociferous signs of independence had their effect on foreign powers, on the government in Tokyo, on Chungking, and on the Chinese public.

As progress toward the establishment of the new government continued, Great Britain, still under Chamberlain, showed signs of wavering in her policy of opposition to Wang and support of Chungking. In mid-November there was a report in the *New Statesman* that Britain had proposed to exchange support for Wang's regime for recognition of British interests in south China.[107] A week or so later a British spokesman, according to the Japanese ambassador, gave an off-the-record interview, stating that Britain might deal with both Wang's and Chiang's regimes.[108] On December 4 Ambassador Shigemitsu cabled from London that the British government was observing the establishment of the Wang regime with great interest and would change her policy toward China if the Wang regime were to succeed. On the other hand, according to Shigemitsu, Ambassador Kerr had reported from Chungking that Chinese resolution was firm and that the Japanese situation in China was precarious.[109]

About this same time, Wang Ching-wei told the Japanese that the French ambassador, Henri Cosmé, had closely questioned Chu Min-i about Wang's intentions, whether Wang was going to head a central government including the Chungking government as well as the Provisional and Restored Governments. Wang asserted that Cosmé's recent trip to Chungking was motivated by the possibility of mediating in favor of the peace movement in consultation with the British. If the British and French ambassadors recommended Chiang's resignation, Chiang might not accept the advice, but the recommendation of the powers would cause upheavals in the Chungking government; Chiang would have to flee to the Communists in the Northwest. Thus, said Wang, forces in favor of the peace movement would come to power in Chungking.[110]

It is difficult to weigh these various reports accurately since the archival information is not yet available. Nevertheless, it seems fair to assume that Wang's appearance of having made a compromise peace with Japan caused Great Britain and France to consider swinging their support to him and thus pacifying the situation in the Far East.

In November and December rumor had it that Lung Yun would declare for Wang as soon as the new government was established.[111] Lung was reportedly opposed to Chiang's orders to transfer a portion of the Yunnan Provincial Army to Hunan in order to make room for several divisions of Chungking troops, who would have solidified Chiang's control of Yunnan.[112] These rumors may have been entirely manufactured by the Japanese, since it was their delight to purvey any sort of information or misinformation about dissension within the Chungking camp or conflict between the Communists and the Kuomintang. But judging from the history of Lung's relationship with Wang, he was watching the plans for the new government with interest. In any case, Chiang and Lung settled their differences for the moment. In the end of December Lung accepted an appointment as director of Chiang's newly established headquarters in Kunming.[113]

The Wang group was making intense efforts to contact the Chungking side directly, and even high councils in the Japanese government thought there was hope for peace. On December 9 Konoye told Harada that it was essential to deal with Wang Ching-wei as the only party in the negotiations. Whatever the appearance, Konoye was assured that the Wang group had close contact with Chungking. And despite the personal animosity that had developed between Wang Ching-wei and Chiang Kai-shek, there were, so Chou Fo-hai had informed him, many on the Chungking side who wanted to join Wang. However, he warned that if Japanese conditions were too harsh, then Chungking forces would naturally not participate. Konoye had, however, received reports that Itagaki was making progress in persuading the hard-line clique to accept some modification of the Japanese position.[114]

Hope for the success of the Wang kōsaku had also extended as far as the incumbent cabinet. In the middle of December the question of whether or not war should be declared came up again. Prime Minister Abe's view was that a declaration of war would simplify things. However, those who were supporting Wang Ching-wei resolutely opposed this plan because they still considered Wang Ching-wei as, in a sense, a plenipotentiary for the Chungking government and negotiations were going on between him and the Japanese. Even though relations between Wang and Chiang were bad, contact was still continuing between their followers.[115] A declaration of war would mean the end of the hope that peace could come through coalition of some or all of Chungking's forces. Moreover, it was difficult to declare war on a regime Japan had asserted did not exist.

Finally the public learned through press reports that the agreement for basic peace terms had been approved by the Kōain on January 6 and by the Five Ministers' Conference on January 8. Most Chinese leaders in Shanghai were convinced that the rumors that Wang's stubbornness had wrung widespread concessions from the Japanese, including an agreement to withdraw, were true, according to the *New York Times* correspondent.[116] The details according to a United Press dispatch from Tokyo were: Chinese recognition of Manchukuo; signing of an anti-Comintern alliance between Wang, Japan, and Manchukuo; the stationing of Japanese troops in north China and Inner Mongolia under the anti-Comintern agreement; joint development of Chinese economic resources; Japan's pledge to withdraw her troops from central and south China within two years after a peace agreement; and national ownership of the railways. We know that these provisions, although accurate, were contradicted by far-reaching Japanese demands and caveats which substantially nullified them. If these terms had been actually and sincerely offered, undoubtedly the majority of Chinese in public and private life would have favored accepting them.

The Wang movement had also grown in stature through two factors: the death of Wu P'ei-fu and the foundation of a military academy. On December 4 Wu P'ei-fu died of blood poisoning from an infected tooth. He had refused medical attention until it was too late. Some thought that the Japanese poisoned him; others thought, perhaps correctly, that Wu chose to die in order to escape from his difficult position between the Japanese and the Nationalists. Both the Chungking government and the

Japanese vied in fulsome eulogies; the one claiming that he held out to the end, the other, that he was devoted to Sino-Japanese cooperation. Both joined in praising his old-fashioned virtues. However, Wang's great rival for leadership was dead. The Japanese had no alternative now for leadership of an Incident-solving new central government.

Throughout Wang's entire political career, he had been frustrated in his political objectives because unlike Chiang and the warlords, he had no military power to back him up. Unfortunately, guns replaced votes in republican China. He determined, therefore, as he had told Kagesa aboard the *Hokkōmaru*, to build an armed force for his new government, not to engage in civil war but to endow his regime with strength, independence, and prestige. Consequently, he had organized in Shanghai a Military Affairs Council and a Central Military Officers' Training Academy. The training academy was inaugurated on December 9 under the leadership of General Yeh Peng, formerly a commander at Hankow who had been cashiered before the Incident at Japanese demand.

Wang Ching-wei himself made the opening address before about a thousand cadets, taking a gentle dig at Chiang Kai-shek and the Whampoa Military Academy by asserting, "The Central Military Academy is the foundation of a modern army in a modern state and must not allow itself to be utilized to maintain a personal dictatorship." This, like Wang's Kuomintang Congress of August, was a completely Chinese affair. The inauguration of the academy was the first occasion when Ch'en Kung-po publicly associated himself with the Wang movement.[117]

Chou Fo-hai, and assumedly Wang with him, believed that the only reason to establish a peace government was to bring Chungking to merge with it and to make peace with Japan. Chou envisioned two possibilities: either Chungking joined the peace movement and Chiang Kai-shek resigned, or Chiang Kai-shek decided to participate in the peace movement without resignation. The latter case could come about through either of two roads: either a third power or powers would mediate and urge Chiang to come to peace, or Chungking could demand a modification in peace terms, withdrawal of the Japanese army and cancellation of the "new central government."[118] While the peace government was in existence, it would constantly at-

The Inauguration of the Central Military Officers' Training Academy, Shanghai, December 9, 1939.

From left to right: Chu Min-i, Chou Fo-hai, Wang Ching-wei, and Ch'en Kung-po.

tempt mediation. "After the Chinese central government is set up, I will try to have contact and make compromises with Chungking. We must try every means to have harmony with the Chungking government in order to unify the country and to realize peace. I will be responsible for the duty of negotiating with Japan. There is no need to ask Chiang Kai-shek to step down. But Chiang must decide himself that he has the determination to have peace. Otherwise all my efforts will be fruitless. Therefore the future of peace is not in our hands but in Chungking's hands. Chungking is the one place responsible for all peace movements."[119]

Wang had asked himself the question that we must ask: in the light of the shallowness of Japanese promises, would not the foundation of a new regime hinder rather than help with Chungking? Wang felt, as he told the Gaimushō's Sado Kadomatsu, that as Sun Yat-sen's Provisional Government in Canton had facilitated peace between north and south, so might his regime bring about peace.[120] Wang emphasized, however, that his movement could only play an effective mediatory role if Japan coordinated her approaches to Chungking with him; otherwise, Chungking would be able to play one against the other.[121] As Wang may have suspected, the Japanese were already bypassing Wang and opening up new direct routes, so they hoped, to Chungking.

The success of the conspiracy between Wang and Kagesa to launch a peace government with the appearance of Japanese cooperation depended on the content of the yōkō remaining secret. The Ume kikan urged in a telegram of December 22 that all care be exercised to prevent revelation of its content, especially in response to questions in the Diet.[122]

The problem of security was much more complex on the Chinese side. Chungking's confidence could not be won without free unhindered contact between Wang's agents and Chungking. The Japanese could never really bring themselves to accept this direct contact; they constantly suspected Chou Fo-hai, who was in charge of this work, of betraying them.[123] At the same time that Chungking was sparing no effort to infiltrate Wang's group and destroy him,[124] there was a deep split among Wang's comrades. At least three could not stomach signing the yōkō, acquiescing in Japanese imperial designs, and proceeding with the plans for government establishment.

Thus Japanese suspicions of the "loyalty" of Wang's comrades were not without basis. Kao Tsung-wu was most suspect. He was a former agent of Chiang Kai-shek; he had for a long time urged upon both Chinese and Japanese comrades his view that Wang's accepting Japanese demands and forming a government would contribute nothing to the solution of the Incident. Despite this difference of views, his personal relations with his comrades continued good, and Chou and Wang protected him from those who desired to allay their suspicions by disposing of him.[125] T'ao Hsi-sheng, unlike Kao, continued to participate in the *naiyaku* negotiations and made known his opposition neither to Wang nor to the Japanese. He came under suspicion partly because he had not been included in Chungking's arrest order.[126] Ch'en Kung-po, whose only tie to the movement was pity for Wang, excited Japanese suspicion not only by his long wavering but also by his vigorous defense of Chinese rights.[127] All these men were bound to Wang by the deepest sense of loyalty. All three were personal friends; yet each, unbeknownst to the others, was planning to leave Wang if he should sign the *yōkō*. Because it was Kao who possessed the photographic copy of the original Japanese demands, it was his defection that proved decisive.

Kao had always said that he would work for peace only within certain limits. Before he had left Hong Kong to come to Shanghai, he had told Tu Yüeh-sheng, underworld lord and Kuomintang stalwart who had advised him against it, that he must join his comrades whose movement he had started, but when and if Wang became a puppet, he would return to Hong Kong.[128] Kao saw his mission after Hanoi as saving Wang Ching-wei; he exercised every faculty of persuasion on Wang and several times Wang seemed ready to accede, admitting that Chiang Kai-shek had been right.[129] In November Kao's mentor, the aged politician Huang Chün, visited Kao in Shanghai and also met with Wang. Wang told Huang he would rather die than become a puppet.[130] When Wang signed the *yōkō*, however, it seemed to Kao that Wang had no intention of turning back; he had crossed the line of treason. Therefore, Kao felt that he could delay no longer. In late December he asked Huang Chün and Tu Yüeh-sheng to act as his emissaries to Chiang; he had a copy of the Japanese demands which Wang was about to accept; they were treasonous; he would give Chiang the draft; he asked nothing in return nor set any conditions, but he prayed that Chiang would persuade Wang himself to reveal the conditions. His objective was not to betray Wang but to frustrate Japanese intentions.[131] Chiang's reply was simply "come to Hong Kong."[132]

Meanwhile, as the comrades met just before the signing of the *yōkō*, Wang made a curious statement which seemed like an oblique threat: the differences between the comrades might result in bloodshed and murder. T'ao feared Ting and Li were about to take action. Shortly thereafter, Ch'en slipped away to Hong Kong intending to give up the peace movement.[133] The anxious T'ao avoided signing the *yōkō* by reporting in sick.[134]

On New Year's Day, both Kao and T'ao separately paid the traditional call to extend season's greeting to Chou Fo-hai. Their conversations obliquely conveyed a certain grief at parting from their friend and comrade.[135] T'ao also visited Mr. and Mrs. Wang. Ch'en Pi-chün, with her characteristic directness, pressed him to sign the *yōkō*, but Wang, solicitous for T'ao's indisposition, suggested that he defer it.[136] The next day Kao visited T'ao, still confined to his bed. T'ao warned Kao of the danger he was in. Kao proposed that they flee together and they discussed the details of their flight.[137] Kao, however, told T'ao nothing of the fatal document he possessed. Kao felt that if T'ao could be persuaded to join him, the blow to Japanese schemes would be the greater.[138] It was on January 4, 1940, that they made good their escape.

When Kao arrived in Hong Kong, he gave the draft of Japanese demands to Tu and Huang to convey to Chiang, as he had promised. Intending to ask Ch'en Kung-po to join them in publicly breaking with the peace movement, he invited Ch'en to meet with him and T'ao Hsi-sheng at the home of a mutual friend. "Tsung-wu," said Ch'en, "I expected that you would leave, but, Hsi-sheng, your departure is completely unexpected. Now I must go back to help Mr. Wang."[139] And so he did, sacrificing both his life and his reputation for his friend.

From Hong Kong, Kao and T'ao cabled an explanation of their actions to Wang Ching-wei: "We too have believed in peace for the past three years. We withdraw from your movement only because of the unacceptability of Japanese terms and the inadvisability of organizing a government. If these terms and that government can be called the basis of peace and national reconstruction, then we are indeed disheartened. For the sake of China you should immediately abandon the movement. The success of your government could only mean the destruction of China. . . . Please do not interpret our love for you as enmity. We left without taking leave because we were overcome by your signing the Japanese treaty. We had no alternative."[140] Kao did not inform Wang that he had the text of the *naiyaku* draft, and apparently Wang did not suspect it.

Wang told Sado Kadomatsu that Kao and T'ao had written him that there was no hope of solving the situation in the Far East at the present time; they would not hinder the establishment of the "new central government" by revealing Wang's plans to Chungking but would stay in Hong Kong and observe the situation.[141] In response to Kao's and T'ao's telegram, Wang sent an emissary urging them to return and discuss the points that they had raised.[142] Wang told Sado that he, like the other comrades, was sympathetic to the point of view of Kao and T'ao. He realized that the present peace conditions were inadequate, but nevertheless, he was determined to proceed. He foresaw difficulties with the allocation of posts to the members of the existing regimes at the Ch'ingtao Conference, but his major concern was the work toward Chungking. Those who favored peace in their hearts were skeptical that the Japanese would offer viable conditions of peace. Comrades in Chungking were watching the situation, and if it improved, then they would come out. But unless they did come out, peace could not be realized. Thus there was a vicious circle that could only be broken by convincing them that there were channels of peace between China and Japan and thus an alternative to continued resistance.

In January, concern about whether or not Japan would recognize his new government loomed larger and larger in Wang's mind. He proposed that if Kawagoe had not resigned, then Japan need take no other step to indicate recognition of Wang's government as the legitimate Chinese government than to return Kawagoe to Nanking.[143] Unfortunately, this was not a possibility, since Kawagoe had formally retired in December 1938 "on account of ill health." At that time it had been stated that a new ambassador would be appointed when a new government of China had emerged.[144] Wang stated that the recognition of the other powers depended upon Japan's recognition. The Italian ambassador, with whom he had met several times, had declared that Italy would follow suit. Italy had not dispatched her ambassador to Chungking but was awaiting the formation of the new government. It was assumed that Germany would follow Italy's lead. Recognition by the United States, Great Britain, and France might be difficult, but if Germany, Italy, and Japan recognized the new government, then the Western powers would undoubtedly accord some sort of de facto recognition as they had in the case of Franco's Spain.[145]

The Japanese must have given Wang the premonition that Japanese formal recognition would not be easily acquired, for on January 20 he declared to Japanese reporters that formal recognition of his new government by Japan would not be necessary because the government of China would not be changed. Japan, he said, recognized the Kuomintang government of Sun Yat-sen and his government would be that government. "We are not establishing a new nation," he said, "we are restoring the nation."[146] Wang had previously professed indifference concerning the question of whether foreign powers recognized the new government or not: the republican government founded in 1911 was not recognized for two years; the Kuomintang government founded in Canton in 1925 had waited a similar period.[147] Without recognition by the powers, however, the new government would have neither that essential attribute of sovereignty, free intercourse with foreign nations, nor the essential resource for maintaining that sovereignty; foreign interests to balance against the overweening Japanese interest.

Accordingly, on the afternoon of January 19 Chu Min-i visited the American ambassador, Nelson Johnson, to seek support from the United States. He had previously visited the British and French ambassadors. The constantly reiterated policy of the United States toward the prospective Wang regime was that it was primarily set up to serve the interests of Japan, would serve to deprive third powers of their rights in China, and would make adjustment of Japanese-American relations more difficult.[148] Therefore, Chu had little chance for success. He tried to convince Johnson of Wang Ching-wei's patriotism and asked

Johnson to make representations to his own government and to Chiang Kai-shek. He tried to sell Johnson on the notion that Wang was serving United States' interests in opposing communism and the Soviet Union, while Chiang Kai-shek was embracing the same. Johnson, as could be expected, coldly rejected Chu's advice.[149] The Wang group wished to use the foreign powers to help them attain independence; but the powers, since they were convinced with good reason that Wang had no freedom, felt that Wang was a tool being used by the Japanese to attempt to manipulate them, as indeed was Japan's intention but not Wang's.

The only cheering note from abroad was a congratulatory telegram to Wang on January 16 from Ciano, the Italian foreign minister, with whom Wang had a long relationship. Wang responded with a grateful reply to the one nation that had steadfastly supported him. This exchange, however, was looked upon by the Japanese with their usual jealousy, and they increased their surveillance of Wang.[150]

Just before the Ch'ingtao Conference, Wang made a final appeal to Chiang Kai-shek to join him in making peace with Japan.[151] He asserted that he and his comrades had held "many frank and open-minded discussions with Japanese leaders" and "both sides, having in mind the future prosperity of East Asia, have been willing to make concessions and so have arrived at a mutual understanding. The foundations of peace have been laid, and China will secure terms which not only will not lead to national extinction but will also preserve her independence and freedom and enable the reconstruction of the nation on the basis of the *San-min chu-i* (Three People's Principles) to be completed." He did not claim that the Japanese had promised withdrawal but he hinted at the possibility: "In regard to the evacuation of the Japanese troops, the Chinese people hope that this can be achieved as early as possible. Nor does Japan wish to have to retain troops outside her own territory longer than can be helped. If you, however, continue to advocate armed resistance, how can evacuation be talked about?"

He continued: "Should you persist in your opposition, I may be compelled to proceed myself with all my efforts to establish the foundation of peace . . . If, however, you, putting the fate of the nation and the livelihood of the people before all other considerations, would make a bold decision to end a futile war and to negotiate an honorable peace with Japan on the basis of the Konoye Declaration, then it will be possible for myself and all the comrades to join with you in a united endeavor to secure the early and concrete realization of a nationwide peace."

Wang's policy was one of make-believe. Wang's assertion that the Japanese were willing to offer conciliatory terms was an unvarnished lie. Wang deeply believed that it would be far better for China to make terms with the Japanese and suppress the Communists. Nevertheless, lying to others "for their own good" is an enormously arrogant act. In this case, if Chiang had believed Wang's assertions of Japan's generous terms and had sued for peace, baring China to its implacable enemy, Wang would have been responsible for betraying his country as surely as if he had opened the gates.

On January 21 Wang and his remaining cadres flew to Ch'ingtao. The long-awaited, oft-delayed Ch'ingtao Conference, foreseen as a major step toward China's salvation, was about to take place. No care or expense had been spared to perfect every detail; the scene of the conference was the palatial former residence of the German viceroy. The press had been assembled to memorialize every detail of this historic occasion. Liang, Wang K'o-min, and their attendants and "advisers" arrived on January 22. On that day, two days before the conference was formally opened, the Kōain text of Japanese demands appeared in the Hong Kong *Ta kung pao* under the names of Kao and T'ao.[152] Chiang had rejected Kao's request to persuade Wang himself to release it. In a moment carefully timed to create the greatest embarrassment to Wang, Chungking had arranged for its publication.[153]

The wind slipped out of the sails of the great theatrical which had been prepared. The Japanese government at first decided to deny that the text exposed by Kao and T'ao was authentic.[154] They branded it "Chinese propaganda";[155] Chou Fo-hai declared that it was "only a private draft prepared by a group of Japanese and not based upon the wishes of the Japanese government."[156] He claimed that the document which had been revealed differed greatly from that which had been agreed upon by the Chinese and Japanese negotiators. (Indeed, it differed, but not in fundamentals.)

Chungking, which had not been cheered by a triumph for a long time, made the best of its coup. Kao's revelation not only discredited Wang but also, by revealing the full extent of Japanese aims, encouraged both Chinese citizens and China's foreign friends to rally behing Chiang. The propaganda mills lost no time in spelling out the message for Chinese and foreign audiences. Wang wished to make China a "second Manchukuo," himself a "second Henry Pu-i," declared the Chungking Ta kung pao. Chiang himself issued statements for consumption at home and abroad declaring that Japanese imperialism was insatiable, the only possible policy continued resistance.[157]

Many petitions were circulated to pardon Kao and T'ao and restore them to office.[158] Kao, in the agony of spirit that he had undergone, vowed when he left Shanghai never again to engage in politics and never again to deal with the Japanese.[159] Barely thirty, Kao abandoned his political career for quiet exile in the United States. Despite the disappointment of seeing the peace movement which he had started fail, he had the consolation of having his good name with Chiang and his countrymen restored. While he was in Hong Kong before he left for exile in March, Chiang sent him a letter written in his own hand calling Kao the "strong man of eastern Chekiang." Chiang and Kao were both from that area, famous for men of strong character. Chiang was praising in a literary way Kao's courage.[160] T'ao spent several years in Hong Kong, then returned to Chungking where he rose to some eminence as a political theorist and ghost writer for Chiang.

The powers reacted swiftly and firmly to the revelation of the terms to which Wang had acceded. On January 24 Prime Minister Neville Chamberlain declared in the House of Commons that "the only government in China recognized by the British Government is the National Government of China, of which General Chiang Kai-shek is the president of the Executive Yuan."[161] Britain would have nothing to do with Wang's planned regime. On January 30 an official of the French Foreign Ministry stated that France would adopt the same policy of nonrecognition that it had adopted toward the existing Nanking and Peking puppet administrations.[162]

Chinese who had supported Wang or who had at least watched the development of his movement with hope were

The Ch'ingtao Conference

From left to right: Wen Tsung-yao, chairman of the Legislative Yuan of the Reformed Government; General Ch'i Hsieh-yüan, minister of public security of the Provisional Government; Liang Hung-chih, chairman of the Executive Yuan of the Reformed Government; Chu Shen, the minister of justice of the Provisional Government; and Wang Ching-wei.

deeply disappointed. Fifteen educational leaders in Shanghai issued a telegram announcing their departure from the peace movement.[163] A Japanese intelligence report from occupied Nanking reported that prior eager anticipation of the new regime had been replaced by the feeling that the new government could be little different from the old Restored Government.[164]

Chou Fo-hai reacted to the revelation by breaking into tears of anger and disappointment. He vowed to kill Kao.[165] Wang, however, remained visibly unruffled. His comrades, and even Wang K'o-min, urged him to press for the release of the yōkō in order to demonstrate the concessions that Japan had made since the original draft released by Kao. No, said Wang, he would abide by his prior agreement and announce if after the Central Political Conference in consultation with the Japanese.[166] Imai describes Wang's demeanor at the Ch'ingtao Conference as epitomizing the gentleman and statesman. As Wang stood coatless in the winter wind, his elegant dress and handsome face captured the hearts of the crowd.[167]

Despite all that had happened, the conference went on. At the opening banquet, Wang and Itagaki competed for the palm of eloquence in their discourses upon "Far Eastern morality" and "Sino-Japanese cooperation." The decisions previously reached were endorsed. The North China Provisional Government would become the North China Political Administrative Committee and continue to handle affairs in north China. The Restored Government was to be dissolved and its employees absorbed by the new government. Liang Hung-chih was to be president of the Control Yuan, Wen Tsung-yao was to be president of the Judicial Yuan, and Ch'en Chün was to be the minister of the interior. A "preparatory committee for returning to the capital" was established under the chairmanship of Chu Min-i.[168] The "return" was scheduled for March 26.[169]

A representative from the "Mongolian Confederated Autonomous Government" managed to weasel in and out before the conference opened, gaining Chou Fo-hai's signature on a document guaranteeing "Mongolian Autonomy."[170]

The most sagacious reaction to Wang Ching-wei's peace movement now that Kao had revealed elements of its secret history came from an unexpected quarter, the mouth of Saito Takao, a seventy-one year old member of the Japanese Diet who addressed that assembly on February 2.[171] Saito reviewed the course of events since Marco Polo Bridge and the sad failure of Japanese statesmen to cope with them. He asked some hard questions. Through miscalculations on both sides, said Saito, a so-called incident had broken out in China which was really the greatest war in Japanese history. Japan, at a massive cost in blood and gold had come to rule an area in China two and a half times larger than Japan itself. There was no question who would win the war; Japanese and Chinese statesmen must resolve the questions between the nations and lay the foundations of a lasting peace. What were to be the terms for peace?

Japan had declared that her "immutable policy" was based on the Konoye statement. Wang Chiang-wei had emerged in response to this statement and had been sacrificing himself to realize the conciliatory peace that had been promised — as Wang saw it, an abandonment by Japan of her imperial ambitions, including withdrawal of Japanese troops from all occupied areas except Inner Mongolia. Saito felt that Wang had correctly interpreted what Konoye had promised. If Japan did not fulfill her promises, she would be betraying Wang. On the other hand, Saito said, Japanese politicians were talking about a "new order in East Asia." He understood the application of the term "new order" in Europe, where "have-not" nations were supplanting "have" nations, but he could not see its applicability to East Asia. Did Japanese statesmen consider it consistent with Konoye's statement?

Now a new government was about to emerge in China. Was this government to have armed forces? Without armed forces it could scarcely administer the vast area committed to its charge. Did Japan intend to recognize this government? What would be its relation to Chungking? How could establishing this government make any contribution to solving the Incident? Saito was constantly interrupted in the course of his speech. Finally the tumult erupted into a general melee. Whether the legislators were demonstrating for or against Saito's sentiments, or were divided, is not clear. In any case, the military was able to apply sufficient pressure to have Saito expelled from the assembly several days later. He had dared to speak the truth.

What Saito alone perceived was that the variously motivated attempts of Konoye and the China clique to buy a cheap peace through political maneuvers had only served to muddy the whole question of war aims and peace terms. Japan was neither willing to pay the price for peace nor for victory. Chiang sought to preserve his nation. Wang Ching-wei was but a chip of the wave. He had tried to interpose himself between the two warring nations as a mediator, but since on neither side was there a desire for mediation, he could only be crushed between them.

Return to Nanking

8 Kao's revelation of the demands Japan had forced upon Wang convinced all observers who were unaware of the secret history of the *kiroku* that Wang was and had been a traitor, a puppet who danced to the Japanese tune. Wang's pretensions to an independent position — the sine qua non of mediation — had been destroyed.

Once again, as after Konoye's resignation and the failure of the statement, Wang had arrived at a juncture from which he could readily neither proceed nor retreat. Chou wrote in his diary at the end of February that previously the peace movement's prospects had been bright before Kao's action; now there was little hope. It was touch-and-go whether the movement could continue; if the new government could not be established in March, then the peace movement would be gradually dissolved.

Wang was in a dilemma, but so this time were the Japanese. Their objective was to "solve the Incident." Now, however, that Wang was exposed as a puppet, every step toward establishing and supporting a government under his leadership in the occupied territories would further calcify the situation. Peace, as Chou and Wang were the first to say, lay not in their hands but in the hands of Chiang Kai-shek. For Japan to set up and support a regime parallel and distinct from Chungking not only meant that seeking direct peace with Chungking would betray Wang Ching-wei, but also it meant that if Japan chose to open direct negotiations, the existence of the Wang Ching-wei regime would be yet another issue that had to be resolved before peace could be realized. Japanese war planning documents make it clear that the Japanese well realized that the establishment of a competing Kuomintang government under Wang's leadership would mean an abandonment of the hope for using Wang to bring Chiang to peace; it would mean a policy of "long protracted war" rather than the political solution which had been the premise of all peace *kōsaku*.[1]

If, despite the probability that setting up a rival government would make settlement with Chungking more rather than less difficult, the Japanese determined to go ahead with the plan, then Wang's regime could only be useful to them if they gave that regime every appearance of substance and support. They would have to keep strictly away from direct dealings with Chungking, making Chungking understand that the road to peace with Japan was through Wang. This would mean that Japan's freedom of action for good or for evil would be curtailed. Only then would either Chiang or the foreign powers have any interest in dealing with Wang, and by so doing, recognizing the legitimacy of the political situation established by Japanese arms. The dilemma in which the Japanese found themselves was completely of their own making, caused, as Saito had said, by the inconsistency between the "new order" and the promises made to Wang at the highest levels of the Japanese government.

The Japanese chose the worst of both worlds. They had not the courage to abandon the scheme to set up a "new central government" headed by Wang. The "central government" idea had a life of its own; Wang Ching-wei was too big a fish to let go; Japan had made promises to him; the China clique and others still entertained great hopes for the Wang *kōsaku*. On the other hand, the Japanese did not have the courage to grant him even the *appearance* and form of autonomy and support, much less truly cede to him the capacities he would need to mediate for peace as he had dreamed. The compromise solution that the Japanese chose was to give Wang just enough encouragement to keep him active, not a bit more. Thus it was thought that Japan would lose nothing if Wang failed, whereas any activity by Wang could not fail to harm Japan's enemies.

The method Japan used to keep Wang going was to apply rather bizarre logic to the half-understood conventions of international law. They could measure out and limit their commitment to Wang by distinguishing establishment of the regime from recognition of it by Japan, and when Wang pressed them on this, they were further able to distinguish dispatch of an ambassador "plenipotentiary" from recognition. Recognition itself could be by the back-door method of concluding a "basic treaty."

Because of the specious distinction between establishment and recognition, this chapter focuses on two crises: would the new government be established, and would Japan extend it diplomatic recognition? In each of these crises the same drama was played out. Japan conducted direct negotiations with Chungking while simultaneously proceeding with preparations to establish or recognize the government, using the threat of doing so in order to blackmail Chungking. Chungking employed in each case the same weapon by hinting that, as the deadline approached, they were about to return a favorable response — if only Japan would delay or cancel establishment or recognition.

Establishment and recognition are essentially a single problem, artificially separated. Wang early feared that Japan would string him along by letting him set up a "government" but deny to it recognition as she had her previous client governments in China. Chou told the Japanese in February that unless the Japanese agreed in advance to recognize their government, then the comrades would stop their preparations for its establishment.[2]

The plan would give the new government "face" in dealing with internal and external elements and would at the same time provide another means for supervision and guidance of the new regime. The ambassador could negotiate with the Wang government a formal peace treaty which would be signed when and if Japan chose to recognize the government. The Japanese tried to chisel just a little bit more; Chou heard they were going to send an ambassador but that he would not submit credentials.[3] This Chou rejected — no credentials, no government.[4] Finally on March 4, Kagesa told Chou that the Japanese would dispatch an ambassador who would submit his credentials to Wang.[5] This decision to send an ambassador without extending recognition, first proposed by a Gaimushō official in Shanghai on February 12, had not been reached without intense debate amidst the Japanese military bureaucratic structure.

As usual, it was not exactly clear what had been decided. Was the ambassador dispatched to Wang to be of greater or less stature than an ordinary ambassador? Those who wished to limit Japan's commitment to Wang said less; those who looked to the "establishment of the new central government" to "solve the Incident" felt more. A compromise was reached which each side could believe represented a triumph for its views.

General Abe Nobuyuki, the former prime minister, was prevailed upon to become an "ambassador plenipotentiary" to Nanking. Said Abe, "If I am just to be an envoy to congratulate the new government, then I will not accept the post."[6] He took his new mission very seriously: "I expect many criticisms of the results of my work in China, especially in view of the difficulties in the way of the smooth development of the new regime in the future. I may be shot during my duties in China and return in ashes like a soldier killed on the battlefront."[7] That such a ponderous and influential personage as Abe should become Japan's first ambassador not only meant that Wang had acquired an important new ally, but also it meant that those who believed that Japan should tie herself closely to the new government scheme had prevailed.

Abe's instructions, on the other hand, made it seem, contrary to his protestations, that his mission was decorative. He was instructed to obey the directions of the Kōain and the army rather than those of the Gaimushō, which in theory was responsible for directing diplomats. Abe was thus less rather than more than a conventional ambassador. Further limiting the appearance of Japanese commitment to Wang in the dispatch of Abe, his arrival in Nanking was delayed until April 23,[8] nearly a month after the government had been established. His departure had been scheduled for March 20, and then, when the Chinese could no longer reverse their course, was canceled.

The Japanese attitude toward recognition of Wang's regime by third powers was marked by the original contradictions in Japanese policy. Japan regarded third power recognition as tantamount to recognition on the part of the powers of the new order and attempted to pressure them into it. For example, on March 5 War Minister Hata declared that the Yangtze would not be reopened for navigation unless the powers showed favor to the new government.[9] But ever jealous of her assumed special relationship with China, Japan could not brook contact between Wang and the foreign powers. Contrary to her public statements, Japan actually *opposed* recognition of the new regime by third powers. In a cable prepared for dispatch on February 17, the Japanese ambassador in Rome was urged to intervene with the Italian and Spanish governments to prevent their recognition of Wang before they received prior approval from the Japanese; Japan's démarche was to be kept strictly secret. At the same time, Dōmei, the Japanese wire service, kept sending back reports predicting that Italy was about to recognize the new government immediately and Spain would follow suit a week later. The reasons for delaying recognition were given to the ambassador as the feeling of the army that recognition by foreigners would allow them to hinder military operations, and that recognition would stiffen Chungking's attitude.[10] The ambassador cabled on March 13 that Ciano acknowledged the "exclusive" status of Japan in China and promised that Italy would only extend recognition to the new government after consultation with the Japanese.[11]

The Japanese sought to escape from their dilemma with respect to Wang by a cautious compromise policy which only involved them in further complications and deceit. What about the dilemma of Wang and his group? Why did they choose to go on? As the possibility of being peace heroes seemed to dim, Wang and Chou came more and more to see themselves as peace martyrs. Even though, wrote Chou, he knew that the peace comrades would be murdered within a year of a settlement with Chungking, they would sacrifice everything, even the peace government, for such a settlement.[12] He told J. Leighton Stuart, still serving as an intermediary to Chiang from the viceroys of north China, what he told a succession of petty agents: Plans for the peace government were continuing, but the comrades would not stand in the way of direct Chungking–Tokyo conversations. He warned Chiang to beware of the Japanese but not to allow personal animosity toward Wang and the comrades to influence his decision for peace or war.[13]

Wang and Chou, however, were not stupid. They knew that they had been discredited, that they were hated and distrusted by all but the most rabid of the anti-Communists in Chungking, that the Japanese had no intention of giving them anything, and that a Nanking government had little chance of improving the prospects for peace. Despite their protestations to the contrary, Wang and Chou, unemployed politicians, deeply wanted to establish a government and to play the game of politics that they loved on the great stage. There is no other explanation for their persistence. Their price was not high and they were willing to settle for less; they accepted Japan's phoney compromise on recognition, and while they strove during February and March to gain concessions from the Japanese on the questions of announcement of the yōkō and the unhindered display of Sun Yat-sen's Kuomintang "blue-sky white-sun" flag, they accepted defeat on these issues too.

It had been Wang's understanding that before the convocation of the Central Political Conference, the Japanese and Chinese sides would announce the conditions of the yōkō which included a promise for eventual withdrawal of Japanese troops, limitations on troop stationing, Chinese management of the railroads. Even though these concessions were a "postdated check" to take effect only after the solution of the Incident, nevertheless, Japanese announcement of them would offer some justification for Wang's collaboration. On February 14 Kagesa told Wang that if the Chinese wished to make a statement, the Japanese would not deny it but neither would they confirm it. Kagesa said that if the Japanese government issued a statement affirming Wang's proposed declaration, then rightists and imperialists in the Japanese government would oppose the new government.[14]

Chou Fo-hai did not share Wang's enthusiasm for a declaration, joint or otherwise. He said: "I personally never advocated that we should discuss our plans openly. I feel that if the conditions were beneficial to the Chinese, then they would be harmful to the Japanese. If they were beneficial to the Japanese government, then they would be harmful to the Chinese. If the declaration is beneficial to the Chinese, then the Japanese people and government must oppose this declaration. If our declaration is favorable for the Japanese government, then the Chinese people must oppose our plan. And also, if we announce our plan, then in the future we may have difficulties in carrying them out. Our purpose is to carry out what we can do, not to make a lot of propaganda."[15]

For Chou the *primum bonum* was to keep playing the political game for its own sake. Wang had finally to confine himself to issuing on March 12, the birthday of Sun Yat-sen, with Japanese approval,[16] a statement in which he assured "the whole nation that the peace schemes do not go beyond the scope of Prince Konoye's Declaration nor contradict the basic principles laid down in that Declaration."[17] The one Japanese concession was to "respond" to Wang's scarcely credible declaration with a vague promise of "support" for the new government.

Actually, the question that was debated with the greatest acrimony between the Wang group and the Japanese was that of the least importance, namely, the flying of the national flag. In June Wang had agreed, although with the greatest reluctance, that the national flag could only be flown accompanied by a yellow triangular pennant bearing the slogan "Peace, anticommunism, reconstruction." Although Wang had swallowed all of the other Japanese demands, on this one he choked. The Italian ambassador told Chu Min-i that the pennant would discredit Wang's claim to be continuing the old Kuomintang government and make Italian recognition difficult.[18] Without a solution of this issue, the comrades were reluctant to continue. On February 10 Inukai expressed a very pessimistic view of the possibility of the Japanese government's changing its mind on this issue. That evening Kagesa held out to Chou the hope that a compromise might be reached after the establishment of the government. Chou did not want to wait. "If we cannot solve this national flag problem, I will be very disappointed. There would be no reason for me to participate in the government."[19]

On March 3 Wang agreed with Chou that without a resolution of the flag problem, as well as the recognition problem, they would not convoke the Central Political Conference, which was to initiate the new government.[20] But since on March 4 Kagesa had reported to Chou that Japan would yield on the recognition question to the extent of sending an ambassador who would submit his credentials, Chou told Wang on March 5 that they could not insist on Japanese concessions on the flag question because the peace comrades had agreed to the yellow pennant the previous June. Wang Ching-wei agreed.[21] On March 13 Kagesa and Inukai confirmed to Chou that for the moment the yellow pennant must remain. But they decided to make a further attempt when Wang arrived in Nanking for the Central Political Conference. At that time Wang could make a personal appeal to General Itagaki, the chief of staff of the Sōgun.[22] On March 17 he implored Itagaki to suspend the requirement of the triangular pennant in the main cities of the titular jurisdiction of the new government: Nanking, Shanghai, and Canton, or at the very least in the capital, Nanking.[23] Or, according to another account, his plea was to permit the yellow pennant to be flown on a separate pole next to the national flag.[24] Itagaki and his staff at the Sōgun supported Wang's request and relayed it to Tokyo, where it was rejected.[25] Wang then returned and begged Itagaki at least to let the flags be hung on separate poles at the gates of the government offices and to let the pennant be altogether eliminated when the "blue-sky white-sun" flag was hung inside the buildings. Itagaki acceded on his own authority.[26] In a rare demonstration of defiance, the comrades dared to fly the "blue-sky white-sun" flag without pennant throughout Nanking on the day of inauguration of the new government. Recriminations from the army followed, and Mei Ssu-p'ing was obliged to "apologize."[27]

All the talk about the flag was pointless when it came to occupied China outside Nanking. Local Japanese military officials were determined to ignore the new flag just as they planned to ignore the new government, regardless of any promises made to Wang. The north China authorities only agreed to fly the "blue-sky white-sun" flag on a few office buildings belonging to the Provisional Government. Elsewhere the old five-bar flag and the Japanese flag would be used.[28] In Hankow, however, the most the local authorities would permit was the hanging of the flag within the ceremonial halls on the day of the inauguration of the new government.[29]

On top of Wang's discouraging "foreign affairs" problems of dealing with the Japanese, he was faced with various problems within his own ranks, first among them the perennial problem of patronage. Because of the aura of failure and collaboration that had come to surround the Wang movement, the coin with which Wang and Chou were forced to buy supporters was promise of prestigious position. There were many who felt that their loyalty should be thus rewarded. Not only did the rivalries within the Wang group need to be reconciled, but also officials of the existing governments, especially of the Restored Government, which Wang's new government was to replace, had to have both their names and their rice bowls protected.

Ting and Li, the two ambitious young gangsters who conducted "special work" from their headquarters at 76 Jessfield Road, engaged in a fierce rivalry for the post of minister of police in the new government. Wrote Chou Fo-hai: "Not long ago we had Kao and T'ao's defection and now we have the Ting and Li dispute. We really lose a lot of face! I feel very angry."[30] A somewhat uneasy compromise was finally reached whereby Chou Fo-hai himself was to have a concurrent post as minister of police, Li Shih-chün would be vice-minister, and Ting Mo-ts'un would be "minister of social welfare."

Uneasy compromise was all that could be achieved with the existing governments as well. The personnel of the Restored Government were resentful of the domination that Wang Ching-wei and his "Kuomintang" had engineered for themselves on paper. Wang was conciliatory, but discontent and tension seethed below the surface.[31] As the day for the establishment of the "new central government" and dissolution of the Restored Government approached, antagonism mounted between the military units of the Restored Government and the forces which the Wang group were trying so hard to build up.[32]

The contradictions between the policy of dissolving the Restored Government and establishing a government on a somewhat different basis but inheriting the commitments and personnel of the old government became steadily clearer. The Restored Government had legions of Japanese "advisers." According to the yōkō, political advisers were not to be dispatched to the central government. The Kōain could not tolerate the dismissal of its minions. Despite Kagesa's protests, Wang inherited the Restored Government's "advisers" as well as those who had spread themselves out over the countryside.[33]

In north China, Wang was faced by the hostility not only of the Japanese military, who prepared puppet troops to act against him,[34] but also of his old friend Wang K'o-min. "Wang," said Wang K'o-min, "has an uncompromisable hostility against Chiang Kai-shek and he has also an ambition to be a leader of China. These two emotions have caused him to become a puppet of Japan."[35] Wang K'o-min would have nothing to do with the new government. He became increasingly cheeky in his dealings with the Japanese and announced on February 2 that he would retire as soon as the "North China Political Administrative Committee," — into which the Provisional Government was to be transmogrified when Wang's government was established — came into being.[36] Wang attempted to dissuade him from retiring by offering him appointment as Nanking's ambassador to Japan.[37] This he rejected and shortly thereafter he retired.[38]

While Wang labored to "return the Kuomintang government to the capital," the Sōgun, ostensible backers of the Wang *kōsaku,* had lost faith in Wang's capacity to solve the Incident and turned to direct contact with Chungking. The original idea of negotiating with Wang Ching-wei was that he was in some sense representing Chungking. But after the Japanese forced upon Wang a treasonous agreement, Wang lost all plausibility as a representative of Chinese interests and as a possible intermediary with Chungking. The Japanese rightly felt that Wang's contacts with Chungking were not very good and that Chungking was prepared to disbelieve and distrust anything Wang might say. The Sōgun, therefore, proceeded to open direct contact with Chungking in December 1939. They offered Chungking directly, however, the same terms that they had offered Wang; the only concession to Chiang was the possibility of throwing Wang over.

The content of these talks with Chungking, if the remarks of the Chungking negotiators are to be taken at all seriously, reveals that in many ways the positions of Chiang and Wang were not very different; Chiang, it appears, would have made virtually the same concessions as Wang had in the Jūkōdō *kiroku* if he could have obtained a promise of Japanese withdrawal. But a promise of a promise would not do for Chiang. It may be, however, that the sole purpose of Chungking in these negotiations was to confuse the Japanese and confound Wang Ching-wei's plans for a new government. For their part the Chinese suspected that Japan's only interest in negotiations was to compromise them. If the word got out that Chiang was talking with the Japanese, then the Communists, as well as the fervid Nationalists, would instantly rebel, and Japan would have her cheap victory.

The initiation of the Sōgun's route to Chungking came when Colonel Suzuki was sent in December to Hong Kong to contact "Sung Tze-liang." The real Sung Tze-liang was the younger brother of T. V. Sung and the two Sung sisters, Sung Ch'ing-ling, the widow of Sun Yat-sen, and Sung Mei-ling, the wife of Chiang Kai-shek. Therefore, negotiations with Sung Tze-liang, the Japanese hoped, would be directly with Chiang Kai-shek himself. The Sung Tze-liang with whom the Japanese dealt, however, was an agent of Tai Li's "Blue Dress Agency" (the Kuomintang intelligence organ), as the Japanese later came to suspect.[39]

In conversations during December and January "Sung" told Suzuki that the Chungking government desired a peace conference but that it must take place before the recognition of Wang's government. Chungking desired peace through mediation by third powers. In any case, it was a precondition of a formal peace conference that a truce take place before the beginning of the conference. Japan must promise the withdrawal of her troops. "Sung" emphasized that in no case would the Chungking government incorporate with that of Wang Ching-wei.[40]

Suzuki opposed negotiations through a third power, but he told "Sung" that if the Chungking side treated Wang Ching-wei in an honorable way, the Japanese would leave the relations between Wang and Chiang as an internal Chinese matter. Suzuki proposed that representatives of Chiang Kai-shek meet with representatives of the Japanese in informal talks in Hong Kong to explore the possibilities for agreement. "Sung" returned to Chungking on February 5 with this proposal and reported on February 9 that the Supreme Defense Council had decided to proceed with the talks which the Japanese had proposed. The Chinese suggested that three representatives be dispatched from each side and meet in Hong Kong at the end of February. Madame Chiang would be present in Hong Kong while the talks were in progress and would assist from the side, although she would not be formally involved in the negotiations.[41] Her presence in Hong Kong would nevertheless lend credence to the claim of the Chinese negotiators that they actually spoke for Chiang Kai-shek and his government.

The news that Chungking had accepted the proposal for informal talks crept up and down the interstices of the military bureaucracy. The Sōgun, the sponsor of the approach, was delighted. Konoye, who had tried so long to win peace in cooperation with the China clique now controlling the Sōgun, was also made aware of the breakthrough,[42] but the incumbent prime and foreign ministers were kept in the dark.[43] The chief of the General Staff and the war minister approved,[44] and the emperor himself, always alert to signs of peace, was also informed.[45] The bureaucrats, however, were determined that the basis of their discussions with Chungking would be the *hōshin* of November 1938, the same as it had been of the discussions with Wang. Colonel Usui was dispatched from Tokyo as the representative of the General Staff, and Colonels Imai and Suzuki were to represent the Sōgun. Madame Chiang arrived as promised on March 5 and the talks were held from March 7 through 10. Each evening a courier from the Chinese side flew to Chungking with reports.[46] The talks were very nearly sabotaged at the beginning by a leak to the press from Colonel Wachi who ran his own competing *kikan* aimed at suborning leaders from southwest China.[47]

As in the Jūkōdō talks, the points at issue between the two sides were the Japanese desire for Chinese recognition of Manchukuo and the Chinese desire for the withdrawal of Japanese troops. The Chinese wished to defer the question of Manchukuo in silent acquiescence with the status quo. China would be willing to make Manchukuo a joint protectorate of China and Japan in a secret agreement, but they would enter into this agreement only after peace had been restored. Otherwise, the Communists would rebel and Chiang would not have an opportunity to reorganize his forces to contain them.[48]

The Chinese negotiators from Chungking, like Kao and Mei long ago in Shanghai, pressed for a public announcement by Japan of her intention to withdraw. Once that was made, they would be perfectly willing to discuss postponing the withdrawal of the troops or stationing them in Mongolia (but absolutely not in north China) in accordance with an anti-Communist agreement. Contrary to the effusions of their propaganda, Chungking was quite willing to forgive and forget its differences with Wang Ching-wei if the Japanese would make concessions on the substantive issues of withdrawal and Manchukuo recognition.

Without promising any concessions on the basic questions, the Japanese proposed a further conference at a higher level. On March 10 the two sides signed their own respective memoranda, since they could not agree on a joint memorandum, and retired to report to their respective governments.[49] "Sung" promised a reply within a week. Imai felt there was hope that the Japanese side might compromise on the army stationing and Manchurian recognition questions, but he found even Itagaki, who had strongly supported the conference and the peace movement, could not compromise on the Manchukuo question.[50] Meanwhile, plans for the establishment of the Wang government were proceeding, and no reply was forthcoming from Chungking.

The Sōgun seems to have entertained extensive hopes for the success of the *Kiri kōsaku* because Inukai, informing Chou on March 19 for the first time of the Hong Kong talks, said that peace conditions seemed settled and by March 23 or 24 there would be some signs of stopping the war. Therefore, the Sōgun desired to delay the establishment of the new government until April 15.[51] The Chungking side had informed the Japanese that the final Chinese reply could not be forthcoming until that date because of the difficulty in reaching internal agreement on the question of Manchukuo recognition.[52]

Whether or not the establishment of the new government should be delayed was a very difficult decision. Chou felt that if Chungking were really going to make peace, then the plan for establishing a new government should be given up.[53] But delegates to the Central Political Conference to open on March 20 had already begun to gather in Nanking, and other preparations were at such a state that delay would mean effective cancellation. Was not this just Chungking's intention? Why should they settle on terms that they had rejected for three years? It could be as well that the plan for delaying, that is, canceling the Wang government found supporters among those Japanese who wished to see Wang dropped and saw in the Chungking feint a chance to do it.

It is true, on the other hand, that at this very time relations between Chiang's forces and the Communists had considerably worsened. According to a report from Shanghai, Kuomintang military leaders in northwest China had accused the Communists of establishing independent regimes, which refused allegiance to the provincial authorities, in eighteen hsien of Shensi, Kansu, and Ninghsia. These regimes were accused of driving out central government and provincial troops, rejecting central government orders, arresting and executing Kuomintang officials, collecting illegal taxes, issuing illegal banknotes, torturing innocent people, kidnaping merchants for ransom, and monopolizing the smuggling of Japanese goods. The report concluded, "The Communist forces, under the guise of joining the common struggle during the existing national crisis are in fact endeavoring to strengthen their position, expand their armed forces and develop their organization to the detriment of the country's welfare."[54] The Supreme Defense Council, composed of China's top military leaders and chaired by the Generalissimo himself, determined upon retaliatory measures against the Communists.[55] Some in the Kuomintang felt perhaps that Wang's policy of a temporary acquiescence in Japan's plans might indeed be better than, under the policy of resistance, allowing the Communist party to fasten its hold on the countryside. Japanese intelligence, usually pretty good, as well as the reports that Chou Fo-hai received from his agents, indicated that Chiang Kai-shek himself was the major hindrance to a turn by Chungking toward peace and anti-communism. Further, the war in Europe was intensifying, making aid to China seem less likely from that quarter.

These factors, plus a love of intrigue, perhaps even boredom with Wang, led the Sōgun to hope for a favorable reply from Chungking and to press for a delay in Nanking. Kagesa and Chou Fo-hai firmly opposed delay of the establishment of the government by more than a few days without more substantial evidence that Chungking was really interested in peace on Japanese terms.[56] A compromise was reached whereby Itagaki himself on March 19 called on Wang Ching-wei and requested that the establishment of the government be delayed from March 26 to March 30.[57] Wang gracefully acceded. It is difficult to see what this compromise accomplished except the saving of face all around.

Wang and Chou were intoxicated by the prospect that the government for which they had striven for so long seemed about to emerge. All the difficulties of the past and those in view for the future for the moment disappeared in the elation of once again being on stage. Having arrived at last in Nanking for the ceremonies of return, Wang and Chou together made a pilgrimage to the tomb of Sun Yat-sen on March 19. As Chou describes it in his diary, it was a very sentimental occasion. "On that day it was cold and windy and raining. On November 20,

Wang arrives in Nanking

Top: Wang Ching-wei arrives in Nanking to establish the new government. Chu Min-i is the figure to the far right.

Center: Wang is greeted by Kao Kuan-wu, the "mayor" of Nanking.

Bottom: General Nishio of the Sōgun is host at a "celebration banquet."

1937, before we left Nanking we also came to visit this tomb. Now looking back on the intervening events, it seems like a dream. Wang read Sun Yat-sen's will and he cried, tears running down. I cried also. After we visited Sun Yat-sen's tomb, the sun came out. This seemed to me a kind of a good sign for a bright future."[58]

On the next day, March 20, Wang opened the long-awaited Central Political Conference with a stirring speech. He praised the distinction of the members of the conference and looked forward to the realization of peace and constitutional rule in China.[59] But despite his brave words, the conference was a rather shabby and pathetic affair. It was attended by thirty members: Wang Ching-wei as chairman, eleven members of his Kuomintang, five members from the North China Provisional Government, five members from the Restored Government, two members each from the so-called National Socialist Party and Young China Party, plus four "non-party national leaders."[60] Needless to say, these representatives represented no one but themselves. At best the support that this disparate group of superannuated Ch'ing officials and low-ranking Kuomintang defectors gave Wang was conditional and grudging.

The hall where the Central Political Conference and succeeding press conferences were held for the small battery of foreign journalists invited up from Shanghai, as well as for an enormous crowd of Japanese reporters, was the only sign of life in the town. The streets outside were desolate; the population was greatly reduced from prewar size; there was no sign that the war damage inflicted by the invading Japanese and retreating Chinese had begun to be repaired. In the hall, however, all the paraphernalia associated with "great events in the modern world" were present: klieg lights, press releases, booths and telephones for reporters, and the like, as if decisions were really being made there.[61]

Everything went according to plan, despite an attempt by guerrillas to blow up a train bearing the delegates to Nanking. The conference "decided" that the new government should be a coalition under the Kuomintang using the "blue-sky white-sun" flag and the *San-min chu-i*. The Restored Government would be abolished; the North China Provisional Government

Wang Ching-wei addresses the Central Political Conference, March 20, 1940.

would become the North China Political Administrative Committee, and so on. The "Organic Law of the National Government" was similiar to the Kuomintang constitution except that the statement specifying party rule: "Prior to the proclamation of the Constitution the Executive Yuan, Legislative Yuan, Control Yuan, and Examination Yuan shall be directly responsible *to the Central Executive Committee of the Kuomintang*" was changed to read "responsible to the Central Political Council." This council consisted of members from the same groups that made up the Central Political Conference. Even though one-party rule was thus ended in theory, it was declared that the "Central Political Council shall not directly issue orders or administer political affairs. Its resolutions shall be transmitted to the National Government for execution.[62] Moreover, "the office of the President shall, during the preparatory period of Constitutional Government, be held by the President of the Central Executive Committee of the Kuomintang,"[63] that is, Wang Ching-wei. The President was empowered to act in case of emergency, without consulting the Council beforehand. In other words, as in Chungking, so under Wang, the period of "constitutional rule" was deferred to the future, despite the claims he had made in his opening speech. Essentially, on paper, the new regime was a Wang dictatorship. Wang occupied the chairmanship of the Central Executive Committee of the Kuomintang and the chairmanship of the Executive Yuan in addition to that of the Central Political Council.

During the third and final day, March 23, the Central Political Conference announced the "liquidation" of the Chungking government. All agreements entered into by the Chungking government after the return of the National Government to Nanking were declared void. Orders were to be given to the men in the field to cease hostilities immediately. All government employees were to report to Nanking where they would be reinstated with their original rank and salary.[64] The personnel of the new government were announced. Wang's associates held the most important posts. Wang Ching-wei was to be acting president until Lin Sen could come from Chungking to take up the post. Chou Fo-hai was minister of finance and concurrently minister of police; Ch'en Kung-po was chairman of the Legislative Yuan; Mei Ssu-p'ing, minister of industry and commerce; Lin Pai-sheng, minister of publicity; and the silent Li Sheng-wu, minister of justice. Chu Min-i was appointed minister for foreign affairs. As agreed at Ch'ingtao, high officials of the Restored Government for the preservation of their "face" were granted the chairmanships of the Judicial and Control Yuans as well as of the Ministry of the Interior. All in all, the ranks were pretty thin for the "National Government of China."

The great day — the "return of the National Government to Nanking," as the Chinese called it, or "the establishment of the 'new central government,'" as the Japanese termed it — dawned on March 30. Chou Fo-hai was filled with a sense of pride and exultation. "Everything, the National Government returning to the capital, the 'blue-sky white-sun' flag flying all over Nanking, is my personal success. This is all only because of myself. In the future I will be the center of the movement. If a person can have two successes like this, I would say that life was not in vain. Of course there will be many difficulties in the future, but I still feel very proud of today."[65] There were throngs of Japanese personalities from public and private life in a holiday spirit in Nanking to celebrate. Wang gave an interview to the president of the *Asahi* newspapers, reciting to him a poem that he had composed for the occasion: "The war has already stopped. A violet cloud falls in the south of China. The hearts of four hundred million are shown a flower of freedom."[66]

The new government announced its ten-point political program, which emphasized its desire for good relations with foreign powers and its aspirations toward securing China's sovereignty and toward democratizing China's political life.[67] The inauguration was celebrated by a flag parade, a mass meeting, and free theatrical performances, with a lantern procession in the evening. Japanese airplanes scattered thousands of leaflets proclaiming the new government's program over the city.[68] The Japanese government issued a statement of support for the new regime.

In addition to the official pledge of cooperation, there was a spate of other congratulatory messages: from Prime Minister Yonai, War Minister Hata, and Foreign Minister Arita — in the cabinet; from Admiral Oikawa, commander of the China Seas Fleet;[69] General Itagaki, the chief of staff of the Sōgun; and General Ando, the commander of the Japanese army in South China

Celebration of the "Return to the Capital," March 30, 1940.

Top: Celebration of the "Return to the Capital."

Bottom: From left to right: Liang Hung-chih, Ch'en Kung-po, Wang Ching-wei, Wen Tsung-yao, Wang I-tang.

— in the military.[70] Prince Konoye also made a statement on the occasion of the inauguration of the new regime, somewhat out of tune with the others. It expressed his usual bystander's attitude: "I hope everything goes well in China, but it must be remembered that this is just the beginning of the real affair."[71]

Chungking's reaction to the new government was not surprising: heaping vitriol on the head of Wang and his supporters on the one hand and using the occasion for cementing foreign and domestic support for the regime on the other.

On March 29 Wang and his wife were burned in effigy before a mass meeting in Chungking (see photograph). Cast iron statues of the two were erected to perpetuate their memory as traitors. A chain letter campaign got underway, in which individuals were requested to send contributions to local Kuomintang offices to be used as a reward for Wang's assassin.[72]

On March 30 the Chungking government ordered the arrest of seventy-seven "traitors," in addition to a previously proclaimed twenty-eight, making a total of one hundred and five, which included all the members of the former existing governments as well as Wang's collaborators.[73] President Lin, who according to Wang's constitution was supposed to join the new regime, began an intensive campaign of speechmaking, followed by Chiang Kai-shek and practically every official of importance. Lin demanded Wang's execution as a traitor.[74] Chiang, speaking before the opening meeting of the fifth session of the People's Political Council, once led by Wang, declared: "Any regime set up by Mr. Wang in whatever form, under whatever name, cannot be anything else than an instrument of the Japanese Army. Such a regime cannot affect China's resistance, nor will it be recognized by the world."[75] The voices of those who had been suspected in the past of ties with Wang rose high in the chorus. Lung Yun declared, somewhat mildly in comparison with most: "I am for peace but I do not like Mr. Wang's way of getting it. The Central Government [Chungking] alone can make peace, not an individual like Mr. Wang."[76] Chinese envoys abroad, who had been importuned by the Wang group in their search for support, cabled their unanimous support of Chiang's government.[77]

Either out of exaggerated fears or the desire to utilize this fairly blatant attack on Chinese sovereignty to commit foreign

Wang Ching-wei and Ch'en Pi-chün being burned in effigy in Chungking, March 29, 1940.

powers to its side, Chungking instructed its diplomatic staff to transmit to every nation to which they were accredited a statement denouncing the Wang government and declaring that "any manifestation of . . . recognition [of the Wang regime], in whatever form or manner, would be a violation of international law and treaties, and would be considered an act most unfriendly to the Chinese nation, for the consequences of which the recognizing party would have to bear full responsibility."[78]

The United States led the foreign powers in denouncing the new regime and expressing its support for Chiang Kai-shek. The Chinese had been pressing the United States for a formal condemnation of Wang Ching-wei ever since the Kao–T'ao revelations in January.[79] This had not been forthcoming, but Chinese diplomats in both Chungking and Washington kept up their efforts to increase American moral and financial support. And certainly the development of the Wang movement, which was seen in American eyes as a plot primarily to expel foreign interests in China, propelled the United States government into a stronger pro-China policy than it would otherwise have taken in light of isolationist opinion at home and the crisis in Europe where American policymakers thought the nation's primary interest lay. A sign of this increased support was the extension of a $20,000,000 loan in March.

On March 27 a Japanese official visited Maxwell M. Hamilton of the State Department to express to him the Japanese view, or rather the view that the Japanese wished the United States to take, toward Wang Ching-wei. Hamilton's response was less than diplomatic, stating that the United States government made policies based on the reports of American officials and would not be influenced by lectures from the Japanese.[80] On March 30 Secretary of State Cordell Hull made a formal declaration stating that the attitude of the United States toward the Far Eastern situation remained unchanged and that the United States continued to recognize the Chungking government as the government of China.[81]

Great Britain was less prompt and less heated in its response to the new government. The British position was made ambiguous by a singularly ill-timed speech by Ambassador Craigie on March 27 suggesting that, since Japan and Great Britain were both sea-going island empire nations, they should cooperate;

that Japan had been maligned and misunderstood. Craigie said his speech had been misinterpreted[82] and London disavowed it.[83] On April 3, R. A. Butler, the parlimentary secretary for foreign affairs, announced in the House of Commons that there had been no change in British policy of continuing to recognize the Chungking government.[84] Nevertheless, the British attitude as expressed to American officials was far more a policy of "wait and see" than the firm American stand.[85]

The voiceless populace of occupied China looked back on chaos and oppression and looked forward to chaos and oppression. In April 1940 a Chinese-speaking foreigner traveled up the Yangtze to Hankow asking the views of local leaders about Wang Ching-wei. Half expressed the view that he had sold out to the Japanese and the other half that he had an understanding with Chiang Kai-shek and would double-cross the Japanese.[86]

Japanese popular opinion tended to exaggerate the importance of the establishment of Wang's regime. Both official and nonofficial circles had come to believe that the "establishment of the 'new central government' " would somehow "solve the Incident." They too were weary of the war.

Unfortunately, the new government had not changed political realities one bit. In fact, even in the capital city of the new government, Chinese, including officials of the new government, had to alight from their cars, doff their hats before Japanese sentries, and otherwise be subject to humiliation by Japanese soldiers. The Sōgun made some effort to disguise the Japanese presence in Nanking to the end of allowing the new government at least some of the formal attributes of power. It ordered Japanese shops to retire from the main street and tried to clear the Japanese from the government offices and official residences which had been commandeered. The Sōgun, despite its title of "supreme headquarters," was little more than a *kikan* among *kikan,* at most *primus inter pares.* It was unable to stop the tide of Japanese who hoped to collect in China the fruits for which Japanese blood had been shed, Japan's racial destiny. With the occupation of China vast numbers of Japanese civilians had migrated to China where they established themselves under the patronage of the Japanese army in virtually every shop and business enterprise. It was no wonder that Japanese promises to restore Chinese enterprises to their owners, like so many Japanese promises, failed of fulfillment.[87]

Wang and his colleagues, now leaders of a regime at last, strove with renewed hope and energy to build on the flutter of prestige that the ceremonies in Nanking had conferred upon them. Wang himself spent most of the month of April campaigning throughout the length and breadth of occupied China to win support for the new regime. His first voyage, to north China and to Mongolia, must have been very disheartening. Several days before Wang's arrival in Peking on April 8, a local (naturally Japanese-controlled) Chinese newspaper published a "manifesto" of a self-styled "China Youth Party," which asserted that Wang was an ineffectual windbag who had accomplished nothing. The "manifesto" went on to denounce the *San-min chu-i*, the fundamental ideology of the "new central government." The *San-min chu-i*, said the manifesto: "are indeed full of conflicting ideas. The birth of the Chinese Communists, the formation of the Chiang Kai-shek regime, the alliance with Soviet Russia and the Communists, the surrendering to American and European interests, and the resistance to the Japanese would all be traced to the *San min chu i*. Now Mr. Wang is revising these Principles. We cannot help but shiver when we think of it."[88]

Wang arrived in Peking on April 8 accompanied by Lin Pai-sheng and Li Shih-chün.[89] Despite the obvious insult that he had received, he affirmed his commitment: "To save China, East Asia, and perhaps the whole world, from calamity, there is no other way except to carry out Dr. Sun Yat-sen's Three People's Principles."[90] On April 9 Wang flew from Peking to Kalgan in Mongolia where he had an interview with Prince Te, the head of the Mongolian puppet government. He was received there as coolly as he had been in Peking. Wang and Te "agreed" that Mongolia should be in no way subordinate to the "new central government" but that the two regimes should both cooperate "for the construction of Asia."[91] From April 12 to April 14 Wang paid a surprise visit to Canton. There he made a speech appealing to the Cantonese for support and referring to his own birthplace in Canton and his long connection with the province.[92] A visit to Hankow followed on April 16.[93]

At the end of the month Wang returned to his capital where General Abe presented his credentials as Japan's ambassador-plenipotentiary to the Nanking government on April 24. A large delegation of prominent Japanese accompanied Abe and joined in a four-day celebration. Wang responded to Abe's congratulations and promise of Japan's "whole-hearted" support by a paean to Sino-Japanese cooperation, claiming that the "new order" which the Japanese hoped to construct and Sun Yat-sen's "pan-Asianism" were at heart the same.[94]

Wang actually entertained no such notion; though he believed that the two great nations had much in common, could do each other much good, and that it was foolish for them to fight, he had nothing but contempt for the Japanese military and their dream of a new order. Wang expressed these sentiments in a letter to a former colleague in Chungking, which fell into the hands of Japanese intelligence. "The thought and ideals of the Japanese people are very simple, those of the military most of all. The present political authority does not lie with the Emperor or cabinet or *genro* or Diet, but with the soldiers; not with the minister of war or commanding generals, but with the middle rank officers on the various staffs. Therefore all — emperor, cabinet, *genro*, Diet, high-ranking officers — are puppets and obey the orders of the young officers. These young officers have no knowledge whatsoever except of military affairs. Since they have won in battle, they have become arrogant. They love profit, they are lecherous and they have broken the old customs of thrift and diligence."[95]

Despite the theatrics of the "return to the capital" and of Abe's arrival, the actual substance of Japanese support for Wang was as thin as ever. The Japanese military was divided between those who "supported" Wang and those who hoped for direct contact with Chungking. For the most part, except for Kagesa, even those who "supported" Wang supported him only as a puppet for enforcing Japanese desires on Chungking.

The policy of the Sōgun, as expressed in a planning document dated May 5, was to restrict the growth of the new government and hamper every effort on the part of the Nanking regime to expand their government quickly and beyond their actual power. The Japanese were to encourage for conspiratorial purposes the Nanking government in the belief that it would soon receive recognition from Japan, but the real decision on recognition would not be made until the end of the summer, depending on how contact with Chungking was proceeding and other developments.[96] "We must be careful lest the 'new central government' become closer to the Chung-king government than to us. Since they are closer to the Han [Chinese] race than to the Japanese race, we must be cautious in order to prevent Nanking government contact with the Chungking government for the purpose of expelling Japan."[97]

Wang and his associates were not blind; they could see clearly that the Japanese had confidence in neither their competence nor their sincerity. Consequently, Wang's peace government could do little to promote peace. "The young Japanese military faction still insists on conquering all of China. This is very harmful to us,"[98] wrote Chou. "The new government has been established for two months. We have not really accomplished anything. If we continue like this, people will really look down on us. I am really concerned about the future of the new government."[99]

Ch'en Kung-po took charge of Wang's next attempt to win from the Japanese partial realization of the new government's hopes. He and Chu Min-i led a "goodwill mission" of twenty-two officials to Tokyo, where they arrived on May 21, "to offer thanks to the Japanese government for the recent dispatch to Nanking of General Abe Nobuyuki as Japan's special envoy."[100]

On May 23 Ch'en Kung-po had the honor of being received by the emperor.[101] And on that same day he interviewed Prince Konoye and then in succession the prime minister, the war minister, the navy minister, and the finance minister. The next day Ch'en had an interview with the foreign minister. Ch'en expressed the desire that the oft-announced negotiations for a basic treaty to be signed at the time of recognition begin soon, since the public was becoming convinced that Japan was not sincere in her support of the Nanking government. Second, he asked for word of the direct negotiations toward Chungking (the kiri kōsaku), which had been revived, and sought assurance that the new regime would not be suddenly sold out. Third, he protested against the complete lack of freedom permitted even the officials of the new government in occupied China and bitterly complained about the independent direction being pursued by the North China Political Administrative Committee.[102]

The only effect of Ch'en's démarche was further to sharpen Japanese distrust of Nanking. On June 18 the president of the Kōain complained to Ambassador Abe that the Wang regime was not concentrating sufficiently on weakening Chiang Kai-shek's government and was rather attempting to increase its own power by demanding that Japan make concessions to China.[103]

The Sōgun, observing, as many of its staff had predicted, that Wang's government was a cipher and fearing lest Japan be cheated of a settlement with Chungking through being bound to Wang, reopened the *kiri kōsaku,* the negotiations with "Sung Tze-liang" in Hong Kong which had been broken off at the time of the "return to the capital."

The Japanese acted completely behind Wang's back. Chou Fo-hai had manifested to Ambassador Abe Nanking's adamant opposition to direct Japanese-Chungking negotiations before Japanese recognition of the new regime; Chungking would speculate that the Japanese had abandoned Wang Ching-wei and they would consequently despise Japan as well as Wang. Recognition of the Nanking regime, said Chou, was a precondition for reopening Chungking *kōsaku;* negotiations for concluding the "basic treaty" which would constitute recognition should be commenced immediately.[104]

Because the Wang *kōsaku* was one conspiracy among many others hatched by military intelligence and never had been more than a ruse, the Japanese hesitated not at all in reopening another route that might gain their objectives more expeditiously. It would have been foolish for them to let a commitment to Wang get in the way of peace, but in fact they sold out Wang without any hope that in return they could buy peace.

The *kiri kōsaku* was thus reopened on Japanese initiative in early April, but it was mid-May before a real response was received from the other side. "Sung" proposed that the same representatives who had met in Hong Kong before the Wang government had been established reconvene in Amoy for another conference. If agreement on terms could be reached, the two armies could declare a truce; Chiang Kai-shek would make a declaration of anti-communism; and formal peace talks between the leaders of the two nations would begin. The two basic questions of Manchukuo and the stationing of Japanese troops would be resolved after peace had been restored.

The Chinese would be in a much stronger bargaining position if the Japanese ceased fighting and agreed to talk. They could be kept talking a long time and could only with difficulty resume fighting. They would inevitably have to make concessions to reach agreement. Moreover, it would appear that the war had ended in a draw and that Japan was not in fact able to make her will prevail in China through force. If this procedure had been followed, the Chinese side would have procured nine tenths of what it wanted before the formal talks began. They would have achieved the cessation of fighting without any humiliating concessions.

Imai's counterproposal was that the top leaders of the two countries meet before arrangements were made for a truce, eliminating a preliminary conference. Thus the Japanese would have got nine tenths of what *they* wanted without the necessity of concessions, for as soon as Chiang committed himself to negotiations with Japan, the fragile coalition between the Kuomintang and the Communists would be transformed into civil war between the two factions. The Japanese would have China at their mercy. The Japanese demanded, moreover, as a precondition to truce that the Chinese yield on the two questions of Manchukuo recognition and stationing of Japanese troops. Imai was again hopeful that if the Japanese military leadership were faced with the immediate prospect of peace in direct conference with Chiang Kai-shek, they would be willing to relinquish at least their insistence on Chinese recognition of Manchukuo. After all, Manchuria had been completely under Japanese control since 1931, and the Chinese had neither the desire nor the ability to challenge that control. They were willing to tacitly acquiesce in the status quo. Moreover, if the Japanese acceded to the principle of withdrawing their troops from China, the Chinese were quite willing to let them delay this withdrawal in intramural China and to make secret agreements for stationing troops indefinitely in Mongolia under a joint anti-Communist agreement.[105]

However, "Sung" told Imai that for the reasons given above it would be impossible for Chiang to enter a peace conference without prior agreement on all major issues. "Sung" dined with Imai on a boat in the Hong Kong harbor and made every effort to convince Imai of what may well have been the truth, that, whatever the appearances, Chiang Kai-shek greatly desired peace, and if Japan would be willing to defer the two points at issue, he would come out strongly for peace, overriding internal opposition.[106]

Imai reported the Chinese position to his superiors, but Japanese policy remained inflexible. However, they did agree to accede to the Chinese request for another informal conference. This took place in a deserted house in Amoy during the first week of June. The conferees soon confirmed that the position of neither side had changed. They decided to defer discussion on basic issues and move on to more fruitful topics: the details for the prospective top-level conference.

Two weeks after the close of the conference, "Sung" on June 22 told Suzuki that Chungking agreed in principle to a conference between Chiang Kai-shek, Itagaki Seishirō, and Wang Ching-wei to be held at Changsha, at that time controlled by Chungking.[107] It is unlikely that Chungking had really withdrawn its requirement of agreement on terms before a top-level meeting; it could not afford to withdraw this requirement without an impressive demonstration of Japanese sincerity which it had so many reasons to doubt. Therefore, Chungking was attempting to draw out the Japanese.

The Sōgun, and its China clique, who had been trying to engineer political victory over the Chinese for so many years, felt that Chungking was in fact turning toward peace on Japanese terms. Wang Ching-wei was not quite so naive. Imai and Kagesa immediately told Chou of the Chungking reply. Would Wang agree? Chou promised to discuss it with Wang and conjectured that Wang would go. When Chou faced him with the proposal, Wang reacted coolly; he suggested that Itagaki alone meet with Chiang. If he were to go, he desired to meet previously with a Chungking representative, like Chang Ch'ün, in Shanghai.[108]

Itagaki himself came to visit Wang on June 24 to discuss the proposed conference and Wang put on his best barbarian-taming performance for the general. He expressed his appreciation to Itagaki for the Japanese willingness to go into occupied territory to confer with Chiang, despite the fact that it was the Chungking army that had been defeated. He felt that this would save Chiang's face. As a Chinese he was deeply grateful; however, with regard to his own attendance, he said that he would willingly go if the meeting was to be known to the public. "If the meeting is to be public I am willing to depart tomorrow with a suitcase. However probably Chungking will demand that the conference be secret, saying that it is still too early for an open conference. In that case we must take precautions for our safety and security."[109]

Two days later on June 26 Wang, revealing his true feelings, told Imai, after consultation with Chou, that in case Chiang Kai-shek did not wish to meet with Wang they should "hold a conference between Itagaki and Chiang Kai-shek. I would not mind if everything could be decided without my presence."[110] Perhaps after all that had happened, Wang was afraid to face Chiang. Wang, however, was no coward. Probably his coolness toward the conference stemmed from the fact that he knew there was no intention on either side to concede on the basic issues; therefore, the proposal for the conference was a political provocation on the part of both. Whether because Wang's remarks had awakened a real concern for personal safety or because they hoped to obtain evidence to expose Chungking's participation in negotiations, the Sōgun demanded, as a condition for the conference, that the Chinese furnish a written guarantee for the safety of the Japanese delegates.[111]

Chungking's predictable refusal did little to quell the Sōgun's optimism; Chou was told on July 3 that the conference would probably begin on July 5.[112] The vice chief-of-staff was dispatched from Tokyo to help in making the arrangements.[113] It was agreed that the Japanese delegation would come to Changsha in an unarmed passenger plane. Local truce would be declared in the area; two fighters might escort the aircraft.[114]

The Sōgun's project was regarded in Tokyo as just another military plot like all the others. When the emperor asked Kido, the Lord Keeper of the Privy Seal, if he should delay his departure for his summer residence in light of the conference, Kido advised him that the preparations for the conference were only a conspiracy. It would not be appropriate for the emperor to take notice of it.[115]

No further word came from Chungking until July 25. Chiang would not meet with Itagaki until Japan repudiated Konoye's *aite to sezu* statement. Further, the Japanese must agree to allow the fate of Wang Ching-wei to be decided solely by the Chinese.[116] Even the Sōgun came to have doubts whether

Chungking was about to fall prey to their conspiracy. They attempted to ascertain if the Chinese had any intention of holding a conference by requesting them to repair the Changsha airfield, but Japanese aerial reconnaissance was unable to detect whether or not the Chinese were complying with their request.[117]

Meanwhile the political situation had greatly changed in Tokyo and the Sōgun's freedom to conduct negotiations with a foreign power on its own initiative and responsibility was greatly constricted. Konoye had been kept informed of the *kiri kōsaku;* whether his role was active or passive is not known. On July 16 the Yonai cabinet fell and Konoye once again had the opportunity to form a cabinet and to attempt again to bring to an end the war that had begun under his tenure. He placed his hopes for peace with Chungking in his friend, the clever and dynamic Matsuoka Yōsuke, who joined his cabinet as foreign minister. Matsuoka, through Nishi and others, had been involved in peace work from the beginning. He had great confidence in his own abilities, in his understanding of Chinese character, and in the quality of his private contacts with Chungking. Before he accepted the post, Matsuoka won the promise of the prospective war minister, Tōjō Hideki, that all the military's separate *wahei kōsaku* would be suspended in favor of Matsuoka's own.[118]

Konoye, because he had been involved in the *kiri kōsaku* in association with the Sōgun's China clique, could scarcely take responsibility for suspending it; the army was not used to taking instructions from the prime minister anyway. When Imai, the Sōgun's key operative, visited Konoye on July 30, Konoye encouraged the continuation of the *kiri kōsaku* and agreed to write a letter in response to the Chinese demand that he abrogate his *aite to sezu* statement.[119] The next day, however, when Imai met with Tōjō, the new army minister, and briefed him on the Sōgun's negotiations, Tōjō severely rebuked him, asserting that the Sōgun was in no way authorized to conduct peace negotiations with China.[120] The Sōgun, however, with Konoye's approval and with that of certain elements in the War Ministry and General Staff, was not responsive to Tōjō's rebuke. Suzuki, the resident Sōgun agent in Hong Kong, presented "Sung" with letters from Konoye and Itagaki, which were intended to meet the Chinese requirements that Japan abrogate the *aite to sezu* statement and promise a hands-off policy toward the settlement of the Wang Ching-wei question.

Konoye's letter was intended to meet the first demand. It was artfully designed to fein a commitment by Konoye to the new negotiations. It read: "To His Excellency Chiang Kai-shek: Greetings. I have heard that as a result of the exchange of opinions concerning questions of Japan and China between a representative of Lt. Gen. Itagaki and a representative dispatched by your Excellency at Hong Kong for over half a year, soon a conference will be held between Your Excellency and Lt. Gen. Itagaki. I do not doubt and do believe that this conference will establish a foundation for readjustment of the relations between the two countries. [Signed] Konoye Fumimaro.[121] The Chinese saw through the artifice of Konoye's phrasing instantly. "Sung's" response was that "The Konoye letter does not positively deny the first Konoye statement. And Konoye does not totally support the Changsha Conference which Itagaki was to attend. Thus the attitude of Konoye is like that of a spectator."[122]

Itagaki's letter on the subject of Wang Ching-wei was a little more responsive to the Chinese demand. "Guarantee in regard to Wang–Chiang Cooperation: In regard to questions on Wang–Chiang cooperation, Japanese may have suggestions of good will in order to assist a smooth peace between China and Japan and particularly for the Chinese themselves. However, based upon the principle of non-interference in internal affairs, we will not handle this question as a part of truce conditions. I hereby guarantee this."[123]

Chungking had already much evidence that the Japanese would not hesitate to betray Wang Ching-wei. The real question with regard to Itagaki was whether he had the mandate of the Japanese government to negotiate. Chungking had seen Wang betrayed as a result of negotiating with Imai and Kagesa at the Jūkōdō; there was nothing to indicate that Itagaki was not trying to lead Chiang down the same path. "Sung" reported on September 19 that the Chungking government had decided to suspend consideration of the Changsha Conference unless Japan should concede on the Manchukuo and troop-stationing questions.[124]

The war in China, now over three years old, was further from solution than ever. The errors of Japanese statesmen and soldiers had bound Japan indissolubly to the *aite to sezu* and "new order" policies. Japan would not deal with Chiang; only Chiang had the power to decide for peace; he could not accept the "new order." Further negotiations between the two nations were pointless. Matsuoka, however, busied himself in preparing several gimmick solutions which he hoped would cut through the deadlock.

Chiang chose to resist the "new order" to the end; Wang judged it wiser to acquiesce in it for the moment. Their differences were as much a matter of the future as the present. The goal, said Wang, in a series of speeches in August 1940,[125] of both the resistance clique and the peace clique was a peace consistent with maintaining China as a sovereign state. A settlement with Japan one way or another was inevitable. The peace clique believed that Japan was then offering the best terms that it would; the resistance clique believed that better terms would be offered later. In fact it was only Pearl Harbor and the Pacific War which justified Chiang.

Wang, though he craved tragic martyrdom and apotheosis, took the pragmatic view, while the far less theatrically minded Chiang took the idealistic view. Wang had always urged that China face facts, in particular the fact that China was weak and Japan was strong. The patriot Pétain had yielded to the "new order" in Europe as Wang in China; nothing could be more foolish than Chiang's policy of depending on weak friends far away to defend him against strong enemies at the gates.[126] China, said Wang, should adjust itself to the situation in which it found itself.

There was much logic in Wang's argument; yet contrary to logic, despite British closure of its lifeline — the Burma Road — in July, despite recrudescence of civil war and the spread of Communist control over the countryside, Chungking was able to fight on while Wang's arguments sounded more and more like those of a coward and a traitor rather than those of a hero.

The *kiri kōsaku* had been the Sōgun's summer amusement; Matsuoka and others attempted to cut it off and start up their own plans for "solving the Incident." Meanwhile, back in Nanking, the Ume kikan and Wang's other supporters were urging that the Wang *kōsaku* be carried through; it might yet be the key to peace, and moreover, Japan had made promises; Japan's honor was at stake. Generals Kagesa and Abe joined forces with Chou, Ch'en, and other Nanking officials in urging that the long-delayed negotiations leading to the "basic treaty" constituting Japanese recognition be commenced promptly. These advocates could not be completely denied. Consequently, on July 5 Wang and Abe formally opened negotiations. The sixteen conferences were extremely dreary.[127]

The one item of the negotiations which was not formal was the timing of the withdrawal of Japanese troops. Wang resolutely insisted that the withdrawal be completed within two years as peace and order were reestablished (*chian kakuritsu to tomo ni ninen inai teppei o kanryō suru*). Finally, Wang agreed to the Japanese draft upon exchange of a secret document which declared, " 'within two years after the restoration of peace and order' does not imply stationing the army perpetually. As soon as tranquillity is restored, then withdrawal may be carried out at any time."[128] The final conference was held on August 31. Wang and Abe made optimistic statements, Wang once again declaring that the agreements were based on the three principles of the Konoye statement.

By autumn Matsuoka's schemes had matured. He hoped to use a "one-two" punch, engineering German pressure on Chungking at the same time as he pushed direct contact through his agents. The tripartite Axis alliance of Japan, Italy, and Germany, signed on August 27, would, he thought, both enlist German cooperation and discourage American interference in East Asia. He quite miscalculated the effects of this alliance, however. The United States became more intransigent rather than more docile. Hitherto, American policy makers had hoped to avoid confrontation with Japan, but now that Japan seemed to have tied herself firmly to the tail of the Nazi kite, the defeat of Japan was as necessary as the defeat of Germany. The alliance bound the solution of the Far Eastern crisis even more tightly to the outcome of the European war. No longer could the Western powers take a bystander's attitude toward Chungking's plight, for it seemed now that the cause of Free China was the cause of the Allies. The effect of the alliance on the Japanese domestic scene was to shift the thoughts of the Japanese military even further from thoughts of a compromise peace with China toward

General Abe Nobuyuki and Wang Ching-wei meet as negotiations for the "Basic Treaty" open.

schemes for taking advantage of the weakness of the colonial powers and of the support of their new allies to realize the "new order." Chungking, stiffened by the increased support of the Allies, the first token of which was the reopening of the Burma Road by Great Britain, was to be less interested than ever in submission to Japan.

Matsuoka was also mistaken in believing that Germany would act as Japan's cat's-paw in East Asia, softening Chungking up for surrender. On November 7 Matsuoka put the following request before the Germans: "Would the Reich Government advise Chiang Kai-shek of its impression that recognition of Wang Ching-wei by Japan was imminent? German and Italian recognition would follow in accordance with the Tripartite Pact, so that the position of the Wang Ching-wei government would have a strong foundation. In order to forestall this development it would be advisable for Chiang Kai-shek to arrive at an understanding with Japan regarding termination of the conflict."[129]

In response to the Japanese request Ribbentrop called in the Chinese ambassador in Berlin and asked him if Chiang considered there was any hope of peace. The ambassador replied that his government was interested in "a speedy conclusion of this conflict that had already been going on for 40 months and that he felt there was no use in fighting any longer. However, for the Marshal [Chiang Kai-shek] the prerequisite was the unconditional evacuation of Japanese troops from Chinese soil.[130] Ribbentrop said that he felt that this was "hardly the basis for a solution."[131] Germany was not prepared to "assume the role of mediator" unless asked by both sides, and he would deny any press reports to the contrary.[132]

After the Axis alliance had been concluded, Matsuoka set up his own kōsaku, his own route to Chungking, using veterans of the early days of Wang's peace movement who had close connections with himself and with Konoye. Matsumoto Shigeharu and Nishi Yoshiaki were once again involved. The conversations were to be between Consul General Tajiri Yasuyoshi in Hong Kong, and those sincere friends of peace and true Sino-Japanese cooperation who were respected by Chiang as much as by both Chinese and Japanese peace comrades, the Shanghai bankers Ch'en Yung-ming and Chou Tso-min.

The Matsuoka kōsaku was a completely civilian kōsaku; in

contrast to the *kōsaku* of the military for which no one was responsible, the Matsuoka *kōsaku* led directly from the foreign minister and, assumedly, from his superior Konoye, to a legitimate diplomat, Tajiri. The Matsuoka *kōsaku* offered Chiang a direct and honorable route to the top of the Japanese government. Such a route had not existed before. Mechanically, therefore, Matsuoka had taken a great step forward. The real problem was that he could not offer Chungking any better terms than had the military *kōsaku;* he could only offer a more honorable way for Chungking to accept them. This was not enough. Second, there is considerable question about the success that Matsuoka's envisaged mediators Ch'ien Yung-ming and Chou Tso-min enjoyed in actually getting through to Chiang.[133] Whereas the *démarche* got underway in early September,[134] there was no clear response from Chungking until November 18.[135] The putative reply of Chiang Kai-shek to Matsuoka said: "For the time being, we demand the postponement of recognition to Wang Ching-wei. First execute total withdrawal, and thereafter we would be willing to discuss stationing of the army."[136] China's terms — repudiation of the "new order" — had not changed. Matsuoka continued to hope. There was a stinger in the tail of the Chinese reply — no recognition of Wang Ching-wei. The highest organs of the Japanese state had already acted. On November 13 the Imperial Conference (Gozen kaigi) had ratified the Wang-Abe "basic treaty"; the treaty would be signed, recognizing the new government on November 30. Matsuoka did not have much time for his miracle.[137]

Essentially, the two governments were engaged in the same mutual squeeze play as they had been in March before the establishment of Wang's government; the Japanese side threatened to establish or recognize Wang if Chungking did not yield; Chungking threatened to break off negotiations if Japan established or recognized Wang. This was a dangerous game; but since there was no possible agreement on basic terms, it was political provocation on both sides.

Matsuoka and even elements in the military were inspired by the Chungking responses to believe that there was hope Chungking might come around — if only the Wang government recognition were delayed. Debate raged amid the General Staff and War Ministry over a proposal to delay recognition at least until December 5 in order to permit officials to come from Chungking for further discussion.

General Kagesa, who was aware that he was dying, had focused his life's hopes on Wang's movement, and General Abe, the former prime minister who had committed himself to negotiating the "basic treaty," were appalled at the possibility that the Tokyo regime might scuttle Wang by delaying recognition. A colleague articulated their views: "Unless we recognize the new government, we will lose the meaning of the new government made by Wang Ching-wei. So far we have done our work in accordance with the instructions of our government. If the government insists that they will not recognize the [Nanking] government, this means we are killing Wang Ching-wei. No one would trust Japanese politics any more. We would not know why the government has sent General Abe as our ambassador."[138]

Abe and Kagesa came from Nanking to Tokyo, stationed themselves before Matsuoka's residence, and announced that they would not leave until he had agreed to sign the basic treaty.[139] "We cannot go back to Nanking in the present situation . . . If you do not recognize [the Nanking government] we have no choice but to die here."[140]

Matsuoka felt that Kagesa, Abe, and others who had been involved with the Wang kōsaku and who were insisting on the recognition of the government, were, like all soldiers, narrow-minded, only conscious of their own concerns. They were not considering the broader picture: that recognition of the Nanking regime would make settlement with Chungking much more difficult and that Wang's regime had no capacity to "solve the Incident." Thus those who insisted upon recognizing Nanking were putting the interests of Wang Ching-wei before the interests of Japan.[141] The emperor himself shared Matsuoka's misgivings. He told Kido on November 29 that in his view recognition of the Nanking government meant breaking off efforts to make peace with Chungking and hence a commitment by Japan to a long-term war.[142]

Civilians had to yield to the tantrums of soldiers; Abe and Kagesa had their way and plans for the signature and recognition proceeded. Both Nanking and Tokyo realized that chances for merger were dim. Consequently, Wang himself took the post of president which had been held vacant for the day when Lin Sen would come from Chungking.[143] On November 27 Wang made a final public appeal to Chiang Kai-shek, the gist of which was the assertion that if Chiang had listened to Wang in 1938, then peace would already be at hand.[144]

On November 28 a Liaison Conference was held between the Japanese cabinet and high military officials in Prime Minister Konoye's mansion. Matsuoka reported that according to a telegram from Tajiri, Chiang's proposal to delay the recognition of the Wang government was nothing more than a conspiracy on the part of the Chungking side. It was decided at this conference to proceed as planned with recognition of the Nanking government on November 30, even if a truce proposal were received from Chungking before that time. After the recognition of the government, contact with Chungking would be suspended.[145]

As scheduled, the "basic treaty" was signed on November 30, accompanied by a joint declaration pledging cooperation in the "new order." The ebullient Chou Fo-hai wrote in his diary: "Perhaps this may be the best way for the Chinese people. We have two governments now. It would be preferable if Wang and Chiang worked together. But one government belongs to the camp of Japan, Germany, and Italy. The other belongs to the British-American camp. Therefore, no matter who wins, China is there."[146]

Chungking used the occasion of the "basic treaty" as she had used the establishment of the government to mobilize support at home and abroad. Chiang in a speech on December 2 led Chungking officials in blasting the Japanese action. On that same day, the Chinese foreign minister made it known privately that Chungking would break relations with any power which recognized Nanking.[147] Chiang advised Anglo-American officials that those countries should "take steps to prevent this action from affecting China's ability to continue resistance . . . If at this time America does not show a positive attitude and give positive assistance, our war of resistance will be gravely imperiled."[148] The response of the United States to Chiang's plea and Wang's recognition was a restatement of America's pro-Chungking attitude by Secretary of State Cordell Hull and the announcement of a credit to Chungking of $100,000,000.[149]

There is no question that the establishment and recognition

of Wang's Nanking government did nothing to further peace. The real question is whether it actually hindered or prevented peace. This would be a heavy burden of guilt for Wang to bear. Although the Wang *kōsaku* encouraged foolish hopes on the part of the Japanese, there is no reason to believe that these schemes stood in the way of peace. The basic issue between China and Japan was the "new order." Neither side showed any sign of compromising on this issue; they both showed willingness to settle on Wang Ching-wei. The judgment that his activities had done nothing to affect the settlement of the Incident would give little comfort to the proud shade of Wang Ching-wei.

The Peace Government in Action

The Peace Movement and Shanghai

9 Although Wang Ching-wei's peace government aspired to become the "Nanking government" in continuation of the prewar regime, in reality Wang's movement was based upon Shanghai and premised upon the peculiar conditions there. Even though Shanghai was China's largest city, she was scarcely a century old, and had all the rawness of a boomtown. Shanghai was unique even among the treaty ports both for her opulence and for her freedom, even looseness. Her wealth had been generated by commerce and commercial values prevailed. Her legal status was never certain, always evolving in tune with the Sino-foreign relationship of which she was a creature. Since the International Settlement, the heart of Shanghai, involved most of the powers, none could rule by fiat. Western law offered protection for commerce and from extradition for political offenses, but otherwise, nearly everything was licit.

Political schemes, as well as financial, were the lifeblood of the city. Agents of every persuasion conferred and sparred. Thus Shanghai was the only place where the private and public activities essential to Wang's movement could have been undertaken. Privately, Wang could be in contact with the political agents of East Asian factions and the powers. He could build his own political machine. Publicly, he could project his appeal not only to a large and wealthy Chinese constituency but to the world, for diplomats and newsmen transmitted from Shanghai the news of China to the world and its governments.

Shanghai began by being Wang's sanctuary; she ended by being Wang's prey. The Japanese failed to grant him any real power or concessions, the Kuomintang did not rally to him, the powers dismissed him. There was now only one way to move: against the foreign concessions in Shanghai. Foreign forces in China were true paper tigers, their homelands engaged in death struggle. The real powers in China, the Japanese militarists and the Chinese nationalists, were united on one thing at least: their opposition to Western privileges in China. At the Jūkōdō, the comrades had discussed a joint offensive against Western imperialism. Perhaps the Japanese, unwilling to grant to Wang anything that they possessed, might acquiesce if he could displace the foreigners, thus acquiring the "real power" he craved.

Wang came to Shanghai in order to take advantage of the opportunities that it offered. However, Wang and his original comrades, who were motivated by broad political conceptions, were very few in number. They had neither money nor power. The movement had to be fleshed out with the human resources to be found in Shanghai to meet the exigencies of the Shanghai scene. Thus it became in reality a Shanghai movement, and it was inevitable that Shanghai morality came to dominate it. This meant vice and violence. To organize a conspiracy based on Shanghai meant necessary alliance with the underworld forces there who were willing to offer their "support" but for a quid pro quo.

When Wang arrived in Shanghai after the assassination of Tseng Chung-ming, his first requirement was security. Chungking's "special work" organ, the "blue shirts" organized and active since 1932 and commanded by General Tai Li, had been successfully liquidating collaborators or suspected collaborators since the beginning of the war. They had funds, good organization, and the support of the general populace as well as a certain amount of sympathy from the foreign authorities, who were certainly not pro-Japanese.

The life of a collaborator was never secure against attack, even from the most trusted quarters, because anyone might be tempted, either by political passion or by money, to betray him. If Wang and his movement were to be protected from Chungking attack without depending upon enemy soldiers, the only course was to ally with the gangsters who had guns for hire in Shanghai. Consequently, in the spring of 1939 before Wang's arrival, Chou Fo-hai contracted an alliance with Li Shih-ch'ün and Ting Mo-ts'un to provide protection. With Japanese assistance, Ting and Li had succeeded by June in building up an effective terrorist apparatus. While participants in the other Japanese-sponsored regimes were picked off by assassins with great regularity, no major figures in the Wang government met their end in such a fashion.

The "special work" organ, "76," as it came to be called, with its headquarters at 76 Jessfield Road, undoubtedly did its work well. Widening its sphere from defense to offense, "76" was the only "real force" that Wang, who so desired armed backing, was able to acquire. The motive for the alliance with Ting and Li was the same that had caused him, Sun Yat-sen, and other Chinese politicians to ally with warlords in the past. This policy had always suffered from the disparity of aims between soldiers and politicians. In this case, it was absolute. Ting and Li had turned traitor long before Wang emerged. They had no concern for the goals of the peace movement. Their only interest was their own aggrandizement. Not only did they use the cover of the peace movement to extend their widespread racketeering, but they also expanded into politics. The peace comrades, dependen' upon them for protection, became their captives. T'ao Hsi-sheng relates that as the comrades were meeting in August 1939 to choose members of the Central Political Committee, Li Shih-ch'ün, armed with a pistol and accompanied by a squad of hoodlums, demanded that more of his agents be included on the committee.[1]

Ting and Li also played a cool game with their former colleagues in Chungking's "special work." Although the two sides exchanged assassinations, a journalist for a journalist, a businessman for a businessman, the agents of the opposing side were killed only in cases of "necessity."[2] While Wang was justified in providing for his security, the indulgence of his movement in counter-terror was completely hostile to his purposes and ideals.

In the same way that Wang's requirement for security enmeshed him in the peculiarities of the Shanghai situation, so did his need for a residence. Wang had originally desired to live in his own house in the French Concession; he had acquiesced in the Japanese desire that he reside in the western "outside roads" area. This area was one of the many anomalies of Shanghai's erratic development. Without any treaty sanction and largely at the behest of real estate promoters, the International Settlement had extended its administrative services—roads, police, and the like—into the "outside roads" area. When the fighting broke out in Shanghai in the late summer of 1937, the Japanese occupied this area as well as the parts of the city under Chinese administration. The Shanghai Municipal Police of the International Settlement continued to claim the right to police the roads as they had before. Many prominent residents of the International

Settlement lived in the "outside roads" area and were naturally quite eager that this protection be continued. The Japanese and their client Shanghai Ta Tao Government, however, claimed jurisdiction over everything else but the highways. The result was a no man's land soon dubbed in popular parlance the "badlands." Criminals who enjoyed Japanese support had merely to duck down an alley or into a building to escape the Shanghai Municipal Police. There was constant tension between the government of the International Settlement and the Japanese on this issue. The "outside roads" area provided a safe zone for the growth of an enormous vice industry. Gambling palaces of the most elaborate sort became frequent. They employed their own private armies for "protection"; often the thugs of rival houses clashed in armed combat. Opium houses with such colorful names as "Peach Blossom Palace" and "Good Friend" flourished. Pickpockets, petty thieves, and the like preyed on the patrons of these establishments.

The "badlands" early provided a sanctuary for the peace movement. The Jūkōdō itself was in the "badlands." Wang's official headquarters at 1126 Yu Yuen Road was in close proximity to several of the more notorious clubs. The Japanese urged Wang to make his residence in the "outside roads" area so that Japanese forces could contribute to Wang's security and yet he would not appear to be their captive. Inevitably, however, Japanese "protection" also meant Japanese control.

After security and habitation, Wang's third need was money. This requirement also dragged him into connection with Shanghai lowlife. The movement in the early days received contributions from well-wishers, but as failure became more likely, voluntary contributions dried up. The only source of legitimate revenue was a Japanese dole from the customs revenue of the occupied ports. After the establishment of the government, expenses increased enormously—Wang had to support the staff of the old Restored Government as well as his own.[3] The new government was permitted no real tax base; it could only collect fees for the few services it was allowed to perform. Thus it was that Wang had to turn to a tax on "badlands" gambling houses and associated enterprises, not only to keep the vultures at "76" happy but also to meet the basic expenses of his government and movement.

The comrades did not have a clear conscience about this reliance and from time to time they attempted to repress the gambling houses — Chou tried in July 1940;[4] Ch'en Kung-po tried after he became mayor of the Chinese sector in November 1940;[5] and a third suppression campaign was mounted in June 1941. These campaigns had no permanent effect; the vice interests were too strong to oppose, too indispensable to do without.

Shanghai was chosen because it offered an apt forum from which to disseminate Wang's convictions about a conciliatory peace between China and Japan. After the basic housekeeping tasks had been taken care of, he moved to launch his appeal through acquiring the prime instrument of mass communication, his own press. Thus he became enmeshed in the peculiar cutthroat world of Shanghai journalism. After the decision to bring the movement to Shanghai, Lin Pai-sheng metamorphosed his Hong Kong *Nan-hua jih-pao* (South China daily) into the Shanghai *Chung-hua jih-pao* (China daily) which, Wang-funded, became a large-scale publishing operation. T'ang Liang-li, an Indonesian-born, German-educated journalist whose *People's Tribune* had always supported Wang, brought his well-edited English language publication over to Wang's camp in October 1939, just after having collected a large subsidy from Chungking.[6] T'ang was a veteran of the wars of Shanghai journalism; his acid pen had won him many enemies and he was not a man to forget a grudge. The publications of Lin and T'ang put Wang's point of view effectively before the Chinese and foreign public. Their success in selling Wang's version of the *naiyaku* negotiations has already been recounted.

The freedom of the press which Shanghai enjoyed at this time was unique in East Asia. Both sides took advantage of this freedom to back publications of their own persuasion. In light of the political tensions and the current of violence that always ran through Shanghai, it was inevitable that the war of words and dollars should soon become a war of bullets and bombs. Journalists were shot and presses wrecked. The Japanese had pressured the authorities of the International Settlement into suppressing newspapers with a direct Chungking affiliation. New papers with American owners sprang up to present the Chungking point of view. Since the freedom to publish was one of the privileges the foreigners had acquired under extraterritoriality, there was little that either the Japanese or Wang's journalists could do except fulminate. Wang's propagandists became further convinced that the United States was the primary enemy of the peace movement.

Wang's policy toward foreign powers was the traditional Kuomintang policy: to seek friendship and aid from all those who were willing to give it and, within the framework of legality and using diplomatic methods, to work for the abolition of the unequal treaties which gave the foreigners special personal, political, and commercial privileges in China. The success of Wang's whole project for setting up a government which would in time become recognized as the "legitimate" Chinese government depended on the friendship of the powers. The United States had the greatest interest in China, and therefore it was the United States which Wang must woo. The United States, however, as a friend of China, had set her face against Japanese imperial designs in China, which she saw as indissolubly linked with fascist designs in Europe. The Americans saw Wang as the cat's-paw of these designs. The Japanese would not permit Wang to be other than a cat's-paw. Therefore, despite the nobility of Wang's desire for peace and the sincerity of his devotion to Chinese interests, it was inevitable that the United States should oppose Wang's schemes at every point. Chu Min-i, and with him we suppose Wang, deeply regretted that the attitude of the United States toward the peace movement had become so profoundly bound to Japanese-American relations, and he eagerly looked for an improvement in those relations.[7]

This of course was a vain hope. By the summer of 1940 it was clear that Wang had no friends among the Western powers. From this point on, the Nanking government was used as the vehicle for a campaign against the foreign powers in Shanghai and Chungking interests there which enjoyed foreign protection. There was logic in this move; the only common interest between Chinese nationalism and Japanese imperialism was opposition to Western privileges in China. The Japanese would yield nothing to the Nanking regime; perhaps it could gain real being through displacing the foreigners in Shanghai and tapping the wealth and power of that great city. The weakness in this reasoning was that, since the alliance between Japanese imperialism and

Wang's version of Chinese nationalism was a radically unequal one, it was inevitable that the Wang regime become a Japanese jackal.

Who was responsible for the anti-foreign campaign of the Nanking government is not certain; the visible evidence suggests a coalition between T'ang Liang-li and the Ting-Li "76" faction. They shared a common interest in getting what they could out of their investment in the now hollow Wang government. Wang himself never made any anti-foreign statement nor did he express support for the policies conducted in his name. He really only had concern for the great issues of war and peace; he had little interest in the sordid affairs of his puppet government. Fear of assassination and his declining health caused him to withdraw into isolation.[8]

To judge from his diary, Chou Fo-hai, who had tirelessly promoted and overseen the practical and administrative aspects of the peace movement ever since Hanoi and who was responsible, in collaboration with Wang, for shaping its policy, held no anti-foreign views nor did he participate in the campaign to harass foreigners and expel them from Shanghai in the summer of 1940.

T'ang had procured for himself the empty titles of "ambassador at large" and "director-general of the International Publicity Board" and from this eminence endeavored to expel the foreigners and to pay off the grudges he had accumulated through the years. His first move was to suggest that all his old competitors be put under his thumb. Foreign news agencies would be expelled from China. They would be replaced by a central news agency in Nanking, which might buy the news of foreign wire services but which would take responsibility for its distribution within China.[9] In June, heartened by the successes of the Nazis — whom he intensely admired — in Europe, he escalated his own offensive; foreign rights must be altogether abolished. The Nanking government, he said, would demand the immediate return of the foreign concessions and settlements and abolition of extraterritorial privileges.[10]

The Japanese had always intended their client governments as tools for use against Westerners; they wished, however, to manipulate these instruments against the foreigners solely in accordance with their own diplomatic objectives. On June 13, in accordance with Japanese instruction,[11] the "Foreign Ministry of the National Government" reiterated the demand that the Japanese had been pressing since the outbreak of the European war: that the belligerent nations withdraw their forces from China.[12] The government also expressed its opposition to transfer of treaty rights by belligerent powers to nonbelligerents.[13] On June 15 and 19, Fu Hsiao-en, the mayor of the Japanese-controlled Shanghai Special Municipality, also addressed notes to the British, French, and Italian consuls general requesting them to withdraw their armed forces from Shanghai.[14]

T'ang wished to seize the initiative and go beyond these controlled Japanese-inspired démarches. On June 13 the *Chung-hua jih-pao* declared that the new government would not hesitate to use force if the colonial powers did not yield diplomatically.[15] T'ang gained the support of "76" and, armed with only his own bluster and a printing press, set out to translate his words into deeds. The newspaper war, the campaigns of terror and assassination, and the attack on the foreign settlements coalesced when, according to T'ang's announcement, Wang's "National Government" ordered Mayor Fu Hsiao-en to arrest eighty-four Chinese residing in the International Settlement and the French Concession. Fu of course, like his Kuomintang predecessors, had no jurisdiction in the extraterritorial areas. The arrest order challenged the principle of the judicial independence of the concessions. Extradition to Chinese authorities was possible only after rigorous legal proceedings and never for political offenses. The offenses, if any, of the eighty-four accused of being Chungking agents were manifestly political. About forty of them were employed by American-owned English and Chinese language newspapers which had been critical of the Nanking government. Undoubtedly some of the eighty-four were indeed on the Chungking payroll; others were victims of error, mistaken identity, and personal grudges on the part of "76" agents.[16] The occasion for the "arrest order" had been the murder on June 29 of one Mu Shih-ying, a pro-Wang journalist. Taking blood for blood, secret police of "76" proceeded to "enforce" the arrest order by assassinating on July 19 Samuel H. Chang, pro-Chungking journalist who was a director of the American-owned Post Mercury newspapers.[17] Chang's name had been on Nanking's list. He was alleged by T'ang to be receiving a $9,000 per month subsidy for *Ta Mei pao*, a Post Mercury paper.[18]

The surprising lesson that T'ang drew from Chang's assassination for the benefit of the Associated Press was: "Only the submission of the local authorities to the National Government at Nanking and the assumption of direct authority over the entire Shanghai area by the National Government, can restore the rule of law."[19] Efforts to persuade the authorities in the French Concession and International Settlement to turn over those on the Nanking government's list of eighty-four undesirables were supplemented by efforts to bribe the police forces in those two areas.[20]

On July 16, without Japanese approval, T'ang demanded not only the extradition of Chinese who had found sanctuary in the foreign settlements but also of seven foreign journalists who enjoyed extraterritorial rights — six Americans and one Englishman. On July 17 the various Japanese authorities — representatives of the military organs, the Kōain, and the Gaimushō — met and roundly expressed their displeasure that the Wang regime had taken such an action without prior consultation. They regarded these "arrest orders" as destructive of the Nanking government's chances of gaining support in Shanghai from both Chinese and foreigners. The Japanese authorities determined that since the order had already been given, Mayor Fu was to relay the demand for the extradition of the Americans and the Englishman to the American and British consuls general respectively. Thus the order would quietly fade away while something of the Nanking government's face would be saved.[21]

Virtually admitting the complicity of Wang's regime in Chang's murder, T'ang, in a letter to the prestigous *North China Daily News*, threatened the concession authorities with more of the same if they continued to be recalcitrant in dealing with the new government: "The National Government of China at Nanking had . . . every right to issue its recent order for the deportation of the seven foreign newspapermen, and to expect the cooperation of the British and American authorities in its execution. The only excuse that those authorities can make for not executing it is that they do not recognize Nanking as the National Government of China. That, of course, they may do, but it should be with full realization of the fact that in so doing they leave no other course open to the Chinese authorities but to take their own measures to see that their order is carried out."[22]

T'ang's blusterings in themselves served rather to discredit the Wang government than to enhance its strength. Time, however, was running against foreign administration in China; after the fall of France, the Western powers had no longer at their disposal the military force upon which their position there was based. The foreign authorities had no choice but to yield to Wang diplomatically when he was supported by the Japanese, since Japan was in a position to expel them at will by force. Naturally, they were more willing to concede Chungking's interests which had found protection in the settlements than their own. This was the case when on November 8 the French Vichy Government transferred the Chinese courts in the French Concession, which hitherto had been operated by the Chungking government, into the hands of the Nanking government.[23] The Japanese had been demanding the surrender of the Chinese courts in the concessions for a long time; but the powers, especially the United States, had expressed their firm opposition. Chungking reacted with a protest to the French and a declaration that "Hereafter, any organs that may style themselves as Chinese courts in the French Concession will be regarded as illegal and all decisions and any other acts of such organs shall have no validity."[24] The former Chungking-appointed judges refused, of course, to serve and were replaced by appointees of the Nanking government. Most Chinese and foreign lawyers began to boycott the new courts, and a war for lawyers in Shanghai was opened between the Nanking and Chungking regimes. Lawyers who wished to practice before the new courts were forced to register with the Nanking Ministry of Justice. If they did so, they were dropped from the directory of the Chungking Ministry of Justice. Thus lawyers were forced to decide between their patriotism and their livelihood.[25]

In the same way that the Japanese had supported the Nanking government's take-over of the Chinese courts in Shanghai, they undoubtedly concurred in the Nanking regime's efforts to take over offices and assets of the Chinese banks there which had hitherto continued their connection with the Chungking government. The first move on the Wang side was the seizure of the Central Bank of China building in Shanghai on November 9,

1940. Chungking responded to force with force; in March 1941, fighting between agents of the two regimes for control of China's banks in the International Settlement of Shanghai netted a total of fourteen killed, sixty wounded, and one hundred and forty-eight captured.[26]

The purpose of capturing these banks was to acquire for the Nanking regime a banking system and a currency of its own, an essential attribute of a sovereign government and a vital political weapon in the complex economic warfare that prevailed in war-torn China.

After the take-over of the Central Bank of China in November, Chou Fo-hai, that factotum of many functions who was also finance minister, drew together a staff and began issuing a new "National Government of China" currency early in January 1941. This currency was to be the only one accepted for government obligations, and as such, it was hoped that Chungking and Japanese currencies and those of the various occupation regimes would be undermined to the prestige and profit of the new government. This currency, like the other wartime currencies, was issued without financial reserves as backing; it was worth no more than the paper that it was printed on, except insofar as the Wang regime could inspire confidence in it.

Chou's development of a national bank and currency was one of the last real efforts to give the Nanking regime some actual strength as a government. Chou wished the Peking Federal Reserve Bank to be placed under the control of his Central Reserve Bank, Japanese military currency to be readjusted and phased out, and the Central Reserve Bank to be the nucleus of control over Chinese industry and commerce.[27] Japan was quite happy to let the Wang forces fight with Chungking in Shanghai but was completely unwilling to allow Chou's currency and bank to expand in the occupied areas under her military control. The new bank was only allowed to function in certain limited areas of the Yangtze Valley.

Perhaps the greatest success that the Wang movement had in gaining power and influence in the Shanghai area before Pearl Harbor was not at the expense of either Chungking or the foreigners but of the rival Japanese-sponsored regime in the area: the Shanghai Special Municipality (formerly the Ta tao government) established shortly after the Japanese conquest, which held sway in the parts of the city which surrounded the concessions. Fu Hsiao-en, the capable and respected mayor of this government, was brutally hacked to death in his bed in the early morning of October 11 (ironically after celebrating China's independence day, "Double Ten," the evening before) by a trusted servant of a decade.[28] Undoubtedly Fu was a victim of Chungking's anti-collaborator campaign, but rumor had it that Fu might have been murdered by Wang's agents, since relations between the two governments, rivals for control of Shanghai under the rising sun, were none too good. The Special Municipality, having been founded long before Wang's government with the support of a rival group of intriguers from the Japanese army, had no connection with and little sympathy for Wang and his movement. However, this government and its supporters did not have another candidate strong enough to replace Fu, and thus the office fell to the Nanking government. It was first reported that Chou Fo-hai would get the post. Perhaps because of the strongly adverse reaction from the foreign press in the International Settlement, which saw Chou as Wang's evil genius, Ch'en Kung-po, who enjoyed a certain prestige among the foreigners, took the post. Inaugurated on November 20, 1940, Ch'en vowed clean and honest administration. He reached in February 1941 an agreement with the Shanghai Municipal Council for the formation of a joint police force in the western area "badlands," which would have the right of "hot pursuit" and which would suppress gambling and other illegal enterprises in that area.[29]

The vice industry continued to flourish. Undoubtedly no mayor, much less a puppet mayor, could have made much headway. The vice interests, well-armed and solidly entrenched, had intimate ties not only with the Japanese army but also with Ch'en's own government.

The notion of a peace government had its birth in Shanghai; there the peace movement struggled to grow; there it fed and was fed upon. It was a creature of that strange overheated Sino-foreign climate; perhaps nowhere else could it have come into existence and maintained itself. Wang Ching-wei's peace movement ended tragically, not only because of Wang's character and that of the Sino-Japanese relationship itself, but also because Shanghai, which became the movement's matrix, inevitably put its own impress upon it.

To the Pacific War and the Grave

The decision of the Japanese to sign the "basic treaty" "recognizing" the Nanking regime was a decision for "long, protracted war." The harsh terms of the "basic treaty" forswore the possibility of using Wang Ching-wei to make a conciliatory peace with China. Furthermore, the Japanese did not trust Wang and his followers sufficiently to allow them a real role in the administration of the occupied areas.

After the signing of the "basic treaty" on November 30, 1940, the task which he had been assigned, General Abe resigned his post as ambassador plenipotentiary and returned to Japan on December 12. In consequence of Japanese recognition, the two governments were to exchange ambassadors. Chu Min-i, the Nanking foreign minister, was appointed to serve concurrently as ambassador to Japan. Honda Kumatarō, a former ambassador to Germany and Turkey, became ambassador to Nanking, taking up his post on December 26.[30] Honda's instructions made it clear that he was not to act as a normal diplomatic representative to a sovereign nation but was to subordinate diplomatic considerations to the objective of a military victory over Chiang Kai-shek. He was consequently to cooperate closely with the Japanese military authorities in China.[31]

Despite these instructions, Honda became a partisan of the Nanking regime and in cooperation with Wang — and, we must assume, like-minded Japanese like Kagesa and Konoye — engineered a bold campaign in May and June 1941 to bring Japanese performance up to her public promises. Unfortunately, we do not yet have the inner sources for this maneuver. The first move of the campaign was a trip by Honda to Japan. He sailed from Shanghai to Kobe on May 10, arriving on May 11. May 12 he spent in Kyoto reportedly composing a "memorial to the throne" on Japan's China policy. In a press conference on May 13, he demanded that Japan fulfill the "fixed policy" of support for Wang Ching-wei that had been decided with the "basic treaty" and before. Japan must render the Nanking regime the support necessary for its stabilization. Japan should request her

Foreign Minister Matsuoka Yōsuke welcomes Wang Ching-wei at the Tokyo railway station, June 17, 1941.

Far left, Chu Min-i; third from left, Wang Ching-wei; fifth, back to camera Matsuoka Yōsuke (?).

allies, Germany and Italy, to recognize Wang's government. Only by making the regime strong could Wang win the support of the Chinese people for peace. Honda accused the Japanese army of misrule, abetted by politicians and financiers, and criticized "Shanghai political brokers" who were attempting to negotiate directly with Chiang, bypassing and betraying Wang.

Matsuoka met Honda upon his arrival in Tokyo on May 14 and the next day the two men had a two-hour conference at which they were reported to have exchanged "free frank views." Honda was said to have presented Matsuoka with a "concrete plan" drafted by Japanese army, navy, and Gaimushō officials in Nanking. According to the Japanese spokesman, "complete agreement" was reached at this interview.[32] On May 16 Honda interviewed War Minister Tōjō Hideki and then called again on Matsuoka to exchange "free frank views on the international situation with China problems as the center."[33] Tōjō himself declared that the army backed Honda's policy of strengthening the Wang regime.[34] The following day Honda called on Prime Minister Konoye and submitted his "memorial." That same day the acting president of the Kōain praised the achievements of Wang's regime and urged Japan to extend all possible assistance to it.[35]

Apparently, in coordination with Honda's representations, Wang Ching-wei in Nanking publicly demanded the immediate end of Japanese control of trade and finance in the Yangtze valley. He demanded also Japanese assistance in arming Nanking government troops and in persuading the Axis-allied nations to recognize the Nanking government. He threatened to retire if the Japanese did not meet his demands.[36]

Building on the groundwork laid by Honda and his other Japanese supporters, Wang Ching-wei made a state visit to Japan in June accompanied by the leading officials of the regime. Perhaps the moribund Nanking government could yet be resuscitated. When Wang and his group docked at Kobe, their boat was met by throngs of banner-waving and cheering Japanese. Wang arrived in Tokyo on June 17 to receive what was reported as one of the greatest welcomes ever accorded a foreign visitor. Foreign Minister Matsuoka and other officials greeted him at the station. On June 18 Wang was formally received by the emperor. The emperor expressed great sympathy for the Chinese

Ceremony on Sun Yat-sen's birthday, March 12, sometime during the Pacific War.

people and strengthened Wang's confidence in his deep and sincere desire for peace.[37]

On the succeeding days Wang held discussions with Prime Minister Konoye, Foreign Minister Matsuoka, War Minister Tōjō, the navy minister, the finance minister, and others. With Konoye, Wang discussed the problems of achieving over-all peace. Wang said that in addition to winning the support of dissident generals like Li Tsung-jen and Pai Chung-hsi, it was necessary in the end to win Chiang's support also. The best way to succeed in this was to gain the support of the pro-American clique in Chungking through American mediation. As for solving the problem between Wang and Chiang, Wang felt that Tōyama Mitsuru, the now aged revolutionary who had so aided Sun Yat-sen in the days before the first Chinese republic, should be entrusted with determining an appropriate settlement. Wang also expressed to Konoye his chagrin at the lack of agreement between the various military authorities in China, which made his work in dealing with them doubly difficult.[38]

In addition to the topics of international affairs and Chungking *kōsaku,* discussions ranged over the whole field of disagreements between Nanking and Tokyo: the independent policy pursued by the North China Political Administrative Committee, the independent policies pursued by local units of the Japanese army, the unfulfilled promise to return Chinese factories and to cede ownership of railroads to the Nanking government, the restrictions placed on the expansion of Nanking's Central Reserve Bank, recognition by the Axis powers, and Nanking's need for arms and financial aid.[39]

On June 23 Konoye and Wang issued a joint statement reaffirming that the new order was to be constructed through Sino-Japanese cooperation. In this spirit Japan would allow the Nanking government freedom to exercise her sovereign authority. Japan would extend a 300,000,000 yen loan to the Nanking government for armaments and would return the houses and factories which had been confiscated by the Japanese army.[40]

No one had better reason than Wang Ching-wei to know that Japanese promises were cheap. These new promises were not kept; the armies in China knew nothing of them.[41] Perhaps the promises were never intended to be kept. If Konoye, Matsuoka, and their fellows could offer Wang nothing substantive, they could at least give him a ceremonial face-lifting.[42] Wang, a brilliant ceremonialist, had always put a lot of faith in ceremonies and trappings.

If Japan had really contemplated aiding Wang's regime which she had hitherto ignored, her plans were shaken by a great event which occurred during Wang's visit: on June 22 German armies invaded the Soviet Union. Japanese policy makers turned to take advantage of the opportunity presented by the difficulties of their old enemy to the north. Matsuoka had signed a neutrality pact with the USSR on April 13, which Japan continued to honor. But the fact that Russia would be in no condition to interfere in East Asia greatly improved prospects for the realization of the new order. Wang and the possibility he represented of a cooperative "solution of the China Incident" — that gravest of all Japan's problems — were pushed to the side once again as the military sought to utilize the favorable turns in the world situation to achieve their most grand ambitions. Wang left for Nanking on June 25. Chou Fo-hai remained in Tokyo to continue discussions, presumably dealing with financial matters. Chou had to return, however, with a virtual admission of failure.[43]

Only one of the demands that Wang and Honda had made for the strengthening of the Nanking government was translated into reality, namely, recognition of that government by the Axis powers as a result of Japanese diplomatic pressure. On June 21 Matsuoka had told Ott, the German ambassador in Tokyo, that Japan intended to press for German and Italian recognition if a further discussion with Wang seemed to reaffirm that this course was desirable.[44] On June 25 Matsuoka said that Wang had requested recognition; Japan supported this request and desired that recognition be extended before July 1. Ott forwarded this demand to Berlin with his personal caveat that Germany demand a quid pro quo: recognition of German economic interests in China.[45] German officials in China strongly opposed recognition of the Wang regime. Their view was that the Nanking government was a nonentity. It was a vain attempt on the part of the Japanese to get out of the difficulty they had got into in China through their own lack of discipline. Moreover, since now Germany was fighting the Soviet Union and Chiang's own greatest problem was the Communist menace, Germany's relationship with Chungking was thrown into a new light. Perhaps the German tradition of cooperation with Chiang could be continued with mutual profit.[46] On June 27 von Ribbentrop decided, however, with the consent of the Führer, to recognize the Nanking government, probably because Japanese assistance in attacking British holdings in Asia was deemed more critical at the moment to the Reich's plans for conquest than any aid Chiang might give them in the future. Von Rippentrop told the Japanese ambassador that he assumed that Germany would enjoy a preference over third powers in her trade with China.[47] On june 28 the Chinese ambassador attempted to persuade the German government not to yield to Japanese pressure, threatening a break in relations.[48] True to their word, albeit with some reluctance,[49] the Chungking government broke relations with Germany on July 2. Italy had never instructed her ambassador in China to present his credentials; consequently, no formal break was necessary.

Konoye, in the underhand way characteristic of his nature and demanded by circumstances, had been ceaseless in his efforts to find some solution of the China Incident, for the outbreak of which he himself must have felt a grave responsibility. Despite his third statement, which had so disappointed Wang's hopes, he did persist in his efforts to bring peace through Wang Ching-wei. It must have been clear to Konoye by the summer of 1941 that Wang was not capable of solving the Incident. The problem of Japan's terms for peace in China was no longer an issue merely between the two countries but, more seriously for Japan's ambitions, had become a bitter issue between Japan and the vastly more powerful United States.

Konoye's effort to reach a settlement with the United States was similiar to and could be called a direct outgrowth of the Wang kōsaku. On one side were the intransigent generals who would settle for nothing but their whole cake; on the other side was, in one case, Chiang Kai-shek; in the second, the no less rigid Cordell Hull. Konoye's plan was in the first case to have Wang be the honest broker; in the other, to play that role himself, in somehow reconciling the irreconcilable. As in the first case, he won the "consent" of the military to the kiroku; in the second case, he won the consent of the military to a meeting between himself and Roosevelt in the Pacific. In both cases, he seems to have felt that if once he could make a bold gesture and reach directly to the center of the opposing country, a compromise could be found that would compel the extremists on both sides to accept it.

The American ambassador, Joseph Grew, argued that the United States, like Wang, should cooperate with Konoye against the extremist elements in the Japanese military. Roosevelt, like Wang, could only have been won by a promise to withdraw Japanese troops from China. Konoye had no authority to make such a promise; the imperial mystique would not allow Japan to retreat. No amount of talking or maneuvering could conceal the fact that Japanese war aims, vacillating though they were, had no limit other than complete subjection of East Asia. This eventually was unacceptable to American policy makers, as it had been to Chinese.

Wang himself was delighted at the prospect that Japan might reach an accommodation with the United States and thereby with Chungking, thus bringing about Sino-Japanese peace. On the other hand, he feared that if Japan were to offer Chungking through the United States better terms than it had offered Wang Ching-wei, Wang's whole "peace, anti-communism, reconstruction" movement, as well as Konoye's own "new order in East Asia," would be discredited. Therefore, he requested in a letter to Konoye dated October 5, 1941, that during the negotiations with the United States, the proposed terms of the peace settlement between China and Japan be kept secret. When Japan and America had reached agreement, then Japan should consult with the Nanking regime and revise the "basic treaty" of the previous year. This new treaty could be announced several days before the announcement of the Japanese-United States agreement.[50]

Wang's pious hope for peace was in vain, and with the attack on Pearl Harbor on December 7, 1941, a veil descends on our knowledge of the Wang regime. The Japanese had lost interest in Wang and indeed, to a large measure, in China. Therefore, the torrent of documents upon which the previous account has largely been built petered out to a trickle. And the foreign publications in the concession areas, which are such an important source for our understanding of modern Chinese history, came to an abrupt halt. The publications in occupied China itself, of which an unclassified mountain remains, seem after some examination to be nothing more than the most mindless and trivial sort of propaganda with little historical value. Therefore, we get only glimpses of the activities of the Nanking regime in the war years.

The major objective of Wang Ching-wei's peace movement was to save China for the Kuomintang; a major objective of the peace government was to save the occupied areas for the Kuomintang. Neither was achieved. The Japanese, Wang complained, would not allow Nanking government forces to battle the burgeoning Communist guerillas; further, Japanese troops themselves were unable to keep Communist expansion in check.

The Japanese army was only able to hold "points and lines," as he put it, that is, roads, railroads, towns, but the Communists held the "surface" in between.[51] Neither Chungking nor Japan, much less the negligible Nanking government, was able to prevent the expansion of the Communists over this "surface." Wang warned the Japanese that if this continued much longer they would have to deal with the Communists rather than the Kuomintang for the settlement of the Incident.[52]

Wang had hoped to gradually bring about "local peace" in the occupied territories which would be followed by "economic reconstruction." These dreams fell prey to the woeful incapacity of the Nanking government. He did set up a "rural pacification commission" in May 1941 in connection with his attempt to resuscitate the government. The official account, which notes the need to depend on Japanese troops and to concentrate on "peace work," that is, propaganda, suggests that it was little boon to the hard-pressed peasantry.[53]

As the war went on, morale among the personnel of the Nanking government, despite the appearance for a time that Japanese victory would justify Wang against Chiang, became lower and lower. In February 1942 Ch'en Kung-po reiterated his deep pessimism. The peace movement had not made one step towards peace; the "return to the capital" had been a seed planted before the ground was cultivated. The "basic treaty" had gained no support from Chungking. The Japanese wahei kōsaku had been narrow-minded from beginning to end. The Nanking government, hemmed in on every side by Japanese guidance organs, attracted only short-sighted opportunists.[54] Wang Ching-wei himself, following a trip to north China in October 1942 pronounced his movement a failure. The various areas of occupied China were becoming more and more locally oriented; he could see no point in the continued existence of the "national government."[55]

Decline of morale among the original peace comrades accompanied by the rise of "real power" allies from the Shanghai underworld led to the development of that traditional security system of Chinese politics, factions. Tani Masayuki, who became ambassador to Nanking in 1943, prepared for his government in March 1944 an elaborate chart and analysis of the factional structure of the Nanking government. Tani saw the first main division between the non-Kuomintang — those from the Restored Government plus various splinter groups — and the Kuomintang. The non-Kuomintang members were without influence. The Kuomintang had the military, the Wang Ching-wei, and the Chou clicques. The Wang clique was further subdivided into four factions: the "official mansion faction," *kung-kuan p'ai;* the "new official mansion clique," *hsin kung-kuan p'ai;* the direct Wang faction; and the "reorganization faction," *kai-tsu p'ai.* The "official mansion faction" centered around Ch'en Pi-chün, her friends and relatives, Lin Pai-sheng, and various underworld elements. The "new official mansion clique" included retainers of Li Shih-ch'ün who had deserted Chou Fo-hai. After Li was poisoned by the Japanese, his followers tended to redistribute themselves either to Madame Wang or back to Chou Fo-hai. The direct Wang faction was composed of those who, like Chu Min-i, had direct blood or other connections with Wang Ching-wei himself. The "reorganization faction" was Ch'en Kung-po's group, which dated back to 1928. It had been expanded by followers who joined after Ch'en became mayor of Shanghai. In almost symmetrical counterbalance to the Wang clique, Tani saw those surrounding the other strong figure in the regime, Chou Fo-hai, divided into three factions: the C. C. clique which was based on membership in that group prior to the war; an underworld clique under Ting Mo-ts'un; and a personal clique around Mei Ssu-p'ing.[56] A polarization around the two centers of power in the regime was perhaps inevitable. There is no reason, however, to doubt Chou's fundamental loyalty to Wang. Chou declared to his diary: "Wang and I can only die together. I will never try to do anything against him."[57] Tani was the same man with whom Wang had hoped to conduct peace talks in Paris in January 1939. As ambassador to Nanking, he succeeded Shigemitsu Mamoru, former ambassador to Great Britain, who had, in turn, succeeded Honda.

Japan's defeat in the Battle of the Coral Sea in May of 1942 signalled that the crest of Japanese expansion in the Pacific had passed. Japan now had a vital interest in mobilizing her empire, since the war was being more hotly contested. Therefore, Japan turned, too late, to a "new China policy." If the Wang regime could be strengthened, it might be able to win Chungking's co-operation. At any rate, puppet troops could take over occupation duties, freeing Japanese soldiers for the South Pacific.

Wang's movement was a peace movement, his government a peace government. He had declared aboard the *Hokkōmaru* that he would never bear arms against Chiang; he had announced in March 1942 that his regime would not participate in the Pacific war.[58] He could not completely reject Japanese demands, but he could hope through negotiations not only to moderate them but also to gain a quid pro quo. During July 1942 various dignitaries exchanged visits between Nanking and Tokyo, and Japan extended a 100 million yen loan for currency stabilization.[59] Apparently, as a result of these negotiations, Nanking was able to win Japanese consent that the regime's participation in the war be limited to a declaration of war against the Western allies, not Chungking. In exchange, Japan would at last return the concessions to the Nanking government, consent to the abolition of all extraterritorial rights in China, and revise the "basic treaty" with Wang. These decisions were ratified by an Imperial Conference (Gozen kaigi) on September 21.[60] The Japanese government made it clear, however, in dispatches to their ambassadors in Berlin and Rome that concessions to Nanking were only a practical expedient; they had no intention of allowing the Nanking regime to join the Axis.[61]

Abrogation of foreign privileges had little practical effect because after Pearl Harbor the Japanese had taken over the concessions, interned or expelled the foreigners, and had no intention of yielding substantively their own position. Nevertheless, abrogation of extraterritoriality — the goal of generations of Chinese nationalists — had a tremendous symbolic value. The allies had declared in 1941 their intention to relinquish extraterritoriality after the restoration of peace.[62] They could not afford to have it said that Wang had won more for Chinese nationalism than Chiang. Thus the Japanese move caused them to move up their relinquishment of these privileges to January 11, 1943.[63]

Wang met with Prime Minister Tōjō in Tokyo on December 21 and 25[64] and, agreement having been reached, the Nanking government declared war upon the United States and Great Britain on January 9, 1943. The declaration was carefully phrased to make the move appear consistent with Chinese nationalism and to avoid hostilities with Chungking. "The National Government has called the national movement to life to strengthen peace and order. On the other hand, America and England have finally succeeded in drawing Chungking to their side . . . and have sent their aircraft stationed in Chungking to bombard Wuhan, Canton, and other regions of China. America and England desire to rule in Eastern Asia or even to annex it . . . It is our aim to liberate China from Anglo-Saxon tyranny, to build it anew and to fight for the liberty of the whole of Eastern Asia."[65]

Japanese propaganda endeavored to hide the fact that war had not been declared against Chungking. According to a Tokyo broadcast, "The most important point is that the government now enters into a complete state of hostility to the Government of Chungking and will wage war à l'outrance against the power of Chiang Kai-shek."[66]

This time the Japanese carried through on their promises. During February and March agreement was reached for the rendition of various Japanese concessions and the subjection of Japanese residents in China to Chinese taxes.[67] The Vichy government agreed to formally retrocede French concessions and extraterritorial rights.[68] Tōjō told the Diet on June 15 that Ambassador Tani had been instructed to begin negotiations for revising the "basic treaty." Finally on August 1 the Nanking government celebrated with patriotic fervor what it represented as a great victory for Chinese nationalism, the take-over of the Shanghai concessions. At last Japan allowed the "blue-sky white-sun" flag to fly, unencumbered by the yellow pennant, all over occupied China. Relations were improved with the hitherto autonomous north China regime,[69] which, in consequence of Communist expansion on the "surface" was less significant than ever.

Japan conceded in the "new China policy" more than ever

Celebration of the rendition of the Shanghai Concessions, August 1, 1943.

before, but nothing changed the fact that the hard-line milita-rists were in command. The China clique who had initiated and carried through the Wang *kōsaku* and with whom Wang had established a certain degree of trust and rapport had all been transferred to distant and dangerous places — Kagesa to Rabaul, New Guinea; Imai to the Philippines. Wang found it difficult to deal with these new men who had not even the China clique's understanding of Chinese nationalism.

In July 1943 Wang sent a car at night for Tsuji Masunobu, who had recently been transferred to Nanking and who was a fol-lower of the China clique's chief ideologist, Ishiwara Kanji. Wang expressed to Tsuji in this midnight interview, conducted without interpreter through Chinese characters, his desire that the China clique return to Nanking: Itagaki as commander-in-chief of the Sōgun, Ishiwara Kanji himself as chief-of-staff, Abe Nobuyuki as ambassador, and Kagesa as military adviser. This could only be brought about, advised Tsuji, through a direct appeal by Wang to Tōjō.[70]

Therefore, in mid-September 1943 Wang went to Japan, osten-sibly to discuss with Tōjō the possibility of peace with Chung-king. Sun Fo, the son of Sun Yat-sen, had led Wang's agents to believe that Chungking at last desired Wang to mediate with Ja-pan for total peace.[71] Chu Min-i and Ch'en Pi-chün had met with Sung Ch'ing-ling in Amoy to discuss this possibility.[72] Tōjō con-veyed to Wang the Japanese position: Japan would consider withdrawal only if Chungking, prior to conclusion of peace, severed relations completely with Great Britain and the United States.[73] Chungking would have liked to be able to turn to crush the Communists; she had certain disagreements with her allies; but she knew better than to cut her own throat. Tōjō's reply thus cut short this peace approach, if that is what it was. On a more conciliatory note, Tōjō reassured Wang that treaty revision would continue as promised and he acceded to Wang's request that these new agreements be divided into two parts: a treaty of alliance based on equality and, separate from it, concessions by the Wang regime to remain in force only for the duration of hostilities.

After these matters had been discussed amicably, Wang pro-ceeded, in the fashion of Far Eastern etiquette, to bring up what

Tsuji represents as the true purpose of his visit: the presentation of his request for the reassignment of his old comrades to duty with the Nanking government. As with Tsuji, Wang put forth his request privately to Tōjō in writing. Tōjō rudely rebuffed him, telling him "not to interfere in the personnel problems of the Japanese Army."[74] Wang returned discouraged and beaten to Nanking and told Tsuji he did not feel that he could speak to Tōjō again. He realized that there was no hope. "We are all predestined for defeat, but let us fight to the end."[75]

Wang did not falter in his efforts to tame the barbarians, even expressing to them how he was "striving to make manifest the virtue of the emperor."[76] Finally, five years after the Jūkōdō, Japan made the public commitments that she had promised in the Konoye statement of December 22, 1938. In a protocol to the new treaty of alliance signed on October 30, 1943, Japan agreed to withdraw her troops from China as soon as peace was restored; further, Japan even renounced her rights under the Boxer Protocol to station troops in north China.[77] It had been Wang's endeavor for all these years to bring Japan to make public the private promises which had caused him to leave Chungking. Now that Japan was on the road to defeat, these promises no longer had any political meaning.

The research of Yoji Akashi into the Japanese archives of the Pacific War period reveal that Japan continued to be boxed in by the *aite to sezu* statement and by the establishment of the Wang Ching-wei regime.[78] Because Japan would not deal directly with the Chiang Kai-shek government, she was forced to communicate with that government through a succession of uncertain and often shady and unreliable intermediaries. Because Japan had set up Wang and made commitments to him, many respectable Japanese decision-makers felt it would be dishonorable to deal with Chiang behind Wang's back. But that Wang had no capacity to mediate had been proven all too clearly by events. Thus the decisions of late 1937 and 1938 — intended to "solve the China Incident" — brought an eight year war instead. Yet it must be noted too that even when Japan's military victory became increasingly unlikely, she never was prepared to offer Chungking through any intermediary peace terms consistent with Chinese nationalism.

Shortly after the paper victory represented by the "new China

Japanese leaders salute Wang's corpse. Third from left, Konoye Fumimaro.

policy," Wang came to the end of his long road, perhaps fortunately, because it spared him the humiliation of suffering a public trial. With failing health he entered Nagoya University Hospital in March 1944, where he received the best medical care Japan had to offer. The Japanese suspected that he would not go without a departing blow; they gave orders that he was to see no journalists; all reports about him were to be censored. They denied him the treatment customarily accorded a head of state.[79] His condition remained stable during the summer, but in September he entered an irreversible decline, dying on October 10 — the anniversary of the 1911 Revolution — about 3 PM, perhaps of pneumonia contracted in a bomb shelter.[80]

In a last testament, the authenticity of which is not entirely certain, Wang proclaimed once again that all that he had done was at one with the aims of his comrades in Chungking; he urged the union of the two factions of the Kuomintang, and he expressed the hope that some day Sino-Japanese cooperation could be realized.[81]

Wang's death was the death of the dream of Sino-Japanese peace for which many in both China and Japan had striven in vain. Prince Konoye himself may be seen in the photograph here reproduced, paying, along with other Japanese leaders, their last respects to the man who had given his life to rescue Japan from her own political dilemma.

His corpse was flown back to Nanking where, contrary to his wishes, it was given a massive public funeral modeled on that of Sun Yat-sen's. He was buried as he wished near Sun Yat-sen and others who had fallen in the revolutionary cause.[82]

Wang's government could not long survive him. Ch'en Kung-po performed his final service for his friend by overseeing its last days. A conference was held to determine future policy: should Wang's followers, in the Chinese tradition of banditry and rebellion, gather what troops and treasure they had and retreat to a mountain stronghold, hoping to deal with Chiang and the Communists as a force to be reckoned with, or should they throw themselves on the mercy of Chiang and their old colleagues in the Kuomintang? Ch'en and Chou, distrusting Chiang, favored the first course. Li Sheng-wu, a scholarly official and longtime follower of Wang who had attempted to preserve the quality of Chinese education under the occupation, elo-

Wang's coffin, draped in the "blue-sky white-sun" flag.

quently opposed the bastion proposal. The goals of the peace movement had been to preserve China's unity and to spare China's people suffering. Would not such a proposal perpetuate strife and betray Wang's ideals?[83] The peace comrades had at times acted foolishly, self-indulgently, out of opportunism and personal ambition. Yet beneath their mortal flaws ran a conviction that they had acted and were acting to do what was best for China. Li's argument prevailed.

It only made sense to try to square themselves with Chungking, nevertheless, while they could offer a quid pro quo for the preservation of their lives. Contact between the intelligence organs of the two Chinas had never ceased. It was Chou Fo-hai who had borne most of the responsibility for maintaining this contact. As Japanese defeat approached, the Communists and Nationalists were tensing for the civil war that was to follow. The Nanking government with its army on the spot might be in a position to throw the occupied areas into the hands of one camp or the other. Chou Fo-hai was reportedly approached by a Communist representative who offered him a guarantee of his life and position in return.[84] Chou rebuffed this offer, putting his hopes in a plan to coordinate Nanking troops with those of Chungking in the final offensive against the Japanese.[85] The Communists could be eliminated at the same time, thus restoring Chinese unity under Kuomintang rule.

That deus ex machina, the atom bomb, wrecked the calculations of all the world's statesmen. Japan surrendered on August 14, 1945, leaving most of China without civil authority. Nanking did what it could to capitalize on its willingness to cooperate. On August 17 Dōmei reported that Ch'en Kung-po had made a million troops available to Chungking.[86] Chungking, however, was no longer interested in Nanking's aid. There was nothing to do but dissolve the government and run. Thus on August 16, the Nanking government was brought to an end, having served five years four months and sixteen days. The Central Political Council of the Nanking government announced its dissolution: "The government, under the leadership of Mr. Wang Ching-wei, returned to the capital and proclaimed far and wide the need for the realization of peace. We hereby dissolve the government which did not realize its goal during the past six years."[87]

The Japanese did what they could to save those Chinese who

had tried to cooperate with them in the client regimes. But the Japanese at this time were in no position to do other than execute the desires of the victors. Chungking had made it amply clear that there was going to be no mercy for collaborators. The Communists were more subtle, encouraging the populace to discriminate between those collaborators who were traitors and petty oppressors and those who had tried to serve the interests of China and her people.[88]

Ch'en Kung-po, although he asserted that he was not afraid to die, felt that his chances for justice would be much enhanced if he could conceal himself until the furor died down. He persuaded Imai to engineer his escape, along with a few followers, to Japan, saying that his presence in Nanking would hinder the transfer of authority to the Chungking government. The next day, August 25, the Chungking forces were due to arrive to take control of Nanking. Moreover, the allies had ordered that by noon of that day all flights into and out of Japanese airfields were to be suspended. Despite these manifold difficulties, Imai was able to arrange for Ch'en and his wife and five associates to fly to Japan.[89] Ch'en left a letter before his departure in the hands of a Japanese officer for delivery to General Ho Ying-ch'in, declaring that his intention was not to flee prosecution but to aid, the smooth take-over of power by General Ho.[80] This letter, however, was not delivered. The first demand of the Chungking officers when they arrived in Nanking was for the whereabouts of the officials of the Nanking government. The Japanese replied that Ch'en had committed suicide.[91] Chungking, however, had learned of Ch'en's escape. Under Chiang Kai-shek's order, Ho Ying-ch'in on September 9 issued a subpoena demanding Ch'en's extradition.

Ch'en and his comrades had been staying at the Kyoto Hotel and then moved at his request into Kinkakuji Temple in Kyoto. There Ch'en had a tragic last conversation with Konoye, soon to die by his own hand to avoid trial as a war criminal.[92]

Ch'en and his comrades, with the exception of his wife, were returned to Nanking in a special plane sent by the Nationalist government. He and most of the other ex-members of the Nanking government were transferred to Hsüchou for trial. He offered an eloquent and dignified defense: he had acted only out of loyalty to his old friend.[93] He calmly accepted the death verdict and was executed on June 3, 1946. His last words to his comrades in prison, Chu Min-i and Ch'en Pi-chün were: "Soon I will see Mr. Wang in the next world."[94] Most of the subordinate members of the Nanking government shortly joined Ch'en there.

Ch'en Pi-chün, rather than trying to exonerate her actions as Ch'en had done, defended the peace movement to the last. She declared to her judges on April 16, 1946: "The actions of my husband Wang Ching-wei all were based on the virtuous ideal of saving the country. Even now I sincerely support him. In the face of the Japanese invasion following the Marco Polo Bridge Incident, all the leaders of the government fled, renouncing their duty to protect the people. We had to take charge of protecting the people and attempt to handle the situation, even though our hands were empty. During this period what did the Chungking Government do to help? Japan was defeated in the Pacific. If the Pacific war had not come about, we might have become the saviours of our country. If our actions are condemned as violating the policy of the government, I will gladly be put to death, for what we did was for the people."[95] Sentenced to life imprisonment, she died, her bulk much reduced by prison regimen, in what had become Communist China in June 1959.[96]

For a while it looked as though Chou Fo-hai would successfully weather the storm. Eight days after the Japanese surrender, on August 19, Chungking had appointed Chou Fo-hai commander of the Nanking-Shanghai Area Special Action Unit in recognition of Chou's organization of the Wang military forces in collaboration with Chungking and his other services. On the next day Chou and several of his cohorts, including Ting Mo-ts'un, were flown to Chungking and ensconced under comfortable house arrest. Popular opinion was greatly incensed; Chou's association with the activities of "76" had made him an object of special hate. Tai Li, the Chungking intelligence chief who had been protecting him, died in a plane crash, and subsequently, Chou was put on trial in Nanking in September 1946.[97] He declared before the court: "Although I participated in the Nanking Government, since 1942 my loyalty has been in Chungking. For the second half of the war I was preparing, in coordination with the Supreme Defense Council of the National

Government, to respond to the Chungking counterattack against the Japanese Army."[98] The fact that he was in their eyes a double traitor did not extenuate Chou's actions in the eyes of the court, and he too was sentenced to death. It is said that through Ch'en Pu-lei, Mrs. Chou gained an interview with Chiang and persuaded him to spare her husband's life. In any case, Chiang ordered the commutation of his sentence to life imprisonment.[99] He died, some say by his own hand, in prison in April 1947.[100]

Chungking's revenge could not be complete unless it could reach Wang Ching-wei, who had escaped to the other world. Following the secret order of Ho Ying-ch'in, on January 21 Wang's concrete tomb was demolished with 150 kilograms of TNT, and his coffin was removed, trucked out to the countryside, and burned.[101]

According to a popular story, Ch'iu Wei-ta, the commander of the 74th Army which had been responsible for the desecration of Wang's remains, was constantly tortured by his conscience for the deed. He was transferred to Shantung to fight against the Communists. One day in broad daylight the ghost of Wang Ching-wei appeared before him. Shouting "Wang hsien-sheng, Wang hsien-sheng" (Mr. Wang, Mr. Wang) Ch'iu shot himself.[102]

At this writing, Wang Ching-wei has been dead, if not resting in his grave, for over a quarter of a century. In evaluating Wang's peace movement, there are certain questions that the historian can resolve and certain that he cannot.

The basic question of whether Wang was a traitor or a patriot, the historian cannot resolve, except in one sense: Wang was no Pétain or Quisling; he did not love the Japanese; he was not hostile to the institutions of his country; he sought nothing for himself but the honor of saving his country. "We had good intentions from the beginning," said Kao Tsung-wu, "but it all came out the wrong way."[103] If one believes that China's real enemy was not Japan but the Communists, then one sees Wang a patriot. If one believes that in the presence of insatiable Japanese aggression, domestic political quarrels should take second place to defense of the homeland against the foreign invader, then one sees Wang a traitor.

The question of whether Wang was wise can more easily be resolved. Wang's original plan was rationally defensible, namely, that, assuming the Japanese wanted to withdraw from China despite their military victories, he could provide them a face-saving way to do so.

But when the first assumption proved vain, his decision to establish a regime in the occupied territories with the hope of future Japanese concessions was foolish. A reversal of Japanese intentions toward China, which was the premise of the "peace government" notion, was wildly improbable. Even if Japan had succeeded in conquering China, the existence of another Kuomintang government which had acceded to Japanese demands would have further perpetuated the division of nation and party.

Notes
Bibliography
Glossary
Index

FRUS refers to the series *Foreign Relations of the United States,* selections from the diplomatic papers of the United States published at irregular intervals by the Department of State, Washington, D.C.

JMFA refers to documents from the Japanese archives captured at the end of the war and available on microfilm at the Library of Congress, Washington, D.C. The documents are for the most part from the Ministry of Foreign Affairs (Gaimushō). The references are to document numbers which are stamped on the documents themselves. The number of the appropriate microfilm reel on which each document is reproduced may be found by referring to the following two handbooks:

Checklist of Archives in the Japanese Ministry of Foreign Affairs, Tokyo, Japan, 1868–1945, comp. Cecil H. Uyehara, (Washington, D.C., 1954).

Checklist of Microfilm Reproductions of Selected Archives of Japanese Army, Navy, and other Government Agencies, 1868–1945, comp. John Young, (Washington, D.C., 1959).

1. Prelude to Tragedy

1. Unless otherwise noted, for information on Wang's life until the Manchurian Incident, I have relied on James Shirley, "Political Conflicts in the Kuomintang: The Career of Wang Ching-wei to 1932," Ph.D. diss. (University of California, Berkeley, 1965) and for the period until 1937, upon Lin Han-sheng, "Wang Ching-wei and the Japanese Peace Efforts," Ph.D. diss. (University of Pennsylvania, 1967). See also Howard L. Boorman, ed., *Biographical Dictionary of Modern China* (New York 1970), III, 369–376 and Boorman, "Wang Ching-wei: China's Romantic Radical," Political Science Quarterly, 79.4:504–525 (December 1964).

2. Tang Leang-li, "Wang Ching-wei — leader of China Renascent," *People's Tribune*, 4.5:241–251 (April 1, 1933).

3. Wang Ching-wei, "On Agrarian Policy," *People's Tribune*, 6.1:4 (Jan. 1, 1934).

4. Royal Institute of International Affairs, *Documents on International Affairs 1937* (London, 1939), pp. 632–638.

5. Dorothy Borg, *The United States and the Far Eastern Crisis of 1933-1938* (Cambridge, Mass., 1964), pp. 37–38.

6. Ch'en Kung-po, "Pa-nien lai-te hui-i" (The reminiscences of the past eight years), p. 187, quoted by Lin Han-sheng, p. 132.

7. Kao Tsung-wu, Conversations with Gerald Bunker, p. 45.

8. Ibid., pp. 1–3.

9. *FRUS, 1936*, IV, 351, 357, 433; and Takagi Rikurō in *Jikyoku geppō* (Current affairs monthly; February 1939) quoted in *Contemporary Japan*, 8.1:138 (March 1939). Kao states, however, that he was not personally involved in the Ho-Umezu Agreement (1935) or the Ch'in Doihara Understanding (1936) but learned of them later. Kao Tsung-wu, p. 58.

10. Kao Tsung-wu, p. 4.

11. *FRUS, 1935*, III, 409.

12. *New York Times*, Dec. 23, 1936, p. 8.

13. Howard L. Boorman, ed., *Biographical Dictionary of Republican China* (New York, 1967), I, 407.

14. Imai Takeo, *Shina jihen no kaisō* (Tokyo, 1964), p. 71.

15. *New York Times*, Jan. 19, 1937, p. 16.

16. *FRUS, 1937*, III, 40.

17. *Contemporary Japan*, 6.2:329 (September 1937).

2. Opening Moves

1. James B. Crowley, "A Reconsideration of the Marco Polo Bridge Incident," *Journal of Asian Studies*, 22.3:277–292 (May 1963).

2. *FRUS, 1937*, III, 170.

3. *FRUS, 1937*, III, 230.

4. *New York Times*, Dec. 11, 1937, p. 3.

5. Crowley, "A Reconsideration," pp. 282–284.

6. Lin Han-sheng, pp. 217–218.

7. Ibid., p. 218.

8. Text: *FRUS, 1937,* III, 216–218.

9. *FRUS, 1937,* III, 257.

10. Hu Shih, "Hu Shih jih-chi chai-lu," *Chin-tai-shih tzu-liao* 2:209–210 (1955).

11. Francis Clifford Jones, *Japan's New Order in East Asia* (London, 1954), p. 44.

12. Wang Ching-wei, "Frankness and Responsibility in Facing the Crisis," *People's Tribune,* 18.4:252 (Aug. 16, 1937).

13. Hu Shih, p. 210.

14. *FRUS, 1937,* III, 192.

15. *FRUS, 1937,* III, 192.

16. Kao Tsung-wu, p. 5.

17. Kao Tsung-wu, pp. 34–37; and Hu Shih pp. 211–212.

18. Nishi Yoshiaki, *Higeki no shōnin: Nikka wahei kōsaku hishi* (Tokyo, 1962), p. 76; and Kao Tsung-wu, p. 6.

19. Ibid., p. 37.

20. *FRUS, 1937,* III, 474. The date that Hu told Ambassador Johnson that he met with Chiang in Nanking cannot be correct since Hu was in Kuling at that time.

21. *FRUS, 1937,* III, 329.

22. *FRUS, 1937,* III, 130.

23. *FRUS, 1937,* III, 146, 329.

24. Kao Tsung-wu, pp. 52–53.

25. Ibid., p. 52

26. Ibid., p. 6.

27. *FRUS, 1937,* III, 368.

28. JMFA, IMT 610:5–20 and IMT 610:23 respectively.

29. Kao Tsung-wu, p. 58

30. JMFA, IMT 610:32.

31. *New York Times,* Sept. 12, 1945, p. 3; and Yabe Teiji, *Konoye Fumimaro* (Tokyo, 1952), I, 403–404.

32. Yabe, I, 405–406.

33. *Contemporary Japan,* 6.3:560 (December 1937).

34. Kao Tsung-wu, p. 7.

35. Kao Tsung-wu, p. 38.

36. Royal Institute of International Affairs, *Documents, 1937,* pp. 676–677.

37. *FRUS, 1937,* III, 636.

38. Royal Institute of International Affairs, *Documents, 1937,* p. 709.

39. U.S. Department of State, *Documents on German Foreign Policy, 1918–1945,* Series D, (Washington, D.C. 1949–1964), I, 779.

40. U.S. Department of State, *Documents on German Foreign Policy, 1918–1945,* Series D, I, 778–779, 793–794.

41. U.S. Department of State, *Documents on German Foreign Policy, 1918–1945,* Series D, I, 780–81.

42. U.S. Department of State, *Documents on German Foreign Policy, 1918–1945,* Series D, I, 794–795.

43. Wang Ching-wei, "Facts about the Peace Proposals," *Oriental Affairs*, 11.5:274–276 (May 1939).

44 Wang Ching-wei, "Facts about the Peace Proposals," p. 275.

45. U.S. Department of State, *Documents on German Foreign Policy, 1918–1945,* Series, D, I, 788.

46. U.S. Department of State, *Documents on German Foreign Policy, 1918–1945,* Series, D, I, 788.

47. *People's Tribune,* 27.1–6:43 (August–October 1939).

48. U.S. Department of State, *Documents on German Foreign Policy, 1918–1945,* Series D, I, 799.

49. *New York Times,* Nov. 27, 1937, p. 6.

50. *New York Times,* Dec. 11, 1937, p. 3.

51. *FRUS, 1937,* III, 767.

52. *New York Times,* Dec. 8, 1937, p. 4.

53. T'ao Hsi-sheng, "Luan liu," *Chuan-chi wen-hsüeh* 2.4:6 (April 1963).

54. *FRUS, 1937,* III, 537.

55. *FRUS, 1937,* III, 447.

56. *FRUS, 1937,* III, 628–629.

57. *China Weekly Review,* 83.1:14 (Dec. 4, 1937).

58. Hollington Tong, *Dateline: China* (New York, 1950), p. 13.

59. Galeazzo Ciano, *Ciano's Hidden Diary 1937–1938,* tr. and ed. Andreas Mayor, intro. by Malcolm Muggeridge (New York, 1953), p. 33.

60. *China Weekly Review,* 83.5:118 (Jan. 1, 1938).

61. Wang Ching-wei [?], *Ō Sei-ei jijoden,* tr. and ed. Andō Tokuki (Tokyo, 1941), pp. 181–182.

62. T'ao Chü-yin, *Wang cheng-ch'üan tsa-lu* (Macao, 1963), p. 27.

63. U.S. Department of State, *Documents on German Foreign Policy, 1918–1945,* Series D, I, 803.

64. U.S. Department of State, *Documents on German Foreign Policy, 1918–1945,* Series D, I, 803, 812.

65. U.S. Department of State, *Documents on German Foreign Policy, 1918–1945,* Series D, I, 815.

66. *People's Tribune,* 27.1–6:44–45 (August–October 1939).

67. Horiba Kazuo, *Shina jihen sensō shidōshi* (Tokyo, 1962), I, 122–128.

68. Royal Institute of International Affairs, *Documents 1938* (London, 1942), I, 341; and Horiba, I, 131.

69. Yabe, I, 526.

3. *Japanese Intentions, Chinese Prospects*

1. Masao Maruyama, *Thought and Behavior in Modern Japanese Politics,* ed. Ivan Morris (Oxford University Press, London, 1963), p. 8.

2. James B. Crowley, *Japan's Quest for Autonomy: National Security and Foreign Policy, 1930–1938* (Princeton University Press, Princeton, New Jersey, 1966), p. xvii.

3. Maruyama, p. 16–17.

4. James B. Crowley, "Japanese Army Factionalism in the Early 1930's," *Journal of Asian Studies*, 21.3:277–292 (May 1962).

5. I am indebted to Mark Peattie, the biographer of Ishiwara, for much of the following.

6. The royal family was maintained in a vestigial state in Korea and lower-level offices were staffed by Koreans but there was no attempt to give Korea the appearance of independence and sovereignty.

7. Horiba, p. 133.

8. International Military Tribunal, Far East, Testimony, p. 31, 463.

9. Yabe, I, 469, 527.

10. Crowley, *Japan's Quest*, pp. 358–375.

11. Yabe, I, 526.

12. Ibid., 469–470.

13. *New York Times*, Jan. 20, 1938, p. 6.

14. *FRUS, 1938*, III, 85–86.

15. Inukai Ken, *Yōsukō wa ima mo nagarete iru* (Tokyo, 1960), p. 41.

16. Imai, *Shina jihen no kaisō*, p. 152.

17. An independent analysis of Japanese client regimes in China is presented in Boyle, John H., "Japan's Puppet Regimes in China, 1937–1940," Ph.D. diss., Stanford University, 1968. Professor Boyle seeks to find common elements in the client regimes established under the auspices of the Axis powers and to see the East Asian regimes in the light of East Asian circumstances. Unfortunately this valuable work reached me too late to assist me in research for this volume. He has summarized his findings in an article: "The Road to Sino — Japanese Cooperation: The Background to the Defection of Wang Ching-wei," *Monumenta Nipponica*, 25. 3–4: 207–301 (September-December 1970).

18. Norman D. Hanwell, "Economic Disruption in Occupied China," *Far Eastern Survey*, 8.6:61 (March 15, 1939).

19. International Military Tribunal, Far East, Exhibit No. 463, p. 1.

20. *China Weekly Review*, 84.6:151 (Apr. 9, 1938).

21. *Taiheiyō sensō e no michi*, ed. Taiheiyō sensō gen'in kenkyūbu, vols. III and IV, *Nitchū sensō* by Hata Ikuhiko, Usu Katsumi, and Hirai Tomoyoshi, IV, 212 (Tokyo, 1963).

22. *FRUS, 1938*, III, 130–131.

23. JMFA, S1611–7:66.

24. International Military Tribunal, Far East, Exhibit No. 463, p. 6.

25. *FRUS, 1938*, III, 193–194.

26. *FRUS, 1938*, III, 228–229.

27. JMFA, IMT 145:54; and Imai Takeo, *Shina jihen no kaisō*, pp. 98–99.

28. W. V. Pennell, "The Passing of Marshall Wu Pei-fu," *Oriental Affairs*, 13.1:42–45 (January 1940).

29. *FRUS, 1939, III*, 134.

30. *FRUS, 1939*, III, 131.

4. Tung and Kao Go to Japan

1. *FRUS, 1936,* IV, 346.
2. Nishi, p. 77.
3. Nishi, pp. 79–80.
4. Nishi, p. 96.
5. Kao Tsung-wu, p. 13.
6. Nishi, p. 96.
7. Nishi, p. 98.
8. Inukai, p. 41.
9. Inukai, p. 771.
10. Kao Tsung-wu, p. 10.
11. Kao Tsung-wu, p. 9.
12. Nishi, pp. 113–115.
13. Kagesa Sadaaki, "Sozorogaki," in *Gendaishi shiryō,* XIII, 358.
14. Kagesa, p. 358.
15. Imai, *Shina jihen no kaisō,* p. 66.
16. Inukai, p. 42.
17. Kao Tsung-wu, p. 13.
18. Kagesa, p. 359.
19. Kagesa, p. 359.
20. Wang Lun headed a mission to Jurchen to make peace during the Southern Sung. Lin Han-sheng, p. 269.
21. Nishi, p. 116.
22. Ibid., p. 119.
23. Kao Tsung-wu, p. 13.
24. Ibid., p. 10.
25. Ibid., p. 15.
26. Yabe, I, 579.
27. Nishi, p. 210.
28. Kao Tsung-wu, p. 8.
29. Nishi, pp. 127–130.
30. Inukai, p. 79; and Nishi, pp. 135–136.
31. Nishi, pp. 135–136.
32. Kao Tsung-wu, p. 15.
33. Nishi, pp. 135–136.
34. The information contained in this paragraph was relayed to the author by an anonymous source considered by the author to be reliable. Therefore the author cites it on his own responsibility and warns the reader of its character as hearsay evidence.
35. Yabe, I, 526–527.
36. Nishi, p. 203.
37. Shigemitsu Mamoru, *Shōwa no dōran* (Tokyo, 1952), I, 213.
38. Kazami Akira, *Konoye naikaku* (Tokyo, 1951), p. 174.
39. Harada Kumao, *Saionji-kō to seikyoku* (Tokyo, 1952), VII, 27.
40. Kao Tsung-wu, p. 16.
41. Nishi, p. 188.
42. Inukai, p. 72.
43. Kao Tsung-wu, p. 17.

44. Inukai, p. 44.

45. Kao Tsung-wu, p. 16.

46. Ibid., p. 18.

47. Ibid., p. 18.

48. Ibid., pp. 17–18.

49. Inukai, p. 24.

50. Imai, *Shina jihen no kaisō,* p. 69.

51. Nishi, p. 190.

52. Yabe, I, 578.

53. Kao Tsung-wu, p. 29.

54. Ibid., p. 9.

55. Nishi, p. 203.

56. Ugaki Kazushige, "Sino-Japanese Peace Talks, June–September, 1938; Extracts from the Diary of General Ugaki," tr. E. H. M. Colegrave, *St. Anthony's Papers,* 2:100 (1957).

57. Ugaki, pp. 98–99.

58. International Military Tribunal, Far East, Record of Proceedings of the Commission Taking the Deposition of Kagesa, Sadaaki, at First National Hospital, Tokyo, Japan, May 22–23, 1947. (World War II War Crimes Records, Record Group 238, The National Archives, Washington, D.C.), p. 56.

59. Kao Tsung-wu, p. 44.

60. Inukai, p. 63.

61. Kao Tsung-wu, p. 18.

62. Ibid., p. 16.

63. Inukai, p. 48.

64. International Military Tribunal, Kagesa Deposition, p. 13.

65. Harada, VII, 43.

66. Harada, VII, 43.

67. Harada, VII, 43.

67. Harada, VII, 43.

68. Inukai, p. 67.

69. Kao Tsung-wu, p. 18.

70. International Military Tribunal, Kagesa Deposition, p. 56.

71. Ibid., p. 59.

72. Kao Tsung-wu, p. 18.

73. Ibid., pp. 18–19.

5. *The Peace Movement Quickens, Approaches Victory, and Is Betrayed*

1. *FRUS, 1938,* III, 220; and T'ao Hsi-sheng, "Luan Liu," 2.4:6.

2. Wang Ching-wei, "Guerilla Warfare and the Scorched Earth," *People's Tribune,* 21.5–6:209–216 (June 1938).

3. *FRUS, 1938,* III, 247; *North China Herald* (Shanghai), Aug. 24, 1938, p. 310; *News Chronicle* (London), Aug. 20, 1938, p. 2; and *China Weekly Review,* 86.6:17 (Oct. 8, 1938) from a report by O. M. Green in *North China Daily News* (Shanghai), Sept. 25, 1938. See also Lin

Han-sheng, pp. 251–252, and his source, Ts'ao Chu-jen, *Tsai-fang wai-chi* (Other records of a reporter; Hong Kong, 1954), pp. 97, 108.

4. Imai, *Shina jihen no kaisō*, pp. 68–69.

5. *FRUS, 1938,* III, 375–376.

6. Kao Tsung-wu, p. 19.

7. Ibid., p. 5.

8. Ibid., p. 5.

9. "Low tone" is either in contrast to the high tone of those who favored the war, or a reference to the meeting place in the bomb shelter, or as related in chapter 2, derived from Kao and Hu's conversation.

10. Kao Tsung-wu, p. 5.

11. Ibid., p. 19.

12. Boorman, I, 407; and T'ao Hsi-sheng, 2.4:6.

13. *China Weekly Review,* 87.10:310 (Feb. 4, 1939).

14. *FRUS, 1938,* III, 395.

15. Kagesa, p. 360.

16. Text: Horiba, I, 190–196.

17. Nishi, p. 209.

18. Text: *FRUS, Japan, 1931–1941,* I, 479–480.

19. Imai, *Shina jihen no kaisō*, p. 78.

20. T'ao Hsi-sheng, 2.4:6.

21. Kao Tsung-wu, p. 60.

22. Yabe, I, 579.

23. Kao Tsung-wu, pp. 19, 60.

24. Ibid., p. 60.

25. Yabe, I, 579.

26. Imai, *Shina jihen no kaisō*, p. 73.

27. Yabe, I, 579.

28. Imai, *Shina jihen no kaisō*, p. 78.

29. Imai, *Shina jihen no kaisō*, p. 73.

30. Yabe, I, 579; and Imai, *Shina jihen no kaisō*, p. 73.

31. Kao Tsung-wu, p. 20.

32. Ibid., pp. 9ff.

33. Inukai, pp. 67–87.

34. Imai, *Shina jihen no kaisō*, p. 73.

35. Inukai, p. 87.

36. Inukai, p. 87.

37. Inukai, p. 95

38. Nishi, p. 213.

39. Kao Tsung-wu, pp. 19, 61.

40. Ibid., p. 20; and Imai, *Shina jihen no kaisō*, p. 78.

41. Kagesa, p. 361; and Imai, *Shina jihen no kaisō*, p. 77.

42. Text: Imai, *Shina jihen no kaisō,* pp. 80–81.

43. Kao Tsung-wu, pp. 20, 61.

44. Imai, *Shina jihen no kaisō*, p. 79. Professor Yoji Akashi informs me that Imai has erred in his recollection of the names and posts of several persons reported attending this meeting.

45. Kagesa, *Deposition,* p. 68.
46. Imai, *Shina jihen no kaisō,* p. 97.
47. Text: Imai, *Shina jihen no kaisō,* pp. 82–83.
48. Kao Tsung-wu, pp. 20, 60.
49. Ibid., p. 11.
50. T'ao Hsi-sheng, 2.4:7.
51. Boorman, II, 458.
52. Imai, *Shina jihen no kaisō,* p. 83.
53. Kagesa, 361.
54. *FRUS, 1938,* III, 397.
55. Horiba, I, 224.
56. Kao Tsung-wu, p. 21.
57. Harada, VII, 235.
58. Inukai, pp. 105–106.
59. International Military Tribunal, Far East, Testimony, p. 31, 479.
60. Kazami, p. 170.
61. Kido Kōichi, *Kido Kōichi nikki* (Tokyo, 1966), p. 687.
62. T'ao Hsi-sheng, 2.4:7.
63. Kao Tsung-wu, p. 25.
64. Ibid., p. 52.
65. Ibid., p. 20.
66. Nishi, pp. 219–220.
67. Imai, *Shina jihen no kaisō,* p. 83.
68. Inukai, p. 98.
69. Text: Imai, *Shina jihen no kaisō,* p. 84.
70. Kao Tsung-wu, p. 22.
71. Nishi, pp. 219–220.
72. Yabe, I, 588.
73. Horiba, I, 229.
74. Inukai, p. 99.
75. Yabe, I, 588.
76. Harada, VII, 233.
77. Yabe, I, 588.
78. Harada, VII, 233–234.
79. Yabe, I, 588; Kao, Tsung-wu, p. 70.
80. *North China Herald* (Shanghai), Dec. 14, 1938, p. 438.
81. T'ao Hsi-sheng, 2.4:7.
82. Imai, *Shina jihen no kaisō,* p. 87; and Wang Ching-wei [?], *Ō Sei-ei jijoden,* p. 199.
83. T'ao Hsi-sheng, 2.4:7.
84. Imai, *Shina jihen no kaisō,* p. 85; *Oriental Affairs,* 11.2:100 (February 1939); *People's Tribune,* 27.1–6:46 (August–October 1939), Lu, David J., *From the Marco Polo Bridge to Pearl Harbor: Japan's Entry into World War II* (Washington, D.C., 1961), p. 80, and Boorman, "Wang Ching-wei," p. 517.
85. Imai, *Shina jihen no kaisō,* p. 87.
86. *Taiheiyō sensō e no michi,* IV, 204.

87. JMFA, IMT 310:18; and Imai, *Shina jihen no kaisō*, p. 87.

88. Chu Tzu-chia [Chin Hsiung-pai], *Wang cheng-ch'üan te k'ai-ch'ang yü shou-ch'ang* (Hong Kong, 1959–1964), I, 6.

89. Kao Tsung-wu, p. 22.

90. "The Meaning of the Sino-Japanese Treaty," *People's Tribune*, 29.8–12:341 (December 1940).

91. *Taiheiyō senso e no michi*, IV, 205.

92. T'ao Hsi-sheng, 2.4:7.

93. Tong, p. 76.

94. *FRUS, 1938*, III, 435–436.

95. *Ta kung pao* (Hong Kong), Dec. 24, 1938, p. 1.

96. *Chung-yang jih pao* (Chungking), Dec. 27, 1938, p. 2.

97. *New York Times*, Dec. 28, 1938, p. 6.

98. Text: *FRUS, Japan 1931–1941*, I, 482–483.

99. *Oriental Affairs*, 11.2:98 (February 1939); and *Ta kung pao* (Hong Kong), Dec. 29, 1938, p. 1; Dec. 30, 1938, p. 1; Dec. 31, 1938, p. 1.

100. Kao Tsung-wu, p. 61.

101. Imai, *Shina jihen no kaisō*, pp. 88–89; and Yabe, I, 590.

102. Inukai, p. 100. Professor Yoji Akashi reports that Tominaga was not appointed to the General Staff until September 1939; therefore Inukai must be mistaken in blaming the intransigency of the General Staff on this occasion on Tominaga.

103. Inukai, pp. 100–103.

104. Nishi, p. 230.

105. Yabe, I, 590.

106. Kao Tsung-wu, p. 23.

107. Kao Tsung-wu, pp. 23–24.

108. T'ao Hsi-sheng, 2.4:7.

109. Kagesa, p. 362.

110. Kao Tsung-wu, p. 24.

111. T'ao Hsi-sheng, 2.4:7.

112. Kagesa, *Deposition*, p. 76.

113. Text: *Oriental Affairs*, 11.2:100 (February 1939).

114. *China Weekly Review*, 87.6:174 (Jan. 7, 1939).

115. *New York Times*, Jan. 7, 1939, p. 5.

116. *China Weekly Review*, 87.7:302 (Jan. 14, 1939).

117. Harada, VII, 249.

118. Harada, VII, 253.

6. From Hanoi to Shanghai

1. T'ao Hsi-sheng, 2.4:7.

2. *FRUS, 1939*, III, 131.

3. *Oriental Affairs*, 11.2:100 (February 1939).

4. *FRUS, 1939*, III, 167.

5. Harada, VII, 261.

6. JMFA, UD 59:69, 71; and Chu [Chin], I, 4.

7. JMFA, UD 59:174.

8. *Ta kung pao* (Hong Kong), Jan. 18, 1939, p. 6.

9. Chu [Chin], I, 114.

10. *China Weekly Review,* 87.11:329 (Feb. 11, 1939).

11. Kao Tsung-wu, p. 24.

12. *Taiheiyō sensō e no michi,* IV, 207.

13. *New York Times,* Jan. 27, 1939, p. 1.

14. Chou Fo-hai, *Chou Fo-hai jih-chi* (Hong Kong, 1955), introduction, p. 2.

15. *FRUS, 1939,* III, 135.

16. Wang Ching-wei, "Facts about the Peace Proposals," p. 276.

17. *China Weekly Review,* 87.11:330 (Feb. 11, 1939); and Chu [Chin], I, 22.

18. *Ta kung pao* (Hong Kong), March 8, 1939, p. 3; March 21, 1939, p. 3.

19. JMFA, IMT 310:23–24; and *Gendaishi shiryō,* IX, 655.

20. JMFA, UD 59:145.

21. JMFA, UD 59:458.

22. JMFA, UD 59:235–239.

23. JMFA, SP 302:53.

24. Nishi, pp. 237–240.

25. *Taiheiyō sensō e no michi,* IV, 207.

26. Inukai, p. 112; and Nishi, p. 246.

27. Kao Tsung-wu, pp. 25–26.

28. Kao Tsung-wu, pp. 53–54.

29. *Taiheiyō sensō e no michi,* IV, 207.

30. Kao Tsung-wu, p. 26.

31. Imai, p. 93.

32. Inukai, pp. 114–116.

33. Kao Tsung-wu, pp. 26–27.

34. Nishi, p. 240.

35. Kao Tsung-wu, pp. 24, 27.

36. Chu [Chin], I, 22–23. This account is attributed to Lin Pai-sheng.

37. Inukai, p. 124.

38. Wang Ching-wei, "Facts about the Peace Proposals," p. 274; and Inukai, p. 124.

39. Kao Tsung-wu, p. 27.

40. Kao Tsung-wu, p. 30.

41. Kao Tsung-wu, p. 61.

42. Kao Tsung-wu, p. 29.

43. Text: *Oriental Affairs,* 11.5:276–277 (May 1939).

44. Kao Tsung-wu, pp. 26, 46, 61.

45. International Military Tribunal, Kagesa Deposition, pp. 139–144; and Kagesa, pp. 373–374.

46. Kagesa, p. 363.

47. *Taiheiyō sensō e no michi,* IV, 207.

48. JMFA, UD 59:144.

49. Inukai, p. 123; and International Military Tribunal, Kagesa, Deposition, p. 87.

50. Inukai, p. 124; Imai, *Shina jihen no kaisō,* p. 94; Imai Takeo, "Taika wahei kōsaku shi" in *Himerareta Shōwa shi,* a supplement to Chisei, pp. 250–258 (December 1956); and *Taiheiyō senso e no michi,* IV, 208.

51. JMFA, UD 59:278.

52. Kao does not recall this. Kao Tsung-wu, p. 29.

53. Inukai, p. 139.

54. Kao Tsung-wu, p. 28; and Inukai, p. 139.

55. Inukai, p. 131; and Imai, *Shina jihen no kaisō,* p. 94.

56. Inukai, p. 135.

57. Inukai, p. 138.

58. Inukai, p. 142.

59. Kagesa, p. 364.

60. Inukai, p. 144.

61. Kagesa, p. 364.

62. Inukai, p. 136.

63. JMFA, UD 59:205; and International Military Tribunal, Kagesa, Deposition, p. 88.

64. Kao Tsung-wu, p. 30.

65. Inukai, p. 148.

66. Exhibit C-1 to International Military Tribunal, Kagesa, Deposition; and Kao Tsung-wu, p. 29.

67. Exhibit C-2 to International Military Tribunal, Kagesa, Deposition.

68. Exhibit C-3 to International Military Tribunal, Kagesa, Deposition.

69. Inukai, p. 152.

70. International Military Tribunal, Kagesa, Deposition, p. 91.

71. Inukai, p. 153.

72. Kagesa, p. 365.

73. Exhibit C-1 to International Military Tribunal, Kagesa, Deposition.

74. JMFA, UD 59:411.

75. Inukai, p. 153.

76. Inukai, pp. 155–156.

77. JMFA, UD 59:133.

78. JMFA, UD 59:351.

79. JMFA, UD 59:399.

80. Exhibit E-2 to International Military Tribunal, Kegesa, Deposition. This document gives the time for re-establishing contact at 1 pm, April 28. I do not believe whether contact was made on the 28th or 29th materially affects the argument.

81. Kagesa, p. 365.

82. Kagesa, p. 365.

83. Kagesa, p. 366.

84. Inukai, p. 159.

85. Kagesa, p. 366.
86. Inukai, p. 158; and Kagesa, p. 365.
87. Kagesa, p. 365.
88. Kagesa, p. 367.
89. JMFA, UD 59:448–449.
90. JMFA, UD 59:408.
91. Nishi, pp. 244–246.
92. Nishi, p. 254.
93. Nishi, pp. 257–260.
94. Inukai, p. 166.
95. Exhibit F to International Military Tribunal, Kagesa, Deposition.
96. JMFA, UD 59:408.
97. Imai, *Shina jihen no kaisō,* p. 95.
98. Exhibit F to International Military Tribunal, Kagesa, Deposition.
99. JMFA, UD 59:419.
100. Inukai, p. 166.
101. Kao Tsung-wu, p. 30.
102. Inukai, p. 171.
103. JMFA, UD 59:209.
104. Exhibit I to International Military Tribunal, Kagesa, Deposition.
105. JMFA, UD 59:210.
106. JMFA, UD SP 302:736–750.
107. Exhibit G to International Military Tribunal, Kagesa, Deposition.
108. JMFA, UD 59:451.
109. JMFA, UD 59:300.
110. Horiba, I, 261.
111. JMFA, UD 59:450–459.
112. JMFA, S 1611–7:522–531.
113. JMFA, S 1611–7:517–521.
114. JMFA, IMT 310:31, SP 302:752.
115. Exhibit K to International Military Tribunal, Kagesa, Deposition.
116. Imai, *Shina jihen no kaisō,* p. 95.
117. Nishi, p. 261.
118. Nishi, p. 261; and Kagesa, p. 369.
119. Nishi, pp. 262–263.
120. *Ta kung pao* (Hong Kong), June 9, 1939, p. 3.
121. Inukai, pp. 173–177; and Kao, "Summary," p. 62.
122. Kagesa, p. 370.
123. International Military Tribunal Far East, Deposition of Shimizu Tozo, Defense Document no. 1352, exhibit 2585, p. 2. Shimizu was the Japanese government's interpreter for the conferences with Wang.
124. International Military Tribunal, Shimizu, Deposition, p. 4.
125. International Military Tribunal, Kagesa, Deposition, pp. 149–150.
126. International Military Tribunal, Shimizu, Deposition, p. 4.
127. *Nichi-nichi* (Toyko, Oct. 11, 1939), p. 1.
128. International Military Tribunal, Shimizu, Deposition, p. 4.
129. Kao Tsung-wu, p. 60.

130. Kagesa, p. 371; and International Military Tribunal, Kagesa, *Deposition*, p. 16.

131. *Gendaishi shiryo*, IX, 652–654.

132. Inukai, p. 195.

133. *Gendaishi shiryō*, IX, 654–659.

134. *Gendaishi shiryō*, IX, 657.

135. *Taiheiyō sensō e no michi*, IV, 210.

136. International Military Tribunal, Exhibit 2588, Defense Document 1298.

137. JMFA, IMT 310:21.

7. From Shanghai to Ch'ingtao

1. Kagesa, p. 372; and Imai, *Shina jihen no kaisō*, p. 98.

2. JMFA, SP 301:907; and Imai, *Shina jihen no kaisō*, p. 100.

3. Harada, VIII, 40.

4. JMFA, IMT 310:22.

5. JMFA, IMT 310:25.

6. Taiheiyō sensō e michi, IV, 211.

7. JMFA, SP 302:659.

8. JMFA, IMT 310:24.

9. JMFA, SP 302:356.

10. W. V. Pennell, "A Letter from North China," *Oriental Affairs*, 12.1:47 (July 1939).

11. JMFA, SP 304:353–356.

12. Morishima Morito, *Imbō, ansatsu, guntō* (Toyko, 1950), pp. 150–151.

13. JMFA, SP 302:224.

14. JMFA, SP 302:217.

15. JMFA, 302:223–225.

16. JMFA, SP 302:245–247.

17. JMFA, SP 302:216.

18. JMFA, SP 302:245–247.

19. JMFA, SP 302:459.

20. JMFA, IMT 310:25.

21. Kagesa, p. 372.

22. *China Weekly Review*, 89.8:244 (July 22, 1939).

23. JMFA, SP 302:204.

24. Morishima, pp. 150–151.

25. Kagesa, p. 372.

26. *China Weekly Review*, 89.7:202 (July 15, 1939).

27. Text: JMFA, SP 302:269, translation in International Military Tribunal, Far East, Exhibit 2591.

28. JMFA, SP 302:621.

29. S. Y. Wang, "Shanghai Schools Thrown into Turmoil as Agents of Wang Ching-wei, with Bribes and Bullets Seek Control of Education," *China Weekly Review*, 90.6:191–193 (Oct. 7, 1939); and *Gendaishi shiryō*, XIII, 243.

30. JMFA, IMT 384:610; and *Gendaishi shiryō*, XIII, 243.

31. JMFA, SP 302:971.

32. JMFA, SP 302:972.

33. JMFA, SP 302:510; and JMFA, SP 302:987–989.

34. JMFA, SP 302:977.

35. JMFA, SP 302:979–982.

36. JMFA, SP 302:993.

37. T'ao Hsi-sheng, 2.4:7.

38. Text: *Oriental Affairs,* 12.3:158 (September 1939).

39. JMFA, SP 302:490.

40. JMFA, SP 302:675.

41. JMFA, SP 302:644.

42. JMFA, SP 302:612.

43. Inukai, p. 262.

44. Inukai, p. 264.

45. *Oriental Affairs,* 12.4:179 (October 1939).

46. JMFA, SP 302:1032, 1052, 1072; Imai, *Shina jihen no kaisō,* p. 101; *China Weekly Review,* 90.2:50–51 (Sept. 9, 1939); and *Oriental Affairs,* 12.4:178–179 (October 1939).

47. JMFA, S 1611–11:159.

48. JMFA, SP 302:1002–1003.

49. *Taiheiyō sensō e no michi,* IV, 214; and T'ao Hsi-sheng, 2.5:6.

50. T'ao Hsi-sheng, 2.5:6.

51. JMFA, SP 302:1144.

52. JMFA, SP 302:1144; and T'ao Hsi-sheng, 2.5:6.

53. T'ao Hsi-sheng, 2.5:6.

54. JMFA, SP 302:1096.

55. Kao Tsung-wu, pp. 40–41.

56. Harada, VIII, 74.

57. Nashimoto Yūhei, *Chūgoku no naka no nihonjin* (Tokyo, 1958), I, 117.

58. *Taiheiyō sensō e no michi,* IV, 214.

59. Horiba, I, 305; and *Taiheiyō sensō e no michi,* IV, 213.

60. *New York Times,* Sept. 7, 1939, p. 15.

61. JMFA, SP 302:1117, 1123.

62. Nishi, p. 268.

63. Horiba, I, 316–317.

64. Nishi, p. 268.

65. Inukai, pp. 196–202.

66. T'ao Hsi-sheng, 2.5:6.

67. *Gendaishi shiryō,* XIII, 249.

68. *Gendaishi shiryō,* XIII, 250.

69. Inukai, p. 266.

70. Inukai, p. 267.

71. Inukai, p. 266.

72. Nashimoto, I, 136.

73. The original text is the one which Kao revealed, *Ta kung pao* (Hong Kong), Jan. 22, 1940, p. 3.

74. T'ao Hsi-sheng, 2.5:6.

75. Kao Tsung-wu, p. 39.

76. Kao Tsung-wu, p. 32.
77. *Gendaishi shiryō*, XIII, 250.
78. *Gendaishi shiryō*, XIII, 251.
79. Inukai, p. 206.
80. Text: *Gendaishi shiryō*, XIII.
81. Horiba, I, 319–320.
82. JMFA, SP 302:1458. See also, in chronological order, SP 302: 1264, 1275, 1288, 1417, 1386.
83. Quoted in *Oriental Economist* (October 1939), and thence in Royal Institute of International Affairs, *Weekly Review of the Foreign Press*, Series C, 10:42 (Dec. 14, 1939).
84. JMFA, SP 302:1420.
85. JMFA, SP 302:1290; and *New York Times*, Oct. 24, 1939, p. 10.
86. JMFA, SP 302:1300, 1405.
87. JMFA, SP 302:1286–1287.
88. *Gendaishi shiryō*, XIII, 316.
89. T'ao Hsi-sheng, 2.5:6–7.
90. T'ao Hsi-sheng, 2.5:7.
91. Kao Tsung-wu, p. 31.
92. Kao Tsung-wu, p. 50.
93. Imai, *Shina jihen no kaisō*, p. 103.
94. Text: Horiba, I, 326–347.
95. Horiba, I, 329.
96. Horiba, I, 348.
97. Inukai, p. 277.
98. *Gendaishi shiryō*, XIII, 302-310.
99. *China Weekly Review*, 91.1:27 (Dec. 2, 1939).
100. *New York Times*, Nov. 23, 1939, p. 18.
101. *New York Times*, Nov. 30, 1939, p. 8.
102. *New York Times*, Dec. 10, 1939, p. 10.
103. *China Weekly Review*, 91.1:28 (Dec. 2, 1939).
104. *China Weekly Review*, 91.3:97 (Dec. 16, 1939).
105. JMFA, UD 59:383; and *China Weekly Review*, 90.3:104 (Sept. 16, 1939).
106. JMFA, SP 302:1451.
107. *China Weekly Review*, 91.1:39 (Dec. 2, 1939).
108. JMFA, SP 302:1495.
109. JMFA, SP 302:1542.
110. JMFA, SP 302:1379.
111. *New York Times*, Dec. 22, 1939, p. 11.
112. *New York Times*, Nov. 19, 1939, p. 30.
113. *New York Times*, Dec. 22, 1939, p. 11.
114. Harada, VIII, 129.
115. Harada, VIII, 132.
116. *New York Times*, Jan. 10, 1940, p. 7.
117. *China Weekly Review*, 91.3:97 (Dec. 16, 1939).
118. JMFA, SP 302:1730.
119. Chou Fo-hai, pp. 9–10.

120. JMFA, SP 302:1721.

121. JMFA, SP 302:1720–21.

122. JMFA, SP 302:1606.

123. JMFA, SP 302:1627.

124. JMFA, SP 302:1272, 1606.

125. Kao Tsung-wu, pp. 41–42.

126. T'ao Hsi-sheng, 2.5:7.

127. Nashimoto, I, 128–130.

128. Kao Tsung-wu, p. 48.

129. Ibid., p. 40.

130. Ibid., p. 55.

131. Ibid., p. 48.

132. Ibid., p. 59.

133. JMFA, SP 302:2397; and *Ta kung pao* (Hong Kong), Jan. 6, 1940, p. 3.

134. T'ao Hsi-sheng, 2.5:7.

135. Chou Fo-hai, p. 1; and T'ao Hsi-sheng, 2.5:7.

136. T'ao Hsi-sheng, 2.5:7.

137. T'ao Hsi-sheng, 2.5:7.

138. Kao Tsung-wu, p. 33.

139. Ibid., pp. 49–50.

140. Ibid., p. 56.

141. JMFA, SP 302:1716–1717.

142. Kao Tsung-wu, p. 56.

143. JMFA, SP 302:1724.

144. *China Weekly Review,* 87.3:70 (Dec. 17. 1938).

145. JMFA, SP 302:1725.

146. *New York Times,* Jan. 20, 1940, p. 4.

147. *Oriental Affairs,* 12.4:179 (October 1939).

148. *FRUS, Japan, 1931–1941,* II, 34, 53.

149. *FRUS, 1940,* IV, 270–271.

150. JMFA, SP 302:2376.

151. Text: *China Weekly Review,* 91.8:269 (Jan. 20, 1940).

152. *Ta kung pao* (Hong Kong), Jan. 22, 1940, p. 3.

153. Kao Tsung-wu, p. 59.

154. JMFA, SP 302:2313.

155. *New York Times,* Jan. 22, 1940, p. 7.

156. *New York Times,* Jan. 24, 1940, p. 2.

157. *China Weekly Review,* 91.9:319–320 (Jan. 27, 1940).

158. JMFA, SP 302:2445.

159. Kao Tsung-wu, p. 48.

160. Ibid., p. 57.

161. JMFA, SP 302:2380; and *China Weekly Review,* 91.13:458 (Feb. 24, 1940).

162. JMFA, S 1611–10:51.

163. Royal Institute of International Affairs, *Weekly Review,* 23:13 (March 14, 1940); and JMFA, SP 302:3488.

164. JMFA, SP 302:2488.

165. Chou Fo-hai, p. 15.
166. JMFA, SP 302:2508.
167. Imai, *Shina jihen no kaisō*, pp. 104–105.
168. JMFA, SP 302:2484.
169. Imai, *Shina jihen no kaisō*, p. 106.
170. JMFA, SP 302:2326; and Imai, *Shina jihen no kaisō*, p. 104.
171. Text: *Gendaishi shiryō*, XIII.

8. *Return to Nanking*

1. Horiba, I, 311.
2. Chou Fo-hai, p. 40.
3. Ibid.
4. Ibid., p. 42.
5. Ibid., p. 43.
6. Harada, VIII, 197–202.
7. *China Weekly Review*, 92.11:394.
8. Imai, *Shina jihen no kaisō*, p. 107.
9. *New York Times*, March, 5, 1940, p. 8.
10. JMFA, SP 302: 2701.
11. JMFA, IMT 384:15.
12. Chou Fo-hai, p. 115.
13. Ibid., p. 38.
14. Ibid., pp. 31–32.
15. Ibid., p. 33.
16. JMFA, SP 302:2595; and Chou Fo-hai, p. 33.
17. *People's Tribune*, 28.5–6:201 (March 1940).
18. Chou Fo-hai, p. 37.
19. Ibid., p. 27.
20. Ibid., pp. 42–43.
21. Ibid., p. 44.
22. Ibid., p. 48.
23. Horiba, I, 385.
24. Imai, *Shina jihen no kaisō*, p. 107.
25. Imai, *Shina jihen no kaisō*, p. 107; and Horiba, I, 385.
26. Horiba, I, 385.
27. Imai, *Shina jihen no kaisō*, p. 107.
28. JMFA, SP 302:2000; and *North China Herald* (Shanghai), April 10, 1940, p. 1.
29. JMFA, SP 302:2002.
30. Chou Fo-hai, p. 36.
31. JMFA, IMT 384:354.
32. JMFA, SP 302:2526.
33. JMFA, SP 302:2611.
34. JMFA, SP 302:2751.
35. Nashimoto, I, 138.
36. JMFA, SP 302:1648, 2496.
37. *China Weekly Review*, 93.4:142 (June 22, 1940).
38. JMFA, IMT 384:445.
39. Imai, *Shina jihen no kaisō*, p. 134.

40. Imai, *Shina jihen no kaisō*, pp. 117–118.
41. Imai, *Shina jihen no kaisō*, pp. 118–119.
42. Harada, VIII, 193.
43. Harada, VIII, 193–194.
44. Imai, *Shina jihen no kaisō*, p. 119.
45. Imai, *Shina jihen no kaisō*, p. 119.
46. Imai, *Shina jihen no kaisō*, p. 120.
47. Imai, *Shina jihen no kaisō*, p. 125.
48. Imai, *Shina Jihen no kaisō*, p. 126.
49. Imai, *Shina jihen no kaisō*, pp. 126–129.
50. Imai, *Shina jihen no kaisō*, p. 130.
51. Chou Fo-hai, pp. 52–53.
52. Imai, *Shina jihen no kaisō*, p. 131.
53. Chou Fo-hai, p. 53.
54. *New York Herald Tribune*, April 23, 1940, quoted by Royal Institute of International Affairs, *Weekly Review*, 32:7 (May 8, 1940).
55. Royal Institute of International Affairs, *Weekly Review*, 32:6 (May 8, 1940).
56. Chou Fo-hai, pp. 52–53.
57. Imai, *Shina jihen no kaisō*, p. 66.
58. Chou Fo-hai, pp. 52-53.
59. Text: *Oriental Affairs*, 13.4:187–188 (April 1940).
60. *Oriental Affairs*, 13.4:192 (April 1940).
61. *Oriental Affairs*, 13.4:186–191 (April 1940).
62. *Oriental Affairs*, 13.4:193 (April 1940).
63. *Oriental Affairs*, 13.4:193 (April 1940).
64. *Oriental Affairs*, 13.4:189 (April 1940).
65. Chou Fo-hai, p. 60.
66. *Asahi Shimbun* (Tokyo), March 30, 1940, p. 7.
67. *Oriental Affairs*, 13.5:244 (May 1940).
68. *Oriental Affairs*, 13.5:244 (May 1940).
69. *China Weekly Review*, 92.6:197–198 (April 6, 1940).
70. *Asahi Shimbun* (Tokyo), March 30, 1940, p. 1.
71. *China Weekly Review*, 92.6:198 (April 6, 1940).
72. *China Weekly Review*, 92.6:199 (April 6, 1940).
73. *Oriental Affairs*, 13.5:244 (May 1940).
74. *China Weekly Review*, 92.6:199 (April 6, 1940).
75. *North China Herald* (Shanghai), April 10, 1940, p. 1.
76. *New York Times*, April 2, 1940, p. 18.
77. *China Weekly Review*, 92.6:200 (April 6, 1940).
78. JMFA, SP 302:2167, S 1611–10:13; and *China Weekly Review*, 92.6:200 (April 6, 1940).
79. *FRUS, 1940*, IV, 279.
80. JMFA, SP 302:2062.
81. Text: *FRUS, Japan 1931–1941*, II, 59.
82. *FRUS, 1940*, IV, 308–309.
83. *FRUS, 1940*, IV, 310.
84. *China Weekly Review*, 92.6:210 (April 6, 1940).

85. *FRUS, 1940,* IV, 309–310.

86. *China Weekly Review,* 92.6:179 (April 6, 1940).

87. Horiba, I, 379.

88. *Oriental Affairs,* 13.5:245 (May 1940).

89. *China Weekly Review,* 92.11:394 (May 11, 1940); *New York Times,* April 8, 1940, p. 10; and *North China Herald* (Shanghai) April 10, 1940, p. 1.

90. *Oriental Affairs,* 13.5:245 (May 1940).

91. JMFA, IMT 384:263; and *China Weekly Review,* 92.12:426 (May 18, 1940).

92. *People's Tribune,* 28.7–10 (April–May 1940).

93. *China Weekly Review,* 92.12:426–427 (May 18, 1940).

94. *China Weekly Review,* 93.1:34 (June 1, 1940).

95. Text: IMT 384:501–505.

96. Horiba, I, 403.

97. Horiba, I, 408.

98. Chou Fo-hai, p. 92.

99. Ibid., pp. 90–91.

100. *China Weekly Review,* 93.5:178 (June 29, 1940).

101. *China Weekly Review,* 93.5:178 (June 29, 1940).

102. JMFA, IMT 384:454–483.

103. JMFA, IMT 384:50.

104. JMFA, IMT 384:534.

105. Imai, *Shina jihen no kaisō,* p. 132.

106. Imai, *Shina jihen no kaisō,* p. 133.

107. Imai, *Shina jihen no kaisō,* pp. 136–142.

108. Chou Fo-hai, p. 104.

109. Imai, *Shina jihen no kaisō,* p. 143.

110. Chou Fo-hai p. 106; and Imai, *Shina jihen no kaisō,* p. 143.

111. Imai, *Shina jihen no kaisō,* p. 144.

112. Chou Fo-hai, p. 110.

113. Kido, II, 796.

114. Horiba, I, 418.

115. Kido, II, 796.

116. Imai, *Shina jihen no kaisō,* p. 144.

117. Horiba, I, 418.

118. Saitō Yoshie, *Azōmukareta rekishi: Matsuoka to sangoku dōmei no rimen* (Tokyo, 1955), p. 81.

119. Imai, *Shina jihen no kaisō,* p. 145.

120. Imai, *Shina jihen no kaisō,* p. 145.

121. Imai, *Shina jihen no kaisō,* p. 145.

122. Imai, *Shina jihen no kaisō,* p. 146.

123. Imai, *Shina jihen no kaisō,* p. 146.

124. Imai, *Shina jihen no kaisō,* p. 147.

125. *People's Tribune,* 29.5–6:171–172, 203–206 (September 1940).

126. Wang Ching-wei, "Chiang Kai-shek's 'Magnetic Warfare,'" *People's Tribune,* 29.1–2:7–10 (July 1940).

127. JMFA, CJ 58–9:2–461.

128. Tanamura Suketaka, *Daihon'ei kimitsu nisshi* (Tokyo, 1952), p. 35.

129. U.S. Department of State, *Documents on German Foreign Policy, 1918–1945,* Series D, XI, 491–492.

130. U.S. Department of State, *Documents on German Foreign Policy, 1918–1945,* Series D, XI, 516–517.

131. U.S. Department of State, *Documents on German Foreign Policy, 1918–1945,* Series D, XI, 517.

132. U.S. Department of State, *Documents on German Foreign Policy, 1918–1945,* Series D, XI, 517.

133. Chou Fo-hai pp. 184, 187–188.

134. Ibid., p. 144.

135. Ibid., p. 186.

136. Tanamura, p. 36.

137. Tanamura, p. 35.

138. Nashimoto, p. 172.

139. Nashimoto, p. 176.

140. Nashimoto, p. 177.

141. Nashimoto, p. 174.

142. Kido, II, 839.

143. JMFA, S 1611–11:471; and Chou, pp. 189–190.

144. *People's Tribune,* 29.11–12:345 (December 1940).

145. Tanamura, p. 37.

146. Chou Fo-hai, p. 191.

147. *FRUS, 1940,* IV, 455.

148. *FRUS, 1940,* IV, 440.

149. *New York Times,* Dec. 1, 1940, pp. 3–4.

9. The Peace Government in Action

1. T'ao Hsi-sheng, 2.4:8.

2. Chu [Chin], I, 61–62.

3. JMFA, IMT 384:236.

4. Chou Fo-hai; p. 80; and *China Weekly Review,* 93.8:278 (July 20, 1940), 93.11:386 (Aug. 10, 1940).

5. *China Weekly Review,* 94.12:383–384 (Nov. 23, 1940).

6. Tong, p. 105.

7. *People's Tribune,* 29.1–2:41–42 (July 1940).

8. *China Weekly Review,* 92.10:412 (May 18, 1940); and Chu [Chin], I, 53–56.

9. *China Weekly Review,* 92.4:108 (March 23, 1940).

10. *China Weekly Review,* 93.8:294 (July 20, 1949).

11. JMFA, IMT 384:512.

12. JMFA, IMT 384:519; and *New York Times,* June 17, 1940, p. 7.

13. *People's Tribune,* 29.1–2:41 (July 1940).

14. Royal Institute of International Affairs, *Weekly Review,* 48:8–10 (Aug. 29, 1940).

15. *North China Daily News* (Shanghai), June 14, 1940, quoted in Royal Institute of International Affairs, *Weekly Review,* 46:6–7 (Aug. 15, 1940).

16. Chu [Chin], I, 61–64.

17. *China Weekly Review,* 93.9:309 (July 27, 1940).

18. *China Weekly Review,* 93.10:356 (Aug. 3, 1940).

19. *China Weekly Review,* 93.10:344 (Aug. 3, 1940).

20. *China Weekly Review,* 94.1:26 (Sept. 7, 1940).

21. JMFA, IMT 384:600–603.

22. *China Weekly Review,* 93.10:356 (Aug. 3, 1940).

23. *New York Times,* Nov. 9, 1940, p. 5.

24. *China Weekly Review,* 94.11:355 (Nov. 16, 1940).

25. *China Weekly Review,* 95.5:155 (Jan. 4, 1941).

26. *China Weekly Review,* 96.4:111–112 (March 29, 1941).

27. *People's Tribune,* 30.1–4:13–16 (January 1941).

28. *China Weekly Review,* 94.7:228–229 (Oct. 19, 1940).

29. *China Weekly Review,* 95.10:330–331 (Feb. 8, 1941).

30. *China Weekly Review,* 95.6:214 (Jan. 11, 1941).

31. Horiba, I, 487.

32. Royal Institute of International Affairs, *Weekly Review,* 86:164 (May 22, 1941); and *New York Times,* May 11, 1941, p. 1; May 15, 1941, p. 7; May 17, 1941, p. 71.

33. Royal Institute of International Affairs, *Weekly Review,* 86:165 (May 22, 1941).

34. *New York Times,* May 17, 1941, p. 71.

35. Royal Institute of International Affairs, *Weekly Review,* 86:165 (May 22, 1941).

36. *New York Times,* May 17, 1941, p. 71.

37. Horiba, I, 592.

38. Kido, II, 885.

39. Horiba, I, 585.

40. Horiba, I, 593.

41. Horiba, I, 593.

42. Horiba, I, 591.

43. *China Weekly Review,* 97.7:201 (July 19, 1941).

44. U.S. Department of State, *Documents on German Foreign Policy, 1918–1945,* Series D, XII, 1057–1058.

45. U.S. Department of State, *Documents on German Foreign Policy, 1918–1945,* Series D, XIII, 17.

46. U.S. Department of State, *Documents on German Foreign Policy, 1918–1945,* Series D, XIII, 29–30.

47. U.S. Department of State, *Documents on German Foreign Policy, 1918–1945,* Series D, XIII, 35–36.

48. U.S. Department of State, *Documents on German Foreign Policy, 1918–1945,* Series D, XIII, 53–54.

49. U.S. Department of State, *Documents on German Foreign Policy, 1918–1945,* Series D, XIII, pp. 79–80.

50. *Gendaishi shiryō,* IX, 722.

51. JMFA, SP 302:1606.

52. JMFA, SP 302:1627.

53. *People's Tribune,* 31.1–6:6 (July–September 1941).

54. JMFA, S 1611–11:505–507.
55. JMFA, S 1611:529.
56. JMFA, S 1611–11:728–740.
57. Chou Fo-hai, p. 155.
58. *New York Times,* March 13, 1942, p. 4.
59. Horiba, I, 671.
60. Horiba, I, 675–676.
61. JMFA, UD 65:390, 409.
62. *China Weekly Review,* 97.3:74 (June 21, 1941).
63. *New York Times,* Jan. 12, 1943, p. 4.
64. JMFA, UD 65:39, 86, 119.
65. Text: Royal Institute of International Affairs, *Weekly Review,* 171:21–22 (Jan. 21, 1943).
66. Royal Institute of International Affairs, *Weekly Review,* 171:21 (Jan. 21, 1943).
67. JMFA, UD 312, 366; CJ 60:1; and Jones, p. 341.
68. JMFA, UD 65:438; and Jones, p. 342.
69. Horiba, I, 689–90.
70. Tsuji Masanobu, "Futari no daitōa soidōsha: Ishihara to Ō Chō-mei" in *Himerareta Shōwa shi,* a supplement to *Chisei,* p. 214.
71. Kido, II, 1053.
72. Kido, II, 1053.
73. Kido, II, 1056.
74. Tsuji, p. 215.
75. Ibid.
76. Kido, II, 1055.
77. Jones, pp. 342–343.
78. Akashi Yoji, "Japan's Maneuvers for the Settlement of the Sino-Japanese War, 1941–1945, unpublished manuscript. (Beaver Falls, Pennsylvania, 1971.)
79. JMFA, S 1611–11:720.
80. Chin Hsiung-pai, *Dōsei kyōshi no jittai: Ō Chō-mei no higeki,* tr. Ikeda Atsunori (Tokyo, 1960), pp. 332–334. This is another version of Chu [Chin], *Wang cheng-ch'uan.*
81. Lin Han-sheng, pp. 485–486.
82. Chin Hsiung-pai, p. 341.
83. Chu [Chin], V, 135–136.
84. Chu [Chin], III, 63–69.
85. Chu [Chin], II, 39–41.
86. *New York Times,* Aug. 17, 1945, p. 5.
87. Imai, *Shina jihen no kaisō,* p. 244.
88. Imai, *Shina jihen no kaisō,* p. 254.
89. Imai, *Shina jihen no kaisō,* pp 244–245.
90. Imai, *Shina jihen no kaisō,* pp. 246–247.
91. *New York Times,* Sept. 9, 1945, p. 5.
92. Imai, *Shina jihen no kaisō,* p. 247.
93. Imai, *Shina jihen no kaisō,* pp. 248–249; and Chu [Chin], IV, 1–31.

94. Chu [Chin], I, 44.
95. Imai, *Shina jihen no kaisō*, pp. 243–254.
96. Imai, *Shina jihen no kaisō*, p. 254.
97. Boorman, I, 409.
98. Imai, *Shina jihen no kaisō*, p. 252.
99. Boorman, I, 409.
100. Imai, *Shina jihen no kaisō*, p. 252.
101. *Ta kung pao* (Hong Kong), April 2, 1962, p. 3; April 9, 1962, p. 3.
102. Imai, *Shina jihen no kaisō*, p. 261.
103. Kao Tsung-wu, p. 49.

Bibliography

Akashi Yoji. "Japan's Maneuvers for the Settlement of the Sino-Japanese War, 1941–1945," unpublished manuscript, 1971.

Asahi shimbun 朝日新聞. Tokyo.

Boorman, Howard L., ed. *Biographic Dictionary of Republican China*. Vols. I, II, and III. New York, Columbia University Press, 1967–1970.

———"Wang Ching-wei: China's Romantic Radical," *Political Science Quarterly*, 79.4:504–525 (December 1964).

Borg, Dorothy. *The United States and the Far Eastern Crisis of 1933–1938*. Cambridge, Mass., Harvard University Press, 1964.

Boyle, John H. "Japan's Puppet Regimes in China, 1937–1940," Ph.D. diss., Stanford University, 1968.

———"The Road to Sino-Japanese Collaboration: The Background to the Defection of Wang Ching-wei," *Monumenta Nipponica*, 25.3–4:267–301 (September–December 1970)

Chin Hsiung-pai 金雄白. *Dōsei kyōshi no jittai: Ō Chō-mei no higeki* 同生共死の實態: 汪精衞の悲劇 (The reality of the shared fate: The tragedy of Wang Ching-wei), tr. Ikeda Atsunori 池田篤紀. Tokyo, 1960.

Chou Fo-hai 周佛海. *Chou Fo-hai jih-chi* 周佛海日記 (The diary of Chou Fo-hai). Hong Kong, 1955.

Chu Tzu-chia 朱子家 (Chin Hsiung-pai 金雄白). *Wang cheng-ch'üan te k'ai-ch'ang yü shou-ch'ang* 汪政權的開場與收場 (The rise and fall of the Wang regime). Hong Kong, 1959–1964.

Chung-yang jih-pao 中央日報 (Central daily). Chungking.

Ciano, Galeazzo. *Ciano's Hidden Diary, 1937–1938*, tr. and ed. Andreas Mayor, intro. by Malcolm Muggeridge. New York, Dutton, 1953.

Crowley, James B. "Japanese Army Factionalism in the Early 1930's," *Journal of Asian Studies*, 21.3:277–292 (May 1962).

———"A Reconsideration of the Marco Polo Bridge Incident," *Journal of Asian Studies*, 22.3:277–292 (May 1963).

———*Japan's Quest for Autonomy: National Security and Foreign Policy, 1930–1938*. Princeton, N.J., Princeton University Press, 1966.

Gendaishi shiryō 現代史資料 (Source materials for modern history). Vols. 9–14, *Nitchū sensō* 日中戰爭 (Sino-Japanese war), comp. Usui Katsumi 臼井勝美 and Inaba Masao 稻葉正夫. Tokyo, 1964.

Hanwell, Norman D. "Economic Disruption in Occupied China," *Far Eastern Survey*, 8.6:61 (March 15, 1939).

Harada Kumao 原田熊雄. *Saionji-kō to seikyoku* 西園寺公と政局 (Prince Saionji and political situations). 8 vols. Tokyo, 1952.

Horiba Kazuo 堀場一雄. *Shina jihen sensō shidōshi* 支那事變戰爭指導史 (History of the war guidance of the China Incident). 2 vols. Tokyo, 1962.

Hu Shih 胡適. "Hu Shih jih-chi chai-lu" 胡適日記摘錄 (Selected records of Hu Shih's diary), *Chin-tai-shih tzu-liao* 近代史資料 (Modern history materials), 2:209–214 (1955).

Imai Takeo 今井武夫. *Shina jihen no kaisō* 支那事變の回想 (Recollections of the China Incident). Tokyo, 1964.

——— "Taika wahei kōsaku shi" 對華和平工作史 (History of peace *kōsaku* towards China) in *Himerareta Shōwa shi* 秘められた昭和史 (Hidden history of the Showa era), a supplement to *Chisei* 知性 (Intellect), pp. 250–258 (December 1956).

International Military Tribunal, Far East, Deposition of Shimizu Tozo. Defense Document no. 1352, Exhibit no. 2585. National Archives, Washington, D.C.

——— Record of Proceedings of the Commission Taking the Deposition of Kagesa, Sadaaki, at First National Hospital, Tokyo, Japan, May 22–23, 1947. World War II War Crimes Record Group no. 238. National Archives, Washington, D.C.

——— Testimony, Proceedings, and Exhibits. National Archives, Washington, D.C.

Inukai Ken 犬養健. *Yōsukō wa ima mo nagarete iru* 楊子江は今も流れている (The Yangtze River is still flowing). Tokyo, 1960.

Jones, Francis Clifford. *Japan's New Order in East Asia: Its Rise and Fall, 1937–1945*. London, Oxford University Press, 1954.

Kagesa Sadaaki 影佐禎昭. "Sozorogaki" 曾走路我記 (Memoirs), in *Gendaishi shiryō*, XIII, 349–398.

Kao Tsung-wu. Conversations with Gerald Bunker.

Kazami Akira 風見章. *Konoye naikaku* 近衞內閣 (The Konoye cabinet). Tokyo, 1951.

Kido Kōichi 木戸幸一. *Kido Kōichi nikki* 木戸幸一日記 (The diary of Kido Kōichi). 2 vols. Tokyo, 1966.

Lin Han-sheng. "Wang Ching-wei and the Japanese Peace Efforts," Ph. D. diss., University of Pennsylvania, 1967.

Lu, David J. *From the Marco Polo Bridge to Pearl Harbor: Japan's Entry into World War II*. Washington, D.C. World Affairs Press, 1961.

Maruyama Masao. *Thought and Behavior in Modern Japanese Politics*, ed. Ivan Morris. London, Oxford University Press, 1963.

Morishima Morito 森島守人. *Imbō, ansatsu, guntō* 陰謀, 暗殺, 軍刀 (Conspiracy, assassination, sabre). Tokyo, 1950.

Nashimoto Yūhei 梨本祐平. *Chūgoku no naka no nihonjin* 中國の中の日本人 (A Japanese in China). 2 vols. (Tokyo, 1958).

Nishi Yoshiaki 西義顯. *Higeki no shōnin: Nikka wahei kōsaku hishi* 悲劇の証人―日華和平工作秘史 (Witness of tragedy: Secret history of the Sino-Japanese peace movement). Tokyo, 1962.

Pennell, W. V. "A Letter from North China," *Oriental Affairs*, 12.1:47 (July 1939).

——— "The Passing of Marshall Wu Pei-fu," *Oriental Affairs*, 13.1: 42–45 (January 1940).

Royal Institute of International Affairs. *Documents on International Affairs, 1937.* London, Oxford University Press, 1939.

————— *Documents on International Affairs, 1938.* 2 vols. London, Oxford University Press, 1942.

————— *Weekly Review of the Foreign Press.* Series C. London.

Saitō Yoshie 齋藤良衞. *Azamukareta rekishi: Matsuoka to sangoku dōmei no rimen* 欺かれた歴史—松岡と三國同盟の裏面 (Deceived history: Matsuoka and the background of the Triple Alliance). Tokyo, 1955.

Shigemitsu Mamoru 重光葵. *Shōwa no dōran* 昭和の動亂 (The disorder of the Shōwa era). 2 vols. Tokyo, 1952.

Shirley, James. "Political Conflicts in the Kuomintang: The Career of Wang Ching-wei to 1932." Ph.D. diss., University of California, 1965.

Ta kung pao 大公報. Hong Kong.

Taiheiyō sensō e no michi 太平洋戰爭への道 (The road to the Pacific War), ed. Taiheiyō sensō gen'in kenkyūbu 太平洋戰爭原因研究部 (Research bureau for the causes of the Pacific War). Vols. 3 and 4, *Nitchū sensō* 日中戰爭 (The Sino-Japanese War), by Hata Ikuhiko 秦郁彦, Usui Katsumi 臼井勝美, and Hirai Tomoyoshi, 平井友義. Tokyo, 1962, 1963.

Tanamura Suketaka 種村佐孝. *Daihon'ei kimitsu nisshi* 大本營機密日誌 (Secret diary of the Imperial Headguarters). Tokyo, 1952.

Tang Leang-li. "Wang Ching-wei: Leader of China Renascent," *People's Tribune*, 4.5:241–251 (April 1, 1933).

T'ao Chü-yin 陶菊隱. *Wang cheng-ch'üan tsa-lu* 汪政權雜錄 (Miscellaneous notes on the Wang regime). Macao, 1963.

T'ao Hsi-sheng 陶希聖. "Luan liu" 亂流 (Disturbed current), *Chuan-chi wen-hsüeh* 傳記文學 (Biographical literature), 2.4:6–8 (April 1963) and 2.5:6–7 (May 1963).

Tong, Hollington. *Dateline: China.* New York, Rockport Press, 1950.

Tsuji Masanobu 辻政信. "Futari no daitōa shidōsha: Ishiwara to Ō Chō-mei" 二人の大東亞指導者—石原と汪兆銘 in *Himerareta Shōwa shi* 秘められた昭和史, a supplement to *Chisei* 知性, pp. 209–217 (December 1956).

Ugaki Kazushige. "Sino-Japanese Peace Talks, June-September, 1938; Extracts from the Diary of General Ugaki," tr. E. H. M. Colegrave. *St. Anthony's Papers*, 2:94–103 (1957).

United States Department of State. *Documents on German Foreign Policy, 1918–1945.* Series D. 13 vols. Washington, D.C. 1949–1964.

United States Department of State. *Foreign Relations of the United States.* Washington, D.C., irregular intervals.

Wang Ching-wei. "Chiang Kai-shek's 'Magnetic Warfare,'" *People's Tribune*, 31.1–2:7–10 (July 1940).

————— "Facts about the Peace Proposals," *Oriental Affairs*, 11.5: 274–276 (May 1939).

———— "Frankness and Responsibility in Facing the Crisis," *People's Tribune*, 25.1:152 (July 1937).

———— "Guerrilla Warfare and the Scorched Earth," *People's Tribune*, 26.10–12 (June 1938).

————汪精衞[?], *Ō Sei-ei jijoden* 汪精衞自叙傳 (Autobiography of Wang Ching-wei), tr. and ed. Andō Tokuki 安藤德器. Tokyo, 1941.

———— "On Agrarian Policy," *People's Tribune*, 6.1:4 (January 1934).

S. Y. Wang. "Shanghai Schools Thrown into Turmoil as Agents of Wang Ching-wei, with Bribes and Bullets Seek Control of Education," *China Weekly Review*, 90.6:191–193 (October 7, 1939).

Yabe Teiji 矢部貞次. *Konoye Fumimaro* 近衞文麿. 2 vols. Tokyo, 1952.

Glossary

Abe Nobuyuki 阿部信行
aite to sezu 相手とせず
Arita Hachiro 有田八郎
Asameshi kai 朝飯會

Baikadō 梅華堂
bōryaku 謀略
bunchi gassaku 分治合作
bunraku 文樂

Chang Chi-lüan 張季鸞
Chang Ch'ün 張群
Chang Fa-k'uei 張發奎
Chang Hsüeh-liang 張學良
Chao Cheng-p'ing 趙正平
Ch'en Ch'ün 陳群
Ch'en Kung-po 陳公博
Ch'en Li-fu 陳立夫
Ch'en Pi-chün 陳璧君
Ch'en Pu-lei 陳布雷
Ch'en Tu-hsiu 陳獨秀
Ch'eng Tien-fang 程天放
Ch'eng Ts'ang-po 程滄波
Ch'i Hsieh-yüan 齊變元
chian kakuritsu go ninen inai ni teppei o suru 治安確立後 二年以內に撤兵する
chian kakuritsu to tomo ni ninen inai ni teppei o kanryō suru 治安確立と共に二年以內に撤兵を完了する
Chiang Kai-shek 蔣介石
Chiang Meng-lin 蔣夢麟
Chichibu no miya 秩父の宮
Ch'ien Yung-ming 錢永銘
Chin Te-shun 秦德純
Chiu-kuo fan-kung t'ung-meng hui 救國反共同盟會
Chou En-lai 周恩來
Chou Fo-hai 周佛海
Chou Lung-hsiang 周隆庠
Chou Tso-min 周作民
Chu Min-i 褚民誼
Chūgoku shuken sonchō gensoku

jikō ni kanshi Nihon ni taisuru yōbō 中國主權尊重原則事項に關し日本に對する要望
Chung-hua jih-pao 日華日報
Chung-hua min-kuo kuo-min cheng-fu 中華民國國民政府
Chūō kōron 中央公論

daijōteki 大乘的
Doihara kikan 土肥原機關
Dōmei tsūshin 同盟通信

Feng Yü-hsiang 馮玉祥
Fu Hsiao-en 傅筱庵
Fu Shih-shuo 傅式說
fu tsung-ts'ai 副總裁
Furukawa (Baron) 古河

Gaimushō 外務省
genrō 元老
Gozen kaigi 御前會議
gunbatsu 軍閥
gunmu kachō 軍務課長
gunmu kyokuchō 軍務局長

Han Fu-chü 韓復榘
Harada Kumao 原田熊雄
harakiri 腹切り

Hata Shunroku 畑俊六
hinin 否認
Hiranuma kiichirō 平沼騏一郎
Hirota Kōki 廣田弘毅
Ho Ying-ch'in 何應欽
Hokkōmaru 北光丸
Honda Kumatarō 本田熊太郎
Horiba Kazuo 堀場一雄
Hsiao T'ung-tzu 蕭同茲
hsien 縣
Hsin kung-kuan p'ai 新公館派
Hsü Mo 徐謨
Hu Han-min 胡漢民
Hu Shih 胡適
Huang Chün 黃群

I-wen yen-chiu so 藝文研究所
Imai Takeo 今井武夫
Inukai Ki (Inukai Tsuyoshi) 犬養毅
Ishiwara Kanji 石原莞爾
Itagaki Seishirō 板垣征四郎
Itō Yoshio 伊藤芳男

Jikyoku geppō 時局月報
Jūkōdō 重光堂

Kachō 課長
Kadomatsu (Major) 門松
Kagesa Sadaaki 影佐禎照
kai-tsu p'ai 改組派
Kan'in no miya 閑院の宮
Kao Tsung-wu 高宗武
Kawagoe Shigeru 川越茂
Kazami Akira 風見章
keizai teikei 經濟提携
kenpei 憲兵
Kido Kōichi 木戸幸一
kikan 機關
kiroku 記錄
Kōain 興亞院
kōdōha 皇道派
kokkō danzetsu 國交繼絕
kokutai 國體
komon 顧問
Konoye Fumimaro 近衞文麿
kōsaku 工作
Ku Cheng-ting 谷正鼎
Ku Meng-yü 顧孟餘
Kung H. H. 孔祥熙
kung-kuan p'ai 公館派
Kung Te-ch'eng 孔德成
Kuo-chi wen-t'i yen-chiu so 國際問題研究所
Kuo-min cheng-fu 國民政府
Kuomintang 國民黨
kyōdō bōkyō 共同防共

Li Sheng-wu 李聖五
Li Shih-ch'ün 李士群
Li Tsung-jen 李宗仁
Liang Ch'i-ch'ao 梁啟超
Liang Hung-chih 梁鴻志
Lin Pai-sheng 林栢生

Liu Hsiang 劉湘
Lung Yun 龍雲

Maruyama (Warrant Officer) 丸山
Matsumoto Shigeharu 松本重治
Matsuoka Yōsuke 松岡洋右
Mei I-ch'i 梅貽琦
Mei Ssu-p'ing 梅思平
Meishi 名啣
Min pao 民報
mushi 無視
Mutō Akira 武藤章

naimen shidō 內面指導
naiyaku 內約
Nakamura Toyokazu 中村豐一
Nakayama Yū 中山優
Nan-hua jih-pao 南華日報
Nashimoto Yūhei 梨本祐平
Nichi-nichi 日日
Nikka kyōgi kiroku 日華協議錄
Nishi Yoshiaki 西義顯
Nishio Toshizō 西尾壽造
Nisshi shin kankei chōsei hōshin 日支新關係調整方針
Nisshi shin kankei chōsei yōkō 日支新關係調整要綱

Oikawa Koshirō 及川古志郎
Oka Takazumi 岡敬純
Ōsuzu (Doctor) 大鈴
Ota Umeichirō 大田梅一郎
Ozaki Hidemi 尾崎秀實

Pa-nien lai-te hui-i 八年來的回憶
Pai Ch'ung-hsi 白崇禧
P'eng Hsüeh-p'ei 彭學沛

ran kōsaku 蘭工作
rengō iinkai 聯合委員會
Renraku kaigi 連絡會議
rōnin 浪人

Sado Kadomatsu 佐渡門松
Saionji Kinkazu 西園寺公一
Saitō Takao 齋藤隆夫

Sanbō honbu 參謀本部
San-min chu-i 三民主義
San-min chu-i, wo tang so tsung 三民主義，吾黨所宗
Satō Kenryō 佐藤賢了
Satō Naotake 佐藤尚武
Shang ch'ing 上清
Shigemitsu Mamoru 重光葵
Shina hakengun sōshireibu 支那派遣軍總司令部
Sōgun 總軍
subete teikoku seifu wa kongo kokumin seifu o aite to sezu 總て帝國政府は今後國民政府を相手とせず
Suga Hikojirō 須賀彦次郎
Sugiyama Hajime 杉山元
Sun Fo 孫科
Sun Yat-sen 孫逸仙
Sung Che-yüan 宋哲元
Sung Ch'ing-ling 宋慶齡
Sung Mei-ling 宋美齡
Sung T. V. 宋子文
Sung Tzu-liang 宋子良
Suzuki Takuji 鈴木卓爾

Ta-ch'ing Ch'ien-lung 大清乾隆
Ta Mei pao 大美報
Ta tao 大道
Tada Hayao 多田駿
Tai Li 戴笠
Tajiri Yasuyoshi 田尻愛義
Takagi Rikurō 高木陸郎
Tanaka Ryūkichi 田中隆吉
T'ang Liang-li 唐良禮
T'ang Shao-i 唐紹儀
Tani Masayuki 谷正之
T'ao Hsi-sheng 陶希聖
Teng Lung-kuang 鄧龍光
Terauchi Hisaichi 寺內壽一
ti-t'iao chü-lo-pu 低調俱樂部
Ting Mo-ts'un 丁默邨
Tōa renmei 東亞聯盟
Tōjō Hideki 東條英機
tokumu kikan 特務機關
tokumu kōsaku 特務工作
Tominaga Kyōji 富永恭二
tōseiha 統制派

Tōyama Mitsuru 頭山滿
Tsai-fang wai-chi 採訪外記
Ts'ao Chu-jen 曹聚仁
Ts'ao K'un 曹錕
Ts'ao Ts'ao 曹操
Tseng Chung-ming 曾仲鳴
Tsuji Masanobu 辻政信
Tu Yüeh-sheng 杜月笙
Tuan Ch'i-jui 段祺瑞
Tung Tao-ning 董道寧
T'ung-meng-hui 同盟會

udon ウドン
Ugaki Kazushige 宇垣一成
Ume kikan 梅機關
Usui Shigeki 臼井茂樹

Von Hohenhoffen フォーレンハーフェン

wahei kōsaku 和平工作
Wai-chiao-pu 外交部
Wakatsuki Reijirō 若槻禮次郎
Wang Ching-wei 汪精衞
Wang Ch'ung-hui 王寵惠
Wang I-t'ang 王揖唐
Wang K'o-min 王克敏
Wen Tsung-yao 温宗堯
Wu Chen-hsiu 吳震脩
Wu P'ei-fu 吳佩孚

Ya-chou-ssu 亞洲司
Yamada Otozō 山田乙三
Yamashita Kamesaburō 山下釜三郎
Yano Seiki 矢野征記
Yen Hsi-shan 閻錫山
yen tien 艷電
yōkō 要綱
Yonai Mitsumasa 米內光政
yukata 浴衣
Yü Han-mou 余漢謀
Yüan Shih-k'ai 袁世凱

zenmin shugi 全民主義
zenmin shugi undō 全民主義運動
zenrin yūkō 善隣友好

Index

131–132; possible negotiations with, 155–156; against peace movement, 169, 174; and Lung Yun, 195; Wang's appeal to, 204–205; government recognized by Great Britain, 206; peace in hands of, 211–212; position compared with Wang, 220; and relations with Communists, 223–224; his reaction to new government, 231; and Japanese-Chungking negotiations, 238–244; and Matsuoka *Kōsaku*, 247–248; commutes Chou Fo-hai's death sentence, 285

Chiang, Madame, *see* Sung Mei-ling

Chiang Meng-lin, 28

Ch'iao Fu-san, 82

Chichibu, Prince, 122

Ch'ien Yung-ming, 58, 76, 247, 248

Chin Te-shun, 23

Ch'in-Doihara Agreement, 31

"China Incident," defined, 1

Chinese American Daily News, 171

Ch'ingtao Conference, 188, 202, 205, 208

Ch'iu Wei-ta, 285

Chou En-lai, 121

Chou Fo-hai, 80, 108, 124, 150, 263; first contact with Wang, 18; as collaborator of Wang, 90–91; and Mei Ssu-p'ing, 95–96; and Jūkōdō conference *kiroku*, 98, 101, 107; plan for Chiang's resignation, 103, 104; and Wang's departure from Chungking, 111–113; goes to Hong Kong, 123; and possible new central government, 132–133, 138, 139, 146–147, 151, 193; and refuge for Wang, 143; and security for Wang, 148, 253; accompanies Wang to Tokyo, 154–155; and new Japanese cabinet, 179; and Japanese negotiations with Wang, 185; on Chiang's joining peace movement, 197–199; loyalties of, 199–200, 273; and defection of Kao and T'ao, 201; and revelation of Japanese demands, 205,

208; on failure of peace movement, 211; and problems of establishment and recognition, 213, 215–219, 223, 224–226, 237; and post in new government, 228; on return to Nanking, 229; and Japanese-Chungking negotiations, 238, 240–241; and "basic treaty," 245, 250; and Shanghai vice, 256; on anti-foreign views, 258; and new currency, 262, 269; clique, 273; after Wang's death, 280–282; death of, 284–285

Chou, Madame, 285

Chou Lung-hsiang, 97, 108–109, 110; accompanies Kao to Nagasaki, 129–130; and Wang rescue mission, 137, 139, 141; accompanies Wang to Tokyo, 154, 158, 160

Chou Tso-min, 58, 76, 247

Chu Min-i, 193–194, 208, 217, 277; seeks U.S. support, 203–204, 257; and post in new government, 229; his goodwill mission to Tokyo, 237; appointed ambassador, 264; and Wang clique, 273; in prison, 284

Ch'ün, Prince, 6, 108

Chung-hua jih-pao, 179, 192, 256, 259

Chung Shan Incident, 9

Chung-yang jih-pao, 14

Chūō kōron, 186

Ciano, Galeazzo, 43–44, 204, 215

Cliques, Kuomintang, 273–274

Communists: as Kuomintang's rivals, 1; and struggle with Chiang, 7–10; policy toward Japanese aggression, 17–18, 24, 25; regimes of, 223–224

Cosmé, Henri, 194

Craigie, Sir Robert, 37, 233–234

Dirksen, Herbert von, 38–39, 41, 44–45, 56

Doihara Kenji, 66; *kikan*, 59, 65, 133, 138

Donald, William, 22–23, 42, 115

Empress of Japan, 81

panies Kao, 128; meets Kao in
Nagasaki, 129; and Wang rescue
mission, 136–137, 139, 140, 141,
144, 146, 148, 150; and "blue-sky
white-sun" flag, 158, 217; on negotiations with Wang, 182, 185;
and Sōgun-Chungking talks, 223
Inukai Tsuyoshi, assassination of,
14, 81
Ishiwara Kanji, 277; on Sino-Japanese cooperation, 51–53, 71–72;
peace efforts of, 75, 76
Ishiwatari Sotaro, 156
Itagaki Seishirō, 78, 79, 183, 195,
277; peace efforts of, 52, 82, 85,
86; and Jūkōdō conference, 100,
105; and Konoye's resignation,
121–122; on Japanese troops in
China, 123–124; meeting with
Kao, 130; and Wang rescue mission, 139; meetings with Wang,
157–160; and Wu Pei-fu, 164;
removal of, 178–179; at Ch'ingtao
Conference, 208; and flag problem, 217–218; and problems of
establishment and recognition,
223, 224; congratulates new government, 229; and Japanese-
Chungking negotiations, 240–243
Italy: Chinese efforts for support
from, 43–44; appeals for mediation, 89, 90; and recognition of
Wang's government, 203, 204,
214–215, 217; and Axis alliance,
245–247
Itō Yoshio: peace efforts of, 72–82
passim, 96; and Jūkōdō conference kiroku, 97, 109; and Wang
rescue mission, 137, 140

Johnson, Nelson, 203–204
Journalism, Shanghai, 256–257, 259
Jūkōdō conference, 97–102; kiroku,
98–101, 105–109

Kadomatsu Shōichi, 137
Kagesa Sadaaki, 52, 121, 129, 152,
164; peace efforts of, 71–86 passim; and new China policy, 93;
and Jūkōdō conference, 97, 100,
101, 102, 105; and Konoye's third

statement, 117–118, 119; transfer
of, 128, 277; his meeting with
Kao, 130; his mission to rescue
Wang, 135–150; and naiyaku negotiations, 179–192; and problems of establishment and
recognition, 213, 216, 217, 224;
and Japanese-Chungking negotiations, 240, 243; and "basic
treaty," 245, 249
Kanin no miya, 56
Kan'in, Prince, 118, 122
Kao Tsung-wu, 102, 123, 124, 184,
285; his relationship with Wang
and Chiang, 14, 16; efforts of, to
avoid war with Japan, 27–31, 34;
peace efforts of, 68–86 passim;
renews peace efforts for Wang,
90, 91, 96; and Jūkōdō conference kiroku, 97–100, 101; and
plan for Chiang's resignation,
103, 104; on Japanese sincerity,
108, 109–110; and Wang's departure from Chungking, 110,
111, 114; and Konoye's third
statement, 117–119; his dealings
with Japanese, 128–130; Wang's
telegram to, 132; loyalties of,
135, 200; and Wang rescue mission, 136–137, 139, 141, 143; and
proposed peace government, 147,
149–150; and Wang's trip to Tokyo, 154; attempted murder of,
155; pessimism of, 156–157; on
Wang K'o-min's failure to cooperate, 176–177; defection of,
200–202; and revelation of Japanese demands, 205–208, 211; exile
to U.S., 206
Kao, Madame, 184
Kawagoe Shigeru, 19, 30–33, 34,
202
Kazami Akira, 57, 70, 97; and
Kagesa Sadaaki, 78–79; breakfast
club of, 81; and Konoye's possible resignation, 107; and Konoye's third statement, 118
Keizai teikei, 93, 94, 116, 120
Kerr, Sir Archibald, 115, 194
Kido Kōichi, 55–56, 107, 241, 249
Kikan (organ), described, 58–59

government, 203–204, 233, 257; and Axis alliance, 245; response to Chiang's plea, 250; and possible negotiations with Konoye, 270–271

Usui Shigeki, 130, 153, 222

Vice, in Shanghai, 255–256, 263
Von Hohenhoffen, 139, 140–141, 143

Wachi Takazo, 59, 222
Wai-chiao-pu (Chinese Foreign Office), 14, 16
Wakatsuki Reijirō, 46
Wang Ching-wei, 18, 47, 59, 67; his peace movement, 2–4, 50–51, 57, 68, 69, 82, 84, 85, 87, 132; his character, 4, 9, 154–155; his idealism, 5–7; and Chiang Kai-shek and the Communists, 5, 7–10; his political style, 5, 12–14; assassination attempts on, 15, 131–132, 136, 166, 168–169; policy toward Japanese, 16–17, 94, 95; on war with Japan, 24, 26–27; talks with Kao Tsung-wu, 29, 30, 80; and Japanese peace proposals, 39–45; as possible replacement for Chiang, 84–86, 90, 99–100, 103–105; rebuffs Japanese, 88–89; takes over peace route, 90–92, 95; and Jūkōdō conference, 97–102; and endorsement of Jūkōdō *kiroku,* 107–109; his departure from Chungking, 109–115; and Konoye's third statement, 115–118; his *yen tien,* 119–120, 123; dismissal of, 121; in Hanoi, 123–140; Hiranuma "secret agreement," 129, 133; his retaliation against Chiang, 133–135; rescue mission, 135–143; decides to establish peace government, 143–154; his trip to Tokyo, 154–162; seeks cooperation of Wu P'ei-fu, 163–167, 168, 171; and Provisional and Restored Governments, 163–165, 167–168; in Shanghai, 169–171, 172–176, 252–264; in

Canton, 171–172; and return to Nanking, 176–177, 229, 235–238; decline of his peace movement, 177–179, 271–279; and negotiations with Japan, 179–192; foreign support for, 193–195, 202–204; his military academy, 196–197; defection of his comrades, 200–202; appeal to Chiang, 204–205; and Ch'ingtao Conference, 205, 208; and revelation of Japanese demands, 205–208; Saito Takao on, 208–210; and problems of establishment and recognition, 211–226; and Japanese-Chungking negotiations, 220–224, 238–244; and Central Political Conference, 226–229; burned in effigy, 231; and response to his new regime, 231–234; and "basic treaty," 245–251; security for, 253–254; in Tokyo, 266–269; death of, 280; desecration of his remains, 285; his peace movement evaluated, 285–286

Wang, Madame, *see* Ch'en Pi-chün
Wang Ch'ung-hui, 39, 45
Wang K'o-min, 56, 132, 162; character of, 60–61; his Provisional Government, 61–62, 64; meetings with Wang Ching-wei, 164–165, 168, 176–177; and Ch'ingtao Conference, 188, 205; and revelation of Japanese demands, 208; hostility toward Wang Ching-wei, 219–220

War Guidance Office (of the General Staff), plan for China, 53–54
Wellington Koo, 34–35, 36
Wen Tsung-yao, 167–168, 208
Western powers: response to China's need, 34–36; and recognition of Wang's government, 203; opposition to Wang, 257
Whampoa Military Academy, 197
World War II, effect on peace movement, 178–179, 271–272, 274
Wright, Mary, 53
Wu Chen-hsiu, 68–69, 71

Harvard East Asian Series

DATE DUE

JE 7 '78			.
GAYLORD			PRINTED IN U.S.A.